Palgrave Studies in Crime, Media and Culture

Series Editors
Michelle Brown
Department of Sociology
University of Tennessee
Knoxville, TN, USA

Eamonn Carrabine
Department of Sociology
University of Essex
Colchester, UK

AF173472

"This book will anger and inspire you, in equal measure. Documenting the complex relations between crime, media and racism across diverse national contexts, media platforms and marginalised populations, it presents empirically rich accounts of the systemic and everyday processes of racialisation across the globe. Offering astute insights into the relations between media and state, economic and social power, and gender, class and race, it provides a model of politically engaged scholarship. *Media, Crime and Racism* is an important and authoritative contribution to the field."
—Professor Greg Noble, *Western Sydney University, Australia*

"In the age of post-truth, a collection which tackles the perennial issues of race and crime in the media is a welcome relief from the torrents of distortions and deception. In bringing together a collection of scholars who offer empirical evidence from a number of contexts, but share an incisive and critical edge in relation to the issues of racism and the media, the editors are to be congratulated in setting a standard for future research in this area."
—Professor Virinder Kalra, *University of Warwick, UK*

"Engaged scholarship that shows how the racialisation of crime and the manipulation of racism are part of the DNA of mainstream culture. *Media, Crime and Racism* demands an end to racist framing and a transformation in our ways of seeing. At last a book that places the bordered thinking of popular culture at the centre of a discussion of the structural processes that, in giving permission to hate, do so much damage to community relations."
—Liz Fekete, Director, *Institute of Race Relations*

This series aims to publish high quality interdisciplinary scholarship for research into crime, media and culture. As images of crime, harm and punishment proliferate across new and old media there is a growing recognition that criminology needs to rethink its relations with the ascendant power of spectacle. This international book series aims to break down the often rigid and increasingly hardened boundaries of mainstream criminology, media and communication studies, and cultural studies. In a late modern world where reality TV takes viewers into cop cars and carceral spaces, game shows routinely feature shame and suffering, teenagers post 'happy slapping' videos on YouTube, both cyber bullying and 'justice for' campaigns are mainstays of social media, and insurrectionist groups compile footage of suicide bomb attacks for circulation on the Internet, it is clear that images of crime and control play a powerful role in shaping social practices. It is vital then that we become versed in the diverse ways that crime and punishment are represented in an era of global interconnectedness, not least since the very reach of global media networks is now unparalleled.

Palgrave Studies in Crime, Media and Culture emerges from a call to rethink the manner in which images are reshaping the world and criminology as a project. The mobility, malleability, banality, speed, and scale of images and their distribution demand that we engage both old and new theories and methods and pursue a refinement of concepts and tools, as well as innovative new ones, to tackle questions of crime, harm, culture, and control. Keywords like image, iconography, information flows, the counter-visual, and 'social' media, as well as the continuing relevance of the markers, signs, and inscriptions of gender, race, sexuality, and class in cultural contests mark the contours of the crime, media and culture nexus.

More information about this series at
http://www.palgrave.com/gp/series/15057

"This dynamic, high-quality collection deepens our understandings of how using racialization as a concept can illuminate the connections between how crime, race and different kinds of borders are made real."
—Professor Steve Garner, *Birmingham City University, UK*

Monish Bhatia • Scott Poynting
Waqas Tufail
Editors

Media, Crime and Racism

Editors
Monish Bhatia
Birkbeck, University of London
London, UK

Waqas Tufail
Leeds Beckett University
Leeds, UK

Scott Poynting
Queensland University of Technology
Brisbane, QLD, Australia

Western Sydney University
Sydney, NSW, Australia

Palgrave Studies in Crime, Media and Culture
ISBN 978-3-030-10108-4   ISBN 978-3-319-71776-0   (eBook)
https://doi.org/10.1007/978-3-319-71776-0

Cover illustration: Rolfo Brenner / EyeEm

Printed on acid-free paper

This Palgrave Macmillan imprint is published by Springer Nature
The registered company is Springer International Publishing AG
The registered company address is: Gewerbestrasse 11, 6330 Cham, Switzerland

Foreword

This book arrives at a crucial moment for the field of criminology. Although debates over 'crime and the media' and 'race and crime' are well established and can be traced back to the ground-breaking work of critical scholarship of the 1970s, the mediated processes that racialise crime and criminalise race have yet to be fully interrogated in the discipline. It is this void that the authors address by exploring the diverse ways that the relationships between the media, crime and racism operate. Covering such issues as the refugee crisis, police violence, riots, Islamophobia, deaths in custody, terrorism and child sexual abuse, the case studies provide a nuanced understanding of the politics of racism at work in each empirical setting.

In some respects, the book picks up the challenge set by Stuart Hall and his colleagues at the Birmingham Centre for Contemporary Cultural Studies (BCCCS) in their major work *Policing the Crisis* (1978), which drew together the centre's research on youth subcultures, media representation and ideological analysis to explore how the themes of race, crime and youth are condensed in the archetypal figure of the 'black mugger'. Yet it also differs from that earlier book in important respects. Each of the contributors here recognises that the crises of the 1970s are significantly different from those experienced now. Implicitly and explicitly they pose important questions over the nature of continuity and change in 'law and order' programmes, the basic contours of social control and the shifting dynamics of media power. Indeed, the key concept that emerges across *Media, Crime and Racism* is that of 'racialisation', and one of the achievements of the text, as a whole, is the way in which it demonstrates the centrality of it to the criminological imagination. In this it chimes with recent attempts to understand the force of representation in the discipline and is full of the transformative possibilities that new ways of thinking bring to bear on old problems.

The concept of racialisation stretches back to the nineteenth century, but it came to more recent prominence in disputes over what came to be known as the 'race relations' paradigm in the UK. Different understandings of racialisation have been advanced, most notably by Frantz Fanon (1961) in his *The Wretched of the Earth*, where it is synonymous with dehumanisation, while for others it describes the constructed nature of racial categories and race-thinking processes, especially in European colonial encounters that sought to legitimate white supremacy. This view is associated with Michael Banton (1977) and his book *The Idea of Race*, which is credited with introducing the term to a sociological audience, where he discusses the racialising of the West initially and then the racialising of the entire world, emphasising how historically contingent the process can be. In the UK 'race relations' had come to be viewed through a public policy paradigm in the 1970s, which was later criticised for ignoring class and nation and for possessing a fixed and colonial understanding of 'race'. Consequently, racialisation was proposed as a radical alternative, and the process is regarded as one of becoming rather than of being.

A pivotal intervention was the publication of the *Empire Strikes Back* (1982) by the Race and Politics group at the BCCCS, which had been formed by Paul Gilroy alongside fellow postgraduate students Valerie Amos, Hazel Carby, Simon Jones, Errol Lawrence and John Solomos. Their collection of critical race essays provoked intense debate and drew criticism from, among others, the sociologist John Rex and criminologist Jock Young, who denounced their work and accused them of writing propaganda. Today it is regarded as one of the most important books written on racism in late twentieth-century Britain and eventually opened up a decisive shift in the sociology of race and ethnicity. Not least since it charged sociology with contributing to the problem of racism by producing pathological accounts of black family life and culture while profoundly criticising the theory and practice of socialist politics in Britain.

In the years since there has been a considerable expansion and extension of the concept in scholarship conveying how racialisation is a complex dynamic connecting the structural dimensions of economic, social and political marginalisation with the cultural representation of social life—the distinctive 'ways of seeing' that frame the experience of social relations. All agree that racialisation is something exercised by the powerful over the powerless and that the concept is an attempt to explain the processes through which races are embodied and bodies are racialised. The processes can be cruel or discreet, destructive or reconciliatory. They may result in genocidal extermination or everyday racism but also in consciousness and empowerment (as in anti-colonial struggles). Outside Europe some attempts have been made to develop the concept beyond the initial 'race relations' disputes, and in this Fanon's work has been especially important. The timeless, universal quality of it has been partly attributed to the 'racial optic' through which he analyses the colonial and postcolonial condition, but also by insisting that race and class co-constitute one another in ways that anticipate intersectional studies of oppression that have since become influential in feminism. This wider legacy of Fanon highlights the psychic and social dimensions of domination, emphasising how subjugated identities can be internalised, even while they are in flux and contested.

Each of the chapters in this book can be read as advancing the terms of these debates. Tina Patel's chapter, for instance, critically analyses the media's coverage of child sexual exploitation in two towns in the north of England, which have received widespread coverage over the period 2010–2015 became racialised where a process of 'browning' was used to construct categories of difference. The crimes were presented as a culturally specific form of deviance, rather than a result of broader inequalities, especially gender and the use of power to reinforce that inequality. Likewise, Waqas Tufail examines the racialisation of Muslims in one of these towns, Rotherham, in the aftermath of the widely publicised child sex abuse scandal, where a popular discourse circulated describing local Muslims as collectively responsible for the crimes. The ways in which racialised criminality is both constructed and reconstructed in the media is explored by Chris Cunneen in relation to the Indigenous peoples of Australia, where he makes the crucial point that processes of criminalisation and penality themselves constitute a significant racialising discourse.

Many of the contributions directly challenge Islamophobia and focus on the ways in which Muslims have been represented since the 2001 attacks on the United States; as Fatima Khan and Gabe Mythen point out, prejudiced and distorting depictions have long been a feature of the UK media landscape. Indeed, this longer view is integral to Colin Webster's chapter, who addresses the changing dynamics of how British Asians have been constructed in the media over a 50-year period, describing how the issues of 'race' and immigration were constructed as 'problems' and 'threats' to social order. The politics of online Islamophobia and misogyny are to the fore in Katy Sian's auto-ethnography documenting her experiences of vitriolic online hate and harassment on social media that followed in the wake of the publication of her first monograph exploring Sikh and Muslim conflict. Innovatively using an analytical understanding of Islamophobia as sustaining violent, structures of governance, she demonstrates the perils and obstacles confronting a woman of colour who seeks to critique racism encounters online, due to the fact that white power, privilege and patriarchy remain unchecked and unregulated on the Internet.

These are only a handful of the chapters in the book, and space precludes a discussion of all the contributions in it, but my point in this foreword is to highlight how the book reconfigures the field. One way in which it does is by making a case for the need to take a greater account of gender relations, and how they intersect with ethnic, racial, generational and class phenomena. All the authors are aware that a racial ascription is always also a social assignation and inevitably involves, in Pierre Bourdieu's terminology, forms of 'symbolic violence' upon those who are ascribed. Both the meaning and possibility of racial ascription vary according to status and context, curtailing considerably the possibility of multiple belongings and mobilising moral evaluation. This moral judgement over the racialised other usually takes a negative form of collective defamation and material assault, where disqualification and stigmatisation can justify discrimination, exploitation and oppression. In other words, questions of cultural representation always have concrete consequences.

According to some commentators not only is it becoming increasingly difficult to distinguish media image from social reality but it is also the case that contemporary forms of sociality are multiply mediated. In such a changing landscape, it is vital that the disciplinary gaze of criminology is enlarged and extended in these challenging times. Imaginative criminology is inevitably transgressive and transformative. Without wanting to minimise the obstacles to doing creative, boundary-challenging work, it is important to recognise that it has always been central to critical understandings of crime and justice, law and order, while challenging criminal justice policies, procedures and practices. In this the book admirably fills the brief that Michelle Brown and I had in mind for the *Crime, Media, Culture* series at Palgrave, which rests upon a desire to break down the often rigid and increasingly hardened boundaries of mainstream criminology, media and communication studies and cultural studies, so that new approaches can flourish.

University of Essex   Eamonn Carrabine
Colchester, UK

Acknowledgements

Edited volumes are deceptively labour-intensive endeavours, and so it has made a world of difference to the editors to have such good people to work with; we have been privileged. We thank all the contributors for their fine chapters, which collectively have made the book, and also for their cheerful support, cooperating with tight deadlines and sometimes unexpected requests.

We thank the original commissioning editor, Julia Willan, for her prompt and enthusiastic response to the volume, and Josie Taylor and Stephanie Carey who saw the project through much of its production in a time of institutional transition, and was patient with our endless requests for flexibility such as more word length and other indulgences.

We cannot express enough thanks to series editors Michelle Brown and Eamonn Carrabine; their encouragement and support has been invaluable; we are especially indebted to Eamonn for his scholarly and generous Foreword. We would also like to thank the three anonymous reviewers, who commented thoughtfully on our original proposal and made helpful suggestions.

Our thanks go to the production team at Palgrave, Springer and copy-editors in India, for their hard work and unfailing courtesy.

Monish would like to thank his colleagues at Birkbeck, University of London and also former colleagues at Abertay University. He would also like to thank his brother, mother, and (late) father for their support. Scott wishes to thank Mabel for her support and forbearance as ever, and teen-ager Lara whose anti-racist instincts since toddlerdom grow ever more conscious and interventionist, and inspire hope in her generation. Waqas would like to thank Joanna for the endless encouragement, and Kareem and Bilal for providing much-needed moments of joy in between writing and editing. May this collection inspire hope and resistance for the anti-racist struggles of the future.

Contents

List of Figures

List of Tables

1

Introduction

Monish Bhatia, Scott Poynting, and Waqas Tufail

For the three editors, this volume marks the broadening out of a conversation that we began together some five years ago or more, about the relationship of the media to the racialisation of crime and the criminalisation of racialised others. We have learnt much from those who have here joined us in this conversation, and of course from those who have bequeathed us all the language and the terms of that conversation.

When we first began our correspondence—across corridors, then between countries and continents—we were all three teaching university courses, primarily of a critical criminological nature, that dealt with the

M. Bhatia (✉)
Birkbeck, University of London, London, UK

S. Poynting
Queensland University of Technology, Brisbane, QLD, Australia

Western Sydney University, Sydney, NSW, Australia

W. Tufail
Leeds Beckett University, Leeds, UK

© The Author(s) 2018
M. Bhatia et al. (eds.), *Media, Crime and Racism*, Palgrave Studies in Crime, Media and Culture, https://doi.org/10.1007/978-3-319-71776-0_1

1

media in relation to racialisation and crime. We drew, in our teaching and our dialogue, on contemporaneous questions. These included how to make sense of the hundreds, thousands of asylum seekers perishing in the Mediterranean, portrayed widely in the media as opportunistic economic migrants, often with state violence exhorted against them, and at best strong social control of them as a 'problem'. The 'illegalisation' of 'boat people' bound for Australia, and also media silence and silencing about unlawful state violence against them. These stories were not monolithic; the same media that can so effectively dehumanise and rationalise injustice can also humanise and demand justice. What of the resident immigrants represented as welfare scroungers and a drain on the economy? What of the purported 'crisis of multiculturalism'? What of 'race riots', such as London in 2011 and Ferguson, Missouri, in 2014, both involving black deaths at the hands of the police, and occasioning much demonisation of 'rioters' in the media, but also the increasing contention there that 'Black Lives Matter'? Racialised 'criminal gangs' of various sorts? How is the 'war on terror' constructed and prosecuted in the media, among other sites; how are (often criminal) wars and warfare mediated? What is the nature of Islamophobia? How does racism 'intersect' with gender relations in specific media reports and story cycles, such as racialised constructions of minority religious practices (e.g. veiling) or of sexual abuse? How is racism in the media resisted, and how is racism resisted in the media—especially the new social media? These were but a few of the questions we discussed with each other and with our students.

In such teaching, we found few publications, and very little in the way of books that dealt contemporaneously with all three factors: media, crime and racism. There were excellent books that dealt with media and crime, or media and racism, or racism and crime, but practically no recent books dealing explicitly and entirely with all three.

Eamonn Carrabine, in his generous foreword to this book, points rightly to the intellectual (and political) legacy that we have inherited from *Policing the Crisis* (Hall et al. 1978). That crisis, of this crisis-ridden capitalist system which is now quite globalised, was four decades ago: at the beginnings of neo-liberalism and before that term was common. Now the current crisis is the crisis of neo-liberalism itself. In making sense of it in relation to media, crime and racism, we have benefited indeed from the understandings of ideology advanced from the 1970s by Stuart Hall and his colleagues from the Centre for Contemporary Cultural Studies (CCCS), and in particular the notion of ideology as the imagined resolution of real contradictions. Another way of putting this is that it involves the systematically distorted perception—distorted by reality itself—of real, underlying social relations: appearances, if you like. In the British 'mugging' crisis of the 1970s, for example, the real shortcomings of social democracy hitting its limits in economic crisis, the exacerbated inequalities in the face of the egalitarian promise, could be projected in ideological processes, working notably through mass media, onto purported 'enemies within' supposedly fomenting social breakdown. Racialised minorities were one such blameable 'enemy'; militant trade unionists were another. This form of projection worked conveniently for, and in the interests of, those who did not by and large suffer the depredations of the economic crisis. It divided, disorganised and confounded those who did experience the sharp end of those contradictions. The construction of the racialised folk devil, the black 'mugger', was just such a form of ideological projection. In following decades, the racialised figure of the asylum seeker, the 'new black' as Sivanandan (2001) put it, served as a screen onto which could be projected, in image, the real insecurities and anxieties occasioned by the winding back of the welfare state in the context of globalisation and the history and continuance of colonialism. (See Lentin and Titley (2011) for a sophisticated analysis of contemporary racism working in this way; see Kundnani (2007) for a perspicacious account of the scapegoating of the asylum seeker in Britain during neo-liberal dismantling of the welfare state.)

Yet 'projection' is just one of the ideological manoeuvres performed by racism, of which there are abundant examples in this book. Another, related, working of racist ideology is what we might call a 'chutzpah' effect. Look at a photograph of a lynching to see the 'dangerous black man' in this light. Who is in danger here? Who is presenting the danger? Consider the depiction of indigenous peoples everywhere, dispossessed of their land, as beneficiaries of the largesse of the dispossessor. Similarly, in the case of Australian Aborigines, the most socially disadvantaged strata on just about any criterion—life expectancy, infant mortality, levels of formal education, income and wealth levels, housing standards, levels of arrest, conviction, incarceration, severity of punishment and deaths in custody as detailed in Chris Cunneen's chapter—their widespread portrayal as receiving 'special privileges'! Note the representation of enslaved peoples as lazy; colonised peoples who have been robbed, cheated and extorted of their wealth and resources as themselves inclined to thievery and other criminality; colonised peoples subjected to rape and sexual exploitation as themselves sexually predatory; those subjected to the violence and barbarism of all forms of primitive accumulation, with its repertoire of mass murder and even genocide, kidnap and forced migration, concentration camps, torture and the whole panoply of state crime, as 'barbaric' and 'uncivilised'. Chutzpah is perhaps too gentle a metaphor for these workings of racist ideologies. More mechanistic, but serviceable, is Marx's and Engel's notion of a 'camera obscura', in which real social relations are inverted in their (nevertheless real) appearances. Thus, who is perpetrating terror in the 'war on terror'? The 'endangered white man' so grieved for by the (violent and even murderous) neo-Nazi 'alt-right' at Charlotteville, Virginia, as we write, is but the latest manifestation of this ideological operation of reversal of victim and perpetrator.

The 'moral panic' model adapted from Stan Cohen and used to such insightful effect by Hall et al. (1978) in *Policing the Crisis* has been much criticised over the intervening decades (a good sample of the debate can be found in Krisnky (2013)) for, among other things, disparaging popular worrying and official responses as disproportionate and diminishing the harmfulness of folk devils to ordinary people; being too conspiratorial as an explanation; being too 'one-way' a model, failing to recognise the extent to which the mass media reflect and take up popular concerns rather than merely plant them in populations; being too top-down a model, overlooking popular resistance and the possibilities for 'taking back' in the media. Most of these criticisms could not be fairly applied to *Policing the Crisis*; the Gramscian model of hegemony infusing the work of the CCCS which elaborated it, was more subtle than that and grasped well the interplay between consent and coercion as well as understanding that the balance of forces routinely did not favour the subaltern. Of particular concern, however, is the potential for 'talking back': the technological means and spaces of doing so have developed exponentially in the intervening 40 years. The internet now exists—everywhere, it seems. It provides valuable tools for anti-racism in the hands of oppositional and progressive social forces, as some of our chapters here demonstrate, and nevertheless a global, ubiquitous, virtually instantaneous and enormously influential medium for the perpetration of racism, a medium not very amenable to regulation, and whose effectiveness is, while not controlled monolithically, concentrated in the hands of the most powerful. Meanwhile, the usual suspects, the press and television and radio, have undergone 40 years more of concentration and are at the same time now thoroughly globalised (and integrated with the internet): witness the Murdoch empire. The effects of these processes on the scale, scope, speed and recurrence of moral panics need nowadays to be taken into account. Morgan and Poynting (2012) argue that, under these conditions, the 'Muslim Other', for instance, is one folk devil that is now globalised and continually recycled. To return to another, often badly travestied, notion of ideology as found in Marx and Engels (notably in *The German Ideology*), the ideology of the ruling class prevails as the ruling ideology through their ownership and control of the means of ideological production; these days that is the internet above all. While masses of people, and perhaps soon most people, may own and operate a computer, laptop or tablet, or smartphone, they cannot own or control a major search engine or widespread social media platform. In as much as the ruling class benefits from deploying and manipulating racism, as sketched above, then we can expect the internet potential to 'talk back' to be one-sided, if certainly not irresistible and eternal.

These are all reasons to return to questions of the relationships between the media, crime and racism some 40 years after *Policing the Crisis*. There is a new crisis and there are new media. The state, as well as the media and indeed some key forms of crime and criminalised activity, is now much more complicated by globalisation. 'Fake news' has become a major political and cultural issue over the period of writing of this book; 'alternative facts' were coined in the last year. Over the last days (as of writing this), US President Donald Trump has refused to denounce an apparent deliberate white supremacist killing perpetrated by driving a car into pedestrians as any form of terrorism, has declined to condemn neo-Nazis for their mob violence including probable homicide and has recommended on Twitter the dipping of bullets used to execute Muslim terrorists, as a (completely fictitious) tactic that he said worked for US General Pershing in the turn-of-the-century Philippines. The Twitter (and other social media and traditional media) exhortations, 'alternative facts' and racist hate crime are causally connected in North America, but also in the British Isles, continental Europe, Australia and other places instanced in this book.

The book begins with an analysis of purported Asian and Muslim criminality as presented in mass media. In Chap. 2, Colin Webster examines the ethno-racist framing of British Asians from 1961 to 2011 and a notable shift in their constructions from victims to criminals. In Chap. 3, Tina Patel discusses the mass media's coverage of child sexual exploitation cases in two North England towns. The cases involve abusers from black and minority ethnic (BME) background, in particular of Pakistani heritage and of Muslim faith. Patel argues the cases were narrated in media entirely through a 'cultural repertoire', drawing on older racialised panics about the brown menace and white victims—portraying abuse as a form of culturally specific deviance, rather than as connected to gender, power and control. This, according to her, has led to a newer category of the black folk devil, and thus ignored white perpetrators and marginalised all victims of such abuse. In Chap. 4, Waqas Tufail examines the construction of 'Muslim grooming gangs' and 'Asian gangs', and the manner in which local media, state actors and institutions framed the child sex abuse scandal in one of these North England towns, Rotherham. Through interviews with British Muslims, Tufail assesses the impact of such media constructions on minority communities and community relations, highlighting the ways in which these representations are challenged and resisted, including through the grassroots, anti-racist feminism that is emerging there. In Chap. 5, Ulrike Vieten uses the case study of New Year's Eve (2015/2016) Cologne sexual violence controversy in Germany and examines gendered anti-Muslim racism in media. Vieten closely scrutinises the media coverage and investigates the portrayal of victims and perpetrators and also sheds light on ways in which criminal investigators, courts and civil society in Germany dealt/deal with the issue of mass public sexual violence.

In Chap. 6, Fatima Khan and Gabe Mythen analyse the labelling and stereotyping of Muslim women in media. They argue that intersecting discourses of gender, identity and faith are based on erroneous assumptions and represent Muslim women as simultaneously victims of gendered oppression and agents of cultural separation. The chapter highlights the importance of resistance as a response to such labelling and stereotyping and ways in which this is made manifest in both counter discourses and everyday practices. In Chap. 7, Katy Sian uses critical auto-ethnography to document online hate, misogyny and the challenges that women of colour face when they engage within online spaces to disseminate research and educate audiences around anti-racist/anticolonial politics. Sian deploys critical race and postcolonial frameworks to examine the Islamophobic/racial harassment of women of colour online, revealing the logic of Islamophobia and its gender dimension in online abuse. In Chap. 8, Anneke Meyer and Scott Poynting draw upon the case study of Muslim cleric Abu Qatada to analyse the Islamophobic moral panic in the British tabloid press. The chapter demonstrates how politicians and tabloids interacted in their exhortation of 'tough' state occasioned by the 'war of terror'. The authors also show how the populist press picked up and propagated the ideology of purported 'failed multiculturalism' and excessiveness of 'human rights' as promoted in recent neo-conservatism.

In Chaps. 9 and 10, Mike Grewcock and Monish Bhatia respectively analyse the portrayal of refugees and 'illegal' migrants in the populist press. Grewcock's chapter focuses on the systemic abuse of the Rohingya ethnic minority in Myanmar and the dominant media narratives of border policing 'crisis'. The chapter shows how media framing of migration crisis in Australia obscures the crisis of the state organised and sanctioned persecution of the Rohingya—crimes which he shows can be characterised as genocide. Bhatia's chapter analyses the racialised portrayal of the refuge seekers of France's Calais 'jungle' and the treatment of so-called illegal migrants in the right-wing and tabloid press, especially in Britain. The chapter highlights the racialised criminalisation of this group and uncovers the media legitimisation of state violence, suffering and deaths of refuge seekers.

In Chap. 11, Kerry Moore and Katy Greenland examine how racism is constructed in crime and law and order news. Drawing upon an extensive study on the representation of racism in UK national newspapers, the *Daily Mail* and *Mail on Sunday*, the *Daily Telegraph* and *Sunday*

Telegraph and the *Sun*, they uncover stories that feature racism; how racism is discussed, positioned and made sense of; what kinds of racist practices are represented as newsworthy and how actors in narratives about racism are characterised. The chapter also highlights the discursive boundaries of racism and their policing. In Chap. 12, Marta Kolankiewicz analyses the media reportage of the murderous and racially targeted attack in Trollhättan, Sweden, in 2015, in a school with a high proportion of immigrants and children from ethnic minority backgrounds. In the hours and days after the event, strategies of both closeness and distance towards those affected by the attack were used in the media. Kolankiewicz argues that news not only represents and/or reports on the suffering but also shapes possible responses to this suffering—the horizons of which are drawn by ethnocentrism and indeed racism. The theme of media denial continues in Chap. 13, where Ryan Erfani-Ghettani discusses media portrayal of black and minority ethnic deaths in custody, and ways in which this denies justice for the bereaved. Instead of investigating police wrongdoings in cases involving suspicious custodial deaths, the dead themselves are smeared as too strong, too volatile or too alien and having brought their deaths upon themselves. The police frame the death in terms of a media narrative that portrays race, and not racism, as the problem. As family and community campaigns for justice emerge, police and the media collude to define their demands as extremist, and therefore illegitimate. In Chap. 14, Chris Cunneen uncovers the ways in which racialised criminality is both constructed and reproduced in the media—specifically racialised criminality constructed around Indigenous people in Australia. Cunneen takes a broad approach to media and includes mainstream media outlets (both print and television) and other media forms including social media and film. The chapter looks at both non-Indigenous and Indigenous media—and expands our understanding of Indigenous resistance and challenges to representations in mainstream media.

In Chap. 15, Sharon Lauricella and Wesley Crichlow examine the coverage of crime and portrayal of black in print news media in Toronto, Canada. By employing framing analysis, together with a conceptual framework called anti-black racism and critical race theory, the chapter analyses a society thoroughly pervaded by violence structured by racism and yet with accounts of guns and gangs prevalent in racially inflected reporting. The chapter engages with the #BlackLivesMatter movement and sheds light on media, crime and racism in Canada. In Chap. 16, Patrick Williams and Becky Clarke explore the racialised construction of gangs and black criminality in Britain in media and through criminal justice discourses. They examine the associated use of joint enterprise law, which has partly contributed to the over-representation of blacks and minority ethnic groups in the criminal justice system. Chapter 17 discusses the foreign national prisoner crisis in the UK press. Using the mechanics of race and gender, Luke de Noronha uncovers the racist construction of non-national criminals and the resultant unjust policies and practices. In the concluding chapter of this book—Chap. 18—Vicki Sentas argues for more focus on the racialising and criminalising practices of the criminal justice system rather than the common approach of seeing racism as perpetuated most saliently through representations in the media.

Together, these chapters offer a range of instructive empirical studies of the nexuses of media, crime and racism, along with nuanced and multi-dimensional analysis using a variety of critical theoretical frameworks. Each chapter addresses all three of these areas of social life and furthers the project of understanding them in their manifold interrelationships. Not only understanding, however, but sharing a commitment to countering racism in its many forms in all of these areas. We hope that this book will prove a useful resource in that struggle.

References

Hall, S., Critcher, C., Jefferson, T., Clarke, C., & Roberts, B. (1978). *Policing the Crisis: Mugging, the State and Law and Order*. Basingstoke: Palgrave Macmillan.

Krisnky, C. (Ed.). (2013). *The Ashgate Research Companion to Moral Panics*. Farnham: Ashgate.

Kundnani, A. (2007). *The End of Tolerance: Racism in 21st Century Britain*. London: Pluto Press.

Lentin, A., & Titley, G. (2011). *The Crises of Multiculturalism: Racism in a Neoliberal Age*. London: Zed Books.

Morgan, G., & Poynting, S. (Eds.). (2012). *Global Islamophobia: Muslims and Moral Panic in the West*. Farnham: Ashgate.

Sivanandan, A. (2001). Poverty Is the New Black: An Introduction. *Race and Class, 43*(2), 1–5.

2

Turning the Tables? Media Constructions of British Asians from Victims to Criminals, 1962–2011

Colin Webster

Introduction: British Asians, the Media and the Race-Ethnicity 'Problem'

Our story really begins with the criminalisation of Asian immigration to Britain in 1971. At the time, a prescient book about the treatment of race in the British press by Hugo Young (1971: 29–41, his emphasis) argued that:

> race only earns its place in the news to the extent that it is bad news... *This is because everything to do with coloured people takes place against an underlying premise that they are the symbols or the embodiments of a problem.*

The context however is the Conservative government's Commonwealth and Immigration Act 1962 beginning the process whereby politicians began to set the terms of debate about race issues. In these terms, most

C. Webster (✉)
Leeds Beckett University, Leeds, UK

© The Author(s) 2018
M. Bhatia et al. (eds.), *Media, Crime and Racism*, Palgrave Studies in Crime, Media and Culture, https://doi.org/10.1007/978-3-319-71776-0_2

notably, Enoch Powell's widely reported apocalyptic 'Rivers of Blood' speech on 20 April 1968 set the trend. Criticising Commonwealth immigration and anti-discrimination legislation that had been proposed in the United Kingdom, the speech resulted in Powell's dismissal from the Conservative Shadow Cabinet despite popular public support.

This chapter describes the processes and mechanisms of media-induced campaigns that construct the issues of 'race' and immigration represented in some sense as public or social 'problems' and 'threats' to order. Focusing on a succession of periods marked by distinctive themes around race and immigration, we can see a dominant media discourse build up about these 'problems' and 'threats'. Although directed at racialised visible minority groups generally, the chapter shows the particular role that British Asians come to play in a transformative drama in which they are at first seen as benign and even victims of injustice, then as coming to represent the greatest threat of all, towards the end of our period. These periods are important as they show the transformation in public perceptions through supposed transgressions by the group of thresholds of public tolerance in which race and ethnicity are increasingly linked to violence and crime.

The theoretical discussion on how to interpret and understand these series of cumulative periods of media representation and imagery is found towards the end of the chapter in the discussion 'from victims to criminals'. The sections to follow summarise the transformation already alluded to in this introduction in how British Asians are seen. The final concluding theoretical discussion firmly locates media treatments of the 'problem' of race and ethnicity within an ideology of populism (Muller 2016). That is the media's paradoxical denial of diversity while celebrating the plurality of 'liberal' individual freedoms within one nation.

Closing the Circle? A Law and Order Campaign Against British Asians

The media through 'accredited or authoritative sources', such as the police, judiciary, experts and politicians, rely on these sources to help define and then reproduce the parameters of the race-ethnicity 'problem', and may connect this problem to other problems such as crime and disorder, through association, repeatedly described and replicated. Once the media have spoken on behalf of the inaudible public, newsworthy deviant and dramatic events become defined and reproduced, authoritative sources and press become mutually supporting and reinforcing, closing off the event to alternative explanations. This 'closure of the circle' becomes the framework of interpretation for all future events and discussion of the problem. In other words, these terms and reference points are those in which all future debate about the topic is conducted and allowed (see Hartman 1970; Carrabine 2008; Ferguson 1998; Van Dijk 1991).

The historical types of media-induced moral panics about the presence of the race-ethnicity problem run in cycles and can escalate. Moral panics run in cycles in which sometimes particular themes and concerns come to the fore, and at other times the same concerns fade. Media-supported anxiety in the case of the presence of immigrants and visible minorities in Britain, though sharing this cycle, can be cumulative and escalate in the negative significance this presence is said to possess, over time. For example, the decision to leave the European Union, in England and Wales, based in part on nativist and anti-immigrant feeling, has been long in the making after decades of public anti-EU immigration discourse. It is not difficult however to see the mechanisms and sequence of this campaign from the 1960s onwards. We can begin to understand how the media through publicly signifying race and ethnicity as 'problems' and associating this with issues of crime and the creation of disorder, the perceived potential threat of an issue escalates. In identifying and problematising the presence of British Asians in certain places as a 'minority', linking by labelling that presence to other problems whereby boundaries are created and 'thresholds' of acceptable values and behaviours are crossed, convergence occurs. That is, as the period we are discussing progresses so that 'there is a tendency to "map" together increasing numbers of problems as constituting one single threat, and for this convergence to contain an increasing purely ideological construction' (CCCS Mugging Group 1975: 63).

Eventually, as thresholds and boundaries staking out societal tolerance limits are progressively broken and thresholds breached—of permissible and acceptable cultural and moral standards and values to legal thresholds to the crossing of extreme violence thresholds—the specific issue and group become perceived as a threat. As the period progresses, there is an increasing tendency for events to be perceived as having pushed beyond thresholds stressing illegality and the flouting of social authority.

The following overlapping periodisation attempts to briefly summarise the main terms and reference points in which the media problematised the presence of British Asians in the United Kingdom from the early 1960s to 2011.

1962–1976 Illegal Immigration, Deportation and Political Protest

The early to mid-1970s were marked by government panic about Asian immigration, following the introduction of the Immigration Act 1971 which granted the right of the dependants of Commonwealth citizens settled in Britain to live in Britain. However, because the rights of entry for dependants was not an automatic one and entry was policed and enforced by immigration officers and the police, who also deal with public demonstrations against Home Office decisions on behalf of individual's appeals, the issue became criminalised (see Guia et al. 2012; Weber 2013).

Ever since 1961 (anticipating the Conservative government's immigration law in 1962), politicians had set the terms of debate about race issues, politicising race relations, and there had been political events around race that hit the headlines (Patterson 1967). These were usually framed by the media as 'the riot story' referring to any sort of affray or the 'illegal immigrants' story in the context of the Immigration Appeals system set up under the 1969 Immigration Appeals Act. Illegal immigration was a running sore in press coverage of race from the 1962 Immigration Act onwards, increasingly around migration from India and Pakistan and the issuing of vouchers for specific jobs in Britain. The 1965 White Paper further reduced legal immigration for unskilled workers. The 1968 Immigration Act for the first time made the failure to submit to examination by an immigration officer a criminal offence. The 1971 Act though made illegal immigration subject to removal or criminal prosecution retrospectively, making it possible to remove people who had immigrated in the past using definitions of illegality brought in later by the 1971 Act. Fear of the Home Office and police was constant. In 1961 no Commonwealth citizen could be deported. Between 1962 and 1969 relatively recently arrived convicted persons could be deported, but after the 1971 Act deportation could happen on grounds of 'general undesirability', and a person being an 'illegal entrant' (Bottomley 1970). Thus, began the criminalisation of immigration reported in the usual ways the media reports any crime.

The media coverage and construction of immigration became frequent and sometimes complicated. From the unambiguously hostile, as the *Daily Mail's* comment section makes clear 'Illegal immigration is a serious crime—because it threatens the whole climate of race relations in this country' (4 May 1973), to more discreet but constant treatment depending on the method and style of individual newspapers. Some papers looked sympathetically to the plight of illegal immigrants' subject to blackmail and exploitation, but as usual, any context was largely missing.

By January 1976 headlines such as ' The Illegal Immigrants of London' (*London Evening News*), 'Ghost Migrant Scandal' (*Sun*), 'Immigrant Survey Shocks Caterers' (*Guardian*), 'The Illegal Workers in London Cafes—84% No Right To Be Here' (*Evening Standard*), 'Illegals in Spotlight' (*Catering Times*) displaced the real issue, summarised at the time by the independent black magazine *Race Today* (February 1976: 32) that 'British workers have refused the low pay and long hours attached to jobs in catering. No worker in Britain, including migrant blacks, unless he/she is defeated and demoralised, would work for £30 for a 100 hour week.'

1970–1972 The Kenyan and Ugandan Asian Immigration Crisis

It wasn't only supposed illegal immigration that raised the press's ire. East African Asians were British citizens because they were given this choice when the African countries they had settled became independent. They were a complicated and 'inconvenient' legacy of the old British Empire. Many chose British citizenship rather than Ugandan or Kenyan citizenship because their future seemed uncertain in the countries they were living. They were then in effect expelled by the new African leaders of those countries in the ensuing nationalism brought by independence.

In response to Britain's responsibilities towards Ugandan Asians, *The Times* leader of 14 August 1972 plaintive cry was:

> Immigrants already settled here stand to suffer more than anyone else from a rate of new immigration greater than the social body of the host country can digest, or that its prejudices can tolerate.

Although most of the British press had been forthright in advocating the acceptance by the government of its responsibilities towards the Kenyan and Ugandan Asians in their leader columns, actual news copy was less sanguine.

1970–1972 'Paki-Bashing' and the Beginnings of Asian Self-Defence

At the time of the East African Immigration Crisis, another, less publicised phenomenon began in the East End of London as the early 1970s witnessed the formation of 'vigilante squads' organised by Pakistanis after several incidents of what became known as 'Paki-bashing'. This was also the case for the later arrived Bengalis (London 1973). Asians beaten up in East London received little protection from the police, and when they began to organise their own defence they were arrested. Until early 1970 there had been few reports in the national press of the numerous incidents in which Asian immigrants had been the victims of unprovoked assaults. In most cases the attackers were white youths—and the police never seemed able to trace them.

There was a reference to the problem as early as 21 October 1968 in the *Guardian* when complaints that the police were not doing enough to protect the Asian community from attack were made. But it was not until April 1970 that reports of such incidents hit the headlines so dramatically that the problem could no longer be ignored by the authorities (Ashe et al. 2016).

The first press reference to Paki-bashing came on Friday, 3 April 1970, when several national daily newspapers carried stories of skinhead attacks on two Asian employees of the London Chest Hospital in Bethnal Green. Five days after the first reports, three young skinheads were televised boasting about beating up Pakistanis. The programme scandalised many people. The very next day, a 50-year-old kitchen porter Tosir Ali was murdered outside his home in Tower Hamlets. The murder was sensational and topical enough to be widely reported (London 1973).

The parallels with the hugely publicised racist murder of a young black man Stephen Lawrence in 23 years later are clear. In the 1990s though, a media campaign by the *Daily Mail* helped identify his killers and forced the police and the government to reform the policing of racist violence. In 1970 the police did nothing.

Again, thinking of media pressure and police inaction, the murder of Tosir Ali took place in a week when reports of 'Paki-bashing' were making headlines in both national and local newspapers, as a murder clearly inspired by racial hatred. An editorial in the *London Evening Standard* of 8 April linked the murder with other attacks on Pakistanis and fascism. On the same day, however, the police discounted any suggestion that this had been a 'skinhead attack', stating that there was no evidence that coloured people were being attacked more often than whites (*Observer*, 5 April 1970) despite almost daily press reports that this was the case. This and other incidents at the time discouraged trust in the legal system, or that the police would protect the Asian community from attack (London 1973).

Tosir Ali's murder was the catalyst to the forming of albeit poorly organised vigilante and defence groups to defend Pakistani communities against attacks from whites. This time papers like the *Evening News* and the *Sun* (8 April 1970) widely reported the reaction of the police and other authorities condemning vigilantism. Furthermore, the police arrested and convicted Asians for carrying offensive weapons which they claimed they had with them for self-protection, again widely reported in the press. Racist murders, violent attacks and increasing police mistreatment of *Asians* (not only blacks) continued apace throughout the 1970s. Police brutality against Asians was perceived to becoming more prevalent in East London at the time. Again, *this* was often not reported by the mainstream press (London 1973).

1974–1977 Policing Asian Industrial Relations

It is difficult today to understand how prominent discussion and reporting of industrial relations by the media was in the 1970s. Both the printed press and the BBC employed armies of industrial relations reporters and correspondents, something which has completely disappeared today (Mills 2016). The 1970s were a time of considerable industrial militancy across the country and different industrial sectors among Asian workers. Often, Asian strikers faced open racism and hostility from white fellow workers when embarking on disputes about pay, conditions and the rights of Asian workers to be trade union representatives at the workplace (Taylor 1974).

Asian women throughout the period of primary migration in the 1960s and 1970s provided a significant reserve of cheap labour. Many of them were employed in low-paid factories and the service industries under extremely poor conditions of long hours and little rest. As an example, cleaners at Heathrow airport were all Asian women, mostly middle-aged and older (Race Today 1974).

The industrial conflict in the Bradford textile industry is a case in point, revealing of mostly local media treatment of race and industrial disputes. The West Yorkshire textile industry was notorious for segregating shifts, facilities, pay and conditions between its Asian and white workers; Asian workers were forced to work for longer and unsocial hours but were paid less. Just as some high-profile industrial disputes attracted a lot of press coverage, especially when this involved the policing of picket lines, many disputes went unreported and unexplained.

The local press in Bradford during the 1960s vigorously debated whether Asian wool textile workers in Bradford constituted 'cheap labour'. The context was to replace white men with white women, then replace white women with Asian men to cheapen wages and increase the intensity of exploitation and insecurity of labour at a time of a general and drastic *reduction* of employment in wool textiles between 1965 and 1980. This response to a cumulative crisis of the wool textile industry in

Britain was employers concentrating their efforts on reducing labour costs through the reduction of employment, maintaining or increasing output without increasing the wages of the workers who remained.

In fact, Asian workers were distributed differently between and within firms according to levels of technological backwardness, size and product so that Asians were overrepresented on night work. Over time Asians were recruited to do the dirtier work and work longer hours with the spread of new machines. A racial division of labour was introduced into wool textiles in the 1950s when Asians were recruited into jobs rejected by other workers and this hardly changed later (Fevre 1984). Racism at work was found most in British managers' and employers' stereotypes of Asians and black workers. Eventually, in the 1970s and early 1980s Asians left the wool textile industry under very different circumstances to the white workers who had preceded them. White workers had left for better jobs, Asians left for unemployment, as they had not benefited from the earlier expansion of alternatives to textile work, nor did they benefit from more limited expansion of service industries in later years (of which white women were the main beneficiaries). Additionally, according to Fevre (1984) Asian men variously vied with white women in their attractiveness to textile employers.

The period 1974–1977 was particularly marked by widely publicised industrial disputes involving Asian workers. The strike at Imperial Typewriters, the inferior treatment of Asian workers at Ford's, Dagenham, and numerous incidents of industrial unrest involving Asian workers throughout the 1970s fought not only employers' discrimination and unfair treatment in the workplace but for recognition by their trade unions to make strikes official and recognise their election as trade union representatives and shop stewards, often amidst white colleague's hostility and a generally divide and rule approach by employers and unions. At Imperial Typewriters, several strikers were arrested and faced criminal charges through picketing (Ramdin 1987).

In May 1977, the strike of the Asian workers at Grunwick Film Processing Laboratories and Mail Order in North London received wide press coverage in their dispute with the white management and only passive support from the TUC (Taylor and Dromey 2016). The industrial struggle of migrant wage earners can be characterised by the trade unions themselves sanctioning race discrimination at the workplace by protecting white privileges in pay and conditions rather than promoting the interests of their black and Asian members. In 1973 and 1974, when two thirds of the work force at Ford's, Dagenham, were immigrant, strikes against redundancies were invariably wildcat and unofficial.

Asian workers on strike at the London Rubber Company demanding union recognition to support underlying issues of low pay, unsocial shift hours and health hazards on the job, were again met by police heavy-handedness on the picket line, escorting strike breakers into the factory. Here as elsewhere, Asian workers were represented as troublesome and militant. Asian workers were disproportionately involved in industrial disputes and strikes very publicly policed at picket lines and publicised in the press (Ramdin 1987). Throughout the 1960s and 1970s, in small textile factories, plastics, electrical components and the larger heavy industry sector, Asian workers struck for union recognition, against racial discrimination that saw them receive lower pay and poorer conditions than white workers and against a system that denied them apprenticeships and safe working conditions. The history of Asian shop-floor industrial action was an indictment of racism in trade unions in Britain (Ramdin 1987).

1976–1987 The Rebellion of the Asian Youth Movements

A strong movement of Asian youth had emerged around the question of deportation and immigration controls in the 1970s. In the 1981 Brixton uprisings, it is often forgotten that Asian youth as well as African Caribbeans and whites were involved in specific public order situations. In particular, the defence by 6000 Asian young people of the community in Southall against invasion by far-right racists and in Bradford in July where 12 young Asian men were arrested and charged with conspiracy to manufacture explosives and conspiracy to cause grievous bodily harm. The defendants were later acquitted after claiming that they armed themselves in self-defence. On 23 April 1979 in Southall, London, 6000 Asians demonstrated and attempted to prevent 59 members of the racist National Front being escorted by the police to hold an election 'meeting' in the area. Clashes with police resulted in the death of a white demonstrator—Blair Peach—clubbed by a police unit (Dummett 1980).

A political demonstration to stop the National Front marching through Bradford's Asian and Caribbean Manningham area in 1976 quickly turned to violent clashes between local young people and the police, receiving no press coverage at all. Clashes in Leeds between young blacks and police the previous year in Chapeltown, Leeds led to a number of arrests. This more or less low-level disorder was becoming more and more common, often beneath the radar of both local and national press.

As Ramamurthy's (2006) political history of Asians in Britain shows, the Asian Youth Movements (AYM) of the 1970s and 1980s based in an ethnic politics of secularism tackled racial violence, police injustice and immigration controls, thus joining media treatments of wider political protest. By this time, the first generation born in Britain, beginning with the Southall Youth Movement, aimed to tackle popular racism and police racism through self-defence. Amidst considerable media publicity, the movement spread to Bradford and elsewhere where the AYM demonstrated publicly, much to the consternation of the police, against incursions into their areas of far-right racist organisations, racist murders and deportation of illegal immigrants and the rights of families to be united.

1988–1989 The Rushdie Affair: Islamisation of Public Protest

Focusing on the representation of race and violent crime in the press, Sveinsson (2008) shows how earlier, cruder, negative *biological* attitudes to 'race' became less strident, and in some ways less acceptable as time wore on, only to be supplemented and in part replaced by a sort of 'cultural' racism—coding 'racial' differences and conflicts as 'cultural' differences and conflicts. The shift from crude biological racism to cultural racism identified by Sveinsson (2008) as the dominant press discourse on race, crime and disorder could probably be located, and triggered by, 'the Salman Rushdie affair', particularly the public 'book burning' in Bolton and Bradford by groups of British Muslims of Rushdie's novel *The Satanic Verses* in 1988 and 1989. Rushdie was subsequently condemned to death by Iraq's leader Ayatollah Khomeini encouraging any Muslim to carry out this 'fatwa'. The typical media response was a series of generalised assumptions that *all* British Muslims supported Ayatollah Khomeini's fatwa. Thus, began a new and particularly strong version of the notion of 'unassimilable cultural difference', only later metamorphosing into the idea of 'self-segregation' (Cantle 2002).

1989–1994 Resurgence of Racist Violent and Asian Self-Defence: Constructing Asian Criminality

This author and others (Webster 1996, 1997) have discussed this period at length elsewhere. It is a period of increasing violent racist attacks on Asians, the increasing defence by Asian young people of the areas in which they lived and increasing violent retaliation against white racists constructing and invading what whites perceived to be areas belonging to Asians. It is in this period particularly when Asian young people are transformed by the media from relatively 'quiet' and 'law abiding' to potentially violent criminals and involved in crime and drugs.

What distinguishes this period from the 1976–1987 period of Asian young people's consciously political leadership against racism under the AYM leadership is its relative lack of overt political ideology and its relatively unorganised, ad hoc defence against violent white racism and everyday racism in smaller towns. It is perhaps the least reported of the periods under consideration here. Or, more accurately, most misperceived by media reporting, as the following themed sections show.

1993–2001 Media Constructions of British Asian and Muslim Criminality

In Malik's (2002) account, television documentary form too has increasingly lent itself to portraying British Asians, and particularly Muslims, as part of an emerging underclass because of crime, drug abuse and family breakdown. Even critically acclaimed documentaries made by black and

Asian producers, such as an edition of *Panorama* entitled 'Underclass in Purdah' broadcast by the BBC in 1993 (cited in Malik 2002), can fall into the trap of Asians-as-social-problem narratives. Social problems are here collapsed into cultural and religious ones ('Purdah' a veil screening or secluding these 'problems') so that images of illegality (drugs, prostitution, family violence, battered women) filmed in parts of the Manningham area of Bradford were presumed to be representative of the entire British Asian community (Malik 2002).

The primary definers, as is often the case, are white police men and professionals. The documentary concluded (cited in Malik 2002: 53):

> In many ways, Pakistanis and Bangladeshis find themselves in a worse position today than when they first arrived in Britain 30 years ago.... Muslim Asians are now asking themselves how they got into this position when other ethnic groups are doing so much better.

The programme was a key marker of, and consistent with the shifts discussed earlier of an escalation throughout the 1990s of identifying and problematising the presence of British Muslims as a threat. As Malik (2002) agrees, a key image of British Asians in the 1990s focused on the threat and manifestations of what was depicted as religious fundamentalism in relation to British Muslims 'who became *the* ethnic folk devils during the 1990s' (p. 54).

1995–2001 Constructing British Muslim Public Disorder

The trope of the hidden, fearful, threat of sudden and extreme violence has become an organising press principle, framework and repertoire, from which the mass media draw. It has become extremely damaging to the fortunes and prospects of the mass of law-abiding, respectable British Muslims. This author (Webster 2011, also see Kundnani 2007) was one of those who argued that the depiction of British Muslims as a community suffering a crisis of parental control over its 'uncontrollable' young people was offered by primary definers as a cause of the first widespread public disorders involving Asian young people in Bradford, West Yorkshire in 1995. At the time, Keith Hellawell, then Chief Constable of West Yorkshire Police, stated that 'Cultural and religious leaders have been worried for the past ten years or so that the younger generation don't follow their teachings and feel that they have great difficulty in controlling them' (quoted in the *Independent* 12.6.95).

The public disorders, again mostly involving Muslim and some black and white young men, in Bradford, Oldham and Burnley—all former textile towns in Northern England—in the spring and summer of 2001, led to widely reported official calls—both mirroring and feeding mainstream media—to end supposed 'self-segregation' and build 'community cohesion'.

2005–2011 The Terrorist Threat and Islamophobia

The ways that the societal control culture and the news media tackled the bomb attacks in London (2005) and Glasgow (2007), the two failed shoe bomb attempts (2001 and 2010) and the 2003 bombing in Tel Aviv, carried out by British-born 'Islamic political terrorists' (Abbas 2007), were terrible harbingers associating individual political violence and terrorism with a particular ethnic and religious group. As argued elsewhere in this chapter, earlier media and crime analysis showed perhaps inevitably that the crossing of extreme violence thresholds leads to the purist form of media construction of law and order campaigns. In particular, those earlier moral panics about British Asian, particularly Muslim, associations with crime and disorder had converged and linked issues and 'problems' focused on this group to one single threat.

Overview: From Victims to Criminals

Over the whole period, what began as non-violent political protest and public demonstrations by British Asians over deportations and the criminalisation of illegal immigration in the 1960s until the mid-1970s was followed by the policing of non-violent industrial conflict and strikes in which Asian workers took a prominent part in the 1970s. During these periods the press and mass media mixed responses and constructions of the 'problem' of Asian immigrant political and workplace protest were ambiguous. Complicated by press sympathy towards a group perceived as *victims* of family disruption through 'inhumane' immigration law preventing family reunion, unfairly exploited at work, and as victims of racist violence defending themselves from attack, Asians were represented at the threshold of legitimacy crossing over to, or pushing, thresholds of legality. As the period progresses, there is a tendency for primary definers and the press to differentiate the original immigrant parent culture as law abiding from its increasingly rebellious youth movement. With the Islamisation of public protest seen in the public burning of books and conflict over the content and ethos of schooling, including its segregation, and the construction of Asian criminality, cultural racism emerges. Eventually, as the 1990s progress, the tendency to 'map' together criminality, public disorder and violence, in which Asians are perceived by whites and the press as crossing the 'extreme violence' threshold—through violent defence and retaliation against white racists attacking their areas—finally gets confirmed in direct public disorders against far-right threats and the police, seen first in the 1995 and especially 2001 public disorders, threatening to undermine the State itself. From these disorders and UK-related 'Islamic political terrorist' bombings from 2001 to 2010 (Abbas 2007; Webster 2011), and taking its cue from the response to the earlier disorders, the government launched its action plan 'Preventing violent extremism: winning hearts and minds' in April 2007, to support the arguably incoherent notion of 'community cohesion' and strengthen the role of faith institutions and Islamic leaders in resisting a particular sort of violent extremism (Webster 2014).

Our story in a sense both ends around 2011 and begins the next twist in the tale of the media treatment of Asians, race and crime. From now onwards there is really only *one* story—a 'master narrative' about the 'terrorist threat' (Kundnani 2014). The turning point is most marked by Prime Minister David Cameron's public criticism of previous government's policies of 'multiculturalism' as a way of governing ethnic and religious relations in Britain, as encouraging segregation and as a threat to community cohesion and shared national identity. Stating that 'Under the doctrine of state multiculturalism, we have encouraged different cultures to live separate lives, apart from each other and apart from the mainstream', Cameron (2011) was asserting, like previous British governments had done, the integration of cultures and values around 'one nation' (see Parekh Report 2000; Cantle 2002). Framed in this way, widely and sympathetically reported, these coded, repeated charges had the connotation of a pervasive obsession with the vulnerability of young Muslims as a group to 'Islamist extremism', as evidenced in Cameron's speech. According to this perspective, the worry is of isolation, of segregation, of a lack of contact, interaction and understanding between different faith and ethnic groups (see Webster 2014). Of course, Cameron's framing and its more or less faithful reproduction by the media was designed to close rather than open debate about the empirical facts of the existence of different 'cultures', and the balance to be struck between equal treatment, different treatment and maintaining social cohesion.

Theory and Populism: Asians, Racism and the Media

Set up in 1968, the Runnymede Trust prioritised the daily monitoring of press coverage of race issues in Britain, explicitly recognising that white attitudes and opinions towards black and Asian people would be influenced and shaped by what was presented in the mass media. This daily press monitoring continued until quite recently. Harman and Husband, in their 1974 book 'Racism and the Mass Media' analysed press coverage from 1963 to 1970. They found that race relations coverage tended to focus on signs of racial conflict and to give very little attention to the access of black people to housing, education and employment. Gordon and Rosenberg (1989) were able to summarise the period over 20 years until the publication of their book, as newspapers treating black and Asian people as a social problem and as a threat to white British society. The stories were of immigration, the speeches and statements of the MP and Minister Enoch Powell from April 1968 warning of serious racial conflict and strife if immigration was not stopped and black and Asian people being encouraged to leave Britain. This extensive and prolonged coverage helped create a climate of racist opinion.

The thread running through all media coverage of race issues over the 20-year period Gordon and Rosenberg covered was illegal immigration—whether of (inaccurate) attacks on the Asian system of arranged marriages supposedly used to obtain British citizenship, press campaigns for tighter immigration restrictions or 'visa cheats'—in effect criminalising entry to Britain. Headlines and stories constantly referred to black and Asian people as 'scrounging' welfare benefits, as a problem of 'law and order', as synonymous with public disorder, while equally consistently ignoring the situation of Asian people as victims of racial violence, and suffering racial inequality in housing, education and employment.

Gordon and Rosenberg (1989) showed how race issues are an urgent and recurrent 'populist' concern. Muller's (2016: 2) highly nuanced discussion of populism allows us to provide a rough definition of populism as a political orientation of politicians and their supporters in the press, on both the Left and the Right, that wants to appeal to 'the people' against the views of the 'establishment' and elites, to tell a story that can be understood by as many citizens as possible, to appear to be sensitive to how 'ordinary people' think and, in particular, feel, while manipulating their political support.

In a version of populist media coverage, the 'New Right' constructs a seemingly new 'common sense' about race that promotes racism through a common set of themes. As we saw in the 1970s and 1980s, very much like today, populism supported and justified policies restricting the entry of black and Asian people into Britain; it questioned the notion of a multiracial or multicultural society; it challenged 'establishment' definitions of racism and anti-racism and finally, offered its own portrayals of different minority groups. Thus, in the 1970s and 1980s 'immigration' was *always* Asian and black immigration not white immigration from the 'White Commonwealth' and Europe. Cultural pluralism, when it is recognised at all, is opposed as a threat to British values and national culture, in which assimilation and integration can only be in terms of the majority British culture as people of different cultures do not get on with one another.

Press commentators and politicians express opposition to anti-discrimination measures and anti-racism, so that 'Nobody is less able to face the truth than the hysterical anti-racist brigade… so-called anti-racists… are only interested in suppressing the truth and the right to free speech' (*The Sun* 26 February 1986, cited in Gordon and Rosenberg, p. 28). The Honeyford affair in Bradford, West Yorkshire, for example, generated many articles from columnists, defending the head teacher Ray Honeyford who resigned following his published attack on multicultural education. By rejecting anti-racism and multiculturalism as ideas, the press undermined the efficacy of opposing racism and the understanding that all societies contain a plurality of cultures and disagreements about values: in effect a refusal to acknowledge, and to deny, the existence of racism and discrimination.

As well as generally reviewing press coverage of race and violent crime, Sveinsson (2008) systematically examined crime articles in the national print media as well as a selection of regional media over a period of two months—1 May–30 June 2007—demonstrating how notions of race tint the lens through which criminality is both viewed and projected. His conclusion was that,

> Culturalist explanations for behaviour have entered crime reporting of the mainstream media in force… The claim that 'culture' is the source of violent crime necessarily attaches violence to certain 'communities' defined by their ethnic 'identity'. This implies that most members of those groups are violent. The effect is that entire 'communities' are criminalized on the basis of their 'cultures'. (p. 3)

Van Dijk (1991) emphasises the role that ideology plays in reproducing the dominance of one ethnic group over another. By 'ideology', here what is meant is simply ideas and meanings that legitimate or promote the power of a dominant social group or class. The press reproduces its own view of hierarchy and the power structure through ideas and meanings. But it also possesses its own autonomous ideology which allows it to deny accusations of racism and impartiality or bias about race. This is because as Chibnall (1977) argued, press ideology internal to news journalism and its organisation hinges on a view of 'professionalism', which organises and integrates a series of largely unconscious perceptions and thoughts. The professionalism of journalism corresponds to 'news value' or the relevance of some news stories and not others. Chibnall (1977: 19) reminds us, despite its emphasis on law and order, press ideology is 'profoundly liberal'. It is a paradox of press populism (which denies a plurality of *societal* cultural values) that it recognises that we live in a plural society of competing *individual* points of view in which no side can claim a monopoly of truth.

Discussion and Conclusion

At each stage and period of the media treatment of Asian minorities, particular press obsessions shift while the master discursive baton of ethno-racist framing of Asian-Muslim criminality, disorder and deviance is passed on. Today, perhaps of greatest significance is the process by which online and social media not only reports and frames 'the problem' of Islam and violent extremism but is *itself* said to be part of the problem, as the major source generating violent extremism.

The brutal killing in May 2013 of an off-duty soldier named Lee Rigby near his barracks in Woolwich, southeast London, by two young British men of Nigerian descent, Michael Adebolajo and Michael Adebowale, was linked to the fact that six months earlier Adebowale had talked on Facebook about his desire to slaughter a soldier. Politicians turned on social networks for not doing enough to stop extremists, accusing Facebook and the like of providing a safe haven for terrorists and of not living up to their social responsibility (Dodd et al. 2014). Internet companies have since faced intense demands to monitor messages on behalf of the state for signs of terrorist intent.

Multimedia and social media platforms, online and offline sources of constructing Muslims as victims *and* perpetrators of violence and abuse are new developments and offer new opportunities. For example, Zempi and Awan (2016) interviewed Muslim men and women who had been victims of both online and offline Islamophobia in the UK. Fears about, and hostility towards, Muslims and Muslim communities, involving abuse and targeted violence against them, are the underlying expressions of Islamophobia and as such are a form of cultural racism. Islamophobia on the internet interacts with media demonisation of Muslims, particularly triggered by local, national and international incidents and events. And of course, overriding everything else is the role that the internet is said to play in the radicalisation of young Muslims. Even though, as Kundnani (2014) argues, radicalisation is best understood through its social and particularly political circumstances, not, as most commentators insist, through social media-induced psychology or theology.

The media treatment of British Asians, crime and disorder, is shaped by a conception of society as an unchanging 'consensus'. Newsworthy events are those which seem to interrupt this consensual calm, challenging some of the major boundaries of that consensus—defined by the law, embodying the 'popular' will of the people—marking 'our way of life' and its connected values. News symbolically reasserts the values of society, public morality and its limit of tolerance, by 'mapping problematic reality.' The eliding of race, ethnicity and violence derives its special status as news value as constituting a critical threshold in society, the violation of which places the racialised perpetrator (and sometimes victim) outside society altogether.

References

Abbas, T. (Ed.). (2007). *Islamic Political Radicalism: A European Perspective*. Edinburgh: Edinburgh University Press.

Ashe, S., Virdee, S., & Brown, L. (2016). Striking Back Against Racist Violence in the East End of London, 1968–1970. *Race and Class, 58*(1), 34–54.

Bottomley, A. (1970). *Control of Commonwealth Immigration: An Analysis and Summary of the Evidence Taken by the Select Committee on Race Relations and Immigration 1969–70*. London: Runnymede Trust.

Cameron, D. (2011, February 5). *PM's Speech at Munich Security Conference*. Retrieved from http://www.number10.gov.uk/news/pms-speech-at-munich-security-conference/

Cantle, T. (2002). *Community Cohesion: A Report of the Independent Review Team*. London: Home Office.

Carrabine, E. (2008). *Crime, Culture and the Media*. Cambridge: Polity Press.

CCCS Mugging Group. (1975 [2006]). Some Notes on the Relationship Between the Societal Control Culture and the News Media, and the Construction of a Law and Order Campaign. In S. Hall & T. Jefferson (Eds.), *Resistance Through Rituals: Youth Subcultures in Post-War Britain* (2nd ed.). London: Routledge.

Dodd, V., MacAskill, E., & Wintour, P. (2014, November 25). Lee Rigby Murder: Facebook Could Have Picked Up Killer's Message—Report. *The Guardian*.

Dummett, M. (1980). *Southall 23 April 1979: The Report of the Unofficial Committee of Enquiry: 23rd April 1979*. London: National Council for Civil Liberties.

Ferguson, R. (1998). *Representing 'Race': Ideology, Identity and the Media*. London: Arnold.

Fevre, R. (1984). *Cheap Labour and Racial Discrimination*. Aldershot: Gower.

Gordon, P., & Rosenberg, D. (1989). *The Press and Black People in Britain*. London: The Runnymede Trust.

Guia, M. J., Woude, M., & Leun, J. (2012). *Social Control and Justice: Crimmigration in the Age of Fear*. The Hague: Eleven International Publishing.

Hartman, P. (1970). The Mass Media and Racial Prejudice. *Race Today, 2*(8), 266–268.

Kundnani, A. (2007). *The End of Tolerance: Racism in 21st Century Britain*. London: Pluto.

Kundnani, A. (2014). *The Muslims Are Coming! Islamophobia, Extremism and the Domestic War on Terror*. London: Verso.

London, L. (1973). The East End of London: Paki-Bashing in 1970. *Race Today, 5*(11), 337–341.

Malik, S. (2002). *Representing Black Britain: Black and Asian Images on Television*. London: Sage.

Mills, T. (2016). *The BBC: Myth of a Public Service*. London: Verso.

Muller, J.-W. (2016). *What Is Populism?* Philadelphia: University of Pennsylvania Press.

Parekh Report. (2000). *The Future of Multi-Ethnic Britain*. London: Runnymede Trust.

Patterson, S. (1967). *Immigration and Race Relations in Britain 1960–1967*. Oxford: Oxford University Press.

Race Today Collective. (1974). Low Pay, Long Hours, and a Small Flames of Rebellion. *Race Today, 6*(5), 137–139.

Ramamurthy, A. (2006). The Politics of Britain's Asian Youth Movements. *Race & Class, 48*(2), 38–60.

Ramdin, R. ([1987] 2017). *The Making of the Black Working Class in Britain.* London: Avebury.

Sveinsson, K. P. (2008). *A Tale of Two Englands: 'Race' and Violent Crime in the Press.* London: Runnymede Trust. Retrieved from http://www.runnymede-trust.org/uploads/publications/pdfs/TwoEnglands-2008.pdf

Taylor, R. (1974, 30 May). Asians and a Union. *New Society, 28,* 608.

Taylor, G., & Dromey, J. (2016). *Grunwick: The Workers' Story* (2nd ed.). London: Lawrence and Wishart.

Van Dijk, T. A. (1991). *Racism and the Press.* London: Routledge.

Weber, L. (2013). *Policing Non-Citizens.* London: Routledge.

Webster, C. (1996). Local Heroes: Violent Racism, Spacism and Localism Among White and Asian Young People. *Youth & Policy, 53,* 15–27.

Webster, C. (1997). The Construction of British 'Asian' Criminality. *International Journal of the Sociology of Law, 25,* 65–86.

Webster, C. (2011). The Construction of Criminality and Disorder Among British Muslim Young People. In M. Farrar, S. Robinson, Y. Valli, & P. Wetherly (Eds.), *'Islam' in 'the West': Key Issues in Multiculturalism.* Palgrave: Basingstoke.

Webster, C. (2014). Negotiating Identities: Ethnicity, Religion and Social Cohesion in London and Bradford. In C. Phillips & C. Webster (Eds.), *New Directions in Race, Ethnicity and Crime.* London: Routledge.

Young, H. (1971). The Treatment of Race in the British Press. In C. Jones (Ed.), *Race and the Press: Four Essays* (pp. 29–41). London: The Runnymede Trust.

Zempi, I., & Awan, I. (2016). *Islamophobia: Lived Experiences of Online and Offline Victimisation.* Bristol: Policy Press.

3

Cultural Repertoires and Modern Menaces: The Media's Racialised Coverage of Child Sexual Exploitation

Tina G. Patel

Introduction

This chapter will discuss the mass media's coverage of child sexual exploitation (CSE) cases in Rochdale (Greater Manchester) and Rotherham (South Yorkshire). These cases gained prominent media attention in the period between 2010 and 2015. The cases involved male abusers of black and minority ethnic (BME) background, in particular of Pakistani heritage and of Muslim faith, who had been abusing young female victims. Although some of the victims were also of the same ethnic background as the abusers, media attention selectively focused on those victims who were of white ethnic background. The chapter argues that the cases were narrated entirely through a cultural repertoire and drew on older racialised panics about the brown menace and white victims. The problem here is that the crime of CSE in these locales (and others like it) became racialised—presented as a form of culturally specific deviance, rather than one about gender and power, this process of 'browning' not only

T. G. Patel (✉)
School of Health & Society, University of Salford, Salford, UK

© The Author(s) 2018
M. Bhatia et al. (eds.), *Media, Crime and Racism*, Palgrave Studies in Crime,
Media and Culture, https://doi.org/10.1007/978-3-319-71776-0_3

created a newer category of the black folk devil, and thus ignored white perpetrators, but also served to marginalise all victims of such abuse. A comment on the media's racialised (re)presentation of these CSE cases takes into account their relative power in modern society, as well as their status, along with other elites, as joint-producers of information about race and racism (van Dijk 2000: 36).

Claiming Cultural Specificity in CSE: Rochdale and Rotherham

CSE can be viewed as a broad term that encompasses a range of activities whereby the child (or young person under 18 years old) receives items, such as food, accommodation, drugs, alcohol, gifts, money or even affection, as a result of them and/or others performing sexual activities. In recent times, the increased use of social media and mobile technology means that CSE can occur without immediate recognition or knowledge. Often violence, coercion and intimidation are used by the abuser. In all CSE cases though, exploitation is based on unequal power relations, associated with the child's social, economic and/or emotional vulnerability (Department for Children, Schools and Families 2009: 9). Despite specialist organisations citing high numbers of reported CSE cases, there had until recently been few prosecutions. The awareness of CSE as a hidden yet widespread occurrence changed somewhat with the release of news in 2012 that the celebrity and (then) British icon, Jimmy Savile, who had died a year earlier, had been sexually abusing young children. Later, as part of a wider police investigation, named 'Operation Yewtree', a number of other high-profile media celebrities including Rolf Harris, Gary Glitter and Max Clifford went on to be sentenced for CSE offences (Shamim 2015). What is interesting about these cases though, and the many others involving white offenders, is that public conversation was based on 'a criminalised narrative'—that is, an "emphasis placed on the criminal intent, not race nor culture, for the motivation behind the sexual exploitation" (Gray and Watt 2013, cited in Shamim 2015: 55).

In May 2012, Rochdale gained prominent media attention for a serious and prolonged case of CSE. The case involved 47 young white female victims and nine offenders—eight of who were of British-Pakistani background and of Muslim faith and the ninth man was of Afghan and asylum-seeking background. Media coverage of the case referred to the 'grooming'[1] of young vulnerable victims by much older offenders, some of who were married and/or fathers, who had used drugs, alcohol, bribery and violence to control and sexually exploit their victims. As one victim reported: "We would get free alcohol and cigarettes, food, free taxis… At first I thought it was great because nothing sexual had happened, I thought I could just get all of this stuff for free. It made me feel like I was pretty. I never thought that they would do what they did to me, because you don't think that would happen… He asked me to come upstairs and I didn't really think anything of it. He then was saying all the things he had bought for me, and he wanted something back for it… I tried to say no in a nice way, but he wasn't having it" (Anonymous victim quoted in BBC News, 8 May 2012).

A few years earlier, Rotherham had been subjected to increased press attention when five men of Pakistani heritage had been found guilty of carrying out a series of offences falling under the CSE category. The offenders received sentences ranging from four to 11 years for abuse against young white girls (the youngest of whom was reportedly 12 years old). However, it was an investigation carried out by *The Times* newspaper after the trial in 2012, which heightened concern and panic—unsurprisingly given that it coincided with the timing of the Rochdale case. *The Times* referred to a 2010 Report by the Rotherham Safeguarding Children Board, in which the term 'cultural characteristics' was used to refer to CSE cases in Rotherham. *The Times* went on to report that there was "a problem with networks of Asian offenders both locally and nationally", but that in areas like Rotherham "there appears to be a significant problem with networks of Asian males exploiting young white females" (*The Times*, 24 September 2012). Later, an independent inquiry into CSE in Rotherham (Jay 2014) estimated that the problem was much higher than expected, stating that 1400 children had been sexually abused in Rotherham between 1997 and 2013 and that most of these cases involved gangs of British-Pakistani men. The report also suggested that there were a number of unknown Asian female victims in the Rotherham case—although this failed to be draw media attention.

The (mis)representation of black and minority ethnic groups in the media is well-documented, as is the recent increase in stories with anti-Muslim narratives (Moore et al. 2008; Saeed 2007; van Dijk 2000). Muslim populations have long been problematised in the media, with an over-zealous tendency to use "race-specific explanations for any criminal activity that is associated with them" (Goodey 2001: 429). In what is claimed to be a post-racial era, anti-Muslim hostility has now focused on what is perceived to be the ever-encroaching cultural, political and religious threat of Islam, and specifically the view that the behaviour of Muslim populations can be seen at best as their refusal and/or inability to integrate into the British 'way of life'. This is illustrated most recently with the media's over-focus and mis-representation of Muslim women who choose to wear the veil (Khiabany and Williamson 2008): "[t]he veil stands for social division, not piety" (*The Times*, 5 July 2014). Parallel fears about Muslim men are also in abundance, and although they have in particular suffered from a 'terror-panic' narrative, recent media coverage of the Rochdale and Rotherham CSE cases re-ignited older sexualised panics about the 'dangerous black body' (Gill and Harrison 2015).

The direction of these narratives is disappointing, albeit unsurprising given the historically Islamophobic depiction of Muslim men as tyrannical and hyper-masculine (Quraishi 2016). This negative depiction is both reflected in and perpetuated by the media. For instance, in an examination of how Muslim populations are presented by the British media, Sian et al. (2012) found that in terms of sexual offending, coverage has focused on 'grooming' stories, notably the grooming of white girls for sex, and allegations of abuse towards Muslim children in Islamic faith schools that are often run by mosques (Sian et al. 2012). In addition, media coverage reported on cases within the specifics of a post-racial era by referring to other/additional socio-variables to add weight to the 'cultural difference' explanation. For instance, in an article on the Rochdale case, Allison Pearson, a columnist for The Daily Telegraph, argued that "[a]ll but one are Pakistani Muslims who come from a patriarchal peasant culture that obviously regards young white British girls as 'easy meat'" (Pearson 2012). As Tufail (2015) notes: "Pearson, noted for her bigoted, outspoken views, took issue with the cultural allowances 'the West' has made to these seemingly backward communities" (p. 32). The suggestion by Pearson, and others who followed suit, was Western (liberal) allowances, combined with fears of being labelled as 'racist', or having been restricted by politically correct agendas, led to failures by professionals in protecting victims and preventing further abuse, as one newspaper reported about the Rotherham case: "Revealed: How fear of being seen as racist stopped social workers saving up to 1400 children from sexual exploitation at the hands of Asian men in just ONE TOWN" [original emphasis] (*Mail Online*, 26 August 2014).

In discussing the Rotherham case and the issue of ethnicity in CSE cases, the Crown Prosecution Service's lead on child sexual abuse, Nazir Afzal, highlighted how the crime is actually about gender (male) power and that ethnicity varies depending on where you are: "I know that the vast majority of offenders are British white male", Afzal stated, going on to cite the figure at between 80 and 90%, before comparing the inconsistent media attention given to cases. "A few weeks after the Rochdale case, we dealt with a case of 10 white men in North Yorkshire who had been abusing young girls, and they were all convicted and they got long sentences. It didn't get the level of coverage" (Nazir Afzal, quoted in *The Guardian*, 3 September 2014). These are claims supported by academic studies—see for instance Cockbain (2013), whose work found that "contrary to popular opinion, CSE is *not* a uniquely Asian threat: in both cases the single largest ethnic group among suspects was white" (p. 28). However, racial reference persists. Indeed, in the case of Rochdale, there was a clear move away from a narrative of CSE being about power and gender towards its re-presentation as something related to ethnic difference and cultural deviance. This is best illustrated with the *Daily Mirror*'s decision to re-release an article several days after it was first published, with an added emphasis on race. For example, the first run of the article ran with the headline of, "Nine quizzed over child grooming", which was later re-published with the headline of, "Nine Asian men quizzed over alleged grooming of white girls for sex" (cited in Cockbain 2013: 24).

The abusive nature of the Rochdale and Rotherham CSE cases is not denied. But what is being critically reflected on is the persistent racialised narrative in which the cases were discussed. Like other CSE cases,

Rochdale and Rotherham were about inequality in society, especially gender inequality, and the use of power and violence to reinforce that inequality. The Rochdale and Rotherham CSE cases had all the hallmarks of other CSE cases, this being the abuse of vulnerable young girls with disorganised and disadvantaged lives, whose vulnerability was targeted by manipulative older men in relative powerful positions, that is, many offenders were business owners with financial stability (Patel 2017). It is argued that from the outset, the cases became presented as a racialised crime. In explaining the offending behaviour, there was an unhealthy reference to the idea of the Pakistani hyper-sexualised predator targeting the ultimate victim—young white girls (Miah 2015: 54–55). This is illustrated in how there was a move away from the term 'child sexual exploitation' and towards that of 'Asian sex gangs'. Indeed, the use of the term 'Asian' in coverage of the case—a term which has traditionally been used to refer to all those of South Asian (Indian, Pakistani and Bangladeshi) heritage—had the immediate effect of widening the group to which the 'grooming stigma' could be applied (Patel 2017). The result of this raciali- sation and net-widening practice resulted in the creation of a new type of racial crime threat (Cockbain 2013: 22) or, as Patel argues, a new(er) racial crime threat which was able to present itself as working within the equality agenda of a supposed post-racial world and, yet at the same time, draw on the idea of a racial hierarchy (Patel 2017).

Observers and 'experts' argued that this particular type of crime was symptomatic of a supposed restrictive Asian culture, which along with its practice of arranged marriages, and a lack of respect for women—espe- cially white women, resulted in young men of Pakistani heritage having pent-up sexual frustrations. Indeed, former Home Secretary Jack Straw argued that such culturally specific sexual frustration was a key cause of the offending behaviour: "there is a specific problem which involves Pakistani heritage men … who target vulnerable young white girls… These young men are in a western society, in any event, they act like any other young men, they're fizzing and popping with testosterone, they want some outlet for that, but Pakistani heritage girls are off-limits and they are expected to marry a Pakistani girl from Pakistan, typically" (quoted in BBC News, 8 January 2011). CSE is not about sexual release, and to suggest it fails to consider the true complexity of cases (Cockbain

2013: 26). Similarly, "Asians, like whites or blacks, do not commit [these] offences *because* they are Asian, white or black" and to suggest this brings the danger of presenting every Asian man as a 'groomer-in-waiting' (Cockbain 2013: 30).

Racialising CSE: Causes, Methods and Consequences

It is not disputed that some CSE in Rochdale and Rotherham involved male perpetrators of Pakistani heritage. What is interesting though is how these cases were solely interpreted through what Miah (2015: 54) refers to as a 'cultural repertoire', and not a 'criminal repertoire' as in Operation Yewtree and others involving white men. The term 'cultural repertoire' is used by Miah to refer to how the men in the Rochdale and Rotherham cases could only be seen through the perspective of race and culture (2015: 55). The construction of Asian criminality in the Rochdale and Rotherham CSE cases was possible because it drew on existing racist foundations and anti-Muslim hostility of a post-racial world. Within the post-racial era (see Patel 2017), we find new forms of racism. Post-race refers to an attempt to move beyond traditional constructions of race, with a specific suggestion that society has so far progressed with race equality, that we have now entered a state where it no longer needs the same amount and/or type of consideration that it warranted in the past. However, as I argue elsewhere (Patel 2017), society continued to be marked out by racialised events, and although these events may be (re) presented as non-racial, their cause and effect continue to divide (and rule) along racial lines. Thus, there is the use of new(er) forms of racism. Balibar (1991) argues that this 'new' racism, or what they call 'neo-racism', is 'racism without races' (p. 21). New forms of racism allowing for an illustrated move away from ideas about racial (biological) inferiority and yet in its place make space for a claim of cultural difference (van Dijk 2000: 34). However, as Semati (2010) points out, the notion of 'difference' remains, and this "conceptualization of 'difference', of 'other' cultures as immutable, fixed, frozen and static essences, is as essentialist as the biological one", with the hateful racial slurs and the more respectful claims to cultural difference amounting to the same thing and both serving to function the preservation of a racial hierarchy in which whiteness is privileged (p. 266).

Within the Rochdale and Rotherham cases, heightened media coverage of the 'Asian groomer' folk devil whet the *post-racial come new racist* appetite of those with wider 'cultural difference', preoccupations about a clash of cultures, failed multiculturalism, problems of mass immigration, problematic family formations (arranged and forced marriages) and the encroaching threat of Sharia Law (Patel 2017). In particular, the media's presentation of these CSE cases normalised the link between race, religion and sexual grooming (Miah 2015: 58). The notion of 'dangerous brown men' (2008) as racialised hyper-sexualised beings actually draws on much older and cruder forms of the 'black folk devil' whose hyper-sexuality has long been presented as a threat to white women (Miah 2015: 62) and, by default, as a threat to the safety, purity and status of the white race as a whole. Within the post-racial era, the 'Asian grooming' moral panic works through slightly different racialised processes—one that uses 'browning' to construct categories of difference. Browning refers to a particular racialised process whereby this population group is constructed as a specific type of deviant category (Patel 2013: 35). Although browning has its roots in the century-old Orientalist visions and narratives of the West (Said 1978, 1993), a surge in the attention given to browning and the brown body occurred in the aftermath of 9/11. In the years before then, brown was an identity (Silva 2010). The brown body had been presented as passive, subservient, inward-looking—and although they were undesirable and unwanted, as illustrated with increasing controls on what was in the past referred to as 'coloured immigration', that is, immigration from the Asian-subcontinent, they were in the main considered to be less of a threat than their black African-Caribbean counterparts. Within a post-race context, brown becomes "re-mapped, re-made, and re-marked … as an identification rather than an identity, distinct from previous articulations of race and identity" (Silva 2010: 173).

Claims about living in a post-race era meant it was no longer desirable in the mainstream to be seen as harbouring racially discriminatory views. Yet, racist views persisted and instead began to be re-presented in more palatable ways. Browning allowed for notions of cultural and non-essential difference to be used to support measures which ultimately resulted in racialised regulation of those perceived to be a threat or, more widely, those who were (in the colonial mind-set of Western society) considered socially undesirable. In recent times this has been the Asian body. It is important to recognise that the term 'Asian' is a term typically used to describe people of South Asian descent. However, the post-9/11 terror-panic context and more recently the 'grooming' scandals have resulted in the term 'Asian' being conflated with 'Pakistani' and 'Muslim' (Cockbain 2013: 23). The end result of this conflation is the wider casting of the deviance net across BME populations, which allows for more BME groups to be stigmatised and subject to enhance surveillance measures. The Asian conflation in media coverage of CSE is considered to be a stra-tegic tactic in the wider 'deviance amplification', to draw on Hall et al.'s (1978) work, of BME populations. Browning of CSE saw newer prac-tices of racial demonisation occur. These *types* of brown bodies were pre-sented as having a unique type of sexual deviance—a predatory preference for young white girls, emerging supposedly from their hyper-patriarchal culture in which the 'off-limits' status of women, which led to confined sexual frustrations. The 'black sexual menace' logic was easy to digest given that it echoed earlier narratives about the black male body (epito-mised in the image of the black penis) and its threat to whiteness. These draw on wider logics about the supposed unruly black body: "the Black body is condemned before it even acts; it has always already committed a crime… Even in the womb, the Black body is already *against the law*" [original emphasis] (Yancy 2008: xxi).

The image of the 'Asian groomer' as a folk devil was so powerful because the image of the menacing black sexual predator was a logic already embed-ded in what Gilroy (2005: 432) refers to as the 'imperial mentalities' of British society. This was illustrated with the former Home Secretary Jack Straw's 'easy meat' comment,[2] suggesting that the best way to understand these CSE cases was not through a criminal model but through a cultural one specific to Pakistani communities (Miah 2015: 57). In addition, the media's victims in these CSE cases were not only white but they were female, young and many came from care homes. They were therefore espe-cially more vulnerable and higher up on the victimhood hierarchy.[3] The media's presentation of the men in the CSE cases echoes its similar presentation of cases involving South Asian men, even in those instances where the victim is also of South Asian heritage. Consider the reporting of the Jyoti Singh Pandey rape in Delhi, in which the international press collectively embarked on selective, biased and sensationalist reporting of the case, which served to damage the reputation of *all* Indian men, presenting them (and Indian nation) as backwards and culturally deficient (Patel 2017). For example, a New York Times Editorial contrasted "India's 'patriarchal village culture' with the ostensibly true cosmopolitanism of Western cities" (*New York Times* Editorial, cited in Roychowdhury 2013: 283–284). Although Pandey was also of South Asian heritage, she became situated in a position closer to whiteness—she was reportedly an attractive woman who dressed in western clothes and wore her long hair flowing and down. She refused to be confined to the home, and instead visited malls and movie theatres (*Mirror* Newspaper 2013, cited in Roychowdhury 2013: 283).

Numerous CSE inquiries, such as that into Rotherham (2014), have stated that "there is no simple link between race and child sexual exploitation and across the UK the greatest numbers of perpetrators of CSE are white men" (p. 91). Yet, the persistent racialisation of the CSE reinforces the notion that the crime is a cultural trait that is hereditary in some groups and not shared with other races (Appiah 1992, cited in Miah 2015: 58). This 'logic' ultimately fails to consider how gender and power relations are key features of CSE. This is illustrated with the findings of a study carried out by Gohir (2013) for the Muslim Women's Network UK, which found that Asian men groom and sexually exploit other Asian children within their own communities—often giving their victims drink and drugs before silencing them with promises of marriage or using threats of honour and shame to conceal the abuse. Indeed, there are more practical reasons, as opposed to cultural ones, for any ethnic factors in the Rotherham and Rochdale cases: the perpetrators were those who were disproportionately employed in the night-time economy, in other words, those places where victims could be offered food, warmth, 'love', transport, drugs and alcohol (*The Guardian* 2014). Failure to consider elements of positionality, gender, power and control in CSE ultimately ignores the needs of all CSE victims.

The racialised misappropriation of the 'victimhood' status enables support for 'white power', or what Cabrera refers to as 'racial hyper-privilege'

(2011: 77). This advantageous status presents white populations as the *true victims* of racial equality agendas, and is used to rationalise any ensuing racially homogenous sub-environments and/or agendas (Cabrera 2014). Interestingly, research by Cabrera (2014) into American white male college students' views about race and racism found that participants forcefully rejected the suggestion that they inhabited a racially privileged position in society. This allows for 'white bodies' to become largely situated as unproblematic, even when they are perpetrators of criminal offences. This is because white bodies are able to draw on the centrality and normality of whiteness in order to detach or play-down labels of deviance (Patel 2013: 34–35). For instance, consider the limited media attention and non-racialised narrative given to those CSE cases involving white offenders, which ran at the same time as Rochdale and Rotherham, such as the 2010 case in West Cornwall involving five (white) men who had groomed and sexually abused children, some as young as five, or the case of the 13-year-old child from North Yorkshire who was sexually abused over a prolonged period by 30 men (Tufail 2015: 34). Part of this whiteness centrality works by hyper-racialising spaces. For instance, in the Rochdale case, it emerged that two of the offenders had worked for a local taxi firm. When the scandal emerged, the firm's owner permitted clients to request a white driver—a decision that was later overturned following protest from Asian drivers. The driver-race selection option illustrates the articulation of spaces in racialised ways, with the taxi-cab being presented here as a 'brown space': a site of danger. In a consideration of the brown taxi driver following 9/11, Sharma (2010) argues that in this brown space, "the knowledge of brown is produced and then disciplined" (p. 185). This also allows for whiteness to become 'normalised' and all else to become presented as deviant.

Concluding Comments

In comparison to white CSE offenders, such as those in Operation Yewtree, concern about the so-called Asian grooming gangs—those CSE cases which involved men of Pakistani heritage in Rochdale and Rotherham—has been processed through a much different logic. This is despite parallels between them, such as how the abuse both largely involved the sexual exploitation of people in care, how similar grooming methods were used and how the victims were considered to have been let down by institutional failures (Miah 2015: 54). Narratives about Rochdale and Rotherham have been packaged through a racial lens—itself presented as being rooted in the 'cultural traits' of not only the offenders but, in addition, the offending community. This racialised narrative has been present from the outset, for instance, in focusing on the 'local Asian community' in Rotherham, Heal argued that taboo and fear probably prevented locals from speaking about perpetrators (2003). In Rochdale too, the CSE case was framed by a racialised narrative, indeed it was claimed that health workers, social workers and the police were 'colour blind' to what one tabloid newspaper argued was an *obvious* racial element of the case: why older Asian men were in relationships with vulnerable white teenage girls (*Mirror*, 20 December 2013). With its over-focus on race (or cultural difference), CSE became used as evidence of 'brown deviance' and was used more widely to support racist agendas around social control. As a result, a newer criminal category became common-sensical in the white imagination and in effect ignored the fact that CSE is about gender, power and control (Budin and Johnson 1988; Hartman and Burgess 1989; Young 1997).

Notes

1. 'Grooming' has been a term commonly used in the media's presentation of child sexual exploitation (CSE) cases. However, it must be recognised that 'grooming' is a 'dubious category'. It is not a distinct sexual offence, as the media would have us believe, but rather it is an 'ill-defined subset' of child sexual exploitation (Cockbain 2013: 22). Grooming is used to refer to the tactics used by sex offenders in attempts to sexually abuse children (Craven et al. 2006, cited in Gill and Harrison 2015: 35).
2. Speaking on the BBC's *Newsnight* programme in January 2011, Jack Straw said about Asian men of Pakistani heritage: "These young men are in a western society, in any event, they act like any other young men, they're fizzing and popping with testosterone, they want some outlet for that, but Pakistani heritage girls are off-limits and they are expected to marry a Pakistani girl from Pakistan, typically…So they then seek other

avenues and they see these young women, white girls who are vulnerable, some of them in care ... who they think are easy meat" (Jack Straw, quoted on *Newsnight*, 7 January 2011).
3. This comment in no way detracts from the victimisation experienced by the girls in these CSE cases.

References

Balibar, É. (1991). Is There a "Neo-Racism"? In E. Balibar & I. Wallerstein (Eds.), *Race, Nation, Class: Ambiguous Identities* (pp. 17–28). London: Verso.

BBC News. (2011, January 8). Jack Straw: Some White Girls Are 'East Meat' for Abuse. *BBC News Online*. Retrieved from http://www.bbc.co.uk/news/uk-england-derbyshire-12141603

BBC News. (2012, May 8). Rochdale Grooming Case: Victim's story. *BBC News Online*. Retrieved from http://www.bbc.co.uk/news/uk-england-manchester-17914138

Budin, L. E., & Johnson, C. F. (1988). Sex Abuse Prevention Programs: Offenders' Attitudes About Their Efficacy. *Child Abuse and Neglect, 13*(1), 77–87.

Cabrera, N. L. (2011). Using a Sequential Exploratory Mixed-Methods Design to Examine Racial Hyperprivilege in Higher Education. In K. A. Griffin & S. D. Museus (Eds.), *Using Mixed-Methods Approaches to Study Intersectionality in Higher Education: New Directions for Institutional Research* (pp. 77–91). San Francisco, CA: Jossey Bass.

Cabrera, N. L. (2014). Exposing Whiteness in Higher Education: White Male College Students Minimizing Racism, Claiming Victimization, and Recreating White Supremacy. *Race, Ethnicity and Education, 17*(1), 30–55.

Cockbain, E. (2013). Grooming and the 'Asian Sex Gang Predator': The Construction of a Racial Crime Threat. *Race and Class, 54*(4), 22–32.

Department for Children, Schools and Families. (2009). *Safeguarding Children and Young People from Sexual Exploitation: Supplementary Guidance to Working Together to Safeguard Children*. London: Department for Children, Schools and Families (DCSF).

Gill, A. K., & Harrison, K. (2015). Child Grooming and Sexual Exploitation: Are South Asian Men the UK's Media's New Folk Devils? *International Journal for Crime, Justice and Social Democracy, 4*(2), 34–49.

Gilroy, P. (2005). Multiculture, Double Consciousness and the 'War on Terror'. *Patterns of Prejudice, 39*(4), 431–443.

Gohir, S. (2013). *Unheard Voices: The Sexual Exploitation of Asian Girls and Young Women*. Birmingham: Muslim Women's Network UK. Retrieved from http://www.mwnuk.co.uk/go_files/resources/UnheardVoices.pdf

Goodey, J. (2001). The Criminalization of British Asian Youth: Research from Bradford and Sheffield. *Journal of Youth Studies, 4*(4), 429–450.

Hall, S., Critcher, C., Jefferson, T., & Roberts, B. (1978). *Policing the Crisis: Mugging, the State and Law and Order*. London: Palgrave.

Hartman, C. R., & Burgess, A. W. (1989). Sexual Abuse of Children: Causes and Consequences. In D. Cicchetti & V. Carlson (Eds.), *Child Maltreatment: Theory and Research on the Causes and Consequences of Child Abuse and Neglect* (pp. 95–126). Cambridge: Cambridge University Press.

Heal, A. (2003). *Sexual Exploitation, Drug Use and Drug Dealing: Current Situation in South Yorkshire*. South Yorkshire: South Yorkshire Police and Partnerships. Retrieved from http://www.lgcplus.com/Journals/2015/05/05/r/b/q/Sexual-Exploitation-Drug-Use-and-Drug-Dealing-the-Current-Situation-in-South-Yorkshire.pdf

Jay, A. (2014). *Independent Inquiry into Child Sexual Exploitation in Rotherham 1997–2013*. Rotherham: Rotherham Metropolitan Borough Council.

Khiabany, G., & Williamson, M. (2008). Veiled Bodies, Naked Racism: Culture, Politics and Race in the Sun. *Race and Class, 50*(2), 69–88.

Mail Online. (2014, August 26). Revealed: How Fear of Being Seen as Racist Stopped Social Workers Saving up to 1,400 Children from Sexual Exploitation at the Hands of Asian Men in Just ONE TOWN. *Mail Online*. Retrieved from http://www.dailymail.co.uk/news/article-2734694/It-hard-appalling-nature-abuse-child-victims-suffered-1-400-children-sexually-exploited-just-one-town-16-year-period-report-reveals.html

Miah, S. (2015). The Groomers and the Question of Race. *Identity Papers: A Journal of British and Irish Studies, 1*(1), 54–66.

Mirror. (2013, December 20). Rochdale Sex Grooming Gang: Police Were 'Colour Blind' to White Girls Exploited by Asian Paedophile Ring. *Mirror*. Retrieved from http://www.mirror.co.uk/news/uk-news/rochdale-sex-grooming-gang-police-2947712

Newsnight. (2011, January 7). *Newsnight*. Broadcasted on *BBC Two*. London: BBC.

Patel, T. G. (2013). Ethnic Deviant Labels Within the 'War on Terror' Context: Absolving White Deviance. *Ethnicity and Race in a Changing World, 4*(1), 34–50.

Patel, T. G. (2017). *Race and Society*. London: Sage.

Pearson, A. (2012, May 9). Asian Sex Gang: Young Girls Betrayed by Our Fear of Racism. *The Telegraph*. Retrieved from http://www.telegraph.co.uk/comment/columnists/allison-pearson/9254651/Asian-sex-gang-young-girls-betrayed-by-our-fear-of-racism.html

Quraishi, M. (2016). Child Sexual Exploitation and British Muslims: A Modern Moral Panic? In S. Hamid (Ed.), *Young British Muslims: Rhetoric and Realities* (pp. 26–38). Farnham: Ashgate.

Roychowdhury, P. (2013). 'The Delhi Gang Rape': The Making of International Causes. *Feminist Studies, 39*(1), 282–292.

Saeed, A. (2007). Media, Racism and Islamophobia: The Representation of Islam and Muslims in the Media. *Sociology Compass, 1*(2), 443–462.

Said, E. (1978). *Orientalism*. New York: Vintage.

Said, E. (1993). *Culture and Imperialism*. New York: Vintage.

Semati, M. (2010). Islamophobia, Culture and Race in the Age of Empire. *Cultural Studies, 24*(2), 256–275.

Shamim, M. (2015). The Groomers and the Question of Race. *Identity Papers: A Journal of British and Irish Studies, 1*(1), 54–66.

Sharma, S. (2010). Taxi Cab Publics and the Production of Brown Space After 9/11. *Cultural Studies, 24*(2), 183–199.

Sian, K., Law, I., & Sayyid, S. (2012). *The Media and Muslims in the UK*. Leeds: Centre for Ethnicity and Racism Studies, University of Leeds.

Silva, K. (2010). Brown: From Identity to Identification. *Cultural Studies, 24*(2), 167–182.

The Guardian. (2014, September 3). Nazir Afzal: There Is No Religious Basis for the Abuse in Rotherham. *The Guardian Online*. Retrieved from http://www.theguardian.com/society/2014/sep/03/nazir-afzal-there-is-no-religious-basis-for-the-abuse-in-rotherham

The Times. (2014, July 5). The Veil Stands for Social Division, not Piety. *The Times*. Retrieved from http://www.thetimes.co.uk/tto/opinion/columnists/article4139405.ece

Tufail, W. (2015). Rotherham, Rochdale, and the Racialised Threat of the 'Muslim Grooming Gang. *International Journal for Crime, Justice and Social Democracy, 4*(3), 30–43.

van Dijk, T. (2000). New(s) Racism: A Discourse Analytical Approach. In S. Cottle (Ed.), *Ethnic Minorities and the Media* (pp. 33–49). Milton Keynes, UK: Open University Press.

Yancy, G. (2008). *Black Bodies, White Gazes: The Continuing Significance of Race*. New York: Rowman and Littlefield Publishers.

Young, S. (1997). The Use of Normalization as a Strategy in the Sexual Exploitation of Children by Adult Offenders. *The Canadian Journal of Human Sexuality, 6*(4), 285–295.

4

Media, State and 'Political Correctness': The Racialisation of the Rotherham Child Sexual Abuse Scandal

Waqas Tufail

Introduction

Over the past decade in Britain, a number of sexual abuse scandals emerged. These ranged from the revelations about celebrity Jimmy Savile, thought to be the most prolific sexual abuser in British history, to the crimes of long-standing Liberal MP Cyril Smith. Both men, now deceased, were left unchecked to commit sexually violent offences against young girls and boys over a period of decades. Operation Yewtree, the on-going Metropolitan Police investigation initiated following the Jimmy Savile scandal, led to the conviction of high-profile sex abusers such as celebrity publicist Max Clifford and entertainer Rolf Harris. Around the same time as the celebrity sex abuse scandal began to make news headlines, another scandal emerged concerning the violent sexual abuse of young girls and women. This related to revelations that groups of men in towns including Rochdale in Greater Manchester and Rotherham in

W. Tufail (✉)
Leeds Beckett University, Leeds, UK

© The Author(s) 2018
M. Bhatia et al. (eds.), *Media, Crime and Racism*, Palgrave Studies in Crime, Media and Culture, https://doi.org/10.1007/978-3-319-71776-0_4

South Yorkshire had been sexually abusing scores of young girls over a number of years. Whilst all of these crimes received widespread news coverage, there was a marked difference in how they were framed and how they came to be understood. In the popular press representations of the Rochdale and Rotherham sexual abuse crimes, issues of violence against women and patriarchy were relegated and decentred in place of a dominant and mainstream narrative that portrayed the child sexual abuse scandal as primarily due to the uniquely dangerous masculinities of Muslim men (Tufail 2015; Gill and Harrison 2015). This chapter examines how local media and state actors and institutions in Rotherham framed the child sexual abuse scandal, the impact this had on minority communities and community relations more broadly and the ways in which these representations were challenged and resisted. This chapter also addresses the inherent tensions between feminists and anti-racists that arise in the context of sexual abuse scandals involving ethnic minority perpetrators (Grewal 2012; Ho 2006) and argues that in Rotherham there is evidence of an emergent, grassroots, anti-racist feminism.

A key feature of the sexual abuse crimes carried out by groups of men in Rochdale, Rotherham and in other towns across the UK was that they came to be understood primarily through race. This was realised through terms popularised by the media in the reporting of these cases, such as 'Muslim grooming gang' and 'Asian gang'. In entering popular parlance, these terms and the related racial signifiers of culture, religion and ethnicity were used as explanatory devices in understanding the motivation for these crimes. Tellingly, this process of racialisation did not take place in the examination of the Operation Yewtree sexual abuse cases, all of which featured criminal investigations into prominent white men. Garner and Selod (2014) have recently called for a reinvigoration of the study of racialisation, a concept they argue has been underdeveloped, particularly in terms of its application to Muslims. Garner and Selod posit that Islamophobia (or anti-Muslim racism) and racism are intimately connected and can be examined and understood further through the concept of racialisation. The concept of racialisation allows for an analysis of Islamophobia on a social, collective and systemic level as opposed to being reduced to analyses focusing on individual psychology. Garner and Selod set out the lack of empirical studies examining the racialisation of

Muslims, and particularly those featuring qualitative interviews with Muslim respondents. This study, in its in-depth, empirical examination of anti-Muslim racism featuring interviews with multiple British Muslim interviewees, responds to this call.

Poynting and Perry, in their examination of anti-Muslim racism in Australia and Canada, point to the practices of the media and the state at an individual and institutional level in creating an 'enabling environment' where violent crimes of hate can flourish (2007, p. 161). This enabling environment, they argue, effectively lends '"permission to hate" to those inclined to commit hate crime against Muslims' (2007, p. 167). Following Poynting and Perry, it is argued in this chapter that a climate of anti-Muslim racism emerged in Rotherham, South Yorkshire, enabled by liberals as much as it was by the more familiar far-right and conservative figures and groups. This anti-Muslim climate resulted in a 'permission to hate' at the local level, demonstrated by a significant rise in attacks on local racialised minority communities. These attacks included the racist murder of an elderly Muslim grandfather, beaten to death whilst walking to his local mosque for early morning prayers.

This chapter demonstrates how the racial landscape of Rotherham was fundamentally transformed in the context and aftermath of the widely publicised child sexual abuse scandal. This landscape was shaped by a popular discourse that variously described local Muslims as in some way collectively responsible for the crimes, as prone to committing them due to cultural deficiencies or as actors representing evidence of the ills of 'political correctness' and 'failed' multiculturalism. Departing from previous studies, this study concentrated primarily on how local media discourses and state and institutional actions (and inaction) shaped the racial landscape within Rotherham. This study highlights how strategies of resistance to both sexual abuse and the racialising of Muslims emerged, demonstrated by the actions of local Muslim women activists, local residents and by child sexual abuse survivors themselves. This chapter is based on an in-depth study centred in Rotherham, South Yorkshire, and uses data collected from a range of sources including semi-structured interviews with British Muslims, critical discourse analysis of media items and documentary analysis of official reports.

From the National to the Local: Race, Culture and Media Framing

In 2011, *The Guardian* reported comments made by the former Home Secretary and Labour MP for Blackburn Jack Straw. Straw, whose constituency is home to a sizeable Muslim population mainly of South Asian origin, attempted to explain the recent conviction of two men for sexual offences committed against girls in Derby by asserting that 'there is a specific problem which involves Pakistani heritage men ... who target vulnerable young girls' (Batty 2011). Straw further commented that young Pakistani men were 'fizzing and popping with testosterone', see white girls as 'easy meat' and that the reason for this is that 'Pakistani heritage girls are off-limits and they are expected to marry a Pakistani girl from Pakistan, typically'. Whilst Straw was later challenged for engaging in crude stereotyping by Keith Vaz, a fellow Labour MP, the comments had already received national attention and served as one of the first notable interventions into what came to be known variously as the 'grooming', 'Muslim grooming gang', 'Asian grooming gang', child sex abuse scandal. Straw's framing of the problem in the arena of race (through the racial signifiers of ethnicity and culture) gave legitimacy to a perspective that may previously have been more associated with the far-right than an ostensibly centre-left politician.

In an article in *The Independent*, following Jack Straw's high-profile comments, writer Joan Smith attempted to challenge the stereotyping by stating that 'these horrific crimes against children are not racially-motivated in the obvious sense' (Smith 2011). However, Smith then proceeded to locate the causes of the crime not in the race of the sexual abusers but in their problematic culture. In doing so, the writer seemingly rejected the unacceptable references to race and ethnicity by replacing them with acceptable references to culture. As Smith informs us:

> Most of the defendants have roots in rural areas of Pakistan, where family structure remains tribal and patriarchal. In such cultures, extra-marital sex is forbidden and girls and women become a potent focus of fear and desire, a circumstance that pimps in this country have skilfully exploited. (Smith 2011)

Whilst it is unclear if Joan Smith is an expert on rural Pakistan or indeed on the nature of family structures and sexual relationships in that country, it is with much conviction that she makes these claims. Smith goes further too in critiquing the role of religious leaders by arguing that 'many imams come from a rural background where such crimes are almost unknown, while their own view of male-female relations tends to be hopelessly out of date'. Aside from the Orientalism that underpins the writer's narrative, it is of note that this intervention is presented as progressive and in opposition to the regressive characterisation offered by Jack Straw. In disavowing the role of race, Smith is content to argue on the terrain of culture, a position that is ostensibly more liberal-minded than the characterisation offered by Straw. However, as Alana Lentin reminds us, 'culture, ethnicity, religion, nationality ... can all stand for race at different times' (2008, p. 490). Solomos and Back elaborate on the emergence of 'new racism' as distinct in its form:

This means that racism may be expressed through a variety of coded signifiers... Contemporary racisms have evolved and adapted to new circumstances. The crucial property of these elaborations is that they can produce a racist effect while denying that this effect is the result of racism. For example, the new racisms of the 1980s are coded within a cultural logic. As a result the champions of this racism can claim that they are protecting their way of life and that the issue of colour or phenotype is irrelevant. (1994, p. 156)

Though Solomos and Back were writing some time ago, the legacy of their assertions are confirmed by more recent studies, such as those examining 'racial cues' in news media reporting of the Hurricane Katrina disaster in the USA (Sonnett et al. 2015) and racist media framing of urban disorder in France (Harsin 2015). The longevity of this concept has also been updated to reflect the racism(s) experienced by Muslim communities, as Dagistanli and Grewal articulate:

In Islamophobic perspectives, the category of 'culture' is often superimposed onto the notion of race whereby racial and cultural differences become interchangeable or at least utilised in the same ways to further an overtly racist agenda. (2012, p. 135)

The above examples from Jack Straw and Joan Smith both aim to offer explanations for the reasons that sexual abuse in some communities occurs and whilst they differed in their articulation, they in fact have a similar if not shared perspective that is only revealed when the racially coded signifiers of 'ethnicity', 'culture' and 'religion' are unmasked.

The above news items were featured in prominent national newspapers, *The Guardian* and *The Independent*, respectively. Whilst studies and analyses of newspapers typically focus on the national press, it is imperative to consider the content of local newspapers too and specifically the ways in which local journalists report on crimes, incidents and behaviours involving British Muslims and individuals and groups from other racialised minority communities (Poole 2011). The following example, taken from an editorial in the *Yorkshire Evening Post* (a daily evening publication considered to adopt a centrist/liberal perspective) in May 2012, highlights a number of issues pertinent to this analysis.

Local Media and Liberal Accounts

In an article provocatively titled 'The truth about grooming?' *Yorkshire Evening Post* reporter Grant Woodward attempted to make sense of the links between 'Asian—and specifically Pakistani Muslim' men and the 'targeting of white girls' (Woodward 2012). Citing one study by the Child Exploitation and Online Protection Centre (CEOP) as the basis for the news article (a study limited by scope, a paucity of accurate data and that the CEOP themselves deemed 'too inconsistent to draw meaningful conclusions'), the story presented is one of a link between ethnicity and crimes of sexual abuse. Attempts such as these to link ethnicity, race, culture or religion to sexual abuse have not been limited to conservative or far-right commentators. Nick Lowles, chief executive of Hope Not Hate, an anti-racist organisation sitting at the liberal end of the anti-racist spectrum, saw fit to pen an article suggesting a link between culture and sexual abuse:

> Of course there is a culture factor to all this in that these paedophiles pick on vulnerable white girls because they think they can get away with this

behaviour as it is being perpetrated against people who are outside their community. (Lowles 2012)

Lowles is at pains in this article to distance himself from fascist, far-right groupings such as the British National Party (BNP) and the English Defence League (EDL). Lowles is seemingly suggesting that it is important for liberal anti-racists to 'accept the facts' and debate the ethnicity link to sexual abuse so that it does not fall into the 'wrong hands' of the far right. The tone of the article is reflected by Lowles' claim that 'we, as anti-fascists and progressives, should not be afraid to speak out'. This characterisation, however, was directly challenged by Liz Fekete, director of the Institute of Race Relations. Fekete highlighted Lowles' selective (and fictitious) use of statistics and recalled the ways in which this tactic was employed by the media and the far right in the 1980s in creating folk devils such as that of the 'young black mugger' (Fekete 2012). Cockbain (2013, p. 30) also robustly challenged the racialisation of the child sexual abuse crimes arguing that the 'construction of grooming as a distinct offence and a racial crime threat has been shown to lie on insubstantial foundations: misconceptions, anecdote, opinion and the deliberate manipulation of limited statistics of dubious provenance'. In her response to Lowles, Fekete recommended a more suitable method through which sexual abuse and racism could be tackled together; 'Instead of ethnicising crime, progressives and anti-fascists could be uniting to create a future for young people free from abuse'. This exchange symbolised not only some of the fissures in the left in a broader sense but also the durability of racist ideas in supposedly anti-racist, liberal left circles.

In the *Yorkshire Evening Post*, Grant Woodward featured an interview with Ann Cryer, a former West Yorkshire MP and who incidentally was cited by Nick Lowles as another brave figure willing to challenge presumed 'uncomfortable truths' regarding 'Asian gangs' and sexual abuse. In articulating her viewpoint, Cryer confirmed 'It is nothing to do with race or religion, it is cultural. There is a culture of having a very macho view of the world among young men in the Pakistani community' (Woodward 2012). This problematic representation of 'young men in the Pakistani community' went unchallenged by the journalist and was thus presented as a legitimate, unproblematic perspective. Beyond Cryer's use of 'culture' as an anti-racist mechanism (to avoid the accusation of racism), she goes further by arguing that in her view the West Yorkshire Police were reluctant to prosecute because of 'political correctitude writ large'. The curious, ahistorical idea that police forces were unwilling to investigate sexual abuse crimes for fear of being labelled 'racist' has been addressed previously (Tufail 2015). However, the idea that police forces and other institutions failed to investigate crimes because of 'political correctness', a claim that achieved prominence in local and national media coverage, requires examination, and it is to this task that this chapter will now turn.

'Political Correctness': A Familiar and Lasting Refrain

In August 2014 Professor Alexis Jay released what came to be known as the Jay (2014) report. This report led to a media sensation that dominated the news agenda and which lasted for several days. Within the report were shocking details of the widespread and long-term sexual abuse of young girls and women by groups of men in the town of Rotherham in South Yorkshire. The author of the report had estimated that at least 1400 young girls and women had been abused in the period between 1997 and 2013. Predictably, much of the tabloid outcry and wider right-wing media narrative focused on the ethnicity of the perpetrators, an issue that has been explored in some detail (Tufail and Poynting 2016; Gill and Harrison 2015; Tufail 2015; Cockbain 2013). Yet there was another thread that ran through both conservative and liberal media accounts concerning the 'grooming' scandal: the issue of 'political correctness'.

Following the publication of the Jay report in 2014 then Home Secretary and current Prime Minister Theresa May argued strongly that 'institutionalised political correctness' on the part of the authorities had played an enabling role in the abuse of young girls and women in Rotherham. May further argued that:

> I am clear that cultural concerns—both the fear of being seen as racist, and the frankly disdainful attitude to some of our most vulnerable children—must never stand in the way of child protection. (Tran 2014)

In the same article it was reported that Yvette Cooper, Labour MP and then Shadow Home Secretary, agreed with the Prime Minister that 'race, ethnicity or community relations should not be used as an excuse not to investigate and punish sex offenders', as if to suggest that it had been so used. The rhetoric of 'political correctness' could be found too in the words of Alexis Jay and Louise Casey, both of whom were independently commissioned by government to write reports into the Rotherham child sexual abuse scandal. Whilst they both reserved significant criticism for state institutions such as the local authority and the police, this was underpinned by a belief that a refusal to investigate the crimes was due, according to Jay, to 'a political fear of tackling the ethnic issue head on'. This claim was bolstered by Casey's official report into Rotherham Council, in which she argued that 'The Council's culture is unhealthy: bullying, sexism, suppression and misplaced "political correctness" have cemented its failures' (2015, p. 9). Both Jay and Casey also criticised the institutional macho and sexist culture that they argued played a role in the abuse being ignored and left to continue for a number of years. Critically, however, despite the myriad reasons presented for the enabling of widespread and long-term abuse in Rotherham, it was the narrative of 'political correctness' that gained most currency in the subsequent press reports and popular discourse.

The following letters, received and published by the *Rotherham Advertiser* (the most popular daily local newspaper in the Rotherham area) in the immediate aftermath of the publication of the Jay report in 2014, shed light on the strength and durability of the 'political correctness' narrative and of how it enabled openly bigoted and racist comments from the public:

> Because this blatant racism is not "in the right direction" all the Pakistani Community appears to know nothing of the events that happened. The fact is that everyone know this.... BUT still no one does anything to stop the onslaught of pathetic political correctness that encourages unfairness, abuse and genuine freedom of speech for everyone. I am not racist either; I am a fair-ist to all. (*Rotherham Advertiser* 2014)

Notable in the above comment is the conspiratorial idea that the 'Pakistani Community' was collectively working in cahoots to keep the abuse hidden. This was a feature that ran through much of the discourse in the aftermath of the Rotherham child sexual abuse revelations and is an issue to which this chapter will later return. Of further note was the assertion by this member of the public that they were not being racist. No such clarifications were made by the following member of the public, who argued in the same edition of the *Rotherham Advertiser* that:

> One thing is for sure, as pressure mounts on the Pakistani communities that caused this outrage, they will soon play the race card with aplomb, they will say we are the victims and we don't deserve this and the pressure to find the perpetrators will stop, the hierarchy will back off and the cycle of political correctness and cover up will be maintained leaving the victims of crime left in the back waters of political correction.

This comment also invokes a version of 'Pakistani community' in framing political correctness at the heart of a supposed 'cover up'. These letters are, of course, only examples but they represent a wider body of public opinion represented in many such comments uncovered during this research in both the *Rotherham Advertiser* and in other local news outlets such as the *Yorkshire Evening Post*. Another comment in the 'Letters to the Editor' section of the 19 September 2014 copy of the *Rotherham Advertiser* portrayed the crimes as representative of a collectively backward culture, the actions of a 'traditional' community:

> The Pakistani community should also take major steps to tackle this. It surely cannot conform to Muslim Holy Scripture to exploit and assault children in this way. Like the rest of us, people from traditional cultures embrace new technology and the benefits of modern society, including education for all children, car and plane travel, the communication advances, the internet and so on. I suggest they also embrace respect for all their fellow humans, irrespective of gender, race or opinions.

According to van Dijk the press play a crucial role in determining how matters pertaining to race and ethnicity are mediated and readers' letters are one crucial avenue through which this can be achieved; 'in order to manipulate public opinion, the Press also tends to select those letters and "spontaneous" opinions of "ordinary people" that are consistent with its own ethnic ideology' (2015, p. 252). The selection of readers' letters, therefore, cannot be seen as a neutral process but rather is closely connected to a newspaper's political identity or 'ethnic ideology'. It is further noted by van Dijk that unfair or inaccurate media portrayals of ethnic minorities are not only the preserve of the tabloid or conservative press; liberal outlets are capable of this too, through perhaps more subtle and nuanced means.

The cry of 'political correctness' has a long history and a resonance that transcends international boundaries. Scott Poynting, for instance, writing on the racist pogrom that came to be known as the 'Cronulla riots' in Sydney, Australia, noted that 'political correctness' related to the apparent 'under policing' of Lebanese youth was cited by politicians as a factor that had led to the disorder (2006, p. 90). Poynting documents how large groups of white men, encouraged and emboldened by nationalist fervour whipped up by a willing media and incendiary comments from politicians, launched racist 'revenge' attacks on those perceived to be 'Middle Eastern' in supposed retaliation for a previous incident. The Cronulla riots are just one example of events in which racialised minorities are the victims of racist violence, yet in subsequent discourse are regarded as in some way culpable and even responsible for the events. The 'political correctness' device and its use by politicians and other commentators is one method through which this is achieved.

Kiran Grewal, writing about the representations of Muslim men in the aftermath of a series of highly publicised gang rapes in Sydney in the early 2000s, highlighted the difficulties faced by commentators attempting to prevent the collective blaming of entire racialised minority communities and the role of the 'political correctness' label in this process:

> Those who attempted to play down the racial element of the crimes or to dispute the legitimacy of placing the blame on a whole community were accused of allowing misplaced multicultural sentiments and political correctness to "morally blind" them, as it was the gang rapists who were the racists and had failed to show tolerance and respect. (2007, p. 120)

The claim of 'political correctness' dominated the media discourse following the publication of the Jay report. There appeared to be a consensus that the local authorities including the council and police failed to properly discharge their duties for fear of upsetting relationships with local ethnic minority communities and to avoid the accusation of racism. This was strongly challenged by several interview participants, including Ahmed, a 38-year-old human resources manager, community volunteer and lifelong Rotherham resident:

> That's absolute rubbish. These cases were not investigated properly because they didn't value the girls. With regard to any other crime there was no PC (political correctness) when someone is dealing drugs, when somebody's got violent, or whatever the crime; there was no PC culture. It's only a PC culture because these investigations cost money… It wasn't value for money to go and protect young familyless (sic) girls in care. That was not value for money. That was the reason; to say it was because of political correctness makes absolutely no sense. We have 63 ward councillors in Rotherham. You had three Asian councillors. How much influence can they have? It defies belief and logic and any sort of rationale.

In his response Ahmed takes issue with the attempts to frame the lack of institutional response in the framework of a culture of 'political correctness'. Rather, Ahmed highlights the well-documented institutional failures and is perplexed at the underlying logic behind the accusation of 'political correctness' which at its root, in this instance, hints at a collective cover up in the local Asian Muslim community. As Ahmed points out, the presence of so few Asian councillors in Rotherham casts further doubt on this claim.

As Lentin (2014) notes, 'political correctness' is a familiar right-wing refrain, attacking in particular the perceived realities and excesses of multiculturalism. Furthermore, the charge of 'political correctness' is aimed at those who, it is believed, suppress criticism and debate and instead allege racism. As Lentin further argues, if the 'anti-multiculturalists'' claims of 'political correctness' were true, 'minority groups would have a disproportionate degree of power in society, where in fact they are consistently under-represented in politics, the media and business, and over-represented among the poor, the imprisoned and the mentally ill' (2014, p. 1277). As the fallout from the 'Rotherham' grooming scandal highlights, long after the death of multiculturalism (Kundnani 2002), the racially loaded language of 'political correctness' remains a powerful tool through which warning and disgust can be expressed at perceived excessive levels of tolerance and diversity.

Collective Blame and Anti-Muslim Racism

Poynting (2006) is correct to note that it is often very difficult to precisely connect popular racialising discourses (and even outright incitement from the media) to acts of racist violence. At times, however, these links can seem to be immutable. An act of extreme violence carried out in Rotherham, South Yorkshire, in August 2015 is a case in point. Mushin Ahmed, an 81-year-old Muslim grandfather of Yemini heritage, was brutally beaten by two white men whilst making his way to the mosque for early morning prayers. As the sustained attack took place, the white men repeatedly referred to Mr. Ahmed as a 'groomer'. Mr. Ahmed died shortly after the attack, and the court later heard that the attack took place 'for no better reason than Mr Ahmed was Asian' (*BBC News* 2016). It is well established that terms such as 'groomer' and 'grooming' are now firmly associated with South Asian and Muslim men due to the circulation of populist racialising discourses (Tufail and Poynting 2016; Tufail 2015; Gill and Harrison 2015; Cockbain 2013). Gill and Harrison rightly contend that the racialisation of South Asian men as sexually violent 'folk devils' is unhelpful as it obscures the prevalence of child sexual abuse across British society and is of no help to the victims. Whilst this is correct, it is further contended that the racialisation associated with the child sexual abuse scandal should also be dissuaded and opposed on the basis that it has resulted in anti-Muslim racism in the form of harassment, abuse, violence and, in the case of Mushin Ahmed, murder.

The increasing hate crimes experienced by the Asian community in Rotherham was highlighted by the launching, in May 2016, of a new dedicated policing operation called Operation Solar (*Rotherham Advertiser* 2016). According to South Yorkshire Police, in the preceding year 377 hate crime incidents were reported in the Rotherham area. Chief Inspector Richard Butterworth confirmed that 85% of the attacks were racist in nature and were mostly directed at Asian people in the area. This operation, however, has to be considered in context. In late 2015, in an unprecedented act of solidarity, a variety of Muslim groups and communities within Rotherham called a meeting to announce they were boycotting South Yorkshire Police. The announcement of the boycott quickly became national news (Sims 2015). The stated reasons for the boycott were varied but centred on the perceived failure of the police to protect the local Asian community from racist attacks and the role of the police in assisting with the scapegoating of local Muslims as collectively responsible for the child sexual abuse offences. Whilst predictably the media reaction to this was sensationalised, it was in fact a local newspaper, *The Star*, that went furthest in its condemnation. An editorial piece on the story described the action as a 'defiant manifesto of anti-police rhetoric … a veiled incitement to vigilantism' (*The Star* 2015). The editorial further accused the boycott of being 'incendiary' yet in the same article referred to the child sexual abuse scandal using the somewhat incendiary language of 'Asian paedophile rapists'. The police boycott was reported by the local press as orchestrated by a few individuals with little community support. The characterisation of the boycott, from both the media and local authority figures, was challenged by several interview participants including Sadia, an employee for a local women's charity in her mid-1950s:

> and then we found the leader of the council having made a press release and in that press release, what he said was that there are a number of young inconspicuous…. He basically said that they were a good for nothing bunch of yobbos who were putting this thing out that the community were upset. The community weren't upset because there's excellent relationships. So when we met again, we were all really, really angry.

At the time of writing, as far as can be ascertained from research, it appears that both of the major local newspapers serving Rotherham, the *Rotherham Advertiser* and *The Star*, do not employ any ethnic minority or Muslim journalists. This is despite Rotherham having an ethnic minority population of 8.1% and a Muslim population of 3.7% (Rotherham Council 2011). This is not to say that Muslim or Asian journalists would necessarily have reported the police boycott or the child sexual abuse scandal any differently, but it does introduce questions about representation and of the ways a diverse press can introduce unique perspectives to news-making (Campbell 1995). Kalra and Rhodes (2013) for instance, in noting the ways in which local media outlets stoked racial tensions prior to the 2001 disturbances in the North of England, highlighted that the *Oldham Chronicle* drew none of its journalists from local ethnic minority communities. Highlighting the under-representation of ethnic minority journalists as a significant, structural and long-term problem, it was recently determined that despite making up more than 5% of the population, British Muslims only account for 0.4% of all journalists (Williams 2016).

Further evidence of the anti-Muslim transformation of the racial landscape within Rotherham was evidenced by reports that a number of parents of schoolchildren from a Catholic primary school had withdrawn their children from visiting a mosque as part of a school trip partly due to fears they may have been sexually abused. As one parent lamented in the 27 February 2015 edition of the *Rotherham Advertiser*, 'The school seems to have forgotten about the local news. I understand that it's not all Muslims that were involved, but how can they be 100% sure that one of them in the mosque wasn't involved?' Interviewees for this study have also spoken about the tensions and divisions caused between communities within Rotherham following the revelations of the child abuse scandal. It has emerged, for instance, that Asian schoolchildren as young as five years old have been bullied and labelled 'groomers' by fellow classmates. Whilst anti-Muslim racism has emerged as a significant feature of local life within Rotherham, there have been considerable efforts from a cross-network of individuals, groups and communities to tackle sexual abuse and anti-Muslim racism at the grassroots level.

Challenging Sexual Abuse and Anti-Muslim Racism

The racist, anti-Muslim narrative that emerged following the revelations of the child abuse scandal did not go without challenge. In the immediate aftermath of the publication of the Jay report, media crews from across the globe descended on Rotherham. There was a media frenzy, and local Muslims in particular were sought out for interviews to provide their perspective. Haleema, an equalities manager in her 1950s and an interviewee for this study, spoke of turning down an interview with prominent broadcaster Jon Snow of Channel 4 News, to be filmed on the steps of the town hall. Haleema felt strongly that the media were out to exploit the situation, and she saw them as 'horrendous' and 'literally part of the problem'. Another interviewee, however, was much more willing to challenge attempts by the media to imply that this was a collectively Asian or Muslim problem that had been ignored or covered up. Through her job Sadia works with abused women from all backgrounds but particularly those from Black and Asian minority communities. She wanted to highlight the overlooked issue of Asian girls being abused by the same men who were convicted as part of the Rotherham child sex abuse cases. Using the same extrapolations as those used in the Jay report, Sadia had determined that at least 100 Asian girls had also been abused. In a little-publicised report titled 'Unheard Voices', the Muslim Women's Network highlighted the under-recognised problem of the sexual abuse of Asian girls and young women, partly due to investigatory methods focusing on white victims (Gohir 2013). Sadia recalls the experience she had with the BBC, which in the end was not broadcast:

> so I was prepared for knowing that I had to push and get this issue out that Asian girls were also abused but what I hadn't been prepared for was the onslaught of, 'You all knew as a Muslim community, your men are all bad and you as women know and stand by them.' It was challenging that. Newsnight didn't play my bit because when he asked me the questions and I challenged him back and said, 'You're a BBC reporter, what about Jimmy Savile?' he didn't like what I said, whereas a number of the others took on board some of the things.

Sadia found that the narrative she wanted to provide did not coincide with the narrative of the BBC journalist interviewing her. Her experience perhaps reflects Fekete's contention that 'Seldom is the "other" given a hearing, expect to confirm our prejudices' (2009, p. 63). Whilst the attempt from Sadia to highlight the double standard of the BBC reporting was met disapprovingly, it was not the only time that such an interaction occurred. Sadia recalled an occasion where she was present at a radio interview where South Yorkshire Police Crime Commissioner Alan Billings was being interviewed on the child abuse scandal:

> So he was asked by the Asian radio presenter, the Asian radio presenter said, 'What is going on in Rotherham?' He said, 'The levels of racism are just sky high. What have you got to say as a white man?' Now Alan, his name is Alan, he immediately reacted and said, 'You can't taint all of us with a few bad men and what they're doing.' I thought you can see the racism but when it comes to the grooming, nobody in authority has ever stood up and said, 'This is a few evil men in our community.'

The collective blaming of the Asian Muslim community in Rotherham was not just challenged by members of the Asian Muslim community. Campaigns led by local Muslims and Unite Against Fascism (UAF) mobilised trade unionists, activists, the Muslim and wider community to counter the repeated far-right marches that had targeted the town. Two individuals who met at one of the UAF demonstrations later went on to author a report titled 'Voices of Despair, Voices of Hope'. The authors decided to write the report as in Rotherham 'an almost unchallenged racist frenzy of abuse and religious hatred has been allowed to develop' since the publication of the Jay report (*Rotherham Advertiser* 2015). The report contains testimony from a number of the survivors of child sexual abuse that took place within Rotherham, detailing the impact it had on their lives. The report also details the impact the fallout and the abuse revelations have had on the town's minority communities, such as 'young children from the Pakistani community being racially abused in the streets and called paedophiles and Muslim and Sikh girls being threatened with "revenge" gang rapes'. The testimony in the report from the survivors of child sexual abuse also features frustration with the way in which the racist, anti-Muslim narrative took hold within the town:

> I never asked for Muslim children and their mothers to be abused or innocent Muslim men but you hear it everywhere now in our town... Even ordinary people think it is ok to shout paedophile down the street at a

seven-year-old Muslim boy, I heard and saw it myself. It doesn't help us, it doesn't help our town.

Consisting of harrowing testimony, poetry and artwork produced by the survivors of child sexual abuse, the locally authored 'Voices of Despair, Voices of Hope' (Harron and Meleady 2015) report offers a complex, grassroots, creative analysis of the Rotherham child sexual abuse scandal that centres the experiences of abused girls and young women whilst simultaneously seeking to challenge the anti-Muslim racism that emerged in the town.

It has not been the intention of this chapter to present an argument that media narratives are monolithically problematic, anti-Muslim or racist. Critical and opposing voices offering dissenting views have been featured by the local and national press, but as Poynting and Perry (2007) note, 'positive' or 'good' news stories concerning Muslims are only notable due to their exceptionality. There is clearly scope for local media to be forced to shift their narratives due to local campaigning work. For instance, on 24 February 2017, the front page of the *Rotherham Advertiser* headline read 'Leave Our Town Alone' as it featured an extract from a letter written by survivors of child sexual abuse to Home Secretary Amber Rudd, urging her to ban the repeated far-right marches that had plagued the town. The letter outlined the trauma survivors experienced at being repeatedly reminded of their abuse and of their experiences being exploited to create 'hatred and fear' in Rotherham. Some of the survivors spoke of the marches bringing back 'horrific memories' of childhood abuse, and the letter included a statement that entering Rotherham and encountering a far-right march brought on more anxiety than bumping into their abusers.

Conclusion

This chapter has offered an analysis of how the circulation of racist discourse was aided and abetted by liberal actors and state institutions offering insights (primarily on the terrain of 'culture') claimed not to be racist, and which, critically, are not actively anti-racist. This ambiguity, it is argued, left the Asian

Muslim community of Rotherham vulnerable to a racist, anti-Muslim narrative that blamed them collectively for the horrific and widespread sexual abuse of children and young girls in Rotherham. This chapter has approached this subject matter via an in-depth empirical case study that has incorporated an analysis of local media, official reports and interviews with local residents. This approach demonstrates the ways in which the racial landscape of Rotherham was transformed by the child sexual abuse scandal. An outcome of this transformation was that racist whites were emboldened with a 'permission to hate' (Poynting and Perry 2007) that resulted in the Muslim Asian community of Rotherham experiencing racist abuse, harassment and even murder.

Writing after the widely publicised Cronulla riots in 2005 in Sydney, Christina Ho highlighted how the racialised portrayal of the events 'criminalised an entire migrant community' (2007, p. 293). This was clearly evident in Rotherham, but as Ho and Grewal (Grewal 2012) have contended, there have proven to be inherent tensions between feminists and anti-racists in attempting to find a position that appropriately addresses the seriousness of sexual abuse whilst preventing the racist marginalisation and criminalisation of minority communities. Grewal correctly situates this debate within the limitations of Australia's liberal politics of multiculturalism arguing that the confines of this flawed framework do not allow for a genuine, anti-racist feminism to emerge. This study has found that in Rotherham, at the local level, there are examples of genuine attempts to practice an anti-racist feminism. This has been located at the grassroots, made up of contributions and campaigning work from sexual abuse survivors, Muslim women's charities and local residents inspired to join campaigns and produce outputs such as the 'Voices of Despair, Voices of Hope' report that seek to simultaneously challenge sexual abuse and racism.

Whether rooted in explicitly anti-Muslim, Islamophobic rhetoric or masked by racially coded signifiers, there is an overlap and some commonality in far-right, conservative and liberal representations of the Rotherham child sexual abuse scandal. At the root of this commonality is an idea that dangerous Muslim masculinities and a disregard for women's rights from within Muslim communities were explanatory factors for making sense of why the abuses took place. Dagistanli and Grewal document how serious crimes of sexual abuse were exploited and represented as just one expression of a backward and inferior Muslim culture. They further contend that 'By constructing sexual violence and misogyny as the preserve of the Muslim man, anti-Muslim and anti-multicultural rhetoric dominant in many Western liberal democracies is reinforced' (2012, p. 138). It has been argued in this chapter that such anti-Muslim and anti-multiculturalist discourses were furthered using the cover of 'political correctness' and that such representations were indulged in by right-wing as well as liberal voices. It has been demonstrated that local discourse and local media are vitally important in shaping the racial land-scape and that in the case of Rotherham, a hostile climate of anti-Muslim racism emerged. It may be wise to follow the words of Christina Ho (2006) in terms of examining the roles of feminists and anti-racists in such circumstances; 'People who are concerned about women's rights should be worried when the language of rights and gender equality is appropriated for an anti-Muslim agenda'.

References

Batty, D. (2011, August 1). White Girls Seen as "Easy Meat" by Pakistani Rapists, Says Jack Straw. *Guardian*. [Online]. Retrieved March 27, 2017, from https://www.theguardian.com/world/2011/jan/08/jack-straw-white-girls-easy-meat

BBC News. (2016, February 29). Mushin Ahmed Death: Two Men Jailed over Racist Rotherham Killing. *BBC News*. [Online]. Retrieved March 30, 2017, from http://www.bbc.co.uk/news/uk-england-south-yorkshire-35688543

Campbell, C. P. (1995). *Race, Myth and the News*. Thousand Oaks: Sage.

Casey, L. (2015). *Report of Inspection of Rotherham Metropolitan Borough Council*. London: Department for Communities and Local Government. [Online]. Retrieved March 29, 2017, from https://www.gov.uk/government/uploads/system/uploads/attachment_data/file/401125/46966_Report_of_Inspection_of_Rotherham_WEB.pdf

Cockbain, E. (2013). Grooming and the "Asian Sex Gang Predator": The Construction of a Racial Crime Threat. *Race & Class, 54*(4), 22–32.

Dagistanli, S., & Grewal, K. (2012). Perverse Muslim Masculinities in Contemporary Orientalist Discourse: The Vagaries of Muslim Immigration in the West. In *Global Islamophobia: Muslims and Moral Panic in the West* (pp. 119–142). Surrey: Ashgate Publishing Ltd.

Fekete, L. (2009). *A Suitable Enemy: Racism, Migration and Islamophobia in Europe.* London: Pluto.

Fekete, L. (2012). *Grooming: An Open Letter to Nick Lowles.* [Online]. Retrieved March 28, 2017, from http://www.irr.org.uk/news/grooming-an-open-letter-to-nick-lowles/

Garner, S., & Selod, S. (2014). The Racialization of Muslims: Empirical Studies of Islamophobia. *Critical Sociology, 41*(1), 9–19. [Online]. https://doi.org/10.1177/0896920514531606

Gill, A. K., & Harrison, K. (2015). Child Grooming and Sexual Exploitation: Are South Asian Men the UK Media's New Folk Devils? *International Journal for Crime, Justice and Social Democracy, 4*(2), 34–49. [Online]. https://doi.org/10.5204/ijcjsd.v4i2.214

Gohir, S. (2013). Unheard Voices: The Sexual Exploitation of Asian Girls and Young Women. *Muslim Women's Network.* [Online]. Retrieved April 6, 2017, from http://www.mwnuk.co.uk/go_files/resources/UnheardVoices.pdf

Grewal, K. (2007). The "Young Muslim Man" in Australian Public Discourse. *Transforming Cultures eJournal, 2*(1), 116–134.

Grewal, K. (2012). Australia, the Feminist Nation? Discourses of Gender, "Culture" and Nation in the "K Brothers" Gang Rapes. *Journal of Intercultural Studies, 33*(5), 509–528. [Online]. https://doi.org/10.1080/07256868.2012.701608

Harron, L., & Meleady, C. (2015). *Voices of Despair, Voices of Hope.* Rotherham: BAA Print and Design.

Harsin, J. (2015). Cultural Racist Frames in TF1's French Banlieue Riots Coverage. *French Politics, Culture and Society, 33*(3), 47–73. https://doi.org/10.3167/fpcs.2015.330303

Ho, C. (2006, October 10). Gang Rapes and the "Cultural Time Bomb". *Australian Review of Public Affairs.* [Online]. Retrieved April 6, 2017, from http://www.australianreview.net/digest/2006/09/ho.html

Ho, C. (2007). Muslim Women's New Defenders: Women's Rights, Nationalism and Islamophobia in Contemporary Australia'. *Women's Studies International Forum, 30*(4), 290–298. [Online]. https://doi.org/10.1016/j.wsif.2007.05.002

Jay, A. (2014). *Independent Inquiry into Child Sexual Exploitation in Rotherham.* Rotherham: Rotherham Metropolitan Borough Council. [Online]. Retrieved March 27, 2017, from http://www.rotherham.gov.uk/downloads/file/1407/independent_inquiry_cse_in_rotherham

Kalra, V., & Rhodes, J. (2013). Local Events, National Implications: Riots in Oldham and Burnley 2001. In *Rioting in the UK and France: A Comparative Analysis* (pp. 41–55). Abingdon: Taylor and Francis.

Kundnani, A. (2002). The Death of Multiculturalism. *Race & Class, 43*(4), 67–72. [Online]. https://doi.org/10.1177/030639680204300406

Lentin, A. (2008). Europe and the Silence About Race. *European Journal of Social Theory, 11*(4), 487–503. [Online]. https://doi.org/10.1177/1368431008097008

Lentin, A. (2014). Post-Race, Post Politics: The Paradoxical Rise of Culture After Multiculturalism. *Ethnic and Racial Studies, 37*(8), 1268–1285. [Online]. https://doi.org/10.1080/01419870.2012.664278

Lowles, N. (2012). *Breaking the Silence on Grooming.* [Online]. Retrieved March 28, 2017, from http://www.hopenothate.org.uk/blog/nick/breaking-the-silence-on-grooming-1893

Poole, E. (2011). Change and Continuity in the Representation of British Muslims Before and After 9/11: The UK Context. *Global Media Journal: Canadian Edition, 4*(2), 49–62.

Poynting, S. (2006). What Caused the Cronulla Riot? *Race & Class, 48*(1), 85–92. [Online]. https://doi.org/10.1177/030639680604800116

Poynting, S., & Perry, B. (2007). Climates of Hate: Media and State Inspired Victimisation of Muslims in Canada and Australia Since 9/11. *Current Issues in Criminal Justice, 19*(2), 151.

Rotherham Advertiser. (2014, September 9). Your Views on Rotherham's Child Sexual Exploitation Scandal. *Rotherham Advertiser.* [Online]. Retrieved March 29, 2017, from http://www.rotherhamadvertiser.co.uk/news/view,your-views-on-rotherhams-child-sexual-exploitation-scandal_8842.htm

Rotherham Advertiser. (2015, February 4). Rotherham "Suffering Resurgence of Racism" in Wake of Grooming Scandal. *Rotherham Advertiser.* [Online]. Retrieved March 31, 2017, from http://www.thestar.co.uk/news/rotherham-suffering-resurgence-of-racism-in-wake-of-grooming-scandal-1-7187792

Rotherham Advertiser. (2016, May 27). Solar System to Fight Hate Crime. *Rotherham Advertiser.* [Online]. Retrieved March 30, 2017, from http://www.rotherhamadvertiser.co.uk/news/view,solar-system-to-fight-hate-crime_2442.htm

Rotherham Council. (2011). *Rotherham Joint Strategic Needs Assessment: Ethnicity and Cultural Identity.* [Online]. Retrieved May 27, 2017, from http://www.rotherham.gov.uk/jsna/info/23/people/54/ethnicity_and_cultural_identity

Sims, A. (2015, October 26). Rotherham Muslims Call for Boycott of South Yorkshire Police over "Demonization" Since Jay Report. *The Independent.* [Online]. Retrieved March 30, 2017, from http://www.independent.co.uk/

news/uk/home-news/rotherham-muslims-call-for-boycott-of-south-york-shire-police-over-demonization-since-jay-report-a6709356.html

Smith, J. (2011, September 1). Joan Smith: Gender Inequality, not Race, Fosters Abuse. *The Independent.* [Online]. Retrieved March 27, 2017, from http://www.independent.co.uk/voices/commentators/joan-smith/joan-smith-gen-der-inequality-not-race-fosters-abuse-2179629.html

Solomos, J., & Back, L. (1994). Conceptualising Racisms: Social Theory, Politics and Research. *Sociology, 28*(1), 143–161. [Online]. https://doi.org/10.1177/0038038594028001009

Sonnett, J., Johnson, K. A., & Dolan, M. K. (2015). Priming Implicit Racism in Television News: Visual and Verbal Limitations on Diversity. *Sociological Forum, 30*(2), 328–347. https://doi.org/10.1111/socf.12165

The Star. (2015). EDITOR'S COMMENT: Muslim Group's Fleeting "Boycott" Has Done Untold Damage to Rotherham. *The Star (Sheffield).* [Online]. Retrieved April 6, 2017, from http://www.thestar.co.uk/news/editor-s-comment-muslim-group-s-fleeting-boycott-has-done-untold-damage-to-rotherham-1-7541010

Tran, M. (2014, February 9). May Blames "Institutionalised Political Correctness" for Rotherham Scandal. *The Guardian.* [Online]. Retrieved March 31, 2017, from https://www.theguardian.com/uk-news/2014/sep/02/theresa-may-political-correctness-rotherham-abuse

Tufail, W. (2015). Rotherham, Rochdale, and the Racialised Threat of the "Muslim Grooming Gang". *International Journal for Crime, Justice and Social Democracy, 4*(3), 30–43.

Tufail, W., & Poynting, S. (2016). Muslim and Dangerous: "Grooming" and the Politics of Racialisation. In D. Pratt & R. Woodlock (Eds.), *Fear of Muslims? International Perspectives on Islamophobia* (pp. 79–92). [Online]. Switzerland: Springer International Publishing. https://doi.org/10.1007/978-3-319-29698-2_6

van Dijk, T. A. (2015). *Racism and the Press.* London: Routledge.

Williams, O. (2016, March 24). British Journalism Is 94% White and 55% Male, Survey Reveals. *The Guardian.* [Online]. Retrieved March 30, 2017, from https://www.theguardian.com/media-network/2016/mar/24/british-journalism-diversity-white-female-male-survey

Woodward, G. (2012, May 17). The Truth About Grooming? *Yorkshire Evening Post.* [Online]. Retrieved April 6, 2017, from http://www.yorkshireevening-post.co.uk/news/the-truth-about-grooming-1-4556658

5

The New Year's 2015/2016 Public Sexual Violence Debate in Germany: Media Discourse, Gendered Anti-Muslim Racism and Criminal Law

Ulrike M. Vieten

Sex-Attacke im Freibad auf 10—Jaehrige—Onkel des Opfers schlug Afghanen (headline)[1]

Introduction

The New Year's Eve 2015/2016 sexual attacks on non-migrant women in German public spaces near the main train stations in Cologne and Hamburg, but also in Stuttgart, have triggered far-right populist debates on the 'integration and gender equality skills' of new immigrants and North African male refugees,[2] in Germany and elsewhere. According to Yilmaz (2015: 38), 'The dichotomous constellation of cultures with gender and sexuality as baselines is symptomatic of the way sociopolitical divisions are imagined, and acted upon, in public discourse.'

Media coverage following the sexual attacks in different cities signify largely an overall moral panic and increase in racialising Muslim men of

U. M. Vieten (✉)
Queen's University Belfast, Belfast, UK

© The Author(s) 2018
M. Bhatia et al. (eds.), *Media, Crime and Racism*, Palgrave Studies in Crime, Media and Culture, https://doi.org/10.1007/978-3-319-71776-0_5

73

Middle East descend, expressing a new scale of 'global Islamophobia' (Morgan and Poynting 2013).

The international public outcry initiated by what appeared to be systematic sexual attacks combined with theft offenses by visibly different, minority men on New Year's Eve 2015/2016 prompted contestations about feminist responses[3] to it and the need to think sexism and racism as intersecting social structures of oppression.[4] Further, the events started a wider debate in society: it pushed the reform of criminal law in Germany,[5] extending the framework of what is regarded as an individual (female) right of *sexual autonomy*,[6] defined in paragraph *177 STGB*. Also, the institutional side of how police reacted initially to the situation on the 31 December became subject of an official inquiry in North Rhine Westphalia (NRW), the federal land of the two cities, Cologne and Dusseldorf. The purpose of this public commission is to interrogate the role of the police in the unfolding of the events.[7] I tried to get hold of records and documents, but this was not possible as this is an inquiry in process.

This chapter discusses some of the national and international media coverage of the New Year's Eve 2015/2016 sexual attacks, and the political, legal and societal responses to it in the period January to July 2016. With this reflection it contributes to international debates on Islamophobia, Anti-Muslim racism and gender (Fekete 2004; Morgan and Poynting 2013; Nelson 2015).

In terms of terminology, I prefer using 'racialising' here in order to emphasise that others are discursively racialised and that racialising is not limited to post-slavery and post-colonial 'race' discourses (Vieten 2011). Arguably, Islamophobia has to be linked to racism as it describes the way Muslims became racialised, particularly post 11 September 2001 (Vieten 2007, 2012; Garner and Selod 2015).

In order to draw on a range of resources in this analysis, I used key words ('Cologne sexual attacks,' 'New Year's Eve 2015/2016,' 'New Year's Eve sexual attacks') while turning to the search engines, 'Google' and 'Bing' (period January to July 2016). Further, I followed the German weekly newspaper, *die ZEIT*, with its coverage of the New Year's Eve events, between January and July 2016.[8] In addition, I included publications by state bodies, critical journalists and feminist activists on this topic.

Using these resources I look at the scandalising of public sexual violence against women recently in Europe (e. g. Germany). It is argued that we are confronted with a gender sensitive but also racist populist outrage on the background of a nativist perception of women as 'German women.'

As it turns out we are confronted with a dilemma: on the one hand, media plays a framing role in displaying, repeating and accelerating racial profiling of Muslim men as potential and actual perpetrators; on the other, media and public outrage pushed the reform of the *177 STGB* in Germany. The latter is demanded by feminist activists and lawyers for a long time, and in that regard the 'moral panic' strengthened the feminist argument and support for a revision of criminal law (e.g. 'sexual autonomy').

First, the phenomenon of 'public sexual violence' is contextualised by looking at social spaces where gendered sexual violence takes place, and asking to what degree *public* sexual violence in Europe is a *new* phenomenon. Second, the chapter looks at how gender and Islamophobia relate to each other and focuses on the ways the New Year's Eve attacks have to be read against gendered culturalism and racism in Europe. Finally, the media coverage will be scrutinised while investigating patterns in the way victims and perpetrators are portrayed, trying to understand how criminal investigators, courts and civil society in Germany dealt and deal with the issue of mass public sexual violence. Here, I will also refer to an expert statement of feminist lawyers in North Rhine Westphalia (NRW), published in direct response to the New Year's Eve sexual offenses.

Gendered Violence: The 'Private' and 'Public' Dimension of Sexual Violence Against Women

Feminists have engaged with institutionalised, everyday sexism[9] and the problematic boundary of the private and the public sphere (see, e.g. McDowell 1983; Fraser 1990; Walby et al. 2014) in terms of gendered violence since the 1970s. The continuity of sexual violence against women, primarily taking place in the domestic sphere,[10] indicates that it is an everyday phenomenon that has been tackled in recent decades but still is endemic and far from been eradicated. A British study, released in

2016, confirmed that slightly more than 50% of women are harassed at work, which includes 'groping, sexual advances and inappropriate jokes.'[11] Sexual violence has to be understood as part of a wider notion of violence against women: according to the World Health Organisation (WHO) some 35% of women experience violence,[12] and thus, it is a global health problem impacting communities and countries beyond the individual cases. Historically, the societal discourse shifted several times since the 1970s: domestic male violence against women was classified among others as caused by 'mental illness,' as 'learned behaviour,' as 'caused by alcohol' or as 'both men and women contribute to violence—victim provocation' (Cavanaugh 2012; Ali and Naylor 2013; Bates et al. 2014; Turchik et al. 2016).

It seems the 'relationship' element dominates cases of domestic sexual violence and contrasts to what might be understood as the defining element of *public* sexual violence, for example, sexual attacks by a stranger. The latter is politicised in the current debate and does need further reflection: to what extend is public sexual violence only been noted recently in European societies, for example, in the context of the emergence of mass immigration of refugees from the Middle East? Having said that it seems that *mass expression of group male violence against women* was first documented in Egypt, in 2005 (Amnesty International 2015: 10). According to Amnesty International (2015) 'in recent years, sexual assaults in public have surged, with women and girls increasingly targeted by groups of men and boys, often at political demonstrations, but also during other large public gatherings … Egyptian human rights organizations have reported that have documented over 500 cases of gang rape and sexual assaults between June 2012 and 2014' (9–10). Though it is reported in Egypt that these acts of public sexual violence also happen at 'religious festival and large public gatherings,' the context of the 'Arab Spring' and the significance of the *Tahrir Square protests* in 2012 introduce a more systematic way of using sexual violence against independent and politically left-wing women at political demonstrations.

Mancini and Pickett (2016: 259–260) pinpoint that women and children are regarded as a particularly vulnerable victim group impacting on the wider public view how to punish the perpetrator. They argue 'It is likely that offenses against this victim base trigger intense moral emotions and, in the public's view, cannot extend from "normal" motives, such as economic gain or interpersonal anger, and thus those who commit them cannot be normal individuals.' Further, they add, 'there is a widely endorsed perception that victims are at substantial risk of being assaulted by stranger perpetrators, a view of reflecting the myth of "stranger danger" (Craun and Theriot 2009).'

Accordingly, the 'stranger danger' is a widely held view in the context of sexual violence. As far as domestic and interpersonal sexual violence is concerned, perpetrators are predominantly male and mostly live in close and private proximity to their victims. In terms of the phenomenon of 'public' sexual violence, the *myth* of the 'stranger danger' does not hold though: here we are talking about the attack of a stranger. It appears the contemporary fear of the oriental stranger needs further interrogation while acknowledging that the stage of public violence, including sexual violence against women, might have reached a new dimension in Europe as elsewhere.

Following the data of the FRA (European Union Agency for Fundamental Rights)[13] 'sexual violence is "an extensive human rights abuse" across Europe. One in three women reported some form of physical or sexual abuse since the age of fifteen. More than half of all European women, including sixty percent of German women, reported that they had experienced sexual harassment or stalking since the age of fifteen. Only thirteen to fourteen percent of the women surveyed across Europe reported their worst incident of partner or non-partner violence to the police.' Though the overall findings confirm the 'personal relationship' aspect and echo the dominance of 'domestic violence,' the report also stresses that '53% of women in the EU avoid certain situations or places, at least sometimes, for fear of being physically or sexually assaulted' (2014). Stalking and cyber harassment as forms of sexual violence are on the rise, too. However, according to this study there is a huge lack in reporting 'publically' experienced sexual violence (ibid.). Overall sexist perceptions affect in significant ways the willingness of women to report cases of sexual violence to the police as far as semi-private and public spaces are concerned.[14]

Further questions result from the outcome of this study, and from broader perceptions of what does count as a sexual attack and how woman (individually) has to respond to it: to which degree is the notion of 'public' sexual violence dismissed in the German, and wider European, contexts for decades, or, to put it differently, did it remain rather under reported as a criminal offense? Is it true that public sexual violence targeting women and young girls as a mass phenomenon is that 'new' as Hannelore Kraft[15] argued? And further, what is the situation for Muslim women in this regard; are they included as female victims in similar ways?

Next, I will look at the perceived 'newness' of public sexual violence in Germany. This has to be read against the notion of 'consent' as embedded in institutionalised sexism: is there a notorious perception of what *female acceptance* of the act itself means, and what a *male perception* of that 'consent' in the act, implies actually? Further, I will relate the gendered culturalist discourse and anti-Muslim racism in Germany and elsewhere to a more symptomatic lack of reported cases of public sexual violence. I argue that Muslim men are grouped and blamed as potential sexual attackers in the public eye falling short in acknowledging a general problem of a rise of male violence in public spaces.

The October Fest or *Taharrush?* Place, Crime, Ethnicity and Gender

Following the New Year's Eve attacks, national as well as international media jumped quickly on the idea to link Cologne to the Egypt mass phenomenon of sexual attacks on women, called *Taharrush*, an Arabic term for 'harassment' that is identified with it. Abdelmonem et al. (2016) argue:

Reflecting these same notions with regards to the New Year's Eve attacks, the *New York Times* reported that in Cologne "groups of young men began encircling young women." Citing *Welt am Sonntag, Deutsche Welle* stated, "A group of young men would encircle the female victim, close the loop, and then start groping the woman." In a Bloomberg News wire piece reprinted in the *Chicago Tribune*, the coverage highlighted how politically commissioned sexual harassment and assaults in Egypt derived from a historical cultural practice of sexual harassment. By situating politicized violence within a "long-standing culture of treating lone women as acceptable targets for harassment" this news agency drew distinctly cultural conclusions about the Arabized and Islamicized "nature" of sexual violence in the Cologne assaults. By means of this associative framing strategy, the coverage managed to align two separate circumstances of sexual harassment and assault and to portray them as manifestations of the same process of collective sexual violence.

Labelling and linking mass sexual violence in Cologne and Hamburg, for example, to attacks in Egypt suggests to the public it might be an 'import' by Middle East and North African/Arab men. Abdelmonem et al. (ibid.) stress that this narrative of the oriental male attacker (oppressor) was employed when making the case for militaristic interventions back to the pre-war rhetoric to interfere in Afghanistan, in 2003. Back then (as today), it was the oppressive regime of the Taliban that triggered a broader international consensus to justify the USA-UK[16]-led war coalition. As argued elsewhere (Vieten 2012: 34).

'The non-veiled Western *modern* woman symbolizes the "positive" in contrast to the "negative" image of the veiled woman.' (Vieten 2011: 69) Either way the secular modern nation state and the orthodox religious community are claiming the female body as a gendered symbol of 'their' community (*Gemeinschaft*). However, this indicates how *woman* in terms of bio-politics (Foucault) is considered patriarchal property (ibid.). It is worth noting too, that the French debate on the headscarf was engendered by President Chirac in 2003, explicitly referring to a national identity crisis torn between the republican 'laïcité' and 'the citizens' of Europe.'

Within a period of 15 years, post 11 September 2011, gendered culturalism and anti-Muslim racism have become normalised in different societies across Europe, particularly in the Netherlands (Vieten 2017), but also in neighbouring European countries such as France or Germany (Vieten 2016). After years of discursively constructing an essentialist and orientalist 'cultural-ethnic' boundary between the Judeo-Christian Occident and the oriental Muslim Other (Vieten 2011, 2012), the new far right takes a by and large mainstreamed 'common sense' racism, to more extreme levels.

This culturalism encompasses mainstream Islamophobic views (Wodak 2013; Wodak and Reisigl 2015), and has turned into a "normalised" gendered lens to view religious-cultural group differences. That means culturalist gendered projection became "normalised" in a few years, and turned into a hegemonic lens yet before far right parties gained significant ground in parliaments across Europe (Vieten 2017).

Whereas the New York Times, *Deutsche Welle* or the Chicago Tribune might count as mainstream liberal media, far-right press uses also blogs and social media to further and install more fear and panic in the audience. In a blog entry, Gatestone Institute[17] Fellow, Soeren Kern (2016, March 5), 'informs' the public about sexual attacks by migrants in Kiel[18] referring to police records. Kern argues that the police officially was instructed not to link sexual assaults directly to the ethnic and national background of current refugee groups. And by that he suggests that the police acts on behalf of a liberal political elite that shies away from the rising levels of crimes, for example, sexual violence against women, enacted by migrant, refugees and other visibly different minority men.

The news coverage in the *Kieler Nachrichten, 29 February 2016*, however, cited different eyewitnesses, who despite confirming that two Afghan men were stalking the girls, clearly stated that the situation was under control and as people were watching also being prepared to intervene. In addition, the police did not receive an actual report of a sexual attack.[19]

It is here where the imaginary of the far-right and nativist mind comes in while generalising individual sexual harassment or stalking as a mode of a culturalist male habit of the Arab foreigner. A racist pattern emerges when sexual violence against women as an everyday phenomenon, introduced above, is mainly problematised in the context of the non-white, non-Christian/stranger attacker. In July 2016, the German Television Broadcast (*Allgemeiner Deutscher Rundfunk/ARD*) aired a documentary looking more closely at the situation of crime investigations in Hamburg, following the sexual attacks. According to official records in Hamburg, 1200 female victims came forward, and the investigators estimated 2000 perpetrators. The juridical procedures, however, indicate that it is almost impossible to get hold of individual perpetrators due to the lack of proof.[20]

Far-right leaders such as Geert Wilders, the leader of the Dutch PVV (*Partij Voor de Vrijheid*; Freedom party), and Marine Le Pen, leader of the French NF (*Front National*), also used the Cologne attacks to make a case for their readiness to defend women's rights. The discussion in Germany also echoes this 'new feminist consciousness': Niejahr (ZEIT online, 4.2.2016) calls this 'Femonationalism'; politicians of the centre right (CDU) out of the sudden felt the need to talk about women's rights. According to Abdelmonem et al. (2016), 'By co-opting feminist demands for women's emancipation and their right to self-defense, these conservative forces instrumentalize the Cologne sexual assaults for their xenophobic ends.'

Given the *discursive* production and co-construction of far-right and mainstream liberal media on this topic, it seems to be relevant to trace how 'public sexual violence' has been reported before 31 December 2015. Also, in concordance with a rather *novel* fury about public sexual violence against women in Germany and Europe, we might wonder whether there have been similar 'moral panic' outrages reported, too, following sexual violence at public entertaining events, such as the annual Munich *October Fest*, the Rhineland Carnival in Cologne, Dusseldorf or Mainz or festivals elsewhere?

In an interview with a feminist activists in Munich, for example, it turned out that sexual violence on the *Wiesn*[21] has been registered over years; the interviewed activist described a rise in numbers of women asking for help and argued that we have to take into account a dark figure (*Dunkelziffer*) as most women are ashamed and do not turn to police for further investigation, ultimately not aiming for a penalty of the perpetrators. The number of their clients (women) rose from 12 to 200 in 12 years (TAZ, 16.1.2016).

In 2012, feminist help groups noted a rise of 40% more victims in comparison to 2011.[22] As far as Britain is concerned, music festivals also have a reputation of becoming highly sexualised and unsafe spaces for women.[23] According to Walby et al. (2014: 193), 'Gang theories of violence have been proposed' in criminology and sociology, previously. While referring to Wolfgang and Ferracuti (1967) here, Walby et al. state that 'there may exist a normative acceptance of violence in some societal groups (Wolfgang and Ferracuti 1967). Such values are transmitted within the cultural groups and individuals can also be born into such a subculture' (Walby et al. 2014: 193).

Walby et al. (ibid.) admit that these theories have been discredited as they were associated with specific visible minority groups, for example, men; however they underline, too, that Wolfgang and Ferracuti (ibid.) also 'identified class as a relevant societal group' (ibid.).

Despite the controversy it sparks, this is a relevant angle for further consideration as it allows to look more closely at intersecting dimensions of gender, class, religion, sexuality and age, for example, and the way 'subcultures' of violence might be generated. In this context, further investigation is needed to understand to what degree cyber space, internet and social media support a new scale of orchestrated public assemblages. These assemblages offer unguarded public spaces for 'spontaneous' mass sexual attacks. As far as Germany is concerned, media and public opinion agree that this kind of enacted public mob mass attacks were a new phenomenon (ZEIT online, 6.1.2016), and there exists no valid resource and research that proves this wrong.

The news coverage discussed so far refers to women as victims; however, attention is payed only to 'native' women, for example, non-migrant and white women. What does media and research say about the experience of migrant women and, particularly, Muslim women when it comes to sexual harassment and violence in semi- and public spaces?

All Women the Same? The Lack of Acknowledging Muslim and Minority Women as Victims of Public Violence

Little is known about sexual violence against migrant and refugee women in German public spaces. However, the news coverage on sexual attacks in refugee shelters sheds some light on the presence of male violence.[24] Though the European Union issued a directive in 2013 (Directive 2013/33/EU),[25] asking Member States for a special protection of women and children, shelters are predominantly provided as *unisex spaces*. Mass accommodations probe to be spaces, semi-public though, where increasing numbers of female refugees experience harassment and sexual violence not only by other male refugees but also by guards.

> More than 440,000 people applied for asylum in Germany last year, with roughly a third of them being women and girls. ...Little is known in Germany about the extent of violence against refugee women and there has been little research into the issue. In one of the few studies that has been undertaken, four out of five respondents said they had been the victims of psychological violence with every second woman saying they had suffered physical violence. The study is now more than 10 years old, but experts believe it is improbable that the numbers have sunk since then. In addition to other refugees, the perpetrators also include security personnel, care-givers and volunteer helpers, all of whom can take advantage of existing structures to easily approach their victims. (*Der Spiegel*, 11 May 2016)

In a move to change this situation, the German government promised about €150 million to equip refugee accommodations with more safe spaces for women and keeping a closer eye on how to protect women and vulnerable children in these state-run institutions. The 'Women's Refugee Commission' released a report[26] in 2016; unlike the situation of 2015 when about 70% of refugees were male, recent figures show that about 60% are women and children. Sexual violence (Sexual and Gender-Based Violence/SGBV) occurs on the journey to and through Europe and is not only limited to the experience in the country of origin (2016: 8).

In general, the reporting and thus official records of violence and sexual violence against minority women, migrant women and female refugees lack reliable figures. Another study was released in 2016: 'Forgotten Women: The impact of Islamophobia on Muslim Women,' commissioned by the European Network Against Racism (ENAR). The authors admit that when it comes to violence against Muslim women or racist crime, official data (statistics) is very limited. Apart from a situation where intersecting dynamics of violence are not fully understood and therefore underreported and researched, for example, 'in the case of hate crime, cases are not often registered as proper complaints (France), are not recorded as an Islamophobic crime and/or the aggravated factor is not recognized (Germany)' (2016: 9).

The ENAR study refers to racist and sexist violence,[27] but sexual violence is not included here. However, the physical and intimidating violence against visibly different and orthodox Muslim women, for example, particularly those wearing a headscarf, takes place in many European as well as German public spaces. As the study makes clear, 'attacks are mostly perpetrated by unknown males' (2016: 26).

A well-known case from Germany might illustrate a tendency to ignore intersecting angles of gender (female), religion (Muslim), ethnicity (minority nationality-Egyptian) and class (middle class—student of pharmacy) divisions feeding a combination of lethal sexism and racism: the 31-year-old Marwa El-Sherbini was stabbed in a court in the city of Dresden, in 2009. El-Sherbini had made a legal effort to sue an ethnic Russian, Alex Wiens, who held German citizenship. Wiens had insulted El-Sherbini for wearing a headscarf and murdered her in court during the trial.[28] He was sentenced to life for murder and attempted murder (Okaz, El-Sherbini's husband) later on. Though this criminal case hit international news, national and local responses rather focused on court security and less on the racist motives of the attacker. Besides, the police shot at El-Sherbini's husband, Okaz, mistaking him for the attacker. Okaz while trying to protect his wife was stabbed several times by Wiens, but unlike his wife survived.

This public violent attack links to a violent history of racist arson attacks in the early 1990s, post-German unification in 1989: in Mölln (23 November 1992) and Solingen (29 May 1993), women and girls died in the fire flames. 'These racist murders provided a landmark within the trauma of many "new" Germans from a Turkish or Kurdish background' (Vieten 2016: 125).

Media had played and continues to play a biased card in the game of 'news' coverage when it comes to sexist and racist thoughts as well as activities. In the 1990s, in the 2009–2011 years (e.g. Sarrazin scandal; see Vieten 2016: 127) as well as in the current moment of 2016, (social) media mirrors dominant gendered and culturalist perceptions. It seems public gendered violence against minority, for example, Muslim women are less acknowledged as an established 'normality' in Germany.

However, the issue of 'sexual' public violence as outlined above is more problematic and cannot be easily subsumed to an affair of either 'minority' or 'majority' ethnic women. The legal framework operates in line with sexist and culturalist stereotypes: criminal law poses particular problems when it comes to track, testify and trial sexual violence against women, and this refers to majority and minority women likewise. The notion of what does count as 'sexual autonomy' is embedded in societal contexts that are channelled through sexist institutions. These sexist institutions are interwoven and framed by racist and racialising state ideologies (Goldberg 1993, 2002).

The final section will look more closely how German criminal law defines the gendered roles of victims and perpetrators as far as perceptions and roles in sexual activity are concerned.

The Criminal Law Debate: Women and 'Sexual Autonomy'

As introduced in the beginning of this chapter, the New Years' Eve 2015/2016 attacks initiated among others a wider public and political debate about a much needed reform of Criminal Law in Germany. The German professional association of feminist lawyers[29]; the *DJB* (*Deutscher Juristinnenbund*—German Association of Female Lawyers) acted as an expert group in the hearing of the Committee mentioned above. The hearing took place at the federal state parliament of North Rhine Westphalia, in June 2016.

The *DJB* argued in detail why the immediate political rush to promise to the public a persecution of the individual perpetrators was due to fail. According to the legal experts, it is the character of these sexual attacks in the public domain, which is not taken into account and regulated in existing Criminal Law.

> It is likely that a significant percentage of the reported cases cannot be penalized according to current law. This is due to a situation where the facts of the case indicate that the attacks were "unexpected" and therefore no "resistance" against the attacker could have taken place. Otherwise, the attacks might not even qualify as "substantial" in terms of the requirements of Criminal Law. Besides, and following here the details that were publi-

cized in the media it might be difficult to get a more adequate understanding of the concrete facts.[30] (Brief Statement of the *DJB*, 29 June 2016).

According to the old version of Paragraph *177 STGB*, the perpetrator must have used what is called in legal terms 'a qualified means of harassment, e. g. force (physical), or an actual (present) threat to the life of the victim, or exploiting the unprotected situation the victim was in; with regard to the latter it is essential that the victim could not resist due to her defencelessness.'[31] Highly problematic is the sequential link between 'threat' and the sexual assault or rape that might follow afterwards. Also, paragraph *184 STGB* requires a certain substantial level of force or actual threat, and as the DJB lawyers made clear some of the temporary insults and harassment (*'flüchtiger Griff in der Kleidung oder an den Po'*—'a volatile reach into the clothes of a woman, or at her bottom') might not even cross this level (*'Erheblichkeitsschwelle'*).

Further they declared that feminist lawyers were demanding the change in positive law for years. Criminal Law fundamentally tends to ignore the *sexual autonomy* of women or any vulnerable person. The DJB asked for legislative change already in 2011[32] and drafted a legislative proposal in 2014. Also, they criticised the notion of 'normal' expectations and 'normal cases': the 'normal case' inscribed in law is that the victim would take measures against the attack, and the attacker-perpetrator would take for granted a consent if the victim does not put up a fight (ibid.).

While challenging populist views, media representation and false promises by politicians, the *DJB* like other feminist activist groups demanded a change of paradigms when it comes to the way female 'sexual autonomy' is approached in society and, as its last resort to defend it, in criminal law.

In April 2016, the second chamber, the *German Bundesrat*, discussed the legal proposal to change 177 STGB.[33] Accordingly, the Criminal Law was changed, on 10.11.2016.[34]

Apart from 177 STGB, it includes further new paragraphs, *184 j* and *184 i STGB*, addressing explicitly sexual attacks of groups and that relate to group assemblages. The incorporation of these new paragraphs has to be regarded as a direct legislative response to the media, social and public debate following the New Years' Eve 2015/2016 events.

Though this sounds positive and could be celebrated as a success to feminist demands, we have to be sceptical to which degree these legal changes combat existing institutional sexism and racism. Certainly, the wider public debate following New Year's Eve 2015/2016 put uncomfortable questions on the table for legislators and the broader society. The more complex dimensions and gendered dynamics of anti-Muslim racism and Islamophobia are not settled by the Criminal Law reform.

Conclusion

As argued in this paper, the consequences of the New Year's Eve 2015/2016 public sexual violence occurrence in Germany[35] are multiple and complex: media coverage, but also discussions and material from social media tools, developed quickly after the events and stirred a racialising of Muslim and Arab men. The controversy about the new character of public sexual attacks also pushed wider debates about the sexual autonomy of women. This led to the actual reform of sexist Criminal Law (Paragraph 177 STGB) that was demanded by feminist groups for years. Still, the dominant profile of the perpetrators as presented in media and public discourse is that of a cultural Other and that of the victim as belonging to the native and ethnic German population. Here, intersecting gendered dynamics of racism and sexism as traced in the public discourse leave aside the particularly vulnerable position of Muslim and minority women.

Though individual and group-led sexual attacks have been noted beforehand, in Germany and elsewhere, these particular events introduced a new phenomenon of mass sexual attacks in Europe. Though it is important not to shy away from how these attacks happened and how to create safer public spaces in future, the actual prosecution of individual perpetrators is complicated. Previously, German criminal law was not sufficiently regulated here, and despite its amendments now in 2016, it is not clear to what degree this will help the case. After all, we have to be cautious that proving someone's guild and using established criminal law might be extremely difficult; profiling, finding the individual perpetrator based on the victim's descriptions and memory, is confronted with a climate and society where loose characterisation such as 'darker skin, eyes and hair' count for all and nothing. The perpetrator's profiling is a reflection of already existing racial and ethno-national stereotypes. At best, the criminal system subscribes to an ethos of 'in doubt pro innocent person' (*in dubio pro reo*); at worse, racial stereotypes are used as the base for judgement and punishment.

Notes

1. *WIEN heute*, kostenlose Tageszeitung, 12.7.2016; text means: 'Sex attack in swimming pool on a girl of ten years—the uncle of the victim beat the Afghan.'
2. Writing in July 2016, it turned out only a minority of three men who have been traced by police were refugees; however the majority of attackers have been of Moroccan, Tunisian and Algerian background. http://www.independent.co.uk/news/world/europe/cologne-only-three-out-of-58-men-arrested-in-connection-with-mass-sex-attack-on-new-years-eve-are-a6874201.html
3. http://www.vice.com/en_uk/read/rape-culture-germany-cologne-new-years-2016-876
4. http://www.spiegel.de/international/germany/german-feminists-debate-cologne-attacks-a-1072806.html
5. https://www.juris.de/jportal/portal/page/homerl.psml?nid=jpr-NLSFADG000716&cmsuri=%2Fjuris%2Fde%2Fnachrichten%2Fzeigenachricht.jsp
6. http://dip21.bundestag.de/dip21/btd/18/090/1809097.pdf
7. https://www.landtag.nrw.de/portal/WWW/Navigation_R2010/030-Parlament-und-Wahlen/015-Ausschuesse-und-Gremien/030-Untersuchungsausschuesse/PUAIV/Inhalt.jsp
8. http://www.zeit.de/suche/index?q=massenhafte+sexuelle+Gewalt+gegen+Frauen&type=article&type=gallery&type=video
9. http://everydaysexism.com/
10. Just put the word 'domestic violence' into an internet search engine (e.g. Google) on 10 August 2016 with 98,200,000 results in 0.43 seconds.
11. https://www.theguardian.com/lifeandstyle/2016/aug/10/half-of-women-uk-have-been-sexually-harassed-at-work-tuc-study-everyday-sexism
12. http://www.who.int/gho/women_and_health/violence/en/

13. http://fra.europa.eu/en/publication/2014/violence-against-women-eu-wide-survey-results-glance
14. I am not going to focus on 'domestic violence' here.
15. Hannelore Kraft is the Social Democratic Minister of North Rhine Westphalia: http://www.n-tv.de/politik/Kraft-entschuldigt-sich-bei-Silvester-Opfern-article18094201.html
16. It might be worthwhile to mention that Spain and Poland were also involved whereas Germany (Chancellor Schroeder) was reluctant to join the 'war of the willing,' mainly because of the German history and a moral reluctant to engage in warfare. That said 'morality' seems not that much to matter when it comes to international warfare industry.
17. https://www.gatestoneinstitute.org/
18. http://www.kn-online.de/News/Nachrichten-aus-Kiel/Nach-Belaestigung-im-Sophienhof-Kiel-Einkaufen-unter-Polizeischutz
19. http://www.kn-online.de/News/Nachrichten-aus-Kiel/Belaestigung-im-Sophienhof-Die-Polizei-muss-sich-korrigieren
20. http://www.zeit.de/gesellschaft/zeitgeschehen/2016-05/silvester-uebergriffe-koeln-prozess
21. http://www.taz.de/!5268871/
22. http://www.thelocal.de/20121004/45349
23. http://www.telegraph.co.uk/women/womens-life/11822420/Bestival-UK-music-festivals-have-a-rape-problem-that-needs-action-now.html
24. http://www.spiegel.de/international/germany/refugee-hostels-in-germany-beset-by-sexual-assault-a-1091681.html
25. http://eur-lex.europa.eu/legal-content/en/TXT/?uri=celex%3A320 13L0033
26. http://www.unhcr.org/569f8f419.html?utm_source=Joint+UNHCR-UNFPA-WRC+Press+Release+-+20+January+2016+-+Report+warns+re fugee+women+on+the+move+in+Eu&utm_medium=email&utm_term=Hauenste@unhcr.org&utm_content=http%3a%2f%2fwww.unhcr.org%2f569f8f419.html&utm_campaign=
27. The study also covers 'discrimination at the work place.'
28. https://www.theguardian.com/world/2009/jul/07/german-trial-hijab-murder-egypt
29. https://www.djb.de/Kom/K3/st16-17/
30. 'Ein nicht unerheblicher Teil der angezeigten Taten ist wahrscheinlich—soweit nach den in den Medien bekannt gewordenen Details eine Einschätzung überhaupt möglich ist—nach geltendem Recht gar nicht

strafbar, weil die Taten entweder überraschend erfolgten und daher kein Widerstand seitens der Täter überwunden werden musste oder aber die Taten gar nicht als „erheblich"i.s.d. Strafrechts eingeordnet werden.' (Stellungnahme des DJB zur öffentlichen Anhörung des Ausschusses fuer Frauen, Gleichstellung und Emanzipation des Landtags Nordrhein Westphalen am 29.Juni 2016, Reform des Sexualstrafrechts).

31. '[E]in qualifiziertes Nötigungsmittel, nämlich Gewalt, Drohung mit gegenwärtiger Gefahr für Leib und Leben oder das nötigende Ausnutzen einer schutzlosen Lage, in der das Opfer aufgrund der Schutzlosigkeit keinen Widerstand leistet'. Cited in Landtag Nordrheinwestphalen, 16. Wahlperiode (Vorlage 16/3733).

32. https://www.djb.de/Kom/K3/pm16-03/

33. https://www.bundesrat.de/SharedDocs/drucksachen/2016/0101-0200/162-16.pdf?__blob=publicationFile&v=1

34. http://www.zeit.de/gesellschaft/zeitgeschehen/2016-06/rechtspolitik-sexualstrafrecht-nein-heisst-nein-fischer-im-recht/seite-3

35. This kind of mass attack also happened in other European countries, in cities such as Zurich and Stockholm.

References

Abdelmonem, A., Bavelaar, R. E., Wynee-Hughes, E., & Galán, S. (2016). *The "Taharrush" Connection: Xenophobia, Islamophobia and Sexual Violence in Germany and Beyond*. Retrieved March 12, 2016, from http://religionre-search.org/closer/2016/03/12/the-taharrush-connection-xenophobia-islamophobia-and-sexual-violence-in-germany-and-beyond/

Ali, P. A., & Naylor, P. B. (2013). Intimate Partner Violence: A Narrative Review of the Biological and Psychological Explanations for Its Causation. *Aggression and Violent Behavior, 18*, 373–382.

Amnesty International. (2015). 'Circles of Hell'—*Domestic, Public and State Violence Against Women in Egypt*. Index: MDE 12/004/2015.

Bates, E. A., Graham-Kevan, N., & Archer, J. (2014). Testing Predictions from the Male Control Theory of Men's Partner Violence. *Aggressive Behavior, 40*, 42–55.

Cavanaugh, M. M. (2012). Theories of Violence: Social Science Perspectives. *Journal of Human Behavior in the Social Environment, 22*(5), 607–618.

Craun, S. W., & Theriot, M. T. (2009). Misperceptions of Sex Offender Perpetration Considering the Impact of Sex Offender Registration. *Journal of Interpersonal Violence, 24*, 2057–2072.

Fekete, L. (2004). Anti-Muslim Racism and the European Security State. *Race & Class, 46*(1), 3–29.

Fraser, N. (1990). Rethinking the Public Sphere: A Contribution to the Critique of Actually Existing Democracy. *Social Text*, (25/26), 56–80. https://doi.org/10.2307/466240

Garner, S., & Salod, S. (2015). The Racialisation of Muslims: Empirical Studies to Islamophobia. *Critical Sociology, 41*(1), 9–19.

Goldberg, D. T. (1993). *Racist Culture: Philosophy and the Politics of Meaning*. Hoboken, NJ: Wiley.

Goldberg, D. T. (2002). *The Racial State*. Cambridge: Cambridge University Press.

Kern, S. (2016, March 5). *Germany: Migrant Rape Crisis Worsens—Public Spaces Are Becoming Perilous for Women and Children*. Retrieved from https://www.gatestoneistitute.org/7557/germany-rape-migrants-crisis

Mancini, C., & Pickett, J. T. (2016). The Good, the Bad and the Incomprehensible: Typifications of Victims and Offenders as Antecedents of Beliefs About Sex Crime. *Journal of Interpersonal Violence, 31*(2), 257–281.

McDowell, L. (1983). Towards and Understanding of the Gender Division of Urban Space. *Environment and Planning D: Society and Space, 1*, 59–72.

Morgan, G., & Poynting, S. (Eds.). (2013). *Global Islamophobia: Muslims and Moral Panic in the West*. London: Ashgate.

Nelson, C. (2015). The Domestic Is Political, and the Political Is Gendered: An Analysis of Veiled Subjects, Gendered Epistemologies and Muslim Bodies. *Islamophobia Studies Journal, 3*(1), 106–114.

Šeta, D. (2016). *Forgotten Women: The Impact of Islamophobia on Muslim Women*. Brussels: ENAR, European Network Against Racism.

Turchik, J. A., Hebenstreit, C. L., & Judson, S. S. (2016). An Examination of the Gender Inclusiveness of Current Theories of Sexual Violence in Adulthood: Recognizing Male Victims, Female Perpetrators, and Same-Sex Violence. *Trauma, Violence, & Abuse, 17*(2), 133–148.

Vieten, U. M. (2007). *Situated Cosmopolitanisms: The Notion of the Other in Discourses of Cosmopolitanism in Britain and Germany*. PhD Thesis, University of East London, UK.

Vieten, U. M. (2011). Tackling the Conceptual Order of Multiple Discrimination. Situating Different and Difficult Genealogies of Race and Ethnicity. In D. Schiek & A. Lawson (Eds.), *European Union Non-Discrimination Law and Intersectionality. Investigating the Triangle of Racial, Gender and Disability Discrimination* (pp. 63–76). Farnham: Ashgate.

Vieten, U. M. (2012). *Gender and Cosmopolitanism in Europe: A Feminist Perspective.* Farnham: Ashgate.

Vieten, U. M. (2016). Notions of Conflict and "New" Citizens' Inclusion: Post-Cosmopolitan Contestations in Germany. In U. M. Vieten & G. Valentine (Eds.), *Cartographies of Differences—Interdisciplinary Perspectives* (pp. 109–134). Bern: Peter Lang Publishers.

Vieten, U. M. (2017). Far Right Populism and Women: The Normalization of Gendered Anti-Muslim Racism and Gendered Culturalism in the Netherlands. *Journal of Intercultural Studies, 37*(6), 621–636.

Walby, S., Towers, J., & Francis, B. (2014). Mainstreaming Domestic and Gender-Based Violence into Sociology and Criminology of Violence. *The Sociological Review, 62*(2), 187–214.

Wodak, R. (2013). "Anything Goes!"—The Haiderization of Europe. In R. Wodak, M. KhosraviNik, & B. Mral (Eds.), *Right-Wing Populism in Europe—Politics and Discourse* (pp. 23–37). London: Bloomsbury Publishing.

Wodak, R., & Reisigl, M. (2015). Discourse and Racism. In D. Tannen, H. E. Hamilton, & D. Schiffrin (Eds.), *The Handbook of Discourse Analysis* (pp. 576–596). Chichester: Blackwell.

Wolfgang, M. E., & Ferracuti, F. (1967). *The Subculture of Violence: Towards and Integrated Theory of Criminology.* London: Tavistock Publications.

Yilmaz, F. (2015). From *Immigrant* Worker to Muslim Immigrant: Challenges for Feminism. *European Journal of Women's Studies, 22*(1), 37–52.

6

Culture, Media and Everyday Practices: Unveiling and Challenging Islamophobia

Fatima Khan and Gabe Mythen

Introduction

In this chapter we wish to broach the issue of the cultural representation of Muslims. While there is now a broad range of literature which documents the ways in which Muslims and Islam are commonly depicted in the Western media, relatively scant attention has been paid to the gendered nature of prejudice against Muslims. Moreover, moving from the plain of representation to material impact, there has been a paucity of studies focused on how Muslims themselves engage with and negotiate distorted representations of their faith, identities and aspirations. Presenting qualitative evidence from a 2015 empirical study with young British Pakistani Muslims living in the North-West of England, in this chapter we consider the associations made between women and Islam at a representational level, focussing primarily on clothing as a marker of identity. We argue that intersecting discourses of gender, identity and faith—which are based on erroneous assumptions—serve to present

F. Khan (✉) • G. Mythen
University of Liverpool, Liverpool, UK

© The Author(s) 2018
M. Bhatia et al. (eds.), *Media, Crime and Racism*, Palgrave Studies in Crime,
Media and Culture, https://doi.org/10.1007/978-3-319-71776-0_6

Muslim women as simultaneously victims of gendered oppression and agents of cultural separation. Further, we posit that dominant ideologies prevalent in the UK undermine Islam and seek to impose upon Muslims narrow, assimilationist notions of British culture and values. Drawing on the data from the empirical study, we contrast common and negative non-Muslim understandings of the meaning and purposes of the veil with the positive attachments and affiliations expressed by Muslim participants. In addition, we emphasise the importance of resistance as a response to labelling and stereotyping, outlining the ways in which this is made manifest in both counter discourses and everyday practices. Before we provide a capsule account of the research methods deployed in the study, it is first necessary to discuss the specificity of the British context in general and a focus on the veil in particular.

Media, Culture and Politics: An Unsettling Context for Muslims?

Muslims and Islam have come under increasing scrutiny within the British media since the 2001 attacks on the USA. In recent years, numerous studies have demonstrated the persistently negative, unfair and discriminatory coverage of Muslims in the news media. For instance, drawing on analysis of hundreds of newspaper articles, a large-scale study by Poole (2002) found that Muslims were routinely associated with social problems and portrayed in a predominantly negative light. A similar media content analysis conducted by researchers at Cardiff University found that 'the bulk of coverage focuses on Muslims as a threat, a problem, or both' (Moore et al. 2008: 3). In a review of large-scale studies oriented towards representation of Muslims, Allen (2012: 9) reports that the most common nouns associated with Islam and Muslims were 'terrorist', 'extremist', 'Islamist', 'suicide bomber' and 'militant'. It is important to note that media representations of Muslims are not uniform nor static. Rather they are relational and indexed to broader social, political and cultural currents. The prevalence of implicit and explicit forms of racism in the mainstream British media against Muslims and non-White

European migrants—in tabloid newspapers in particular—in the lead in to the vote to exit the European Union bears this point out. While this gives a flavour of the ways in which Muslims have been commonly portrayed post 9/11, it should be noted that prejudiced and distorted representations in the UK have a much longer history, variously connecting Muslims to problems around immigration, welfare and civil unrest (see Mythen 2014: 107). Indeed, Islam as a religion and Muslims as a faith group have been a source of fear and fascination in the British news media since the Salman Rushdie Affair. The sensational coverage of the response to the publication of Rushdie's blasphemous book *The Satanic Verses* in 1989 saw Muslims denounced as 'uncivilised', 'barbarians' and 'dangerous fanatics' (Parekh 1990: 5). Since the late 1980s, media discourses have dominantly portrayed Muslims as inherently risky, with Islam frequently being depicted as incompatible with the contemporary 'British way of life'. Over time, these negative trajectories have manifested themselves in various controversies associated with Muslims, for instance, the wearing of the veil, the problem of radicalisation and urban unrest. Since the September 2001 attacks, Muslims have become 'hypervisible' in news media, a fact made all the more notable given their general absence from more 'normalised' representational positions such as in popular soaps, literature and reality television (Jasapal and Cinnirella 2010: 289). In as much as British Muslim men have been associated with a range of ills—including violent extremism, radicalisation and child sexual exploitation (Dagistanli and Grewal 2012; Tufail 2015)—Muslim women have been problematised in other ways. Notably, in the UK and across Europe, the veiled Muslim body has been a source of contention and political debate, with the *hijab* proving to be a 'floating signifier' (Lentin and Titley 2011: 93). In the early days of the disastrous 'War on Terror', it came to represent a potent symbol of the oppression of Muslim women, being used by some media commentators as partial justification for the bombing of Afghanistan and the illegal invasion of Iraq. It is notable that the victimisation of Afghan women by fundamentalist groups had barely been addressed by Western media and politicians until it became expedient to argue for military intervention as a means of liberating the women of that country from oppressive patriarchal rulers (Stabile and Kumar 2005).

The cultural meaning of veiling—in the context of Muslim women wearing the *hijab*, *niqab* or *burka*—has been widely debated in the media. Williamson (2014) observes that media coverage of veiling can be characterised according to three anthropocentric themes: refusal 'of *our* way of life', a sign of *our* excessive tolerance and as a harbinger of terrorism. The shift from the veil as a sign of victimhood to a marker of anti-Britishness can be indexed to comments made by Jack Straw, former UK Home Secretary. In his personal column in the *Lancashire Telegraph*, Straw (2006) called on Muslim women to play an active part in the improvement of community relations, urging them to remove the *niqab*, which he claimed was 'a visible statement of separation and of difference' The then leader of the House of Commons went on to assert that 'wearing the full veil was bound to make better, positive relations between the two communities more difficult'. Straw's comments were eagerly seized upon by the mainstream media, and the veil was summarily added to a stock catalogue of media narratives portraying Muslims as at once problematic and homogeneous: foreign, backward, outside of normal society, tending towards extremism and refusing to integrate into British society (see Said 1997). At the time, the *Daily Mail* columnist Melanie Phillips (2006) insensately claimed that the veil was 'an Islamist symbol which plays a role analogous to the use of the swastika by Nazism'. Such an impoverished view was echoed by several senior political figures, and the veil rapidly became configured as an iconic symbol of cultural difference that required not only public debate but also potential legal restriction. Today, the veil remains a contentious issue, both in politics and media discourse. Nigel Farage, the former UK Independence Party leader infamously called for a ban on the *niqab* in the UK, bolstered by public opinion polls showing support for such action. In a YouGov (2016) poll, 61% of respondents supported the statement 'the burka should be banned in Britain'. Meanwhile, hate crimes against Muslims have risen in recent years, with women who wear the veil being specifically targeted. The annual survey by the anti-Muslim hate monitoring group, *Tell Mama*, reported a significant rise in hate crime incidents against Muslims in 2014–2015 amounting to a tripling of attacks in comparison with the previous year (*Tell Mama* 2015: 6). The group reported the greatest impact of hate crimes being felt by women who were visibly Muslim, with 75% of attacks suffered by those who were clearly identifiable as Muslims, given that they wore headscarves or veils. Of course, it would be erroneous to suggest a causal link between biased media representations, institutional discrimination and Islamophobic hostility directed at Muslims in the public sphere. As Allen (2012: 2) notes, the role and impact of the media is both 'contentious and debatable' and there is no direct evidence that shows media coverage causes Islamophobia or anti-Muslim sentiment. Nevertheless, given that the media is a key source from which information about Muslims is gathered, it is perhaps unsurprising that a cultural climate of suspicion has developed towards Muslims in the UK (see Allen 2012). To illuminate this point, we will go on to consider the experiential impacts of negativity and hostility on British Muslims, returning to the controversy surrounding the wearing of the veil. It is first necessary, however, to provide a brief outline accounting for the methods used to gather the data we discuss below.

The Empirical Study: Purpose, Design and Methods

The qualitative study was conducted in the North-West of England and designed to gather insights into the outlooks of a group of young British Pakistani Muslim, aged between 18 and 26. The first phase of the study involved 32 participants contributing to four focus groups, each including four male and four female participants. The second phase comprised 12 in-depth interviews with participants from the focus group sample. The participants in the study were recruited through existing contacts within the local Muslim community and, thereafter, through snowball sampling. A series of open questions were formulated to act as a compass for the focus groups. After focus group discussion, an iterative phase of thematic data analysis was conducted through which prevalent issues were excavated. The key themes visible in data analysis were further explored during the second phase of semi-structured interviews. It was our intention to deploy a complimentary set of research methods. The focus groups were utilised to capture information through interpersonal debates and were specifically designed to obtain understanding of particular topics and processes which may not emerge from single interactions with the researchers (see Morgan 1996). As such, the focus groups facilitated the discussion of sensitive subjects that have not been adequately represented in wider public debate, in a supportive environment of peers. The semi-structured interviews permitted us to explore further the issues raised in focus groups through probing participant's individual accounts of social experiences and processes (see Silverman 2001). All of the focus groups and interviews were recorded, transcribed verbatim and axial encoding was conducted to organise the raw data into ideas, themes and phenomena as they arose (Strauss and Corbin 1997: 61). The data analysis process then moved into a second phase where the researchers discussed the emergent patterns and comprehensively compared them to the initial coding labels. Following this phase of cross-checking for consistency, final themes were derived from the data set. In line with the objectives of the chapter, we wish to prioritise discussion of three of these themes: attribution of oppression, public property and respect.

Attribution of Oppression: Muslim Women as Passive Subjects

Although the study had not intended to focus specifically on issues of dress, this emerged as a topic raised across the focus groups, being widely discussed by women in particular. One key theme emerging in these discussions revolved around perceived oppression. Several participants reported being frequently party to attitudes that associated veiling with gender inequality. One interesting aspect of this was the relative positions taken by non-Muslim observers and a discernible tendency towards assuming that Muslim women needed to be emancipated:

Naseema: 'Have you ever had the one about, why don't you just try it, you'll never go back? It's about being a free woman'.
Sofie: 'I'm mixed (race) so I have white cousins. I only wear hijab to school, but the times I've had to listen to my cousins talk

about "it's my life" and that I "should choose freedom". The worst thing is they know me, they know I do my own thing'.

Naseema and Sofie's experiences illustrate how the veil is understood as an inhibitor to autonomy that must be removed in order for women to achieve freedom. In these interactions, outside observers feel a responsibility to help 'liberate' Muslim women who are perceived as unable to fully experience a free life without rejecting the veil. Rahila and Samina re-affirm Sofies's concerns, indicating that dominant discussions about the wearing of the *hijab* and *niqab* fail to account for the wearer's choice, instead echoing dominant media and political discourses:

Rahila: 'What does my head in about the veil thing is all these people who talk about it, only know what the papers, politicians and Taliban tell them. So when they talk to you they bring those vibes with them'.

Samina: 'You've hit the nail on the head. First, there's the whole feminism hypocrisy when all I see in the magazines is "how to be young and how to be sexy", never anything else. On top of that these women, who are always trying to make us feminists just like them, don't know who we are. How do they know what we think or why we cover? I don't let anyone push me around and I wear the *hijab*. Actually, if anyone is bullying us it these feminists who just won't mind their own business, they make me feel less strong, if you know what I mean'.

Rahila's comments illustrate that, for her, public discussions about veiling are rooted in normative knowledge about the practice and fail to account for individual choice and agency. Samina underlines this arguing that whilst she feels able to practice veiling without undermining her values as a woman, her self-belief is undermined by outside voices. Moreover, these voices are interpreted as possessing not only popular currency but also an assumed moral superiority. Yet, as Hoodfar (1992: 2) posits, advocates of a 'one size fits all Eurocentric feminism' fail to recognise the compatibility of veiling and gender equality. It could be suggested that media and political discourses connecting veiling to oppression have restricted how the practice has become socially understood, encouraging remarks that might be interpreted as Islamophobic. Samina also introduces another important issue here: many of those who critique the veil as a symbol of patriarchy fail to recognise that they themselves operate within a context of gendered power relations. This is more explicitly discussed by Mariam and Amina, who pointedly remark that many non-Muslim women who are prepared to critique veiling on the grounds of equality fail to turn the same critical lens on wider British society—and indeed their own embodied choices.

Mariam: 'Well … it's like those girls who say they can't understand why we cover up, wear the *hijab*. They always think it's mean … we are under men, controlled by men. Like men have all the power over us. That's why we do it. Sometimes I think about them, how they dress. What they think looks good. I think you're the ones in really tight jeans, wearing short skirts. You're not wearing clothes like that because it's comfortable. It's because it looks good to men'.

Amina: 'It's not just that though, is it. When they're saying things like that to us it's as if they're some kind of feminists, equal to men, just because they're not Muslim. It's not true. It's not like men and women are equal here. Women aren't equal just because they are not Muslim, are they?'

As Mariam's comment suggests, non-Muslim women are subject to hegemonic standards of feminine beauty and its associated bodily choices. In other words, being a non-Muslim British female does not preclude someone from experiencing sexism nor from the micro level disciplinary effects of hegemonic patriarchy. It is understandable therefore that participants should highlight the double standards inherent in certain feminist critiques of gendered Islamic practices. Of course, generalisations regarding individual agency of the women described in the excerpts above cannot reflect the complexity of the debate around individual choice, bodily technologies and patriarchal power. In dominant discourses surrounding the veil, a roll on consequence of insisting that female veiling practices are indicative of

Islamic gender oppression is that Muslim men are universally positioned as oppressors. As Siddiqui (2012) posits, in portraying the Muslim female as the victim, Muslim men are simultaneously located as barbaric, unreasonable and violent dictators. Through his pioneering work on Orientalism, Edward Said (1978) has long argued that the West's perception of Islamic barbarism is encapsulated by apparent maltreatment of women, with Muslim men being normalised as inherently misogynistic oppressors. During a follow-up interview with La-Rayb, her personal frustrations with certain 'feminist' discourses follow this trajectory:

La-Rayb: 'I can't even tell you how many times some woman has asked me if my dad makes me wear the *hijab*. And they use that special soft tone that people save for abuse victims. When they do that I want to make them a victim of abuse there and then! [Laughter]. No, but seriously, you know what I mean, you can't be a Muslim woman and not get that'.

Moderator: 'I think I know what you mean, will you tell me in your own words?'

La-Rayb: 'Well basically they are saying that you are the victim of some type of abuse. I know that seems dramatic but on some level they are saying that you are being forced to do something against your will. But what they are also doing, and this really gets me right where it hurts. They make out that my dad is a monster. How dare they, how dare they say that about my dad. I can't stand them; I mean I literally want to do something to them. They see it on the news about women not getting education in Iran and then they use that tiny bit of information like sheep and come to me with it'.

La-Rayb's frustrations appear twofold. Firstly, she rejects the assumption that her bodily choices are a consequence of forced oppression governed by patriarchal structures. Secondly, she expresses anger that male family members are implicated as perpetrators of abuse against women. The flip side of this coin from a male perspective was articulated by Raheem during a follow-up interview. He has two sisters, both of whom practice veiling and talked about how their decision to dress modestly had been negatively reflected on him during social interactions:

Raheem: 'I've got two sisters and they both wear the *hijab*. Anyway, they came to meet me from work and I was walking down with this guy I work with. You know everything was fine and we are quite good friends. So I meet my sisters and introduced him. Seriously, it's like they had two heads, at first he couldn't help staring, then he said he liked Sanna's turban. He called it a turban, I mean the guy has lived in Manchester all his life. He sees Muslims every day. Well my sisters started laughing and then because it all got so awkward he said, "do you make your sisters wear them? I bet you are a right Osama at home". Do you know what, I just said "bye" and walked off. What a joker, it's just a poor show that. I mean where do they get off? Insulting me and them. I don't tell my sisters what to do, they don't tell me what to do. On top of all that, I just wouldn't be that rude to anyone, but it just seems that you can do and say anything to Muslims'.

Whilst Raheem insists that his sisters' choice to veil is autonomous, he is frustrated by the assumption that his sisters' modest dress is a result of his oppressive behaviour. The suggestion that Raheem is 'a right Osama at home' is symptomatic of an Islamophobic attitude that simultaneously assumes Muslim male misogyny and Muslim female victimhood. Not only does this personally offend him and his sisters, it indicates a shift in interactional dynamics as he introduces his sisters. In effect, Raheem's work colleague assumes that his sisters are objects not subjects, to be talked about and around, rather than to. As we shall see, this is indicative of a wider sense of public ownership of the female Muslim body which permits scrutiny and questioning without invitation and at will.

Public Property, Power and Religion

At odds with personal motivations driven by respect and choice, several participants spoke of their frustrations regarding public discussions about acceptability of dress for Muslim women and, in particular, the wearing of the veil. In the UK, Jack Straw's views about the *niqab* were to be a harbinger of media debates to come, with condemnation of the *niqab* becoming a well-rehearsed position in the British news media (see Meer et al. 2010). At a wider level, media and political narratives have legitimised the idea that embodying Islam through dress is no longer a personal choice, but a public matter with societal ramifications. As such, the regulation of Muslim women's dress has been indexed to debates around national security, multiculturalism, British values and gender equality. The otherwise everyday practice of veiling for Muslim women has thus become pregnant with imputed meanings. Interpreted exclusively as a strong marker of identity, some non-Muslims have erroneously come to view the veil as a symbol of Islamic patriarchy and/or a tacit indicator of extremism. Within such constructions, Islamic embodiment and those who choose to practice it are open to interrogation. *Ergo*, the female Muslim body is deemed beyond self-governance and individual choice. Rather, Muslim women's bodies become a legitimate site of contestation onto which all manner of fears and anxieties are inscribed. While this is a point to which we will return, it is important to note that the production of negative connections between dress and extremism also affect Muslim men. Sartorial and physical choices to embody Islam were frequently described by male participants as being equated with radicalism or anti-Western values. Here Kamran, who chooses to wear a beard, describes his experiences at work.

Kamran: 'Like I said before, working where I do, I'm always on the receiving end of crap about Muslims ... jokes about looking like Abu Hamza'.

The verbal abuse suffered by Kamran is mirrored by the experiences of Sofie and Rahila:

Sofie: 'It's like me. When I'm wearing a *hijab* sometimes, I swear down, the kind of looks I get. I mean, I still get the odd look when I'm in jeans and that, but, you know, put on a *hijab* and *shalwaar kameez* and it's like I'm the devil'.

Rahila: 'I know what you mean. Like when you're wearing Western clothes hardly anyone notices you … you forget about the Muslim thing, completely, but as soon as you're in Asian clothes; my God, some of the looks. I mean, I normally just wear Western clothing, but my older sister, she wears the *hijab* most of the time. When I'm out on my own I don't really get bothered that much, but when I'm with my sister, the amount of dirty looks and comments we get is amazing. Like this one time, we were in town and this group of chav girls started having a go at us, shouting out things like, "Look, Osama's missus". They kept following us, calling us things like "sand niggers". My sister even got shoved. Not that hard. It didn't hurt her, but it was scary still. That's just the way it is, I suppose'.

Not only does this conversation show how Islamic dress is routinely associated with terrorism, it also illustrates that embodied signifiers of Islam increase the likelihood of Islamophobic reactions. The disparate forms of common abuse suffered by Muslims are well documented in the literature and include being verbally abused, physically assaulted, spat on and threatened with violence (see Allen 2012; Poynting and Mason 2006). In line with these findings, the research data from this study suggests that Islamic dress increases the likelihood of experiencing Islamophobia. Some non-Muslim Britons may be less tolerant of individuals who are perceived to be 'Muslim and proud' by virtue of displaying visible in-group symbols. In this way sartorial choices and personal grooming preferences become misinterpreted as a wilful symbol of anti-Britishness. This phenomenon is highlighted by the following interview extract:

Nusaiba: 'Once, when I told a friend that I was called a terrorist by some random on the street, she said something like well you were wearing a veil and people just think you might be "one of them". Well, all I can say is she is not my friend anymore. I can't believe it, it's like, okay well, "you can't help being brown, but at least have the decency to try to fit in". As if wearing *shalwaar kameez* is enough reason to abuse us. It's because they think that if we wear *shalwaar kameez*, or a *topi* or *hijab* we are not grateful for being allowed to live here, that we are against them, they like Muslims who slag off Islam and act like they don't like it'.

Nusaiba's story illustrates anti-Islamic sentiment in operation and indicates a form of social penalty invoked by the wearing of Muslim dress. Nusaiba, Sofie and Rahila interpret this penalty according to the dual constructs of 'Islamist' and 'moderate' Muslim. The 'moderate Muslim' is viewed as being someone who is pro-Western, shuns Islamic bodily choices in favour of Western attire, engages in mainstream British social and leisure time pursuits and performs the part of the good British citizen. Whereas the 'Islamist Muslim' wears traditional Islamic dress and is perceived as being anti-Western, having little in common with British culture and is consequently unaligned with Britishness and rendered 'other'. Nusaiba recognises the impact of Islamic attire, its association with the negative constructs of Islam and the reactions it can elicit. Her former friend, who appears to suggest the act of wearing the veil elicits and implicitly justifies Islamophobia, highlights an attitude that is, in some respects, echoed in the false dichotomy of 'moderate' Muslims versus 'extreme' Muslims inherent in State security narratives and policies. Spalek and McDonald (2010) have highlighted these distinctions, suggesting that the UK Government has sought to legitimise certain theological strands of Islam over others. Further, Kundnani (2009) reasons that this process has been accelerated by marginalising voices that do not align with State security policies and enabling and encouraging those that do. Such State practices and policies have provided frameworks for calibration which identify, measure and stigmatise particular expressions of Islam. One case in point is the British counter extremism strategy, Prevent (2011). While this strategy is formally designed to counter all forms of radicalisation—including from individuals committed to racial violence—the focus of scrutiny is strongly directed towards Muslims, with the Prevent strategy document using the word 'Muslim' in excess of 100 times (see Mythen et al. 2017). Indeed, initial allocations of funding from government to local councils were directly determined by the density of Muslim populations in given regions (see Thomas 2016). While policies such as Prevent 2011) promote moderate forms of Islam, such forms of ideational coercion are coupled to more invasive forms of surveillance and scrutiny (see Awan 2013). Further, counter-productive State security practices that unjustly target Muslim communities are part of a broader fabric of discrimination in which 'permission to hate' (Poynting and Mason 2006: 367) is sanctioned. In this regard, outpourings of public racism and xenophobia which have materialised since the vote to leave the European Union have been alarming. As Burnett (2017: 6) reasons, the upsurge in attacks on Muslims and Eastern European migrants post Brexit has not been matched by a State commitment to proactively challenge racially motivated forms of physical and mental abuse. The data in our study showed negative social attitudes towards Islamic embodiment were, unfortunately, a quotidian part of participant's daily lives. As our data illustrates, the everydayness of Islamophobia means that Muslims cannot but develop adoptive strategies to manage it. Such strategies involve deflection, self-discipline and regulation of dress. Clearly, an absence of overtly visible signs of 'Muslimness' reduces the likelihood of experiencing Islamophobia. This experiential knowledge leads some Muslims to 'perform safety' through dress and display in an attempt to reduce stigmatisation in public (Mythen et al. 2009: 736). Jalal's reflections illustrate the tensions implicit in such sartorial 'choices':

Jalal:	'I wouldn't go to a football match in my *jubba*. Can you imagine … me in my dress? It's not just a dress though, it's a man in a dress. I'd never live it down, but not even in a funny way, they would not stop calling me Osama and that would be it then, you'd just have to go for it'.
Moderator:	'What do you mean? Go for what?'
Jalal:	'Well, have a fight. That's what happens, once it gets to religious insults, you kind of have to. So it's better never to

go anywhere like that, dressed in *apna* [our own] clothes
… best to be as *gorah* [non-Muslim] in those situations,
jeans t-shirt and loads of talk about going out and stuff,
you know?'

The excerpt shows how Jalal actively controls his speech and dress to
manage the stigma attached to overt 'Muslimness'. He chooses not to
embody Islam in certain contexts for fear of verbal attacks that could lead
to more serious conflicts, potentially involving violence.

The pervasiveness of micro level forms of Islamophobia is worrisome
and impacts directly on the everyday lives of young Muslims, as illustrated by the experiences of participants in our study. The need to develop
active strategies of risk management that may involve inhibiting expression is an understandable response to volatile conditions but is nonetheless troubling in terms of freedom of expression and personal liberties.
While Article 9 of the Human Rights Act (1998: 20) defends an individual's right to free expression and ensures 'the freedom to exercise religion or belief publicly or privately, alone or with others', for Muslims
visible markers of faith can only be confidently and freely displayed in
contexts and spaces that are predetermined as safe.

Respect, Modesty and Sartorial Choice

In addition to notions of public property and the attribution of oppression, a third theme of respect was frequently raised in conversations. For
female participants, the symbolic significance of the veil transcends the
two most prevalent discursive interpretations of Islamic subordination
and anti-Western sentiment. In sharp contrast, wearing of the veil was, in
many instances, motivated by a mixture of personal choice, modesty and
respect. Considered in the global context, subordination and resistance
should not be elided from discussions. Nevertheless, for participants in
our study, the veil was variously worn as a fashion statement, a symbol of
religious devotion and a means of upholding familial honour. For some
participants, veiling is considered to be a permanent state that endures
across time and space, whilst for others it is a transient practice, confined

to culturally or religiously significant events. Within the focus groups, participants spoke candidly of veiling as part of a set of subjugatory practices through which women can be controlled in some Muslim cultures. However, distinctions were drawn between 'traditional' and 'modern' approaches towards wearing the veil. Several participants, such as Amina, Rahila and Fazal Jaan, asserted that veiling as a permanent practice was not an appropriate choice for them. Rather, it was considered to be a fluid and context-dependent option:

Amina: 'We all know that women have to cover their heads when they don't want to. No-one is denying that. I mean if someone said there are no women anywhere who are forced to cover their heads, at all. Ever. That's just thick'.

Rahila: 'I don't think anyone's that stupid. I mean we all know about Saudi, and how it is when we go back to Pakistan. I don't mind playing at *Amiran*'.[1]

Fazal Jaan: 'When I'm on my holiday but, I couldn't do it for real. We all know girls who do have to and I just wouldn't want to be like that'.

Other participants rejected outright the practice of enforced sartorial modesty, asserting that this was contrary to the principles of the Koran and thus un-Islamic.

Sofie: 'I can't believe these parents think that they are following Islam, forcing their daughters to cover up. It's so embarrassing, these *jahil*[2] giving Islam a bad name. In the *Quran* women are equal. As far as I am concerned I am as good as any man. The Prophet said so. Let's not forget that they said that women are the twin halves of men'.

Basanti: 'That's because most Muslims don't practice real Islam, they just do what the people at mosque expect. They just expect women to cover up, don't they?'

Here, Sofie is determined to distance Islam from practices that she claims deny Muslim women the gender equality that is enshrined in the

Quran and *Hathidic*[3] teachings, which she uses to reinforce her rights as a Muslim woman. Basanti endorses Sofie's rejection of such practices, claiming that enforced veiling is concerned with covering and regulating women's bodies rather than an act which is rooted in Islamic teachings. Whilst the equality of men and women is explicit in the *Quran* and there is widespread agreement amongst Islamic scholars that it instructs both Muslim men and women to dress and behave modestly in society, there is no unequivocal directive stating that Muslim women must cover their bodies. Contemporary Islamic scholars (Esposito 2005) and Islamic feminists (Ahmed 2011) agree that the veil was not introduced by Muhammad and pre-dates Islam. Esposito (2005) posits that veiling and seclusion were cultural customs assimilated from the conquered Persian and Byzantine societies. Those customs became associated with Islam and, as a result, *Quranic* verses were interpreted to align with and accommodate cultural norms. Contra notions of subordination and resistance, participants described their motivations for veiling in two ways that jar with dominant, normalised interpretations: as a sign of religious devotion and a fashion preference. For Faheema and Sofie, the veil can be a private symbol of respect for Islam during prayer and the holy month of Ramadan:

Faheema: 'But really, I mean I don't know that many girls who absolutely have to wear it. You know, none of us are really forced to wear it. I wear it when I want to wear it. It's like, you can't pray without it, so obviously you're going to wear it sometimes, but nobody's forcing me. It's my choice'.

Sofie: 'Well yeah, no I don't wear it at all out of school. But I do when I pray and during Ramzaan.[4] That's a respect thing. I do when I want to show respect to my religion. It's between me and God, so it's got nothing to do with anyone else. So I wear it mostly when I'm on my own'.

Both young women assert that they do not wear the veil as a symbol of social identity to signify modesty, fashion choices or identity politics. Instead, their veiling is a personal homage to Islam, worn particularly during times of religious significance. In this way, ritualised embodiment of Islam allows them to reach a religiously defined mental space. This transcendental aspect of Islamic embodiment is rarely, if ever, rendered accessible to non-Muslims and conflicts with dominant media and cultural assumptions regarding subordination and male privilege. In addition to utilising the veil as a symbol of respect, several participants spoke of veiling as a fashion style in keeping with lifestyle choices. For younger participants in particular, hybridised forms of fashion display were considered *de rigour*. The blending of traditional Islamic dress with contemporary British fashion is discussed below by Pia and La-Rayb:

Pia: 'Well, I know for the old school *Ammas* it was an *izzat* thing and it is still when I go to Pakistan, but La-Rayb has turned the *hijab* into a catwalk piece!' [laughs]

La-Rayb: 'Why can't I be into fashion and still wear the *hijab*? I'm still covered up. My dad wouldn't let me out if I wasn't. I think yeah, we have changed since the *Ammas* time, but we are still covered up. I could still pray in these clothes…'

Pia refers here to La-Rayb's elaborately folded *hijab*, much like a turban set relatively high on the crown of her head, rather than the more discreet flat to the head style associated with traditional veiling. Such trends amongst 'scarfies' or 'hijabistas' are not unique to La-Rayb and have been tracked in the literature. Tarlo (2007) dates the transformation from traditional to fashion *hijab* to the early 1990s when Muslim women were looking for ways to dress Islamically and fashionably, more as a means of independently managing their own look, rather than being controlled by the fashion industry. La-Rayb alludes to the notable changes in Muslim women's dress that have occurred over a generation, 'amma' being a respectful term for 'mother'. She goes on to make the point that fashion and modest dress were perceived to be mutually exclusive, which is now no longer the case:

La-Rayb: 'Before we took control of how we wanted to dress, Muslims were so un-cool. It was either traditional or modern; we had to make a choice, *niqab* or mini skirt. This way we can do both. We can do what we like, we can mix both things, can't we?'

La-Rayb reflections echo Tarlo's (2007: 131) point, suggesting that the practice of veiling has undergone a metamorphosis in recent years, evolving as a result of 'trans-cultural encounters and experience in a cosmopolitan urban environment'. Whilst indicating both ends of the spectrum here, La-Rayb illustrates the limited choices available to previous generations of British-Muslim women who were dressed *either* traditionally modest *or* unequivocally Western. She goes on to note how not only is modest dressing one of many sartorial choices available to young British-Muslim women but that mainstream fashion norms and traditional dress can be merged. The hijabista is able to 'cherry pick', fusing both cultures to create a 'third fashion' to correspond to life choices that reflect the hybrid nature of her identity: modest and avant-garde. In this way, the *hijabista* trend can be aligned with Homi Bhabha's (1990) notion of hybridity. As Huddart (2005) notes, Bhabha was primarily interested in what happens in liminal spaces of negotiation and transference. For Bhabha (1990), it is spaces on the borders between cultures which are productive and allow the creation of hybridised cultural products and practices. It is clear that many young British-born Muslims are adept at navigating across a range of cultural choices and practices that blend heritage and tradition with contemporary aspects of identity formation (see Mythen et al. 2013).

Conclusion

This chapter has sought to draw attention to the gap between the social construction of the identities and aspirations of Muslims in the British media and the experiences and motivations of a group of young British Muslims. To illuminate this lacuna between representation and practice, we have focussed on issues around dress and the connections made between dress, culture, faith and identity. Having discussed the routine ways in which Muslims are represented in the British media, we have unpacked three salient themes arising out of our study—attribution of oppression, public property and respect—that illustrate the divisive impacts on Muslims of dominant cultural ideologies on everyday life. Regrettably, the present situation is not easily remedied, with Islamophobic attitudes being pervasive across a range of social institutions, from education to the police force, politics and the media. In the case of the latter, the unremitting reproduction of stereotypes and prejudiced representations of Muslims is not helped by a lack of representation within journalism. A recent UK House of Commons Report (2016: 3) noted that, while Muslims make up over 5% of the national population, less than 0.5% of British journalists are Muslims. This is indicative of the need for broad and wide systemic change to tackle anti-Muslim discrimination. To this end, it is vital that the experiences and voices of Muslims are listened to and given credence if Islamophobia is to be tackled, resisted and ultimately vanquished.

Notes

1. Lead character in Mughal era love story, always depicted in modest but glamorous period costume.
2. Islamically uneducated.
3. A record of the teachings and practice of the Prophet Muhammad.
4. Ramadan.

References

Ahmed, L. (2011). *A Quiet Revolution: The Veil's Resurgence, from the Middle East to America*. New Haven: Yale University Press.

Allen, C. (2012). *A Review of the Evidence Relating to the Representation of Muslims and Islam in the British Media*. [Online]. Retrieved September 15, 2016, from http://www.birmingham.ac.uk/Documents/college-social-sciences/social-policy/IASS/news-events/MEDIA-ChrisAllen-APPGEvidence-Oct2012.pdf

Awan, I. (2013). 'Let's Prevent Extremism by Engaging Communities not by Isolating Them', *Public Spirit*, January Edition. Bristol: University of Bristol.

Bhabha, H. (Ed.). (1990). *Nation and Narration*. New York: Routledge.

Burnett, J. (2017). Racial Violence and the Brexit State. *Race & Class, 58*(4), 85–97.

Dagistanli, S., & Grewal, K. (2012). Perverse Muslim Masculinities in Contemporary Orientalist Discourse: The Vagaries of Muslim Immigration in the West. In *Global Islamophobia: Muslims and Moral Panic in the West* (pp. 119–142). Surrey: Ashgate Publishing Ltd.

Esposito, J. (2005). *Islam the Straight Path*. Oxford: Oxford University Press.

Hoodfar, H. (1992). The Veil in Their Minds and on Our Heads: The Persistence of Colonial Images of Muslim Women. *Resources for Feminist Research, 22*(4), 5–18.

House of Commons Report. (2016). *Radicalisation the Counter Narrative: Identifying the Tipping Point*. London: HMSO.

Huddart, D. (2005). *Homi K. Bhabha*. London: Routledge.

Human Rights Act. (1998). (c.42). Retrieved May 18, 2016, from http://www. legislation.gov.uk/ukpga/1998/

Jasapal, R., & Cinnirella, M. (2010). Media Representations of British Muslims and Hybridised Threats to Identity. *Contemporary Islam, 4*, 289–310.

Kundnani, A. (2009, October). *Spooked! How not to Prevent Violent Extremism*. [Online]. Retrieved May 18, 2016, from http://www.irr.org.uk/pdf2/ spooked.pdf

Lentin, A., & Titley, G. (2011). *The Crises of Multiculturalism: Racism in a Neoliberal Age*. London: Zed Books.

Meer, N., Dwyer, C., & Modood, T. (2010). Embodying Nationhood? Conceptions of British National Identity, Citizenship, and Gender in the 'Veil Affair'. *The Sociological Review, 58*(1), 84–111.

Moore, K., Mason, P., & Lewis, J. (2008, July). *Images of Islam in the UK: The Representation of British Muslims in the National Print News Media 2000–2008*. [Online]. Retrieved May 28, 2016, from https://orca-mwe.cf.ac. uk/53005/1/08channel4-dispatches.pdf

Morgan, D. L. (1996). Focus Groups. *Annual Review of Sociology, 22*(1), 129–152.

Mythen, G. (2012). Contesting the Third Space? Identity and Resistance Amongst Young British Pakistanis. *British Journal of Sociology, 63*(3), 393–411.

Mythen, G. (2014). *Understanding the Risk Society: Crime, Security and Justice*. London: Palgrave Macmillan.

Mythen, G., Walklate, S., & Khan, F. (2009). I'm a Muslim, but I'm not a Terrorist: Victimisation, Risky Identities and the Performance of Safety. *British Journal of Criminology, 49*(6), 736–754.

Mythen, G., Walklate, S., & Khan, F. (2013). Why Should We Have to Prove We Are Alright? Counter-Terrorism, Risk and Partial Securities. *Sociology, 5*(3), 1–16.

Mythen, G., Walklate, S., & Peatfield, E. (2017). Assembling and Deconstructing Radicalisation: A Critique of the Logic of Drivers. *Critical Social Policy, 37*(2), 180–201.

Parekh, B. (1990). The Rushdie Affair: Research Agenda for Political Philosophy. *Political Studies, 38*(4), 695–709.

Phillips, M. (2006, December 21). Drawing a Veil over Common Sense. *Daily Mail*.

Poole, E. (2002). *Reporting Islam: Media Representations and British Muslims*. London: IB Tauris.

Poynting, S., & Mason, V. (2006). Tolerance, Freedom, Justice and Peace? Britain, Australia and Anti-Muslim Racism Since 11th September 2001. *Journal of Intercultural Studies, 27*(4), 365–392.

Said, E. (1978). *Orientalism*. London: Routledge.

Said, E. (1997). *Covering Islam: How the Media and the Experts Determine How We See the Rest of the World*. London: Routledge.

Siddiqui, D. (2012). *Islamophobia in Transnational Feminist Discourses*. [Online]. Retrieved June 7, 2016, from http://www.patheos.com/blogs/mmw/2012/04/islamophobia-in-transnational-feminist-discourses/

Silverman, D. (2001). *Interpreting Qualitative Data: Methods for Analysing Talk, Text and Interaction*. London: Sage.

Spalek, B., & McDonald, L. Z. (2010). Terror Crime Prevention: Constructing Muslim Practices and Beliefs as 'Antisocial' and 'Extreme' Through CONTEST 2. *Social Policy and Society, 9*(1), 123–132.

Stabile, C., & Kumar, D. (2005). Unveiling Imperialism: Media, Gender and the War on Afghanistan. *Media, Culture and Society, 27*(5), 765–782.

Strauss, A., & Corbin, J. (Eds.). (1997). *Grounded Theory in Practice*. Thousand Oaks: Sage.

Straw, J. (2006, October 5). I Felt Uneasy Talking to Someone I Couldn't See [Online News Article]. *The Guardian*. [Online]. Retrieved May 18, 2016, from http://www.theguardian.com/commentisfree/2006/oct/06/politics.uk

Tarlo, E. (2007). Hijab in London, Metamorphosis, Resonance and Effects. *Journal of Material Culture, 12*(2), 131–156.

Tell Mama. (2015). Centre for Fascist and Post-Fascist Studies 2014/2015 Annual Monitoring, Cumulative Extremism and Policy Implications. [Online]. Retrieved September 15, 2016, from http://tellmamauk.org/wp-content/uploads/pdf/Tell%20MAMA%20Reporting%202014-2015.pdf

Thomas, P. (2016). Youth, Terrorism and Education: Britain's Prevent Programme. *International Journal of Lifelong Education, 35*(2), 171–187. https://doi.org/10.1080/02601370.2016.1164469

Tufail, W. (2015). Rotherham, Rochdale, and the Racialised Threat of the "Muslim Grooming Gang". *International Journal for Crime, Justice and Social Democracy, 4*(3), 30–43.

Williamson, M. (2014). The British Media, the Veil and the Limits of Freedom. *Middle East Journal of Culture and Communication, 7*(1), 64–81.

7

Stupid Paki Loving Bitch: The Politics of Online Islamophobia and Misogyny

Katy Sian

Introduction

In 2013 feminist writer Caroline Criado-Perez found herself subjected to numerous rape threats following her Twitter campaign calling for Jane Austen to appear as the new face on the £10 bank note. A string of female MPs have also experienced online abuse, death threats and harassment. Furthermore, many celebrity figures and those in the public eye have also complained of sustained online harassment (Jane 2014: 558–570). Cases of women as victims of hate continue to escalate in the unregulated online world, whose sexism and misogyny appears to know no bounds. Symbolic and systemic violence targeted towards women is not new; patriarchy is a staple feature of western societies. However, with the rise of the Internet and new digital technologies, an environment of hate and vulnerability has flourished whereby violence towards women (and minority groups) is increasingly made possible, without restrictions and without constraints. Gendered hatred continues to spiral in cyberspace as it has come to represent a discursive stage in which the distribution,

K. Sian (✉)
University of York, York, UK

© The Author(s) 2018
M. Bhatia et al. (eds.), *Media, Crime and Racism*, Palgrave Studies in Crime,
Media and Culture, https://doi.org/10.1007/978-3-319-71776-0_7

performance and displaying of graphic sexual violence are routine practice (ibid.: 558). Online hate has thus become normalised as media systems continue to facilitate the monitoring, stalking and surveillance of
individuals (Atkinson 2014: 164). These shifts have worked to feed a
(male) predatory relationship with women, whereby many female celebrities have often been targeted because they have gained a few pounds or
lost a few pounds (ibid.). The contemporary mediascape has as such given
rise to a culture of voyeurism, which continues to prop up hetero, white
and hyper-masculine cultural norms that subjugate females (and those
deemed 'other'). Subsequently, more and more individuals are increasingly finding themselves at greater risk of online stalking, bullying, hate
and harassment (ibid.).

The contemporary phenomenon of cyber hate, cyber abuse, cyber
bulling, cyber stalking, cyber threats/incitement, and cyber harassment
continues to grow and spread at a rapid pace (Awan 2014: 134). The
Internet has enabled hate to propagate incognito. Online abuse thus
remains extremely difficult to contain due to the use of anonymous screen
names, virtual private networks and the TOR network.[1] Furthermore
cyber hate is often poorly monitored by law enforcement agencies. For
Awan and Blackmore (2012) cyber hate can be seen as complex nodes of
representation where perpetrators use digital technology and space to target and constrain those they believe to be a threat (Awan and Blackmore
2012 in Awan 2014: 139). Awan (2016: 13) goes on to point out that
such a form of power enables the offender to exercise dominance over
groups they believe to be subaltern. As a relatively low-profile academic,
who occupies a subordinate position as both female and ethnically
marked, I was shocked to have fallen victim to online Islamophobia and
misogyny, which is on-going and continues to circulate across different
sites.

Based on a critical auto-ethnography documenting my experiences of
online hate, this chapter will examine the challenges and burdens that
women of colour are made to carry when they engage within online
spaces to disseminate research and educate audiences around anti-racist/
colonial politics. The chapter is informed by a selection of online materi-
als across a variety of platforms including Internet forums, YouTube,
news comments sections, Twitter and Facebook, collected from 2013 to

2016. This forms what I will refer to throughout this chapter as the corpus, that is, the totality of the linguistic online material that has been documented throughout the aforementioned time period.[2] A discourse analysis of the corpus will enable me to critically examine the logics of Islamophobia—its circulation and manifestation online—as well as the gender dimension involved in the abuse. It will facilitate an exploration of the way in which individuals, actions and language combine to produce meaning through a system of signifying practices (Hall 1992: 275–331). This account situates itself conceptually within critical race and postcolonial feminist frameworks, as a means to unpick and unravel the complex and textured intersection between Islamophobia/racism, gender and online spaces. The chapter will go onto to conclude that the Islamophobic (and more broadly racial) harassment of women of colour online can be seen as the shift from the democratic to the demagogic, and as the replaying of the wider gendered and racialised nature of citizenship.

The Contours of Online Hate

The abuse began in 2013 following the publication of my first monograph examining Sikh and Muslim conflict. As someone who identifies as a Sikh, I researched extensively the notion of Sikh Islamophobia, which ironically became further validated through the online Islamophobia I received from some members of the Sikh community. One of the main components of my research was to challenge the idea of 'predatory' Muslim males targeting 'vulnerable' Sikh girls and forcing them to convert into Islam, what my work has described as the 'forced' conversions narrative (Sian 2013). This is a tale that has been circulating within the Sikh community for some time and one that is underpinned by Islamophobia, racism and Orientalism. The theme of 'forced' conversions to Islam is central within Sikh discourse as it reignites historical tensions between Sikhs and their antipathy towards Muslims (Sian 2013: 55–69). This story emerged in the British diasporic Sikh community in the 1980s; however as it is largely based on anecdotal accounts and hearsay, there is little evidence to suggest that a genuine case of 'forced' conversion exists

(Sian 2011: 115–130). My research has thus been committed to understanding and interrupting anti-Muslim discourse circulating within the Sikh diaspora, and seeks to develop a wider conversation around collectivity and anti-racist politics.

I was invited to participate within a book launch, which was filmed by the organisers and posted online with my full consent; what followed was a barrage of Islamophobic and misogynistic abuse. Since then, almost every written/visual commentary piece I have been involved within has been trolled with a series of Islamophobic comments, all of which seem to bear a resemblance. For the purposes of this chapter, Islamophobia will be defined as a conceptual category to describe not simply 'unfounded hostility' based on the fear or hatred towards Muslims as proposed by the Runnymede Trust in their 1997 report *Islamophobia: a challenge for us all* but rather as "the disciplining of Muslims by reference to an antagonistic western horizon" (Sayyid 2010: 15). Islamophobia in this sense, according to S. Sayyid (2010) can be seen as the upkeep of the violent frontier between the notion of the west and Islam (Sayyid 2010: 15). Through such an analytical understanding of Islamophobia, I will be able to demonstrate the various ways in which the corpus manifests itself through this framework, which is marked by wider structures of governance, rather than a few bad trolls.

Soon after the organisers of my book launch posted the recording on YouTube, the following statements appeared in the comments section:

SuperSos2012:	Who is [this] bitch?? Looks like [a] porn star [.] Why is she [n]ot wearing her burka bitch.[3]
Roar-Sounds Djs:	STUPID PAKI LOVING BITCH ... LOOKS HALF HALAL ... BITCH.[4]
DrSingha23:	Dirty slut.[5]

We see here specific Islamophobic comments, alongside general misogyny, that is, 'dirty slut.' The identifying name given on the third comment in particular, 'DrSingha23' is a clear indicator that this perpetrator is likely to be Sikh, using the common marker 'Singh' denoting a Sikh male.[6] The first two comments are also clearly misogynistic using terms such as 'bitch' and 'porn star.' Such abuse, or 'sexualized vitriol,' exposes the way in which online spaces readily facilitate and host misogynistic rhetoric and symbolic forms of sexual violence (Jane 2014: 566). Furthermore, the combination of racist/Islamophobic abuse is demonstrative of the additional challenges or multiple oppressions around the 'subaltern speaking' online, or rather her (in)ability to speak online (Spivak 1988; Brah 2005: 108). The comment that I should be wearing a burka is suggestive of the anger around my perceived association with Islam; this is further made explicit with the second comment claiming that I am a 'stupid Paki loving bitch' and that I look 'half halal.' The comments seem to try and make a suggestion that I am in some way connected with Muslims and Islam with the inference that I somehow 'look' a bit Muslim, whatever that might 'look like.'

The resentment about my work challenging Islamophobia, both within the Sikh community, and at the state level, is a key trope across the corpus; there appears to be a real sense of anger from the perpetrators around the idea that I somehow align myself with Muslims/Islam. In other words, the notion that I am an Islamophile is a dominant theme that continues to arise in the abuse, with numerous comments claiming I 'sleep around' with Muslim men. Alongside the suggestions that I am an Islamophile, we can see also the way in which the misogyny is equally as present and explicit with the repetitive use of the word 'bitch' and constant references to sex and promiscuity. Other examples of this trope have appeared on several Sikh forums:

Mrggg123:	Sounds like she has already converted to me, the actions and signs are all there to be seen. Apparently she was known to s*** pakis in her uni days....[7]
Chatanga1:	do you know anything about this katy kuty?[8]
HSD1:	Her name is Katy Sian and she is an out and out islamophilic apologist. She was on the 'board for anti-racism' or something at the University of Leeds, a city with a disproportionate number of grooming cases.[9]
Sikh Sangat Forum:	She's allegedly been having relationships with Muslim guys while at university who brainwashed her with Palestine and pro-Islamic nonsense. She calls herself a Sikh, but her name, her tweets, her book, her whole agenda and antics suggest otherwise. She has said nothing pro-Sikh in her whole set up, she has no clue about grooming cases regarding Muslim rape gangs that have been caught a few

months back. The numbers of Muslims caught grooming non-Muslim girls for sexual exploitations is in the thousands … we need to ask ourselves why is it always or mostly the Muslim males that are involved in this? … Katy Sian would probably back out of the debate, she is a politically correct liberal, pro-Islamo-fascist apologist, and might as well wear the burka over her head. She ignores the cases of countless Sikh female victims of Islam … which are probably in their hundreds if we add them up from all the years this has been going on since the 1980s.[10]

The notion that I have engaged in sexual relationships with Muslim men seems to be an issue that the perpetrators are obsessed with. There is a strong voyeuristic element running throughout these comments, with an emphasis on Muslims and rape. The perpetrators appear to desperately try and account for the fact that my work does not subscribe to Islamophobia, and offer different theories and explanations as to why I am not anti-Muslim. They claim however that I am anti-Sikh, a self-loather, who has betrayed her community and allowed Islam and Muslims to 'brainwash' me with the suggestion that I have converted, or rather been forcefully converted into Islam.

Once again we see the misogyny quite clearly, for example, above, 'Chatangal' asks, 'do you know anything about this katy kuty?' kuty referring to the Punjabi word for bitch. Alongside the explicit hatred for Muslims, a very male presence is also prominent on these forums and message boards. The male dominance of space in general has been long documented by many feminist writers. For example, Frances Heidensohn (1985) examined extensively how women are constrained in the public sphere through the dominance of men, that is, outside of the domestic sphere, other spaces have been largely dictated by male codes leaving them excluded, and less able to participate as they tend to be threatening for women (e.g. the workplace, streets at night, pubs) (Heidensohn 1985: 183–188). We can see how over 30 years on, this same logic appears to apply to the online space, a space overwhelming dominated by patriarchal norms.

The Islamophobia is rife throughout these comments; we see the perpetrators referring to Muslims as 'Pakis,' notions that Muslims are more likely to rape 'kufrs' (non-believers), a clear disgust at pro-Palestinian campaigns (and anything deemed 'pro-Muslim/Islam') as well as ideas of global jihad. In her work on digital Islamophobia in the context of Sweden, Karina Horsti (2016) points out that over the past 15 years, the trope of Muslim gang rapes as part of the feared Islamisation of Europe has become prominent in the counter-Jihad movement and in the radical right-wing parties across Europe (Horsti 2016: 2). The comments posted clearly appear to reproduce these fears feeding an Orientalist discourse, which constructs Muslims as sexually barbaric, and as threatening the 'purity' of the west by apparently sexually exploiting non-Muslim women.

The perpetrators are likely to be racialised themselves,[11] but it appears that they have internalised racist, colonial narratives around Muslim 'others.' The idea of threatening racial others has been a central feature in the story of western nations. A brief glance at the history illustrates the way in which the figure of the racially marked male in particular has been mobilised to represent a 'threat.' Vron Ware (1996), for example, examines the way in which British fascist literature became obsessed with the theme of black men raping 'vulnerable' white women in attempts to re-establish white supremacist ideology, in which the sensational portrayal of 'vulnerable' white females besieged by hyper-masculine racial 'others' became one of the most powerful icons of racism in the British landscape:

> These constructions derive their apparently hidden (but no less effective) meanings from the historical memory produced by centuries of slavery and colonization. The image of the defenceless white woman whose safety is threatened by the predatory and violent black male can be traced back to discourses of white supremacy. (Ware 1996: 81)

At the heart of these racist tales of the 'vulnerable' white community at the hands of 'treacherous' black men is the idea of whiteness and the maintenance of white privilege, in other words, the replaying of colonial ideas of whiteness as the norm and 'others' as somehow abnormal. Such narratives are constitutive of western racial histories and have become institutionalised within state practices, as well as internalised and reproduced by not only the majority population, but also ethnic minorities themselves, particularly against the backdrop of the war on terror.[12]

Islamophobia is a topic that has been documented extensively (e.g. Said 1997: 2–69; Rana 2011: 134–175; Sayyid 2010: 5–19; Poole 2009: 28–52; Richardson 2004: 33–53; Allen 2010: 83–187; Tyrer 2013: 21–40). Over a decade since the collapse of the twin towers, public and political discourse remains saturated with negative representations of Muslim populations at both a domestic and international level; the construct of the global Muslim 'threat' is thus a notion firmly entrenched within the psyche of western states (Sian et al. 2013: 80–116). The war on terror heightened the conditions under which ideas around male Muslim bodies as hyper-sexualised flourished across popular and political sites. As Gargi Bhattacharyya (2008) suggests, the construct of the 'savage black rapist' has transformed into the image of the dangerous brown male who is typically seen to have come from a primitive, barbaric culture, rife with misogyny and the oppression of women. To complete this narrative, he is represented as being unsatisfied sexually due to his traditional family structure and devoted to honour killings, regarding females as merely exchangeable objects (Bhattacharyya 2008: 19).[13]

Such a description resonates strongly with the assertions made by the online perpetrators who explicitly feed this Islamophobic discourse. The image of the 'threatening' Muslim male is well established, from debates on honour killings, grooming and forced marriages; the notion that the Muslim male is working to destroy the west appears to hold an ideological appeal in the Global North. This Orientalist fantasy has, unsurprisingly, come to occupy discussions in the online world. For example, Horsti's research found similar expressions of Islamophobia circulating on the blogshere:

> On one hand, the bloggers depict Muslim men as strong agents, who deliberately and strategically rape for the purpose of conquering the West. On the other hand, they depict Muslim men as non-thinking, animal, or virus-like organisms. In the latter instances, the bloggers erase a conscious agency by describing rape as an "infection," "epidemic," and "pathology". (Horsti 2016: 11)

The Islam and rape trope is clearly racialised whereby Muslim male bodies are constructed as sites which require urgent policy intervention. The criminality of Muslim men is read through a cultural prism, so that it establishes an association between culture and crime; such constructions work to both replay racial histories and maintain racial hierarchies. These representations uncover underlying concerns around the governing and managing of 'unassimilated' 'foreign' and 'incompatible' bodies whereby the violation of women by 'impure foreigners' translates into the violation of the nation. It does not matter whether the online abusers are Sikh, non-Sikh, brown, black or white, as they are ultimately subscribing to an Islamophobic language which constructs Muslim as 'other.' These hegemonic forms of Islamophobia, masculinity and patriarchy were made further explicit through a wave of Twitter abuse which I came to experience, with accusations that I am an Islamist sympathiser.

As my work has continued to develop, I have become more engaged within anti-racist politics at both the academic and grassroots level, connecting with networks through social media, particularly Twitter. There appeared to be one dedicated troll under the name, F-Equivalence-Watch, @LiberalCraig, who continued to harass, stalk and abuse me. @LiberalCraig created several fake accounts under my name, or using one very similar, featuring my profile picture to suggest the account(s) belonged to me as offensive tweets were posted (see Figs. 7.1 and 7.2). After reporting the fake accounts to Twitter, both were removed.

The background images on both accounts are used to evoke the notion of Islamic terrorism, featuring pictures of ISIS (Fig. 7.1) and a picture of Cerie Bullivant (Fig. 7.2), who in 2006 was falsely detained by British law enforcement agencies under Section 5 of the 2005 Terrorism Act as a 'terror suspect.' He spent two years under a control order, before being fully acquitted. Bullivant participates within human rights advocacy work and is a spokesperson for the organisation CAGE which seeks to help victims of the war on terror. My alleged links with CAGE appear to have riled @LiberalCraig who also went on to publish a video onto YouTube entitled 'Katy Sian: The Islamist' (see Fig. 7.3).

In this video for around 25 minutes, 'False Equivalence Watch' or @LiberalCraig dissects and trawls my entire Twitter page to somehow reveal my alleged Islamist links. @LiberalCraig represents clear elements

Fig. 7.1 Fake Twitter account 1

of the cyber stalker, which for Michael Pittaro (2007) refers to someone "who uses the Internet as a weapon or tool of sorts to prey upon, harass, threaten, and generate fear and trepidation in his or her victims" (Pittaro 2007: 180–181). On @LiberalCraig's Twitter account, his profile picture features a photograph of Christopher Hitchens to ensure that his real identity remains unknown. For Pittaro, cases of cyber stalking will continue to grow due to the fact that the Internet offers a safe space in which an offender can easily hide and obscure their real identity behind what he describes as a 'veil of anonymity' (ibid.: 181). Pittaro suggests that the anonymity of the online world allows the offender to connect with almost anyone who has access to the Internet, at any time and in any place, without having to fret about being identified or prosecuted by the criminal justice system (ibid.: 181).

Katy Sian
@culturecrafting

Anti imperialism (from white people). Pro Islamism.
Hate Uncle Tom Muslims - only like field Muslims

♀ The Imperialist West

𝒮 youtube.com/watch?v=7dkHXR...

5 FOLLOWING   **0** FOLLOWERS

Fig. 7.2 Fake Twitter account 2

Due to his interest/obsession with my work, @LiberalCraig is likely to be Sikh. This can be confirmed by his many Twitter exchanges around Sikh politics, claiming in one tweet that "his ancestors put up a good fight against the Mughal Empire," which is a strong indicator of his Sikh background. He parades himself as a devout atheist and positions himself politically as 'liberal.' @LiberalCraig constantly harassed me, asking me to direct message him if I wanted the video to be removed:

> @theculturecraft if you want the video removed then DM me and we will discuss.[14]

He clearly found some jouissance in the fact that he felt he had some kind of power over me (Salecl, in Laclau 1994: 229), in the sense of having the authority to remove or keep the video up on YouTube. This feeds Pittaro's analysis of the cyber stalker who is described as being driven by a voracious demand to have power and governance over the victim (ibid.: 182). I ignored and blocked his account, rather than engage, which

Katy Sian - The Islamist
False-Equivalence Watch · 998 views

Fig. 7.3   Katy Sian—The Islamist. Date: June 11, 2015. Source: YouTube. Link: https://www.youtube.com/watch?v=7dkHXRUGhwc

seemed to make him more hostile towards me. After not responding he urged me to 'publically distance myself from CAGE' while threatening that he was planning another video, continuing to play out the predatory cat and mouse game:

> @theculturecraft are you going to publicly distance yourself from CAGE. I am planning another video Katy.[15]

Continuing his routine intimidation and harassment, @LiberalCraig then went onto tag in my university institution calling for them to sack me for allegedly being a racist, pro-Muslim, Islamist sympathiser:

> Hey @UoYSociology—When are you going to sack your Islamist/Terrorist sympathising lecturer @theculturecraft?[16]
>
> @UoYSociology Why do you have the racist & Pro Islamist @theculturecraft as a lecturer in your department?[17]

Tweets posted by @LiberalCraig continued where my so-called Islamist sympathising was emphasised. Alongside this the direct misogyny appeared with the claim that I suck Islamist dick; the tweets became more abusive with the constant use of the f word:

> She's a vile Islamist apologist of the most annoying kind @theculturecraft.[18]
> Fuck Katy Sian—Islamist apologist.[19]
> She wrote a book on Islamophobia in the Sikh community yet she sucks Islamists dick.[20]

Combined with the misogynistic and Islamophobic abuse, @LiberalCraig displayed a clear animosity towards my academic trajectory, claiming that I have a 'clear left agenda.' Furthermore, despite the fact that my work evidently aligns itself with anti-racism, for @LiberalCraig that makes me a racist, with accusations that I have a hatred towards white people and or the west:

> Academia? More like academics with a clear far left agenda—*cough cough* Katy Sian....[21]
> Not surprised to find the racist crackpot Katy Sian '@theculturecraft' at another regressive conference.[22]

He even went as far as posting a long comment in the news comments section of a piece that I had written for the Guardian, claiming once again that I was an Islamist, and he proudly posted this on his Twitter account, it in fact features as his 'pinned tweet' to ensure tweeters are alerted to it. As En-Chieh Chao (2014) argues, commenting spaces provide users with the opportunity to gain popularity and measure their performance by showing the volume of hits a particular comment has received, and as such these spaces become sites of achievement and competition:

> The commenting box invites expressions that can be achieved and quantified with only a few clicks. It has no spatial or temporal limits but is open to everyone who has access to the website. The spirit of the 'quick comment'

that is built into the box is the antithesis of rigorous study and meaningful dialogue but a haven for diatribe. (ibid.)

@LiberalCraig's comments below epitomise this 'haven for diatribe' described by Chao. The comments, or 'cybersmearing' campaign (Pittaro 2007: 187), were not to stimulate a fruitful or constructive exchange, rather they reflect a series of unfounded accusations with the aim to discredit my work and academic standing:

> Katy Sian happens to be a very vocal supporter of the group CAGE, and has shown support for terrorism in the past (She used to have a cover picture of an airline hijacker on her Twitter page). Why does the liberal media apply this double standard? We should fight against BOTH Far Right white supremacists and Islamists (violent and non violent) and we should not provide a platform for their sympathisers.[23]

@LiberalCraig's fulminations share an uncanny resemblance to the discourse articulated by the white supremacist terrorist, Anders Breivik, whose enemy, according to Slavoj Zizek (2011), was a mixture of three key elements: Marxism (or left politics), multiculturalism and Islamism. As Horsti points out, the discourse of liberal nationalism is no longer restricted to the activity of the far right, but rather it has entered the realms of the mainstream. This shift has been facilitated and permitted by the 'misrecognition of racism' (ibid.). The misrecognition of racism is apparent in @LiberalCraig's Islamophobic articulations, whereby European colonial histories of violence and racism are erased, dismissed and ignored, thus the anti-racist challenging structures and histories of white supremacy translate into the Islamist/racist who simply hates white people and white society. @LiberalCraig in his reworking of racism therefore ironically becomes the anti-racist, who claims to be opposed to both Islamism and far right extremism, despite his constant expressions of anti-Muslim hate.

Such a combination of the erasing of racial histories, alongside the misrecognition of the logics of racism, and the trope of the supposed Islamisation of Europe, is symptomatic of the way in which right-wing xenophobia, under the guise of liberal nationalism, manifests itself in contemporary Europe. Cyberspace can therefore be seen as a system which works to transport, reproduce and reinforce wider racist power structures which have already existed and operated in society for centuries (Horsti 2016: 8).

The fact that I am not Muslim also appears to reflect the hostile landscape in which anti-Muslim hate attacks continue to escalate (Ameli and Merali 2015: 123–186), and furthermore points to the way in which those seen to be 'on the side' which challenges racism, xenophobia and Islamophobia become conceptually marked as Muslim, and subsequently 'other.' As such, it appears that the discrimination and hate directed towards those perceived to be Muslim is less to do with the religious origin of the victim, and more to do with the racialisation of Muslims, and the offender's notion of what constitutes 'Muslim-ness' and Islam (Chao 2014: 2). Processes of racialisation generated by the war on terror have thus meant that the Muslim subject is not fixed, that is, the Muslim signifies a category that denotes anything deemed contrary to the idea of the west, the active 'Other' (Weaver 2012: 496). Unsurprisingly then, those like myself who critique ideas of Eurocentrism, western superiority and white supremacy are likely to find themselves more susceptible to expressions of Islamophobia.

The intersection of Islamophobia with misogyny cannot be dismissed from the corpus of online abuse. From porn star, to slut, to bitch, being a woman of colour carries an extra risk and an extra vulnerability. Constant references to my perceived sexual behaviour rooted in baseless allegations; alongside a 'commonplace' string of sexist bile, the online space represents a restrictive and limited place for subordinate voices to exercise their agency. From the banal forms of patriarchy commenting on my appearance (see below) to the more hostile forms as discussed above, we can see the way in which wolf whistles on the street, to direct sexual harassment, projects itself discursively in cyberspace:

...Great shout with Katy Sian—she's fucking fit, no doubt, but her views are hideous. Anti-Hindu, Anti-Jew, open Islamist. Foul.[24]

The misogyny has been both generic and racialised. The examples discussed clearly demonstrate the complex ways in which misogyny works in conjunction with anti-Muslim racism. That is, along with the common expressions of patriarchy, the abuse directed towards me has also been specifically rooted within a racial framework based on the reproducing of cultural essentialisms, particularly around Islam and my alleged sexual engagement with Muslim males. Furthermore, the actual nature of the abuse is reflective of the ways in which hegemonic forms of masculinity/patriarchy are performed, exercised and maintained in western societies. The corpus explicitly reveals a clear gendered power dimension in play whereby from all the statements examined, it would appear that every single perpetrator has been male, where themes of sexualisation, objectification and fetishisation are paramount. The stalking, the harassment and the intimidation thus works to replay, and reinforce, both societal norms of male dominance and female subordination, as well as hegemonic forms of whiteness, westerness and Eurocentrism.

Conclusion

The Internet has often been heralded by liberals as an open, democratic space, free from frontiers, free from regulation and free for all. Connecting, bonding and uniting citizens across the world, the Internet has come to be regarded as an unstoppable, universal force traversing boundaries, barriers and borders (Banks 2010: 233). For cyber-libertarians the Internet provides a platform for free speech and expression, permitting the unrestricted exchange of information and ideas, with very limited government intervention (ibid.). However, this cyber-liberal-utopia may be a dream for the privileged, but a nightmare for the subordinate. As James Banks (2010) reminds us:

> The anonymity, immediacy and global nature of the Internet has also made it an ideal tool for extremists and hatemongers to promote hate. Alongside the globalisation of technology, there has been an incremental rise in the number of online hate groups and hate related activities taking place in cyberspace. (ibid.)

Cyberspace is thus not immune from the workings of power dynamics, oppression and exploitation, and for many it often represents a site of exclusion. The notion of an inclusive digital world supported by libertarians can therefore be seen as an imaginary, or rather a fantasy, which is deep-rooted in a politics of privilege and white, hetero, male normativity, whereby women, women of colour and people of colour more broadly are exposed to a misogyny and racism reminiscent of the 1950s, that is, before the advances of the civil rights and women's movements which helped to reshape the standards of conduct and behaviour in which untrammelled patriarchy was restricted, and white supremacy was challenged.

This chapter has demonstrated the various obstacles and perils that a woman of colour who desires to critique racism encounters due to the fact that white power and patriarchy remain unchecked and unregulated in the online world. In particular, cyberspace facilitates post-racial iterations of racism in the form of Islamophobia (Sayyid 2014: 23). This hatred goes beyond the normal reach of right-wing hate groups and Neo-Nazis, to embrace a wider population who would contest racism but succumb to Islamophobia (ibid.). My experiences of online Islamophobia and misogyny thus demonstrate that, contrary to the ideal of its utopian advocates, the Internet is a space like any other, riven by power relations. As such, its ability to provide platforms for minority views is undermined by the fact that the platform is itself structurally uneven in the distribution of power and privilege. What my experience describes is a structural condition which does not depend upon the identity of the trolls being black, brown or white, nor does it depend on whether I am Muslim, Sikh, non-Muslim or non-Sikh, but rather, the use of a discourse of racialised and gendered privilege by which the offenders articulate themselves and their view of the world.

This chapter has illustrated the narrow range of expression and agency afforded to minority groups seeking to articulate themselves on the Internet. Those women who dare challenge racism (and sexism, homophobia, etc.) often find themselves targets of vilification and abuse. The key difference between the online world and the 'real' world is that western societies have been transformed by the active agency of anti-racist movements and women's movements across the globe. This has resulted in greater regulation both at the formal and informal level. The online world however harks back to European societies prior to the advances of the civil rights and women's movements, in which it wasn't that racist or sexist behaviour was tolerated, rather it was simply the norm. This is not to say of course that western societies are post-racial, or post-sexist, and free from unequal power relations, but undoubtedly more mechanisms are in place to regulate forms of hate and discrimination on the ground. These mechanisms need to be expanded and deepened to cover the Internet to enable it to become an engaging and inclusive space of respectful, robust and mutual exchange, perhaps only then will cyberspace come close to fulfilling the utopian dreams of some of its early pioneers.

Notes

1. Virtual private networks enable users to access a private network securely and encrypt transmitted information (Herscovitz 1999: 214). The TOR network refers to a system that allows online anonymity by concealing identifying characteristics (Ren and Wu 2010: 424).
2. This definition is inspired by the way the late Barthes talks about the corpus in his analysis, see Barthes (1964) *Elements of Semiology*, Hill and Wang: New York, and Barthes (1975) *S/Z*, Cape: London, for further elaboration.
3. Source: Youtube, https://m.youtube.com/watch?feature=youtu. be&v=zJDG7fQ7SE8 (July 2, 2013).
4. Ibid.
5. Ibid.
6. Of course there is no certainty due to anonymity, but the indicators point to Sikh heritage or someone with knowledge of Sikh background. Please note the same applies to discussion later on in the piece related to Twitter user @LiberalCraig.
7. Source: sikhsangat.com, http://www.sikhsangat.com/index.php?/ topic/77183-katy-sian-exposed/ (June 12, 2015).
8. Source: sikhawareness.com, http://www.sikhawareness.com/topic/ 15230-sickening/ (August 29, 2013).
9. Ibid.

10. Source: sikhsangat.com, http://www.sikhsangat.com/index.php?/topic/75213-trying-to-organise-a-debate-katy-sian-vs-sas/ (August 18, 2014).

11. Again due to anonymity there is no certainty, but because such comments were posted on a Sikh forum, it is likely to be the case.

12. For example, Jasbir Puar (2008) illustrates the way in which the assimilation of Sikhs intensified post-9/11, with a string of jingoistic gestures (e.g. National flags outside Gurdwara's) signalling their allegiance with the west in response to the blurring of Sikhs and Muslims.

13. We see this trope frequently circulating in popular and political discourse, for example, in his infamous (racist) statement in 2011, Jack Straw (former home secretary) claimed that Pakistani men viewed white girls as 'easy meat.' He went onto explain that because they are living in a western society, Pakistani men are '*fizzing and popping with testosterone*' and require an outlet for that, but Pakistani women are off-limits so they are more likely to target white women. Straw's comments were circulated and supported by certain media outlets including the Daily Mail and The Sun. See: *Daily Mail*, "White girls are "easy meat" for Pakistani men: Jack Straw under fire for making "offensive" remarks on sex abuse cases," published online (January 8, 2011), available at: http://www.dailymail.co.uk/news/article-1345277/Jack-Straw-making-offensive-remarks-sex-abuse-cases.html and *The Sun*, 'Straw: White girls seen as easy meat,' published online (January 8, 2011), available at: https://www.thesun.co.uk/archives/news/296386/straw-white-girls-seen-as-easy-meat/

14. Source: Twitter (26/07/2015).

15. Ibid. (15/06/2015).

16. Ibid. (13/10/2015).

17. Ibid.

18. Ibid. (08/11/2015).

19. Ibid.

20. Ibid. (06/11/2015).

21. Ibid. (24/07/2015).

22. Ibid.

23. Source: The Guardian, https://www.theguardian.com/higher-education-network/2015/jul/21/how-do-you-spot-a-student-extremist-in-a-university (July 21, 2015).

24. Source: Youtube, https://www.youtube.com/watch?v=7dkHXRUGhwc (June 11, 2015).

References

Allen, C. (2010). *Islamophobia*. Farnham: Ashgate.

Ameli, S., & Merali, A. (2015). *Environment of Hate: The New Normal for Muslims in the UK*. Wembley: Islamic Human Rights Commission.

Atkinson, R. (2014). Stalking and Harassment. In R. Atkinson (Ed.), *Shades of Deviance: A Primer on Crime, Deviance and Social Harm* (pp. 162–165). London: Routledge.

Awan, I. (2014). Islamophobia and Twitter: A Typology of Online Hate Against Muslims on Social Media. *Policy & Internet, 6*(2), 133–150.

Awan, I. (2016). Cyber Islamophobia and Internet Hate Crime. In I. Awan (Ed.), *Islamophobia in Cyberspace: Hate Crimes Go Viral* (pp. 17–22). London: Routledge.

Awan, I., & Blackmore, B. (2012). *Policing Cyber Hate, Cyber Threats and Cyber Terrorism*. Farnham: Ashgate.

Banks, J. (2010). Regulating Hate Speech Online. *International Review of Law, Computers & Technology, 24*(3), 233–239.

Bhattacharyya, G. (2008). Dangerous Brown Men and the War on Terror. In S. Sayyid & A. Vakil (Eds.), *Thinking Thru' Islamophobia: A Symposium*. CERS e-Working Paper, no. 12. Leeds University, pp. 18–21.

Brah, A. (2005). *Cartographies of Diaspora: Contesting Identities; Hybridity and Its Discontents: Politics, Science, Culture*. London: Routledge.

Chao, E. (2014). The-Truth-About-Islam.Com: Ordinary Theories of Racism and Cyber Islamophobia. *Critical Sociology, 41*, 1–19.

Hall, S. (1992). The West and the Rest: Discourse and Power. In S. Hall & B. Gieben (Eds.), *Formations of Modernity* (pp. 275–331). Cambridge: Polity Press.

Heidensohn, F. (1985). *Women and Crime*. New York: New York University Press.

Herscovitz, E. (1999). Secure Virtual Private Networks: The Future of Data Communications. *International Journal of Network Management, 9*, 213–220.

Horsti, K. (2016). Digital Islamophobia: The Swedish Woman as a Figure of Pure and Dangerous Whiteness. *New Media and Society*. https://doi.org/10.1177/1461444816642169 (Available as Online First).

Jane, E. (2014). Back to the Kitchen, Cunt': Speaking the Unspeakable About Online Misogyny. *Continuum: Journal of Media & Cultural Studies, 28*(4), 558–570.

Pittaro, M. (2007). Cyber Stalking: An Analysis of Online Harassment and Intimidation. *International Journal of Cyber Criminology, 1*(2), 180–197.

Poole, E. (2009). *Reporting Islam, Media Representations of British Muslims.* London: I. B. Tauris.

Puar, J. (2008). The Turban Is not a Hat: Queer Diaspora and Practices of Profiling. *Sikh Formations, 4*(1), 47–91.

Rana, J. (2011). *Terrifying Muslims: Race and Labor in the South Asian Diaspora.* Durham: Duke University Press.

Ren, J., & Wu, J. (2010). Survey on Anonymous Communications in Computer Networks. *Computer Communications, 33*(4), 420–431.

Richardson, J. E. (2004). *(Mis)Representing Islam: The Racism and Rhetoric of British Broadsheet Newspapers.* Amsterdam: John Benjamins Publishing Company.

Runnymede Trust Commission on British Muslims and Islamophobia. (1997). *Islamophobia: A Challenge for Us All: Report of the Runnymede Trust Commission on British Muslims and Islamophobia.* London: Runnymede Trust.

Said, E. (1997). *Covering Islam: How the Media and the Experts Determine How We See the Rest of the World.* London: Vintage Books.

Salecl, R. (1994). The Crisis of Identity and the Struggle for New Hegemony in the Former Yugoslavia. In E. Laclau (Ed.), *The Making of Political Identity* (pp. 205–232). London: Verso.

Sayyid, S. (2010). Out of the Devil's Dictionary. In S. Sayyid & A. Vakil (Eds.), *Thinking Through Islamophobia* (pp. 5–18). London: Hurst and Company.

Sayyid, S. (2014). A Measure of Islamophobia. *Islamophobia Studies Journal, 2*(1), 10–25.

Sian, K. P. (2011). 'Forced' Conversions in the British Sikh Diaspora. *South Asian Popular Culture, 9*(2), 115–130.

Sian, K. P. (2013). *Unsettling Sikh and Muslim Conflict: Mistaken Identities, Forced Conversions and Postcolonial Formations.* Lanham: Lexington.

Sian, K. P., Sayyid, S., & Law, I. (2013). *Racism, Governance and Public Policy: Beyond Human Rights.* London: Routledge.

Spivak, G. (1988). Can the Subaltern Speak? In C. Nelson & L. Grossberg (Eds.), *Marxism and the Interpretation of Culture.* Urbana: University of Illinois Press.

Tyrer, D. (2013). *The Politics of Islamophobia: Race, Power and Fantasy.* London: Pluto Press.

Ware, V. (1996). Island Racism: Gender, Place, and White Power. *Feminist Review, 54*, 65–86.

Weaver, S. (2012). A Rhetorical Discourse Analysis of Online Anti-Muslim and Anti-Semitic Jokes. *Ethnic and Racial Studies, 36*(3), 483–499.

Zizek, S. (2011, August 8). 'A Vile Logic to Anders Breivik's Choice of Target' *Opinion: The Guardian Online*. Retrieved June 2017, from https://www.theguardian.com/commentisfree/2011/aug/08/anders-behring-breivik-pim-fortuyn

8

'Ta-Ta Qatada': Islamophobic Moral Panic and the British Tabloid Press

Anneke Meyer and Scott Poynting

The right place for a terrorist is a prison cell. The right place for a foreign terrorist is a foreign prison cell, far away from Britain.
UK Home Secretary Theresa May (2012a)

Global Islamophobia

The racialised 'Muslim Other' has since 9/11 become the pre-eminent 'folk devil' in the global 'West'. Morgan and Poynting (2012) argue that the moral panic framework, suitably developed to recognise the contemporary globalisation of the process, can usefully comprehend this construction of the global Muslim figure of evil and moral threat. This

---

A. Meyer
Manchester Metropolitan University, Manchester, UK

S. Poynting (✉)
Queensland University of Technology, Brisbane, QLD, Australia

Western Sydney University, Sydney, NSW, Australia

© The Author(s) 2018
M. Bhatia et al. (eds.), *Media, Crime and Racism*, Palgrave Studies in Crime, Media and Culture, https://doi.org/10.1007/978-3-319-71776-0_8

chapter examines the media-driven furore in 2012 over the detained London-based Muslim cleric, Abu Qatada, as a case study exemplifying this. The so-called hate preacher and supposed fundamentalist Islamist proponent of terrorism is quite a stock figure in the global iconography of Islamophobia, and Abu Qatada provides a clear instance. The symbiosis between crusading populist media and political leaders determined to outbid each other in their tough profile in the 'war on terror' is well demonstrated by this case. It also illustrates the ideology of purported 'failed multiculturalism' and supposed excessiveness of 'human rights' promoted in recent neo-conservatism, as well as some characteristic ideological elements of contemporary global Islamophobia.

Abu Who?

Abu Qatada is a Palestinian who has Jordanian citizenship, as he was born in Bethlehem in 1960 when the West Bank was under Jordanian control. He held leave to remain permanently in the UK since 1994, when his application for asylum on grounds of religious persecution in Jordan was accepted. Despite this history, the British government moved to deport him to Jordan, where he had been convicted in absentia over his purported involvement in a bomb plot in 2000. Abu Qatada claimed that testimony used in that trial was extracted under torture and that he would face torture if he were extradited there. The European Court of Human Rights ruled that he could not be expatriated there to face trial on evidence obtained under torture, and Britain's Special Immigration Appeals Commission (SIAC) and Court of Appeal concurred. Home Secretary May then secured a treaty between UK and Jordan guaranteeing that evidence obtained under torture would not be used against Abu Qatada, and he was consequently deported to Jordan in July 2013. He has spent over ten years in detention without trial in Britain, including three years at Belmarsh prison in conditions that were described by his lawyer Gareth Peirce as being 'buried alive in concrete coffins', for 22 hours a day without any sunlight (Bright et al. 2002). This incarceration was in 2004 ruled by the law lords to be unlawful. After several brief periods under house arrest subject to stringent control orders, Abu Qatada was released in November 2012 from Long Lartin jail, the government's attempts at extradition to the USA having failed in the courts, pending apparently improbable legal appeals. The conditions of his previous imprisonment there were described by a prisons inspector in 2011 as 'uniquely isolated and uncertain' (Travis 2011: 18). There was manifestly no evidence which could have been used to try him in the UK.

In January 2012, the ruling by the European Court of Human Rights that Abu Qatada could not be deported to Jordan for trial because of torture-tainted testimony, and shortly thereafter the British High Court ruling that he must therefore be released from detention, prompted predictable outbursts from the tabloid media, which railed against meddling in Britain's affairs, and that an irrational and ideologically driven human rights/civil liberties lobby was putting the nation in danger from fanatical Islamist terrorists. There had been previous demonising rants in the media about Abu Qatada; indeed the Islamophobic moral panic which followed 9/11 can be seen as a major reason that he was incarcerated in the first place, given that there was no evidence enough to try him in the UK for any unlawful act. In these and the 2012 round of moral panic, the media across the global 'West' routinely referred to Abu Qatada, without a scintilla of evidence, as 'Bin Laden's right-hand man in Europe'.

The Abu Qatada case was front-page news repeatedly from January 2012 until his deportation, and routinely invoked the exaggeration, demonisation and outrage characteristic of moral panics, involving a symbiosis between tabloid media and opportunistic politicians, pitching to and exacerbating popular fear and prejudice for perceived electoral advantage.

Islamophobic Moral Panic

It is clear that 'dangerous' Islam and the folk devil of the Muslim Other are ongoing themes of sensationalism and moralising by popular media and populist politicians. There is a global dimension to this: across the global 'West', the same discourses are circulated around Muslims (for instance that they are proponents of terrorism, supporters of Al-Qaeda, fundamentalist extremists, preachers of hatred, violence, misogyny, etc.)

and the same concerns expressed. These ongoing, global trends are punctuated by specific or discrete moral panics which are relatively short-lived and usually national in scope. What distinguishes these episodes from the ongoing background concerns is that the interest and attention is intensified, with front-page news, public outrage and condemnation, intense political 'debate' and forceful state reaction. Discrete cycles of UK panic from 9/11 to that over Abu Qatada in 2012–2013 include the reaction to the London bombings in 2005, the controversy around Sharia law in February 2006, the response to the London car bomb and Glasgow airport attack in 2007 and the Abu Hamza case (on and off since 2003) (Meyer 2012). Concurrently, the Muslim folk devil is both global and national, a continuous creation which is personified in many individual figures. These figures such as Abu Hamza or Abu Qatada are central to creating panics about Islam and terrorism in that they give it a 'face of evil'. Of course, the representation of these individual folk devils is shaped out of general discourses about Islam, and draws heavily on stereotypes and iconography: from veils and headscarves on women to long beards on men, to traditional loose-fitting robes on either, to prayer rituals, to food and drink proscriptions and so on.

Moral Panic over Abu Qatada

Campaigns of moral outrage and fear do sell newspapers, but the Abu Qatada story especially involved the conservative media as the most excited and panicky, as Islam and terrorism is one of their current staples and it can moreover be attached to some of their other demonising campaigns such as immigration and asylum seekers, 'scroungers' of the welfare state, as we shall see. In as much as this moral panic involved an element of right-wing political and media campaigning over 'foreign' European courts imposing 'human rights gone mad' on an unwilling Britain, leaving it in peril from terrorists and taken advantage of by 'bogus asylum seekers' and the like, this became an element of what developed into the push for Brexit. It was thus a peculiarly British cycle of national moral panic, while at the same time taking up and circulating quite international tropes of radical Muslim folk devilry.

The Abu Qatada case has a distinctly moral feel—it is about religion, murderousness and hatred, terrorism, asylum, the welfare state and the moral condemnation of an individual labelled as evil. Abu Qatada is a classic folk devil—a threat to 'our' people's lives as well as to the moral order. As Critcher's (2009) typology would suggest, it is no surprise that the Abu Qatada case has fuelled a moral panic: Abu Qatada is portrayed as an immoral figure who has no right to be in the country; he is seen as amenable to social control (at least, if only, the UK government could expel him and the European Union would not keep hindering); and while the regulation advocated concerns only Abu Qatada and by extension all other Muslim 'hate preachers' and terrorism suspects, there is certainly no desire to extend this regulation to the 'us' of the purported moral mainstream bound by 'British values'.

Methodology

We traced the course of the current moral panic from 17 January 2012 when controversy arose over the European Court of Human Rights ruling that Abu Qatada could not be deported to Jordan, which led to his short-lived release from prison under control orders, through to 13 November 2012, the day after his appeal against deportation to Jordan was upheld in the Special Immigration Appeals Commission. Our analysis focuses especially on the first period when the Abu Qatada case became front-page and headline news (as it did again prior to his eventual deportation, in urging and triumphalism rather than outrage, though this will not be detailed here). We look into the populist and conservative press, namely, the three biggest tabloids—*The Sun*, the *Daily Mirror* and the *Daily Star*—the two mid-market papers, the *Daily Mail* and the *Daily Express* and the broadsheet, *The Daily Telegraph*.

The research process involved gathering relevant articles through the Lexis Library database, online newspaper archives and physical hard copies (which allow better analysis of graphics and layout). We believe that we obtained virtually all articles in these organs over the period concerned that mentioned Abu Qatada. We analysed all major types of articles, namely, news articles, editorials and opinion columns. Editorials and opinion columns, in addition to news articles, play a particularly important role in the discursive construction of social problems by openly taking normative positions and offering 'newsreaders a distinctive and authoritative "voice" that will speak to them directly' (Greenberg 2000: 519). All types of articles blend social facts with normative judgements (van Dijk 1998); the difference is merely one of degree and openness.

Our analysis was for meaning and significance, seeking the main themes and ideological elements of the moral panic as it ran its course. We were not interested in a quantitative analysis, classifying and counting words or aggregating column-inches on various topics. Our ideology analysis seeks to draw out the discourses and discursive strategies through which the media—in our research, print and online newspapers—create specific panics around Islam such as this one, and both draw upon and contribute to the maintenance of Islamophobia. The analysis connects the linguistic and visual framing of Abu Qatada in the British press to larger societal issues, such as xenophobia and Islamophobia. We identify the construction of four specific themes and how they link to the creation of a folk devil, how they embody moral outrage and concern to re-establish moral order, and demands for strong state action aimed at social control of the demonised.

Four ideological themes emerged from our analysis of the press coverage about Abu Qatada over this period:

1. Abu Qatada as a figure of evil, terror and hatred associated with Islam.
2. Abu Qatada as an undeserving beneficiary of largesse from 'our' society that, as a 'Muslim extremist', he rejects, and as a manipulative bogus asylum seeker.
3. The theme of 'kicking him out', cleansing our society of this foreign being that does not belong, throwing out the garbage, cutting out the corrupting tumour and sending him back to Jordan where he came from.
4. The notion of a human rights agenda that is indifferent to the dangers of radical Muslim terrorism, offends common sense, is imposed on the nation by European meddling and is often advanced by liberal judges, lawyers and a 'human rights lobby' who are out of touch with ordinary people.

Theme 1: Evil—Abu Qatada as a Figure of Hate

'Al-Qaeda Monster Who Wants Us Dead'

A key way in which Abu Qatada's evil is established is through framing him as part of the larger evil of Islamist terrorism. Firstly, he is directly branded as a terrorist, both by the media and politicians. Witness the *Daily Mail*'s headlines 'Terrorist on the school run' (Doyle and Slack 2012) or 'How to get tough with a terrorist' (Doyle 2012). Home Secretary Theresa May in parliament (May 2012a) and writing in *The Sun* (May 2012b) goes from saying that 'Abu Qatada (…) provides religious justification for acts of violence and terror' to conclude by calling him a 'foreign terrorist'.

Secondly, Abu Qatada is constantly linked to individuals, groups and events which, in the ideology of the global West, signify Islamist terrorism: Al-Qaeda, Osama Bin Laden and 9/11. While there is no evidence that Abu Qatada was involved in the 9/11 attacks, newspapers constantly link him to them. It is frequently reported that videos of Abu Qatada's sermons were found in a flat in Hamburg used by terrorists involved in 9/11; ergo his speeches inspired the terrorism. For instance, the *Daily Mail* describes Abu Qatada as an 'Al Qaeda-linked zealot accused of inspiring terrorist atrocities worldwide' (Slack 2012a), and then the 'accused' is dropped: 'Among those influenced were Mohammed Atta, one of the ringleaders of the September 11 hijackers' (Slack 2012a). The *Daily Star* describes Abu Qatada as an 'al-Qaida cheerleader' (*Daily Star* 2012b), while *The Sun* calls him an 'al-Qaeda sympathiser' (Sabey and Pollard 2012). His words are dangerous and massively destructive weapons:

> British security services now face the most enormous challenge in protecting the public from a hate preacher who would be able to wreak havoc in minutes. …Qatada's role is to provide what the Home Secretary called 'the religious justification for violence'. (Slack 2012b: 4)

In the process, Abu Qatada is represented as a personification of evil, portrayed in words denoting and connoting wickedness or abomination— such as 'monster' and 'vile'. *The Sun*'s headline 'Evil in the shadow of

Wembley' (Sabey and Pollard 2012) uses 'evil' as a noun in place of his name. A *Daily Star* editorial calls Abu Qatada an 'evil nutjob' (*Daily Star* 2012c). Typical of the othering manoeuvres of folk devilry (Asquith 2008), these headlines and expressions position Abu Qatada not only as bad but as inhuman and also as dirt and contamination (which must be 'cleaned up') and as disease (such as a cancer which must be excised). A *Daily Mirror* opinion piece labels him 'scum of the earth' (Parsons 2012).

Abu Qatada's evil is assembled against the background of an 'us' as a taken-for-granted moral community. In this clash, he is *our* enemy. For instance, *The Sun* front page on the day of his release from prison in February 2012 has the massive headline 'Freed: Public enemy no. 1. Skulking in van, evil Qatada is driven from jail' (Newton Dunn 2012). *The Sun* editorial (*The Sun* 2012a) describes Abu Qatada as 'an al-Qaeda monster who wants us dead'. Similarly, an opinion piece in the *Daily Mirror* says that 'Abu Qatada is a malignant tumour on the heart of the nation. He is our sworn enemy, a preacher of hatred and intolerance and murder' (Parsons 2012).

Abu Qatada as the 'Hate Preacher'

Connected with characterisation of Abu Qatada as malevolent, we see his ubiquitous depiction in the tabloid and populist political demonography as a 'hate preacher'. 'The hate escape' (Newton Dunn 2012) was headlined on *The Sun*'s front page as Abu Qatada was released—briefly as it turned out—from prison in February 2012. The hate preacher label is spuriously based, for instance on selective representations of some of his religious rulings from as long ago as the Algerian conflict, taken out of context to present him as violent, vengeful and barbaric. As with the 'terrorist' tag, the term 'hate preacher' becomes a given and is constantly used, often in conjunction with the epithet 'terrorist'. The Muslim 'hate preacher' has become a stock figure across the global 'West', and the media archive photographs present a standardised visual image: religious head coverings, loose-fitting traditional robes, long beards, all of which equally signify Islam and the Middle East and South Asia more generally. These images of the Muslim Other go beyond constructing an evil terrorist network ultimately to demonise entire religious and indeed ethnic communities.

Qatada's being a Muslim does always not need to verbally underlined because it is constantly visually established. Nearly all newspaper articles are accompanied by a photo of Abu Qatada: most commonly a full-body shot showing him from head-to-toe walking along the streets with a rucksack on his back and full supermarket shopping bags in both hands (e.g. Flanagan et al. 2012; Wilson 2012a; Hughes and McTague 2012; McKinstry 2012a; Parry and Pettifor 2012). In this photo Abu Qatada has a long, unkempt beard which reaches half-way down his chest, wears a *taqiyah* (a traditional Islamic head covering for men) and *shalwar kameez* (long shirt over loose trousers), traditionally worn in south and central Asia, as well as many Arab countries. These three signs—his beard, his cap and his outfit—are strong signifiers of his origin (Middle Eastern/ Arab) and his faith (Muslim), determining his identity and foregrounding his ethnicity and religion, his difference.

One notable photograph, which appears several times (e.g. Hughes 2012; Dawar 2012a, b), shows Abu Qatada—again with a *taqiyah* cap, a long beard and wearing a *shalwar kameez*—in front of a library of books with Arabic writing. This last signifier is strongly suggestive of his status of an Islamic scholar, which could be seen as positive, with connotations of being educated, intelligent, widely read and studious. To avoid these readings, the newspapers direct readers towards seeing these signs as proof of Abu Qatada being a Muslim extremist through captions and inset headlines labelling him a 'hate cleric' or 'hate preacher'.

These pictures both personalise and de-personalise Abu Qatada; they both specify and genericise (Van Leeuwen 2008). They are shots of him as an individual but by the same token present him as an instance of a generic category by focusing on stereotypical signifiers of Islam and Middle Easternness to define him, making him stand for a larger group and mass. He emerges as a problem and threat in his own right but also as a metonym for a larger racialised group.

Abu Qatada is invariably referred to through a multi-compound noun (Fairclough 1989), 'hate cleric' or 'hate preacher'—this emphasises both what he does (preach hate) and who he is (a cleric or preacher of hate, who hates). The latter identification is a case of classification: the expression 'hate cleric' is used to describe various other Muslim religious leaders linked to terrorism and extreme religious beliefs (such as Abu Hamza or Osama Bin Laden). This classification adds to the impression that Abu Qatada is part of a group of religious scholars and preachers who hate any faith other than their own form of Islam.

Theme 2: Welfare Scrounger

One of the key themes of the coverage focuses on Abu Qatada as social welfare recipient and benefits manipulator. This theme again asserts the moral element in moral panic and connects themes of Muslim immigrants, the welfare system and asylum. This is a continuing topic from the beginning of the 2012 moral panic and is constantly scattered throughout the coverage (e.g. articles which mostly focus on other issues, such as danger or terrorism, also mention in places how the welfare state supports Abu Qatada and his family and at what cost), and there are many news articles and some op-ed pieces devoted to, or substantially about, this theme.

Abu Qatada's family—a wife and five children—depend upon social security benefits while he is incarcerated or indeed under control orders, and when released on bail, he shares these benefits. The coverage presents Abu Qatada as a welfare scrounger because he obtains benefits from the state which he does not deserve, in a society that he deprecates. For example, an article in *The Sun* headlined 'Freed to sponge off the country he hates' (Phillips and France 2012) states that on his release from prison, Abu Qatada 'will collect a huge benefits bonanza'. The *Telegraph* describes the benefits he and his family receive as 'handouts' (Burleigh and Whitehead 2012). His receipt of social welfare is represented as unjustified, unjust and outrageous: words such as 'sponge', 'benefits bonanza' and 'handout' indicate that he is a lazy person who relies on the state for his subsistence rather than working (which of course he did as an imam before he was incarcerated). This kind of language is common in conservative-populist tabloid and mid-market paper coverage of welfare recipients, who are routinely presented as work-shy and undeserving, yet here the objection to Abu Qatada's moral right to British state support is grounded in the attitude that he does not belong to the nation and is not 'one of us'. 'We pay £5million to keep hate cleric safe' (Spillett 27 2012) is a typical example of how Abu Qatada is not only represented as an outsider but as inimical towards 'us'. The *Daily Express*, for instance, calls Abu Qatada a 'sworn enemy' and 'implacable foe' (McKinstry 2012a), while *The Sun* claims that the UK is a 'country he hates' (Phillips and France 2012). The British state is seen as sustaining a man whose aim is to destroy it. This is presented as an outrage and affront to common sense, indicated by words such as 'madness' (*Daily Star* 2012e) or 'crazy' (Wilson 2012e) in the popular press, while the conservative mid-market press actually goes further and see this as an insult to national identity: 'Only a regime which has lost all sense of justice and patriotism could require its citizens to pay for one of its sworn enemies. It is a form of nationalised suicide. ...[T]he cost of keeping Qatada here is an insult to civic morality' (McKinstry 2012a). The *Telegraph* sees it as indicative of 'the society we have become' (Burleigh and Whitehead 2012), which is one without true leadership and strength, ruled by the EU and timid adherence to unnecessary human rights legislation, too weak to stand up for itself.

The newspapers all emphasise the amounts of money Abu Qatada and his family are receiving in benefits, the size and condition of their rental property and so on. For instance, a *Daily Mirror* article headlined 'Qatada pad busts Cam's welfare cap' describes Abu Qatada's home as a '£400,000 five-bed house [which] has three bathrooms, a reception and a study' (Pettifor 2012a). When Abu Qatada is rehoused in March 2012, the focus is on his home being bigger, better, nicer and more expensive— more bedrooms, larger garden, newer décor inside—as summed up by headlines such as 'A bigger home for Qatada' (*Daily Express* 2012b). The *Sun* writes that Qatada is 'claiming tens of thousands of pounds from the state for himself, his wife and family. That is on top of about £1.5 million the al-Qaeda fanatic has already collected in handouts, legal bills and prison costs from the country he hates' (Phillips and France 2012). The *Sun* article indicates that newspapers conflate benefits received by Abu Qatada with other costs, such as legal aid, police surveillance and even his own imprisonment, thereby inflating the amount of 'benefit' Abu Qatada is seen as 'getting'. This device was prominent in the reports following the ruling on 12 November that he could not be deported to face trial in Jordan because of the likelihood of evidence being adduced that was obtained under torture. The *Daily Mirror's* front-page story, 'Laughing in our faces', calculates that 'Osama bin Laden's flunky [Abu Qatada] will cost £100,000 a week to watch when he is freed on bail' (Pettifor 2012b).

The impression of disproportionality is compounded by comparative references to Jordan, where Abu Qatada would presumedly be living if he had not come to the UK, emphasising its lesser development and impoverished life, such as overcrowded, poor habitats (Kelly 2012; Westcott 2012). All of this is designed to stir feelings of outrage and injustice and is of course particularly likely to incense readers at a time of major cuts in welfare budget. The outrage and resentment is both transferred from, and generalisable to, asylum seekers and Muslim immigrants in general.

Theme 3: The 'Throw Him Out' Campaign

'Must Try Harder to Kick Out Qatada'

As well as exaggeration and demonisation, moral panics are characterised by exhortations of drastic measures by the state. The newspapers' demand in the case of Abu Qatada is that the preacher of Islamist hatred and jihad is to be kicked, booted or thrown out, like a piece of garbage—which he is repeatedly named as.

The Sun launched a campaign on 9 February, heralded by the 'People power' editorial (*The Sun* 2012b), to 'try harder to kick out Qatada' (Wilson 2012b: 13), in the words of the headline occupying almost a full page. A readers' petition to 'kick out Qatada' was included on page 12 alongside the article (Wilson 2012b) and was alluded to in many subsequent issues and online, with a picture of scissors here urging 'cut out this petition' and a picture of a (conveniently advertised) aeroplane from a cut-price airline, whose airfare for Abu Qatada *The Sun* grandstandingly offered to pay. Thereafter, the round (1–2 inch diameter), red-rimmed campaign insignia bearing the colour headshot of the folk devil himself with the slogan 'Must try harder to kick out Qatada' constantly accompanied *The Sun* articles over the course of this moral panic. An early example was alongside the next day's main article 'Boot him out ... or he'll stay here forever' (Wilson 2012c) which also featured the cut-out petition again as well as a smaller article on the same page whose headline declared, based on findings of a YouGov poll commissioned by the tabloid, that 'Majority of Brits want him gone' (Wilson 2012d). The logo reappeared in November 2012 when the moral panic re-emerged as 'Preacher of hate goes free today' (Wilson 2012f). Examples from the other tabloids abounded, even the *Daily Mail*, which presents itself as more respectable than the 'red-tops': 'Kick out Qatada now, demand MPs' (Shipman 2012), in whose editorial that day the desired deportation was more calmly termed 'removal' (*Daily Mail* 2012a). A page-one story on 14 February, however, displayed a stunt from the *Daily Mail*, which had interviewed Abu Qatada's family in Jordan, and misrepresented their anxieties with the headline 'Even his mother wants him kicked out of Britain!' (Kelly and Slack 2012). The *Daily Express*, ever keen to exploit xenophobia, urged the home secretary in the headline to 'Stop kowtowing to European court and boot out hate cleric' (Dawar 2012b) and the next day deployed the synonymous headline metaphor: 'PM calls Jordan's King to help kick out Qatada' (Dawar 2012c). Following Abu Qatada's re-arrest on 17 April and detention pending deportation, the *Daily Mirror* triumphed on its front page, 'At last! Preacher of hate Qatada getting the boot from UK after 10-year fight' (McTague 2012).

There are two points to make in respect of moral panics about the persistent use of the terms 'kick out'/'boot out'/'throw out'. The first is about the demonisation process that is typical of moral panic. In addition to the labelling as 'terrorist', 'hate preacher' and 'scrounger' discussed above, the demonising here involves dehumanisation.[1] Throwing out is what is done with useless (scrounger), noxious and dirty things, such as the 'piece of dirt' that 'lickspittle cowards' (Europe, 'ECHR enthusiasts') allowed to live here (in 'our' otherwise pure and orderly country), 'spouting his hatred of us' (Buchanan 2012).

The second point about 'booting' and 'kicking' is that it is about toughness and punishment. It is equally characteristic of moral panics that they involve calls for punitive, socially controlling, and if necessary violent, response from the state. The exaggerated language of booting or kicking out—rather than deportation, repatriation or extradition—is part of the campaigning aspect of moral panics that is so attractive (since lucrative) to tabloid media. Thus the *Daily Mail* headline: 'How to get tough with a terrorist. As UK agonises over Qatada, Italy simply ignores Euro judges and kicks out fanatic' (Doyle 2012).

Theme 4: Human Rights Gone Mad

'This human rights fiasco needs to be brought to an end' (McKinstry 2012b), resounded the headline of the op-ed column in the *Daily Express* on 13 February 2012, after Britain's Special Immigration Appeals Commission ordered that Abu Qatada must be released, following a ruling by the European Court of Human Rights (ECHR) that he could not be deported to Jordan since he would not face a fair trial there because evidence to be used against him had been obtained under torture. The first three sentences of the column combined all the elements of the 'human rights gone mad' theme in this moral panic:

> The European human rights regime, so adored by Left-wing lawyers and judges, represents a conspiracy against the mainstream of the British public. Thanks to these alien regulations, justice has been perverted, the immigration system reduced to a shambles and dangerous criminals allowed to walk our free on streets.
>
> That process of judicial destruction reached its nadir last week in the appalling case of Abu Qatada, an illegal immigrant and Muslim extremist wanted in Jordan on terrorism charges. (McKinstry 2012b: 12)

Here we see the process of 'extension' that Stan Cohen (2002) refers to, which links a moral panic about a particular folk devil (Abu Qatada himself, and by metonymy, evil terrorist Islamist plotters and Muslim hate preachers in general), with public worrying about wider issues that resonate as indicators of social ills: in this case 'soft touch' human rights legalities, European meddling in national affairs, supposedly uncontrolled immigration and its putative link with crime. As David Garland (2008: 11) observes, in Cohen's model of moral panic, the self-appointed custodians of social order and public morality 'always reach beyond the immediate problem, linking it to other disturbing symptoms of malaise'. Yet this 'reaching beyond' is overdetermined by the conditions that induce an outbreak of moral panic, involving an 'already primed, sensitised public audience' as well as 'the existence of marginalized, outsider groups suitable for portrayal as "folk devils"' (Garland 2008: 14). Islamophobic ideological elements that are more or less continually circulating globally both prime a fearful worrying public for the next cycle of moral panic, and at the same time allow their anxieties to be projected onto the specific Muslim Other that becomes the particular folk devil of that round of panic.

The exaggeration that is characteristic of moral panic is at work in this passage in calling Abu Qatada an 'illegal immigrant' when he has been long since accepted by the UK as a refugee. It provides an ideological link to the notion of criminality, which is found in the many press articles playing on this theme. The fact of Abu Qatada's conviction (in absentia) in Jordan on terrorism charges makes him a 'criminal'. The fact that the conviction was obtained with evidence extracted under torture—precisely the issue for the ECHR—is glossed over in this opinion column passage as in the many articles on this theme.

In the 'human rights gone mad' theme, nationalism trumps the rule of law. Tabloid after tabloid, enthusiastically echoing Conservative backbenchers, urges the government to 'Ignore ECHR and put him [Abu Qatada] on a plane' (*Daily Express* 2012b). Furthermore human rights are conditional: 'Of course human rights are hugely important. But when you spend most of your time cheering for al-Qaida then these rights should go out the window' (*Daily Star* 2012a). Or again in May: 'Deport Qatada now. He doesn't deserve human rights the way he's acted' (*Daily Star* 2012d). Clearly, human rights are seen as for good (British) people, not for the 'evil' and not for 'monsters'.

The *Daily Express* combines its house-style xenophobia and nationalism with anti-cosmopolitan Euroscepticism, to extend the issues of the Abu Qatada moral panic to the blaming of EU immigration for unemployment, in a leader headed, 'Britain is being demeaned by European institutions' (*Daily Express* 2012c). It editorialises, 'The ECHR should be ignored in the case of Qatada. A moratorium should be placed not only on Romanians and Bulgarians coming to Britain to work while we have mass unemployment but on people from other EU countries too' (*Daily Express* 2012c).

The government was careful to uphold European law in this case, while (often not very successfully) pressuring the ECHR to reflect British courts' interpretations more closely in its own—or else allow 'flexibility' of interpretation to national courts. This two-pronged approach is also evident in then Prime Minister David Cameron's official pronouncements which often combined colloquial and tough language with an insistence on the necessity to follow legal rules: 'I sometimes wish I could put him on a plane and take him to Jordan myself. But government has to act within the law. That is what we'll do. We will get this done' (*BBC News* 2012).

While the informal linguistic style and the use of the pronoun 'I' suggest that Cameron *personally* is in touch with the people and would like to simply expel Qatada, he associates the *institution* of the *government* with upholding the rule of law. This may or may not have persuaded the public of Cameron's popular credentials, but it certainly did not satisfy the Conservative Party's more nationalistic MPs, who earned the *Mirror*'s approbation by urging the government to 'Ditch the Euro court' (Little 2012). Similarly, in November 2012, the *Mail* reported that 'Tory MPs … demanded that the government should ignore the verdict and "put Qatada on a plane". There were also calls for the Government to rip up human rights law' (Slack and Doyle 2012). Moral panics invariably involve media campaigns, usually advancing demands for strong action by the government. Here it is necessary to 'get tough' with Europe in order to be allowed to 'get tough' with the folk devil at issue.

In the Abu Qatada case, the campaigning media perceive that the British state can act firmly and oust the folk devil only if it is unhampered by the EU. The ECHR threatens the ability to present Abu Qatada as a problem which can be solved by social control, by ruling that he cannot be deported; the 'kick out Qatada' campaign can be seen as a cry to claim such control, and the 'Ditch the Euro Court' demand is a condition for this.

Thus an unnamed Home Affairs Correspondent in the *Daily Mail* under the headline 'Human rights humiliation' (Home Affairs

Correspondent 2012) quoted Tory MP Charles Walker as addressing the Home Secretary in the House of Commons thus: 'You must not delay in getting this scumbag and his murderous mates on a plane and out of this country. And in so doing would you send a metaphorical two fingers to the ECHR?' That day, under the headline 'Humiliated at home' (*Daily Mail* 2012b), the *Daily Mail* editorialised, 'this case is only one of many in which Britain has been humiliated by that court and its 47 unelected judges from jurisdictions as diverse as Lithuania, Albania and Russia', neatly skipping over the question of where, in fact, judges actually *are* elected (certainly not in Britain) and what this would imply for the separation of powers if they were. The *Mail* concluded: 'A few days ago the Mail asked how Britain can stay in the ECHR if it keeps mocking our courts and our parliament. With our humiliation by Qatada and contemptuous treatment by the judges convening in Brighton that question can rarely have been more pressing (*Daily Mail* 2012b: 14)'. After November's SIAC ruling, *The Daily Telegraph* in its editorial asked rhetorically, 'Would any other country in the world have been willing to demonstrate its judicial impotence in such a humiliating fashion? (*The Daily Telegraph* 2012)'. It concluded, 'the Government must fight this all the way. It would make a mockery of British justice if [Abu Qatada] were allowed to stay indefinitely (*The Daily Telegraph* 2012)'.

Conclusion

While the original model of moral panic offered by Stan Cohen conceived of the phenomenon as occurring in discrete episodes, our examination of the panic around Abu Qatada suggests that contemporary moral panics may occur in series, focusing on similar topics. Firstly, considering the larger context of Islamophobia and moral controversy around dangerous Islam, we conclude that the British media were able to induce a panic about Abu Qatada by drawing on a stock of already established and ready-made discourses around evil and violent Muslims and invoke them without need for explanation. A good example is how the discourse of religious-inspired hatred and murder can simply be invoked through the term 'hate cleric'. Similarly, the media can use the tried-and-tested discursive strategies to frame individuals as folk devils, such as by linking Abu Qatada to key events like 9/11 and figures symbolising Islamist terrorism, such as Osama bin Laden. There is also a vicious circle in operation: by linking together moral panics about distinct issues or individuals, the danger of these individuals and specific incidents is amplified by connecting them to a larger network of Islamist terrorists, whose existence and danger potential is in turn proved and magnified by these specific events and individuals.

Secondly, while specific threats or individuals can be targeted and 'defeated' by the strong state reaction demanded in moral panics, the larger, vaguer menace to which they are connected is not dissipated and if anything emerges as even more threatening now that another element of it has become popular knowledge. In that sense, moral panics around dangerous Islam seem to be self-perpetuating.

Thirdly, crossover and connections are by no means limited to a series of moral panics about a similar issue, such as, for instance, dangerous Muslims. In the Abu Qatada case, the media also borrow heavily from discourses which have been established in the coverage of welfare recipients over the years, especially in the right-wing and populist press (lack of entitlement, over-generous welfare provision, lazy scroungers vs. hardworking taxpayers and so on). These are slightly modified and augmented in their linking to this case, but in essence again we see evidence of (especially tabloid) journalism drawing on and repeatedly reproducing established discourses that are known to 'other', to vilify and to incense. In doing so, and in constructing stock folk devil figures such as the Muslim 'hate preacher' with ideological links that are generalised to wider Muslim communities, the popular media are perpetuating and exacerbating Islamophobia.

Coda

Abu Qatada's deportation to Jordan in July 2013 was allowed under European (and thus British) human rights law because of the treaty ensuring that evidence obtained through torture would not be used against him in Jordanian courts. At trial, Abu Qatada was acquitted in

June 2014 of historic charges of being a party to a terrorist bombing campaign there in 1998 (Travis 2014). He was then acquitted in September 2014 of further charges of plotting a terrorist attack on millennium gatherings, and thus released from custody, remaining presumptively innocent (Malik and Su 2014). His deportation and presumably permanent removal from Britain was secured though the opposite presumption, expressed and disseminated through an Islamophobic moral panic that, for all the media condemnation of 'hate preachers', mobilised and exhorted popular hatred.

Notes

1. We will discuss later how Abu Qatada's human rights are deemed irrelevant; he is regarded as not human in that sense.

References

Asquith, N. L. (2008). Race Riots on the Beach: A Case for Criminalising Hate Speech? In A. Millie (Ed.), *Papers from the British Criminology Conference*, Huddersfield, UK, 9–11 July 2008, pp. 50–64. Retrieved from http://www.britsoccrim.org/volume8/4Asquith08.pdf

BBC News. (2012, April 19). Abu Qatada Appeal: May Defends Removal Delay. Retrieved March 28, 2013, from http://www.bbc.co.uk/news/uk-17776335

Bright, M., Burke, J., & Wazir, B. (2002, January 20). UK Terror Detentions 'Barbaric'. *The Observer*, 1. Retrieved December 31, 2012, from http://www.guardian.co.uk/world/2002/jan/20/politics.september11

Buchanan, K. (2012, April 22). How Lickspittle Cowards Allowed Piece of Dirt to Live Here Spouting His Hatred of Us. *Sunday Express*, 36.

Burleigh, M., & Whitehead, T. (2012, February 11). Evil Let Loose on Our Street. *The Daily Telegraph*, 25.

Cohen, S. (2002). *Folk Devils and Moral Panics* (3rd ed.). Abingdon: Routledge.

Critcher, C. (2009). Widening the Focus: Moral Panic as Moral Regulation. *British Journal of Criminology, 49*, 17–34.

Daily Express. (2012a, March 26). Hate Cleric Is Handed a Bigger Home, 19.

Daily Express. (2012b, April 19). Abu Qatada: Ignore ECHR and Put Him on a Plane. Editorial, 12.

Daily Express. (2012c, April 21). Britain Is Being Demeaned by European Institutions. Editorial, 14.

Daily Mail. (2012a, February 10). The Qatada Question. Editorial, 14.

Daily Mail. (2012b, April 20). Humiliated at Home. Editorial, 14.

Daily Star. (2012a, February 15). It's Plane Sensible. Editorial, 6.

Daily Star. (2012b, April 1). Abu Qatada 'to Cost Millions'. Retrieved June 25, 2013, from http://www.dailystar.co.uk/posts/view/243498Abu-Qatada-to-cost-millions-Abu-Qatada-to-cost-millions-

Daily Star. (2012c, April 20). How About Our Rights? Editorial, 6.

Daily Star. (2012d, May 2). Boot Hate Cleric Out. Editorial, 6.

Daily Star. (2012e, May 9). End Abu Dithering. Editorial, 6.

Dawar, A. (2012a, February 7). Hate Cleric's Deemed a Danger, Send Him Back. *Daily Express*, 5.

Dawar, A. (2012b, February 9). Stop Kowtowing to European Court and Boot Out Hate Cleric. *Daily Express*, 2.

Dawar, A. (2012c, February 10). PM Calls Jordan's King to Help Kick Out Qatada. *Daily Express*, 2.

Doyle, J. (2012, March 28). How to Get Tough with a Terrorist. *Daily Mail*, 24.

Doyle, J., & Slack, J. (2012, February 7). Terrorist on the School Run. *Daily Mail*, 1.

Fairclough, N. (1989). *Language and Power.* London: Longman.

Flanagan, P., Hall, M., & Twomey, J. (2012, January 18). Fury as Radical Cleric Is Allowed to Stay. *Daily Express*, 4–5.

Garland, D. (2008). On the Concept of Moral Panic. *Crime Media Culture, 4*(1), 9–30.

Greenberg, J. (2000). Opinion Discourse and Canadian Newspapers: The Case of the Chinese 'Boat People'. *Canadian Journal of Communication, 25*(4), 517–537.

Home Affairs Correspondent. (2012, April 20). Human Rights Humiliation. *Daily Mail*, 9.

Hughes, S. (2012, January 18). EU Can't Kick Out Qatada. *The Sun*, 7.

Hughes, C., & McTague, T. (2012, February 8). The Right Place for a Terrorist Is a Prison … the Right Place for a Foreign Terrorist Is a Foreign Prison. *Daily Mirror*, 5.

Kelly, T. (2012, March 26). Qatada, the Happiest Man in England. *Daily Mail*, 5.

Kelly, T., & Slack, J. (2012, February 14). Even His Mother Wants Him Kicked Out of Britain! *Daily Mail*, 1.

Little, A. (2012, April 21). Ditch the Euro Court, Say MPs. *Daily Mirror*, 5.

Malik, S., & Su, A. (2014, September 24). Abu Qatada Cleared of Terror Charges by Jordan Court and Released from Jail. *The Guardian*. Retrieved July 14, 2017, from https://www.theguardian.com/world/2014/sep/24/abu-qatada-cleared-terror-charges-jordan-court

May, T. (2012a, February 7). *Speech to the House of Commons*. Retrieved from http://www.publications.parliament.uk/pa/cm201212/cmhansrd/cm120207/debtext/120207-0001.htm#12020774000003

May, T. (2012b, February 8). I'm Doing All I Can to Get Rid of This Man. *The Sun*, 9.

McKinstry, L. (2012a, February 9). Coalition Fails in Its Duty to Protect Us from This Vile Man. *Daily Express*, 12.

McKinstry, L. (2012b, February 13). This Human Rights Fiasco Needs to Be Brought to an End. *Daily Express*, 12.

McTague, T. (2012, April 18). At Last! *Daily Mirror*, 1.

Meyer, A. (2012). Moral Panics, Globalisation and Islamophobia: The Case of Abu Hamza in the Sun. In G. Morgan & S. Poynting (Eds.), *Global Islamophobia: Muslims and Moral Panic in the West* (pp. 181–195). Farnham: Ashgate.

Newton Dunn, T. (2012, February 14). Freed: Public Enemy No. 1. The Hate Escape. *The Sun*, 1.

Noble, G. (2012). Where Is the Moral in Moral Panic? Islam, Evil and Moral Turbulence. In G. Morgan & S. Poynting (Eds.), *Global Islamophobia* (pp. 215–231). Farnham: Ashgate.

Parry, T., & Pettifor, T. (2012, February 15). What Price Freedom? *Daily Mirror*, 10.

Parsons, T. (2012, April 21). It's the Court of Inhuman Rights. *Daily Mirror*, 13.

Pettifor, T. (2012a, February 16). Qatada Pad Busts Cam's Welfare Cap. *Daily Mirror*, 11.

Pettifor, T. (2012b, November 13). Laughing in Our Faces. *Daily Mirror*, 1.

Phillips, R., & France, A. (2012, February 7). Freed to Sponge Off the Country He Hates. *The Sun*, 6.

Sabey, R., & Pollard, C. (2012, February 15). We Find Hate Preacher—Evil in the Shadow of Wembley. *The Sun*, 15.

Shipman, T. (2012, February 10). Kick Out Qatada Now, Demand MPs. *Daily Mail*, 13.

Slack, J. (2012a, February 8). Twisted Ruling Puts Lives at Risk. *Daily Mail*, 7.

Slack, J. (2012b, November 13). Our Courts Are Now the Puppets of Judges in Strasbourg. *Daily Mail*, 4.

Slack, J., & Doyle, J. (2012, November 13). Qatada Out Today … at £5m a Year Cost to Taxpayers. *Daily Mail*, 4.

Spillet, R. (2012, February 27). We Pay £5million to Keep Hate Cleric Safe. *Daily Star*, 8.

The Daily Telegraph. (2012, November 13). A Mockery of Justice. Editorial, 25.

The Guardian. (2013). ABCs: National Daily Newspaper Circulation February 2013. Retrieved March 28, 2013, from http://www.guardian.co.uk/media/table/2013/mar/08/abcs-national-newspapers

The Sun. (2012a, February 7). UK Surrenders. Editorial, 8.

The Sun. (2012b, February 9). People Power. Editorial, 8.

Travis, A. (2011, August 18). Terror Suspects Isolated and in Limbo, Says Prisons Inspector. *The Guardian*, 19.

Travis, A. (2014, June 26). Abu Qatada Cleared in Jordan of 1998 Bomb Plot. *The Guardian*. Retrieved July 14, 2017, from https://www.theguardian.com/world/2014/jun/26/abu-qatada-cleared-terrorist-bomb-plot-jordan

van Dijk, T. A. (1998). Opinions and Ideologies in the Press. In A. Bell & P. Garrett (Eds.), *Approaches to Media Discourse* (pp. 21–63). Oxford: Blackwell.

Van Leeuwen, T. (2008). *Discourse and Practice: New Tools for Critical Discourse Analysis*. Oxford: Oxford University Press.

Westcott, S. (2012, March 26). Hate Cleric Abu Qatada Is 'Happiest Man' as He Gets Bigger Home. *Daily Express*, 19.

Wilson, G. (2012a, February 8). Ta-Ta Qatada: Kick Out Hate Preacher Now, Say MPs. *The Sun*, 1.

Wilson, G. (2012b, February 9). Let's Try Harder to Kick Out Qatada. *The Sun*, 12–13.

Wilson, G. (2012c, February 10). Boot Him Out … or He'll Stay Here Forever. *The Sun*, 13.

Wilson, G. (2012d, February 10). Majority of Brits Want Him Gone. *The Sun*, 13.

Wilson, G. (2012e, April 23). MP: Theresa Misled Us on Qatada Cash. *The Sun*, 6.

Wilson, G. (2012f, November 13). Preacher of Hate Goes Free Today. *The Sun*, 4.

9

Bordering on Denial: State Persecution, Border Controls and the Rohingya Refugee Crisis

Michael Grewcock

Introduction

At this point, the situation of the Rohingya cannot be understood without considering a possible genocide.… The community is cornered and traumatised, forcing them to escape in the worst possible conditions to the open sea, where many perish with the rest of the world scarcely reacting.

> Tomás Ojea Quintana, Special Rapporteur on the situation of human rights in Myanmar, Foreword to Green et al. (2015, 14).

Nope, nope, nope … Australia will do absolutely nothing that gives any encouragement to anyone to think they can get on a boat, that they can work with people smugglers to start a new life … I'm sorry. If you want to start a new life, you come through the front door, not through the back door.

> Tony Abbott, Prime Minister of Australia (2013–2015), outlining his government's refusal to consider resettlement of stranded Rohingya refugees, quoted in Cooke (2015).

M. Grewcock (✉)
University of New South Wales, Sydney, NSW, Australia

© The Author(s) 2018
M. Bhatia et al. (eds.), *Media, Crime and Racism*, Palgrave Studies in Crime,
Media and Culture, https://doi.org/10.1007/978-3-319-71776-0_9

In May 2015, sections of the global media, including in Australia, suddenly took notice of the plight of the Rohingya, a Muslim minority from Myanmar (Burma), described by Amnesty International as "the most persecuted refugees in the world" (Hamling 2016), by the United Nations High Commissioner for Human Rights as the victims of possible crimes against humanity (UNHCHR 2016) and by a growing number of researchers and human rights activists as the victims of an unfolding genocide (Zarni and Cowley 2014; Green et al. 2015). The focus of attention in May 2015 was a crisis that developed as an estimated 5000–8000 Rohingya from Myanmar and Bangladesh were abandoned on boats in the Bay of Bengal and the Andaman Sea after the Thai authorities mounted a major policing operation against illicit migration networks moving people through Thailand into Malaysia (Murdoch 2015a; UNHCR 2015a). The situation was exacerbated by the decisions of the Thai, Malaysian and Indonesian governments to refuse entry to the boats and in some cases push them back out to sea. Some of the passengers on the boats were rescued by Indonesian fishermen but least 70 are estimated to have died as a result of "starvation, dehydration, disease and abuse by boat crews" (UNHCR 2015a).

The crisis eased after the Malaysian and Indonesian governments agreed on 20 May 2015 to admit temporarily those stranded within their jurisdiction with the proviso that they be resettled or repatriated to other states within 12 months (ReliefWeb 2015). It was effectively considered over, for the purposes of mainstream media coverage, following a meeting of Myanmar and regional government representatives convened by the Thai government on 29 May 2015. That gathering agreed to further regional co-operation to rescue those still stranded at sea and to work towards "the comprehensive prevention of irregular migration, smuggling of migrants and trafficking in persons" (Thai Ministry of Foreign Affairs 2016), although at the insistence of the Myanmar government the final communiqué made no direct reference to the Rohingya (Popham 2016, 192).

However, the May events formed part of a protracted crisis of forced migration in the region, in which the Myanmar authorities have played a central role. Since the late 1970s, hundreds of thousands of Rohingya have fled Myanmar to seek protection and security in neighbouring states. This underscores a little acknowledged existential crisis that faces the Rohingya people, who face systemic discrimination, enforced segregation and state sanctioned pogromist violence (Green et al. 2015). The official marginalisation of the Rohingya has been entrenched since 1982 when changes to Myanmar's citizenship laws rendered them stateless and vulnerable to repression by the military regime. This has continued despite Myanmar's political reform process (FIDH 2015): Rohingya representatives were prevented from participating in the 2015 national elections, and the Rohingyas' existence as a distinct ethnic minority remains officially denied, including by former opposition leader, Aung San Suu Kyi (Green et al. 2015; Lloyd 2016; Popham 2016).

This chapter focuses on the systemic abuse of the Rohingya and challenges the dominant media and government narratives of the May 2015 events as primarily a crisis of border policing. It starts by providing an overview of the migration patterns of Rohingya refugees and how these are shaped by regional border controls. It then engages in a discussion constructed around three themes: how the media framing of the May 2015 events, particularly in Australia, as a migration crisis, obscures the more fundamental crisis of the Rohingya; the state-organised and sanctioned persecution of the Rohingya in Myanmar, and why this can be characterised as genocide; and the ways in which the border policing policies of Australia and other states in the region expose Rohingya refugees to further risks and help deny the scale of persecution the Rohingya face.

Forced Migration and the Unfolding Crisis

The people stranded in boats in May 2015 were part of a growing population of Rohingya refugees and internally displaced persons, mostly from Rakhine State in Myanmar, that has emerged since the late 1970s. The Muslim communities in Myanmar are diverse and complex (Crouch 2016), and the history and status of the Rohingya as a distinct ethnic group is highly contested (Leider 2014). The official view of the Myanmar government is that they are Bengali, reflecting the Rohingyas' Muslim ethnicity and the encouragement of migration from East Bengal (now

Bangladesh) to the predominantly Buddhist Rakhine State during the period of British colonial rule. However, such ethno-religious and nationality-based distinctions rely upon state boundaries that were imposed by colonialism and ignore a long pre-colonial history of settlement and economic, cultural and labour exchange between the two regions (Zarni and Cowley 2014, 689–695).

The distinctions also reflect the rising influence of an explicit Islamophobic Buddhist nationalism. In the 1950s, "the Rohingya and their chosen ethnic designation were accepted by the Burmese state" (Green et al. 2015, 28), but in 1978, following a government campaign to register citizens that targeted the Rohingya as "illegal immigrants", an estimated 200,000 Rohingya left Myanmar, mostly for Bangladesh, where they were settled without formal rights of residence in a network of United Nations funded camps. Most returned to Myanmar the following year, but many began leaving again after the changes to citizenship laws in 1982. A further 250,000 Rohingya fled Myanmar after a military operation was launched in northern Rakhine state following disputed national elections in 1991–1992. The majority were returned from Bangladesh to Myanmar by 2000, but there has been a steady flight of Rohingya to other neighbouring states since that time, including many of those who were repatriated (Cheung 2011, 50–53). In 2012, an estimated 140,000 Rohingya were displaced by widespread, orchestrated attacks against them that left an estimated 120,000 segregated in Internally Displaced Persons camps in central Rakhine State (UNHCHR 2016, 3). From early 2014, at least 94,000 "Rohingya and Bangladeshis" embarked on irregular boat journeys from the Bay of Bengal, with "a peak of 31,000 in the first half of 2015" (UNHCRC 2016, 3).

This history of forced migration and displacement has resulted in substantial Rohingya populations in neighbouring states, although precise numbers are difficult to ascertain because many remain undocumented and often are intermingled with other Muslim and refugee communities. In Bangladesh, approximately 32,000 registered Rohingya refugees live in two camps, but the unregistered population living in informal communities outside the camps is estimated to be between 200,000 and 500,000 (UNHCR 2015b). In Thailand, which mainly functions as a transit point to Malaysia and beyond, estimates of the informally settled

Rohingya population have varied between 3000 and 20,000 (ERT 2014b, 17). In Malaysia, which has a much larger documented refugee population, over 135,000 refugees from Myanmar were registered as of 30 June 2014, of whom 37,850 were Rohingya and 11,970 Myanmar Muslims (ERT 2014a, 14). However, some non-government organisations estimate the total number of Rohingya in Malaysia to be as high as 150,000 (Reynolds and Hollingsworth 2015).

The main receiving countries have not signed the 1951 UN Refugee Convention and do not have developed refugee protection frameworks (ERT 2014a, b). Rohingya refugees in Thailand, Malaysia and Indonesia are almost entirely reliant upon the UNHCR and non-government organisations for recognition and support. Statelessness and a lack of legal status leave Rohingya refugees vulnerable to detention, extortion by police and state officials, violent attacks and other forms of abuse (Fortify Rights and BROUK 2016; Loh 2015; Reynolds and Hollingsworth 2015; Szep and Marshall 2013).

It is also widely reported that the networks that facilitate informal travel out of Myanmar and Bangladesh operate with the co-operation and in some cases the active involvement of state officials in Thailand and Malaysia (Alcorn et al. 2015; Chambers 2015; Davis and Cronau 2015; ERT 2014a, b). Analysing these networks is beyond the scope of this chapter, suffice it to say that periodic policing operations can cause considerable short-term disruption (as opposed to the elimination) of their activities. This appeared to be the case in early May 2015, when the discovery of mass graves near smugglers' camps in southern Thailand prompted the Thai Prime Minister to order the crackdown on illicit networks that triggered the boat crisis (UNHCR 2015a).

Many of the bodies exhumed in May were believed to be Rohingya, who had been held in camps subject to their families being forced to pay additional money to take them overland into Malaysia (Alcorn et al. 2015; UNHCR 2015a). However, the Thailand-Malaysia border zone is just one high-risk area for the Rohingya. The maritime journeys out of Myanmar and Bangladesh are particularly dangerous. Up to 2000 are believed to have gone missing at sea between June 2012 and May 2014 (ERT 2014a, 12), and an estimated 1100 lives were lost between January 2014 and June 2015 (UNHCR 2015a). In that context, the May 2015 events reflected the longer-term structural violence (Weber and Pickering 2011) that forced migration has entailed for the Rohingya.

Media Narratives of the Crisis

The media played an important role in constructing the crisis within a specific time frame. An analysis of Australian media coverage during May and June 2015 undertaken for this chapter[1] revealed a heavy reliance on official government and institutional sources and identified two dominant themes that were central to the normative framing of these events: first, this was a crisis defined by a breakdown of border policing, and second, primary responsibility for the crisis rested with the human smuggling and trafficking networks whose activities undermined legitimate border policing in the region.

The ways in which these themes informed the media narratives varied. For example, there was a clear distinction between more liberal approaches[2] that spoke of a humanitarian crisis and provided some insights into the sociology and political economy of forced and irregular migration and the News Limited tabloids[3] that were almost entirely focused on defending the Australian government's border policing strategies. However, despite differences in tone and content, in virtually all the media coverage the essential parameters of the crisis were drawn around the stranded boat passengers, the organised criminal gangs responsible for abandoning them, regional governments overwhelmed by a flow of unauthorised migrants and the need for states in the region to devise border policing measures that somehow would resolve the situation in the immediate and longer term. The dominant conceptualisation of the crisis excluded any questioning of the legitimacy of border controls and related discourses on the deviance of forced and irregular migration. This was consistent with the approach of the main parties at the regional meetings on 20 and 29 May, but it also reflected both a parochial emphasis on Australian border policing (discussed further below) and the close—if not hegemonic— material and ideological links between the mainstream media and the Australian political establishment.

A Border Policing Crisis

The dominant theme of the media coverage was that the crisis was the product of a logjam caused by a surge of irregular migration in circumstances where the neighbouring states were not prepared to allow the boats to land. The crisis was both humanitarian and structural. The humanitarian dimension was brought out by the urgency of the situation, evoked through the language of "spiralling humanitarian crisis" and "horror refugee limbo" and graphically illustrated by images of emaciated Rohingya on crowded boats or desperately clinging to pieces of debris to keep themselves afloat (Murdoch 2015b). This was a cohort who were victims of circumstance and deserving of sympathy, although even that basic human response was condemned by some as "brainless compassion" (Bolt 2015). They were also evidence that the normal structures of border control had broken down. Humanitarian or not, this was a crisis defined by the visibility of irregular migration, by dozens of overcrowded boats in the Bay of Bengal being buffeted by a game of maritime "ping pong" (Murdoch 2015c) and bearing a burden to be managed and contained, preferably through a regional agreement (Alford and Owens 2015).

Within that paradigm, the Rohingya were simultaneously vulnerable and threatening, stranded at sea but with the potential to overwhelm the capacities of receiving states, starving and helpless but posing a threat to orderly regional migration and Australia's border policing regime (Bolt 2015). In this context, there was little acknowledgement of the Rohingyas' motivations for fleeing or the legitimacy of seeking protection. Those trapped on the boats were largely denied any voice or meaningful agency. They could be objectified as victims of illicit networks or dismissed as economic migrants, but ultimately, they were defined in relation to the migration status accorded to them by the states they sought to enter and the fact of their unauthorised travel.

Human Smuggling and Trafficking

The media reports of mass graves and the images of suffering on board the boats reinforced the criminality of the human smuggling and trafficking networks[4] that were assumed to bear primary responsibility for the crisis. There seems little doubt that these networks have been willing to put the safety of irregular migrants at risk through various forms of physical violence, sexual assault, coercion and neglect (Human Rights Watch 2015). However, the focus on human smuggling and trafficking (the terms were used interchangeably in much of the media) detracts from the impacts of restrictive border policies and illicit labour markets in sustaining circuits of illicit migration (Marfleet 2006, 216–239).

Illicit migration circuits are an important subterranean feature of a local political economy in which the distinctions between formal and informal markets often are blurred. Smugglers and traffickers provide the means of travel in circumstances where official travel documents are difficult or impossible to obtain. They also act as brokers into large-scale informal labour markets that draw in labour from across the region to work in key sectors of the economy. This workforce includes refugees with no other means of survival, who can be coerced into working in highly exploitative conditions. In some cases, such arrangements amount to little more than slavery. A Pulitzer Prize-winning series of articles on the lucrative seafood export industry in Thailand and Indonesia in 2015 "found workers [from Myanmar] trapped in cages, whipped with toxic stingray tails for punishment and forced to work 22 hours a day for almost no compensation" on an island in Indonesia (Associated Press 2016). It is unclear whether any of the rescued workers were Rohingya but a similar media investigation into the Thai fishing industry in July 2015 found that "hundreds of Rohingya men were sold from the network of trafficking camps recently discovered in southern Thailand" and that "[i]n some cases, Rohingya migrants held in immigration detention centres in Thailand were taken by staff to brokers and then sold on to Thai fishing boats" (Stoakes et al. 2015).

Such examples raise significant issues about workers' rights, the nature of the global economy and state corruption, and highlight the interrelationships between smuggling and trafficking, labour migration and refugee flight. However, such complexities typically were overlooked or lost in the mainstream media coverage. As the May events progressed, those on board the boats increasingly were described as migrants rather than refugees, and the consequences of forced return to their state of origin downplayed. For the workers found in Indonesia, repatriation to Myanmar was reported as a humanitarian outcome (Goodman 2016). This may have been the case for some of the individuals concerned but various regional government officials, including the Australian Foreign Minister, sought to discredit the stranded Rohingya as mostly "illegal labourers" rather than "genuine refugees" (Borello 2015).

While there is an element of compulsion common to both categories, the casual conflation of irregular labour migration and forced migration delegitimises all unauthorised migration and denies the specific protection needs of the Rohingya and other refugees (ERT 2014a, b). Moreover, structuring refugee policy around restrictive border controls assumes smuggling is a driver rather than a necessary corollary of refugee movement, denies smuggling's humanitarian function in the absence of alternatives and objectively ignores the violent and abusive state policies and practices from which the Rohingya refugees seek protection.

The Crisis of the Rohingya

Viewing the May 2015 events through the prism of border policing obscures the more fundamental crisis of the Rohingya within Myanmar. This is an ongoing crisis characterised by statelessness, social fragmentation and exclusion from civil society. For the Rohingya, the absence of any formal status or acknowledgement as a distinct and legitimate community has normalised a state of invisibility: "In Burma they say we are from Bangladesh…When we come to Bangladesh, they say we are from Burma…People view us as if we don't exist" (quoted, Constantine 2012, 19).

The invisibility of the Rohingya arises in part from direct censorship and repression. Within Myanmar, there is virtually no independent media coverage of events in Rakhine state, and there is sustained pressure on aid and non-government organisations prepared to support the Rohingya or publicise their circumstances. In 2013, for example, the Organisation of Islamic Co-operation was refused permission to open a representative office following protests by thousands of Buddhist monks (Cook 2016, 268). In February 2014, Medécins Sans Frontières, the main provider of health care to the Rohingya in Rakhine state's displacement camps, was ordered to suspend all operations within the country (Hodal 2014). An internal United Nations report in 2015 also extensively criticised the organisation for "self-censorship" and for prioritising economic development over "systematic abuses" of the Rohingya (Stoakes 2016).

The obstacles confronting those seeking to investigate the human rights situation in Myanmar were described by researchers from the International State Crime Initiative (ISCI), who conducted extensive fieldwork research in Rakhine state:

> The Rakhine state authorities have, as much as possible, attempted to isolate the Rohingya from both wider Myanmar society and the international community. Rohingya known to have spoken to journalists and UN Special Rapporteurs have been harassed and beaten by the authorities. In light of this, ISCI visits to Rohingya camps, villages and the Aung Mingalar ghetto were, of necessity, clandestine … [A]ll requests to enter northern Rakhine state were denied and Rakhine state's Security Minister made it explicit to the Attorney-general that ISCI was to be denied access to northern Rakhine state in order to prevent the team from meeting with Rohingya living there. (Green et al. 2015, 87)

Despite such institutional pressures, there is a growing body of research by academics, non-government organisations and official bodies, including the United Nations High Commissioner for Human Rights that documents the systemic persecution of the Rohingya and other minorities (FIDH 2015; Green et al. 2015; Human Rights Watch 2013; International Crisis Group 2013; UNHCHR 2016; Zarni and Cowley 2014). The scale and seriousness of the persecution is reflected by a number of recent reports identifying it as a potential genocide (Green et al. 2015; Yale Law School 2015; Zarni and Cowley 2014). This conclusion has been criticised by some government officials and non-government organisations as an exaggeration and unhelpful to encouraging Myanmar's democratic transition,[5] but the ISCI Report, which is based on the most extensive research to date and whose authors were not compromised by the need to maintain an ongoing relationship with Myanmar state authorities, makes a compelling case.

The ISCI Report draws on the work of Argentine scholar, Daniel Feierstein, who argues that genocide is best understood as a set of social practices that aim "(1) to destroy social relationships based on autonomy and cooperation by annihilating a significant part of the population … and (2) to use the terror of annihilation to establish new models of identity and social relationships among the survivors" (Feierstein 2014, 14; Green et al. 2015, 21). Feierstein (2014) identifies six stages of genocide—stigmatisation; harassment violence and terror; isolation and segregation; systematic weakening; extermination; and symbolic enactment. The ISCI Report adopts this framework and concludes that "we are witnessing Feierstein's fourth stage", that is, the stage of systematic weakening that "includes strategies of physical destruction of the target group through overcrowding, malnutrition, epidemics, lack of health care, torture and sporadic killings; and psychological destruction through humiliation, abuse, persistent violence and the undermining of solidarity" (Green et al. 2015, 23).

In coming to this conclusion, the ISCI Report documents

evidence that the Rohingya have been subjected to systematic and widespread violations of human rights, including killings, torture, rape and arbitrary detention; destruction of their homes and villages; land confiscation; forced labour; denial of citizenship; denial of the right to identify themselves as Rohingya; denial of access to healthcare, education and employment; restrictions on freedom of movement and State-sanctioned campaigns of religious hatred (Green et al. 2015, 15).

The Report also highlights a history of persecution over the past 30 years that has involved "the Myanmar State coordinating with Rakhine ultra-nationalists, racist monks and its own security forces" (Green et al. 2015, 15). In particular, the Report focuses on the "organised massacres" that occurred in 2012 that left over 200 Rohingya people dead, displaced 138,000 into detention camps and isolated 4500 in a "squalid ghetto in Sittwe, Rakhine state's capital" (Green et al. 2015, 15). This underpins a situation where the "escalating institutionalized discrimination against the Rohingya has allowed hate speech to flourish, encouraged Islamophobia and granted impunity to the perpetrators of violence" (Green et al. 2015, 15).

The ISCI Report concludes "with an urgent warning to civil society in Myanmar, to international civil society, to the government of Myanmar and international states" that "[a] genocidal process is underway" and that "[it] can be stopped but not without confronting the fact that it is, indeed, genocide" (Green et al. 2015, 100). Faced with such a desperate situation, it seems likely the Rohingya will continue to seek refuge and stability elsewhere subject to their capacity to travel and survive within informal diaspora networks. However, refugee flight contributes further to the fragmentation of the Rohingya community and cannot resolve the situation within Myanmar itself. In this context, the policies of potential transit or receiving states towards Rohingya refugees are not detached from the conditions of life for the Rohingya within Myanmar. The refusal to acknowledge and challenge the situation in Myanmar—and instead focus on policing refugees who try to leave—constitutes complicity in the state crimes and organised violence committed against the Rohingya.

Border Policing, State Crime and Denial

The systematic weakening of the Rohingya population is exacerbated by the policies of bystander states such as Australia, where the characterisation of the Rohingya principally as unauthorised migrants reflects a calculated policy of indifference that amounts to a form of denial (Cohen 2010, 140–160). Within Australia, this is driven politically by a criminogenic border policing regime that inflicts systemic harm on all refugees who attempt unauthorised entry in order to seek asylum (Grewcock 2009, 2014, 2015) and that specifically seeks to contain the Rohingya within Myanmar or immediate neighbour states. As I have examined elsewhere, this regime overwhelmingly targets refugees from the developing world and sustains and draws some of its legitimacy from the deeply rooted racist ideologies associated with the White Australia policy and the more recent rise of Islamophobia (Grewcock 2009).

The May 2015 events coincided with the Australian government's Operation Sovereign Borders, a highly secretive military-led campaign designed to prevent unauthorised refugee boats entering Australian jurisdiction. Operation Sovereign Borders was established with the stated political purpose of "stopping the boats", and was central to a strategy that included naval interception, boat pushbacks, the use of purpose-built lifeboats to return passengers to Indonesia, the use of navy vessels to return passengers to Sri Lanka, the expansion of Australia's offshore detention and processing regimes on Nauru and Manus Island (PNG) and a refusal to resettle refugees detained on Nauru and Manus Island in Australia (Grewcock 2015).

Operation Sovereign Borders was one of the more unilateral attempts by Australian governments since the late 1970s to influence the border policing strategies of states in the south-east Asian region (Grewcock 2009). Its initial purpose was to physically interdict and prevent unauthorised boat travel into Australian territory at a time when the always relatively small numbers of boats arriving had spiked (Grewcock 2015). Politically, it also sent a signal that rather than wait for a regional agreement to police people smuggling, the Australian government would condone states taking whatever measures were necessary to prevent the Rohingya and others seeking refuge in the region from travelling at all. In this environment, the Australian government's promotion of pushbacks arguably contributed to the intransigent approaches of the Thai, Malaysian and Indonesian governments that triggered the May 2015 crisis and a similar refusal by the Indonesian government to allow a boat carrying 44 Tamils to land in Aceh in June 2016 (Topsfield and Rosa 2016).

For the Australian authorities, reducing the number of refugees able to travel in the region is upheld as a measure of political authority and success. Any lingering concerns the Australian government may have for the Rohingya are filtered through opaque diplomatic processes designed to normalise relations between Myanmar and Australia and to improve border policing co-operation. Meanwhile, the Rohingya remain officially invisible—stateless within Myanmar, unrecognised in neighbouring states or isolated indefinitely, usually offshore, in Australia's immigration detention complex.

One such individual, Imran Mohammad, fled Rakhine state as a teenager and was recognised as a refugee by the United Nations High Commissioner for Human Rights in in Indonesia 2013. With little hope of resettlement, he attempted to reach Australia by boat later that year but was detained by the Australian authorities and forcibly transferred to the Manus Island offshore processing centre. In a 26-page account of his 1000-day detention on Manus Island in April 2016, Imran, then 22, wrote of being stranded in a state of limbo:

> We are already broken, vulnerable and hopeless, damaged physically and mentally. They are striving to show the world that we are criminals and bad people…
>
> We have had more than enough of this torture. We are in a situation in which it is difficult to choose what to do because whatever we do, there are negative consequences…We are not provided with clear answers, not given the right to access legal representation and at every turn, we are manipulated and fed false information, which has built more desperation, mistrust and heartache amongst us…I know that we are already dead as our blood has been sucked from our bodies by enormous pain….
>
> To sum up, this is a message from a place of isolation to the whole world…I have been persecuted and deprived of my basic human rights since I was born right up until now. I have never known safety or peace, and I have never known citizenship or a right to call any country my own. (Doherty 2016)

Imran Mohammed's account not only highlights the individual impact of Australia's border policing practices but also provides a sense of the collective experience of Rohingya refugees. The Rohingya people do not have the option of formal migration out of Myanmar. The calculations they must make about their travel are determined by which irregular option constitutes the least risk in a situation of prolonged and convulsive crisis rather than by political rhetoric emanating from states like Australia demanding they enter through the front—not the back—door. The crisis that engulfs the Rohingya was neither defined by the wretched scenes of May 2015 nor capable of being solved by further restrictions on their movement. Moreover, the denial of their status as refugees or the legitimacy of their attempts to secure long-term stability and protection serves to justify and prolong the potentially genocidal persecution they face.

Conclusion

The May 2015 crisis was a moment of wider public visibility for the Rohingya. However, the dominant framing of the crisis—in which the media played an important role—as a challenge for border policing neutralised its potential to highlight the ongoing underlying crisis within Myanmar. The political priority given by states such as Australia to deterring and containing refugee movement not only prevents refugees from reaching safety but also intensifies the crises from which they are fleeing. Potentially, this has profound individual and collective consequences for the Rohingya. The restrictions on their right to free movement sit within a range of state practices—both inside and outside Myanmar—that threaten their survival. Any "regional solution" must start by addressing that issue.

Notes

1. Based on a survey of 98 news items from the Australian Broadcasting Commission, SBS World News, the Melbourne Age, the Sydney Morning Herald, the Sun-Herald, the Daily Telegraph and the Herald Sun between 1 May 2015 and 1 July 2015. My thanks to UNSW Law student Bronte Richardson for her assistance with the research for this section.
2. For example, the *Guardian* (Stoakes et al. 2015) and the *Associated Press* reports at http://www.pulitzer.org/winners/associated-press
3. The Sydney *Daily Telegraph* and the Melbourne *Herald Sun.*
4. On the distinctions between smuggling and trafficking, see Lee (2007).
5. For a summary of these criticisms, see Lee (2016).

References

Alcorn, G., Reynolds, K., & Simons, M. (2015, December 10). Revealed: Thailand's Most Senior Human Trafficking Investigator to Seek Political Asylum in Australia. *The Guardian.* Retrieved July 4, 2016, from https://www.theguardian.com/world/2015/dec/10/thailands-most-senior-human-trafficking-investigator-to-seek-political-asylum-in-australia

Alford, P., & Owens, J. (2015, May 16). Tragedy, Mayhem as Nations Told 'Stop Bouncing Bots Around'. *The Australian*. Retrieved July 4, 2016, from http://www.theaustralian.com.au/national-affairs/foreign-affairs/tragedy-mayhem-as-nations-told-stop-bouncing-boats-around/news-story/642ba97 90ea4dba25946024bcc26086c

Associated Press. (2016, April 26). *The 2016 Pulitzer Prize Winner in Public Service*. Retrieved July 4, 2016, from http://www.pulitzer.org/winners/associated-press

Bolt, A. (2015, May 25). Let's Stop Moralising and Protect Australia. *Daily Telegraph*. Retrieved July 4, 2016, from http://www.dailytelegraph.com.au/news/opinion/lets-stop-moralising-and-protect-australia/news-story/47f3b8 0a985f424035af7278065aae84

Borello, E. (2015, May 23). South-East Asia Migrant Crisis: Julie Bishop Told by Indonesia Most of 7,000 People Stranded Are Illegal Labourers, not Refugees. *ABC News*. Retrieved July 4, 2016, from http://www.abc.net.au/news/2015-05-23/bishop-says-most-of-7000-stranded-people-are-labourers/6491836

Chambers, P. (2015, October 23). Thailand Must End Its Own Rohingya Atrocity. *The Diplomat*. Retrieved July 4, 2016, from http://thediplomat.com/2015/10/thailand-must-end-its-own-rohingya-atrocity/

Cheung, S. (2011). Migration Control and the Solutions Impasse in South and Southeast Asia: Implications from the Rohingya Experience. *Journal of Refugee Studies, 25*, 51–70.

Cohen, S. (2010). *States of Denial: Knowing About Atrocities and Suffering*. Cambridge: Polity Press.

Constantine, G. (2012). Exiled to Nowhere: Burma's Rohingya. *Author*. Retrieved from www.exiledtonowhere.com

Cook, A. D. B. (2016). The Global and Regional Dynamics of Humanitarian Aid in Rakhine State. In M. Crouch (Ed.), *Islam and the State in Myanmar: Muslim-Buddhist Relations and the Politics of Belonging* (pp. 257–278). Oxford: Oxford University Press.

Cooke, R. (2015, August). Nope, Nope, Nope: Why Australia Won't Help the Rohingya. *The Monthly*. Retrieved June 30, 2016, from https://www.the-monthly.com.au/issue/2015/august/1438351200/richard-cooke/nope-nope-nope

Crouch, M. (Ed.). (2016). *Islam and the State in Myanmar: Muslim-Buddhist Relations and the Politics of Belonging*. Oxford: Oxford University Press.

Davis, M., & Cronau, P. (2015, 23 June). Journey into Hell. *Four Corners*. Retrieved July 4, 2016, from http://www.abc.net.au/4corners/stories/2015/06/22/4257490.htm

Doherty, B. (2016, June 30). 'End This Political Game': Manus Island Refugee Makes Plea to Australia. *The Guardian*. Retrieved July 24, 2016, from https://www.theguardian.com/australia-news/2016/jun/30/end-this-political-game-manus-island-refugee-makes-plea-to-australia

Equal Rights Trust (ERT). (2014a). *Equal Only in Name: The Human Rights of Stateless Rohingya in Malaysia*. London: Equal Rights Trust and Institute of Human Rights and Peace Studies, Mahidol University. Retrieved June 30, 2016, from http://www.equalrightstrust.org/ertdocumentbank/Equal%20Only%20in%20Name%20-%20Malaysia%20-%20Full%20Report.pdf

Equal Rights Trust (ERT). (2014b). *Equal Only in Name: The Human Rights of Stateless Rohingya in Thailand*. Retrieved June 30, 2016, from http://www.equalrightstrust.org/ertdocumentbank/Equal%20Only%20in%20Name%20-%20Thailand%20-%20Full%20Report.pdf

Feierstein, D. (2014). *Genocide as Social Practice: Reorganizing Society Under the Nazis and Argentina's Military Juntas*. Brunswick: Rutgers University Press.

Fortify Rights and BROUK (Burmese Rohingya Organization UK). (2016). *Everywhere Is Trouble: An Update on the Situation of Rohingya Refugees in Thailand, Malaysia, and Indonesia*. Retrieved July 4, 2016, from http://www.fortifyrights.org/downloads/EverywhereisTrouble.pdf

Goodman, A. (2016, April 18). Is the Seafood You Eat Caught by Slaves? *Democracy Now*. Retrieved July 4, 2016, from http://www.democracynow.org/2016/4/18/is_the_seafood_you_eat_caught

Green, P., McManus, T., & de la Cour Venning, A. (2015). *Countdown to Annihilation: Genocide in Myanmar*. London: International State Crime Initiative. Retrieved June 30, 2016, from http://statecrime.org/data/2015/10/ISCI-Rohingya-Report-PUBLISHED-VERSION.pdf

Grewcock, M. (2009). *Border Crimes: Australia's War on Illicit Migrants*. Sydney: Institute of Criminology Press.

Grewcock, M. (2014). Back to the Future: Australian Border Policing Under Labor, 2007–2013. *State Crime, 3*(1), 102–125.

Grewcock, M. (2015). Australian Border Policing and the Production of State Harm. In G. Barak (Ed.), *The Routledge International Handbook of the Crimes of the Powerful* (pp. 331–347). London: Taylor Francis.

Hamling, A. (2016). *Rohingya People: The Most Persecuted People in the World*. Amnesty International Australia. Retrieved June 30, 2016, from http://www. amnesty.org.au/refugees/comments/35290/

Hodal, K. (2014, March 1). Burma Tells Medécins Sans Frontières to Leave State Hit by Sectarian Violence. *The Guardian*. Retrieved July 25, 2016, from https://www.theguardian.com/world/2014/feb/28/burma-medecins-sans-frontieres-rakhine-state

Human Rights Watch. (2013). *"All You Can Do Is Pray". Crimes Against Humanity and Ethnic Cleansing of Rohingya Muslims in Burma's Arakan State*. Retrieved July 14, 2016, from https://www.hrw.org/report/2013/04/22/all-you-can-do-pray/crimes-against-humanity-and-ethnic-cleansing-rohingya-muslims

Human Rights Watch. (2015). *Southeast Asia: Accounts from Rohingya Boat People*. Retrieved July 14, 2016, from https://www.hrw.org/news/2015/05/27/southeast-asia-accounts-rohingya-boat-people

International Crisis Group. (2013). *The Dark Side of Transition: Violence Against Muslims in Myanmar*. Retrieved July 14, 2016, from http://www.crisisgroup.org/~/media/Files/asia/south-east-asia/burma-myanmar/251-the-dark-side-of-transition-violence-against-muslims-in-myanmar.pdf

International Federation for Human Rights (FIDH). (2015). *Half Empty: Burma's Political Parties and Their Human Rights Commitments*. Retrieved July 4, 2016, from https://www.fidh.org/IMG/pdf/burma-bat-5_report.pdf

Lee, M. (Ed.). (2007). *Human Trafficking*. Cullompton: Willan Publishing.

Lee, R. (2016). *Reports on Genocide in Myanmar Highlight the Need for Change*. Retrieved July 14, 2016, from http://www.e-ir.info/2016/01/24/reports-on-genocide-in-myanmar-highlight-the-need-for-change/

Leider, J. P. (2014, June 25). *Rohingya. The Name. The Movement. The Quest for Identity*. Network Myanmar. Retrieved July 4, 2016, from http://www.networkmyanmar.org/images/stories/PDF17/Leider-2014.pdf

Lloyd, P. (2016, June 22). Burma Leader Aung San Suu Kyi Bans Use of Rohingya Name for Oppressed Muslims. *ABC News*. Retrieved June 30, 2016, from http://www.abc.net.au/news/2016-06-22/aung-san-suu-kyi-bans-use-of-rohingya-name/7534410

Loh, F. (2015, January 9). The Rohingya: Who Are They? Why Are They in Malaysia? *Aliran*. Retrieved July 4, 2016, from http://aliran.com/aliran-csi/aliran-csi-2015/rohingya-malaysia/

Marfleet, P. (2006). *Refugees in a Global Era*. Basingstoke: Palgrave Macmillan.

Murdoch, L. (2015a, May 11). Rohingya Muslim Boat People Land in Indonesia, Thousands More Stuck at Sea. *Sydney Morning Herald*. Retrieved June 30,

2016, from http://www.smh.com.au/world/rohingya-muslim-boat-people-land-in-indonesia-thousands-more-stuck-at-sea-20150510-ggygky.html

Murdoch, L. (2015b, May 16). Rohingya Muslims Cry for Help as Horror Refugee Limbo Continues. *Sydney Morning Herald*. Retrieved July 4, 2016, from http://www.smh.com.au/world/rohingya-muslims-cry-for-help-as-horror-refugee-limbo-continues-20150515-gh2cet.html

Murdoch, L. (2015c, May 17). Desperate Killings at Sea: Rohingya Fleeing Myanmar. *Sydney Morning Herald*. Retrieved July 4, 2016, from http://www.smh.com.au/world/desperate-killings-at-sea-rohingya-fleeing-myanmar-20150517-gh3dpo.html

Popham, P. (2016). *The Lady and the Generals: Aung San Suu Kyi and Burma's Struggle for Freedom*. London: Rider Books.

ReliefWeb. (2015, May 20). *Myanmar: Joint Statement: Ministerial Meeting on Irregular Movement of People in Southeast Asia*. Retrieved June 30, 2016, from http://reliefweb.int/report/myanmar/joint-statement-ministerial-meeting-irregular-movement-people-southeast-asia

Reynolds, S., & Hollingsworth, A. (2015, November 17). *Malaysia: Rohingya Refugees Hope for Little and Receive Less*. Refugees International Field Report. Retrieved June 30, 2016, from http://www.refugeesinternational.org/reports/2015/11/17/malaysia-rohingya-refugees-hope-for-little-and-receive-less

Stoakes, E. (2016, May 22). Leaked Documents Show How the UN Failed to Protect Myanmar's Persecuted Rohingya. *VICE News*. Retrieved July 25, 2016, from https://news.vice.com/article/how-the-un-failed-to-protect-myanmars-persecuted-rohingya

Stoakes, E., Kelly, C., & Kelly, A. (2015, July 20). Revealed: How the Thai Fishing Industry Trafficks, Imprisons and Enslaves. *The Guardian*. Retrieved July 14, 2016, from https://www.theguardian.com/global-development/2015/jul/20/thai-fishing-industry-implicated-enslavement-deaths-rohingya

Szep, J., & Marshall, A. R. C. (2013, December 4). Special Report: Thailand Secretly Supplies Myanmar Refugees to Trafficking Rings. *Reuters*. Retrieved July 4, 2016, from http://www.reuters.com/article/us-thailand-rohingya-special-report-idUSBRE9B400320131205

Thai Ministry of Foreign Affairs. (2016). *Summary Special Meeting on Irregular Migration in the Indian Ocean 29 May 2015, Bangkok, Thailand*. Retrieved June 30, 2016, from http://www.mfa.go.th/main/en/media-center/14/56880-Summary-Special-Meeting-on-Irregular-Migration-in.html

Topsfield, J., & Rosa, A. (2016, June 17). Indonesian Police Fire Warning Shot as Stranded Sri Lankan Women Disembark Boat. *Sydney Morning Herald*. Retrieved July 25, 2016, from http://www.smh.com.au/world/indonesian-police-fire-warning-shot-as-stranded-sri-lankan-women-disembark-boat-20160616-gpl2k2.html

United Nations High Commissioner for Human Rights (UNHCHR). (2016). *Situation of Human Rights of Rohingya Muslims and Other Minorities in Myanmar*. A/HRC/32/18. Retrieved June 30, 2016, from http://reliefweb.int/report/myanmar/report-united-nations-high-commissioner-human-rights-situation-human-rights-rohingya

United Nations High Commissioner for Refugees (UNHCR). (2015a, April–June). *South East Asia Mixed Maritime Movements*. Retrieved June 30, 2016, from http://reliefweb.int/report/myanmar/south-east-asia-mixed-maritime-movements-april-june-2015

United Nations High Commissioner for Refugees (UNHCR). (2015b, August). *Bangladesh Fact Sheet*. Retrieved June 30, 2016, from http://www.unhcr.org/50001ae09.pdf

Weber, L., & Pickering, S. (2011). *Globalization and Borders: Death at the Global Frontier*. London: Palgrave Macmillan.

Yale Law School (Allard K. Lowenstein International Human Rights Clinic). (2015). *Persecution of the Rohingya Muslims: Is Genocide Occurring in Myanmar's Rakhine State? A Legal Analysis*. Retrieved from http://www.fortifyrights.org/downloads/Yale_Persecution_of_the_Rohingya_October_2015.pdf

Zarni, M., & Cowley, A. (2014). The Slow-Burning Genocide of Myanmar's Rohingya. *Pacific Rim Law and Policy Journal, 23*, 681–752.

10

Social Death: The (White) Racial Framing of the Calais 'Jungle' and 'Illegal' Migrants in the British Tabloids and Right-Wing Press

Monish Bhatia

In the week commencing 24 October 2016, demolition of the Calais 'jungle' camp was officially initiated. The workers surrounded by the armed riot police[1] tore down the wooden shacks using 'sledgehammers and chainsaws'; bulldozers moved in later during the week, to fully clear out the 'ramshackle shantytown' (*Mirror*). The tabloid press in Britain pursued the subject intensely and obsessively. They reported 'furious refugees' protested against demolition (*The Sun*), set camp on fire (*Telegraph*) and 'fought' a 'pitched battle' with police—terming it 'The Battle of Calais' (*Daily Mail*). The 'jungle' camp was 'finally destroyed' (*Daily Mail*), which was portrayed as a victory over 'invaders', 'illegals', transgressors and security 'threats', who wanted to bring misery and instability to 'soft touch' Britain (*The Sun; Daily Mail*). Immediately after the demolition, the French prefect of Pas-de-Calais Fabienne Buccio released a statement outlining that it is a 'mission accomplished' and 'there are no migrants in the camp'—news largely welcomed by the right-wing and tabloid press. However, this was neither the beginning nor the end.

M. Bhatia (✉)
Birkbeck, University of London, London, UK

© The Author(s) 2018

M. Bhatia et al. (eds.), *Media, Crime and Racism*, Palgrave Studies in Crime, Media and Culture, https://doi.org/10.1007/978-3-319-71776-0_10

181

In the weeks and months leading to the demolition, media cranked up the coverage of Calais, with racism inherent in the reporting. The stories of police violence and state-sanctioned brutality became a regular feature. The tabloids and right-wing press published articles and images of refugee torment, mostly blaming them for their own pain, suffering and deaths. The articles legitimised policing and border control tactics, deploying the language of war, victory and defeat, and further dehumanising, demonising and 'othering' refugees. The 'jungle' was portrayed as a hyper-criminogenic space and 'bandit country'. This was accompanied by images of men (of colour) in balaclavas and faces covered with mask/scarf, who were waiting to unleash violence on the innocent white people and hardworking truck drivers (*The Sun*). The media constructed it not only as a lost territory but also as a territory lost to the foreign vagabonds and invaders, who had unlawfully taken over a civilised and peaceful French costal town. The 'jungle' became associated with 'illegal' migration and 'bogus' refuge seekers—a place where blacks, Arabs and men from the Muslim world exerted their dominance and 'gang' rule and behaved in an uncivilised, pathologically lawless and animalistic manner. The images presented alongside these stories often projected total disorder, in turn re-asserting the need for even tougher policing and border control measures, and further demands to immobilise and discard these undesirable bodies and protect the nation. By portraying (unprotected, vulnerable and at-risk) people of colour in this manner, media circulated, reproduced and maintained the dominant racial frame.

In the book *White Racial Frames*, Feagin (2013: 10) conducts an historical analysis to argue the ways in which white society has adopted frames, by combining its "beliefs aspect (racial stereotypes and ideologies), integrating cognitive elements (racial interpretations and narratives), visual and auditory elements (racialised images), a 'feelings' aspect (racialised emotions), and inclination to action (to discriminate) and strong positive orientation to whites and whiteness (a pro-white frame)". The racial frame is an "overarching worldview, encompassing important racial ideas, terms, images, emotions, and interpretations" (2013: 3). The newspapers and other print media play a role in perpetuating racist framing and circulating frames to the white society (Feagin 2013). They have used this frame to give its readers a tool to understand, interpret and make sense of the situation and also to generate impact. The frame by default gives a strong negative orientation to the racially 'othered'. The criminality image is constantly reinforced, dramatising the crimes committed by the racial 'other' and thus strengthening and maintaining the racial frame.

The journalists shape the news reporting within a given frame reference, according to a latent structure of meaning and stimulation of public to adopt these frames from the journalists' point of view (McQuail 2000: 495). The use of certain frames (by newspapers and white elites) entails calling public attention to selected matters while ignoring others (Iyengar and Kinder 1987). When it comes to the reporting of Calais and refugees, tabloids and right-wing newspapers have used a dominant 'illegal' migration frame.[2] This particular frame is powerful and it criminalises racialised bodies and transforms the way people view, feel, believe and think about those seeking refugee protection.

In this chapter, I will analyse the racialised construction of the 'jungle' and its inhabitants and manner in which the 'illegal' and 'criminal' racial framing is used and strategically deployed to legitimise violence against refuge seekers, deny their suffering, their personhood and distance them from humanitarian discourses. The chapter argues that racial framing and legitimisation of state violence and border control practices have produced a social death of refuge seekers in Calais.

The Racialised Outsider and the Calais 'Jungle'

Calais is a port town and major point of transit, tucked in the North of France, around 20.7 miles away from Dover in Britain, separated by the English Channel (See Image 10.1). In May 1994, the Channel Tunnel opened, connecting Britain with France and continental Europe. The ambition to make land transport for travel and trade expeditious finally became a reality. A staggering 366 million people have passed through this transport network—with around 21 million passengers in 2015 alone (57,000 passengers daily) and the rail shuttle carried more than 2.5 million cars and coaches and 1.5 million trucks (EuroTunnel Webpage[3]). Similarly, Dover-Calais and Dover-Dunkirk remained two of the busiest short ferry routes, carrying roughly 9.8 million and 3.2 million passengers, respectively (Department of Transport 2015). Since Britain is part of the European Union,[4] British citizens can travel freely without restrictions across the Channel into Europe and vice versa (i.e. EU nationals do not require an entry permit or visa to enter Britain). However, unlike most EU countries, Britain is not a signatory to the Schengen Agreement[5] and retains full control of its borders (Peers 2015). Those travelling to Britain go through immigration and legal document checks, and 'third-country' nationals need to seek British visa/entry clearance prior to arriving in the country, and their papers are scrutinised by the authorities at the border. While there was a liberalisation of free movement for EU nationals, this was rather different for 'third country'/former colonial subjects seeking refuge, who were confronted with increasingly restrictive and control-oriented approaches (also see Kostakopoulou 2000; Huysmans 2006).

This complicates the situation at Calais (part of the Schengen zone), which is treated merely as a transit point by undocumented refuge seekers (non-Europeans, 'non-white' and third-country nationals) seeking to enter Britain (not part of the Schengen zone). Once in Britain, people have the right to seek asylum, and cannot be removed until final decision on their application has been reached. In addition, tabloid and right-wing press have repeatedly circulated stories of migrants going underground and living 'illegally', and constructed them as 'threats' (*Daily Mail*, 2014). Therefore, the port of Calais turned into a contradictory space, where desire to retain freedom of movement was contrasted with a racialised securitisation agenda to keep the 'other' out. The British government consistently tried to implement a whole host of strategies to block 'third-country' subjects from entering—and this shaped the borders of Calais, as explained below.

In 2003, the British and French governments signed the Le Touquet Treaty, a bilateral agreement, which established juxtaposed immigration controls. As per the agreement, travellers are required to clear immigration checks in the country of departure (as opposed to arrival). The aim was clear from the outset—exclusion of people seeking asylum. The agreement made it possible for the UK Border Force to

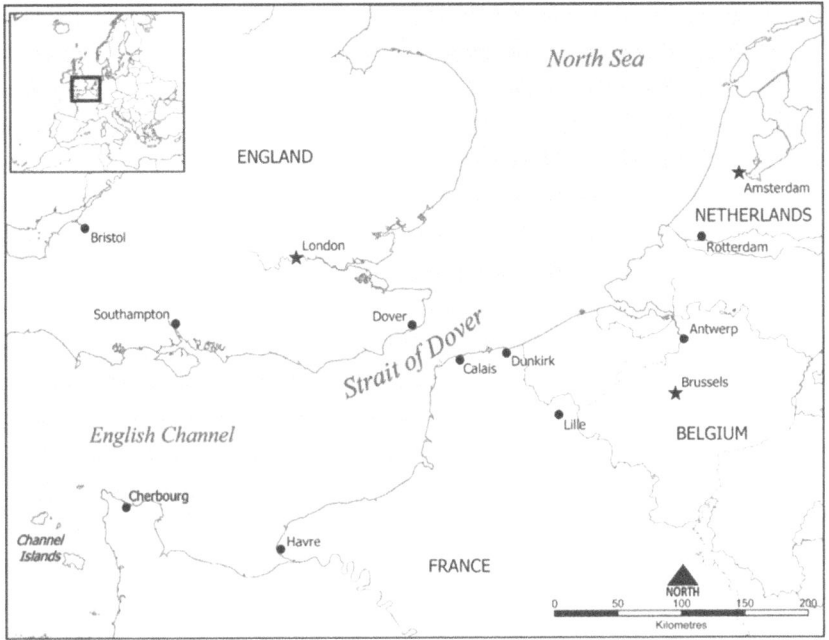

Image 10.1 Geography of Calais and Dover

establish its operations in Calais, send more officers and direct greater resources towards border policing on the French side. These escalating measures were implemented to make sure that only those individuals who are 'eligible' to travel (freely) could enter the country and thereby detect/block all the unwanted, undocumented, 'illegal' and undeserving 'third-country' nationals from entering Great Britain. Despite its relevance in the control of immigration, mention of the Le Touquet agreement in newspapers was extremely low until 2015—when it suddenly grabbed British press attention in the months leading to the EU in/out referendum. This was especially so after Nicolas Sarkozy (former French President) and Xavier Bertrand (current President of the region Hauts-de-France, which Calais is part of) made a series of statements on moving asylum processing and border checks from France to England.

The tabloids and right-wing press immediately turned their focus on the 'dangers' of such a move, which could potentially result in a 'jungle' camp shifting from Calais to Dover and "raising the spectre of a migrant flood into the UK" (*Express* 25 February 2016). As the Brexit campaign and European refugee 'crisis' intensified, along with an increase in 'terrorist' attacks across Europe (explained later), the news articles on the Le Touquet Treaty[6] (published between January 2016 and June 2016) continued to dramatise spatial tensions, the supposed need for maintaining strong controls and protecting sovereignty. They continued to demand the exclusion of 'illegals' and undesirables from the nation state—a racial framing which has occurred throughout postcolonial history (see Smith 1994; Webber 1996; Solomos 2003; Schuster and Solomos 1999; Smith and Marmo 2014).

The events that took place prior to/after the Le Touquet Treaty coming into existence are equally significant in understanding how Calais turned from merely a harbour into contested *borderlands*—that is, zones around and at the periphery of borders in which border, surveillance and migration regimes, all become important elements of spatial governance and control (Schwenken 2014: 171). More crucially, it is important to analyse the ways in which tabloid and right-wing press shaped and re-shaped these borderlands, by renewing and maintaining the racial frames and circulating criminalised discourses of 'illegal' migration, crime and deviance, identity and belonging, inclusion and exclusion, segregation and banishment (also see Gilroy 2013). After all, such racial frames and discourses play a critical role in informing and shaping public debates about consciousness of the racialised politics of immigration and crime (Ibrahim and Howarth 2015; Greenslade 2004; Hainmueller and Hopkins 2014; van Dijk 1983) and disseminate racist ideologies and hatred (Hartmann and Husband 1974; van Dijk 2015).

Around two decades ago in the winter of 1998/1999, a number of Kosovan refugees, fleeing war, arrived in Calais in the hope of seeking safety in Britain. In response to their visible plight, the Sangatte camp opened and was operated by the French Red Cross. It offered basic facilities, a roof over the head and meals twice a day. Over the three-year period, the camp population increased from 209 to 1600. Iraqi Kurds and Afghans joined the Kosovans, as the situation in their home countries turned unsafe. The overwhelming goal of the majority was to reach Britain, due to its perceived 'favourable' and 'humanitarian' asylum regime (Schuster 2003). Initially, the camp received little attention and was irrelevant to the British press and politicians, as it was a matter for the French and located on their soil. However, things changed in the lead up to the 2001 general elections.

Due to increase in the clandestine attempts made by refuge seekers to enter Britain, the Sangatte camp became of immense interest to the tabloid press. In a bid to produce hysterical, fear and impact-generating articles, journalists often 'smuggled' themselves into Britain and then reported about the people smugglers, crime and lax border controls, producing a 'crisis', which according to them was ignored by British politicians (Schuster 2003). The newspapers demanded strengthening of Britain's borders and sending British troops to patrol the French coast, with headlines such as "Stop the invasion"; "We can't take any more asylum seekers"; "Asylum invasion reaches 12,000 a month"; "Asylum: we're being invaded" and "Refugees, run for your life" (Schuster 2003: 8). The tabloids also deployed the terminology of natural disasters, calamities and war, to project Britain as 'victim' of 'floods', 'invasions' and 'tidal waves' of asylum seekers (Philo and Beattie 1999). According to Sara Ahmed (2004: 122), these are 'sticky words', as they create associations between asylum seekers and loss of control, and dirt and sewage. Sticky words work by mobilising fear and/or anxiety of being overwhelmed. Such words construct a nation at an absolute 'breaking point'—one that simply cannot cope with the presence of the other, resulting in calls for immediate action to reverse the uncertainty and 'crisis'.

Under immense pressure from the tabloid press, David Blunkett (Home Secretary 2001–2004) persuaded the French government to close the Sangatte camp (which happened in late 2002; Schuster 2003). A few months after its closure, the British prime minister and French president signed the bilateral Le Touquet Agreement and introduced juxtaposed border checks. However, such controls did not deter refugees from arriving in Calais and attempting to cross the Channel. At the same time, the press in Britain increasingly turned xenophobic, Islamophobic and anti-immigrant and waged a zealous negative campaign on 'bogus' asylum seekers, tainting public opinion further (Kundnani 2001). For instance, Lynn and Lea's (2003) analysis of readers' letters to newspapers showed that 'asylum seekers' by default meant 'bogus' asylum seekers and 'illegals', while 'genuine' refugees were considered as rare and elusive. The very (cold and bureaucratic) term asylum seeker turned pejorative, and regardless of whether tabloid/right-wing press used the words 'bogus', the tone of articles indicated that all refuge seekers were 'bogus', fraudulent and 'illegal'.

Those seeking asylum became associated with 'threats' to security and stability of the country, with their presence portrayed as likely to cause a decay of the social fabric. The tabloids and political figures promoting such views used the racial differences of people arriving in Britain (to ramp up the anti-immigration agenda and introduce a range of restrictionist policies), and in the case of those seeking asylum, it was their 'non-whiteness' (Said 1978; Lynn and Lea 2003). As Kundnani (2001) argues, "we no longer hear of their different values, their alien religion, their strange language. Rather, the image of asylum seekers is defined not by what they are, but simply by the fact that they are 'not one of us', and are, therefore, a threat to 'our way of life'" (p. 52). Over the years, Britain has directed millions of pounds into policing, surveillance and control and constructed physical walls/boundaries around the French harbours, to restrict the flow of those seeking refuge.

Due to the sheer volume of traffic—the large movement of people, the variety of transportation options, the opportunities of clandestine entry (hiding in train/truck/car/ferry or perilous walk through the Tunnel) and the shorter travel distance when compared to other French ports—Calais has always been considered a better transit option for undocumented refugees wanting to seek sanctuary in Britain. By implementing juxtaposed controls, neither of the governments reached for a humanitarian solution but simply made it harder for refuge seekers to make successful entry attempts to Britain. This, when coupled with the closure of Sangatte, created a 'bottleneck effect'. It left refuge seekers unsuccessful at border crossing, stranded and suffering in a spatial limbo. After 2003, politicians made a decision not to create another shelter/camp around Calais, on the grounds that it might constitute a 'pull factor' for 'illegal' migrants. From here on, refuge seekers squatted in derelict buildings in/around the Calais city or created flimsy makeshift camps on wastelands near the Tunnel.

People seeking asylum status started calling these camps the 'jungle' (*Calais Migrant Solidarity website*[7])—a term that not only highlighted squalid living conditions, vulnerability, ongoing trauma and suffering but also became a medium through which suffering and struggles were made visible. Campaigners and activist groups began to use this term to raise awareness about the plight of this group, urging the governments to act compassionately and find sensible solution to a complex humanitarian situation. The 'jungle' began to shed light on the hypocrisy of the British government, which on one hand continued to project itself as a beacon of human rights and refugee protection—and on the other, left refugees to suffer in wastelands. The 'jungle' showed the disposability and disregard for refugee lives. The word demonstrated sheer immorality, inhumanity and racism of the British and French states—which gave scant regard to meeting basic needs of the vulnerable population and only focused on directing higher investments into 'security' measures and controlling, or deterring the entry of, racialised bodies. The term 'jungle' highlighted the resistance and resilience of humans in adversity, in the zones of extreme exclusion, making visible the invisible (for instance, see Godin et al. (eds) 2017—book *Voices from the 'Jungle': Stories from the Calais Refugee Camp*).

In a bid to stop any state-sanctioned or NGO camps from re-emerging, tabloid and right-wing press circulated stories of those who had arrived in Britain under the Sangatte deal.[8] For instance, *The Telegraph* (2006) published an article highlighting that *Most Sangatte migrants are out of work*. Similarly, other articles were published, labelling those seeking asylum in Britain as 'welfare scroungers', 'cheats' and an inherently criminogenic group of people, exploiting the generosity of 'soft touch' Britain (Malloch and Stanley 2005; Greer and Jewkes 2005). The stories continued to reproduce the age-old white racial frames, depicting migrants as lazy, unemployed, stupid and a burden on taxpayers (Smith 1994; Anderson 2013). Such representations through language and discourses are important in the meaning-making process, and it constructs a tainted version of social reality (Barlow 1998; Hall 1997). The newspapers constructed people seeking asylum as a problem, as opposed to people who have a problem (Welch and Schuster 2005), and highlighted 'dangers' of the 'Sangatte 2', and 'fresh build-ups of migrants' seeking to enter Britain clandestinely (*The Telegraph* 2007; *Daily Mail* 2014; *Express* 2014). They started using the 'illegal' migration racial frame to convey this message, thereby criminalising those seeking refuge and rapidly moving the focus away from the human rights lens (Howarth and Ibrahim 2012). The newspapers hijacked the term 'jungle', which was used by this group to highlight squalid living conditions, powerlessness and limbo, and gave it a new meaning. Initially in 2007, it was used sparingly, but from 2009 onwards, it became the dominant term (Howarth and Ibrahim 2012: 207).

The populist newspapers turned the 'jungle' into a powerful metaphor loaded with hyper-racist, criminalised and other negative connotations. The aim was to generate a greater impact, creating a wider distance between 'them' and 'us'. It was re-defined as 'a ghetto', 'notorious', 'a hiding place' for 'criminals', where there were ethnic 'turf wars', 'rampant' criminality and 'vicious battles between armed migrants and people smugglers' (Howarth and Ibrahim 2012: 207–208). The 'jungle' came to represent the dirt, savageness and ferocity of its inhabitants, lack of restraint and adherence to the law, where the only law perceived was the survival of the fittest. The inhabitants of the 'jungle' were now turned into inferior 'other', sub-humans, who did not deserve to exist in the civilised West. The 'jungle' not only became spatially but also symbolically bordered. As Edward Said mentions in *Orientalism* (1978): "the imaginative geography which distinguished our land from barbarian land is enough for 'us' to set up the boundaries in our own mind, whether 'the barbarians recognise them or not'. The Orient, in particular the near-Orient is regarded as the complementary opposite to the West" (Said 1978: 54–58). It can therefore be argued that the tabloid and right-wing press used this old Western-centred racial framing and constructed a powerful 'truth' about the 'jungle', which strongly reproduced and maintained the West/rest dichotomy, demarcated boundaries and further removed 'the other' from compassion and humanity mind-set of its readers (Hall 1992; Mills 1997).

In 2009, the French government demolished the 'jungle', and the event turned into major news in the British media and tabloid press—a racial 'spectacle' devised by the authorities to impress their spatial control over Calais (Ibrahim and Howarth 2016). The new camps re-emerged within a matter of days to replace the ones destroyed. There were five further camp demolitions between 2014 and 2015 (Ibrahim and Howarth 2016) and a partial demolition in July 2016; the camps continued to re-emerge. The events in the Mediterranean and unprecedented numbers of refugees arriving in Europe's frontier countries seeking safety renewed and retained tabloid interest in the 'jungle' (Ibrahim and Howarth 2016). This was topped up by the political hysteria about Brexit, with strong anti-immigrant wings on both sides of 'leave' and 'remain' camps drama-tising and dominating tabloid headlines and disproportionately focusing on the situation at Calais and (refugees turned) 'illegal' migrants. The pro-Brexit camp argued that leaving the EU would result in tightening of 'porous' borders, a drastic reduction in 'illegal' immigrant numbers and a consequent decline in crime (Bhatia 2016). Whereas, the anti-Brexit camp warned about leaving the safety and protection of the EU, which could result in a weakening of borders, a huge influx of 'illegal' immi-grants from the 'jungle' coming into Great Britain and consequently a rise in crime. Both discourses on anti-immigration attempted to outma-noeuvre each other by presenting extreme, ideologically biased, mislead-ing and faulty scenarios, lacking robust research and evidence (Bhatia 2016). Despite the numbers of refuge seekers in the 'jungle' not reaching beyond 10,000 people in total (which is 0.07% of those seeking protec-tion in Europe), the tabloids and politicians portrayed it as the tip of the iceberg, that everyone coming to Europe wanted to enter the Great Britain 'illegally' and that, given half a chance, they would (Crawley and Clochard 2016).

With the increase in the 'terrorist' incidents across Europe, and warn-ings of further imminent attacks high on the public agenda, tabloids rep-resented 'illegal' migrants and those seeking refuge as extremely 'dangerous' and associated the group with violence (e.g. Malloch and Stanley 2005; Bosworth 2008). By repeatedly linking 'illegal' migration with crime, the press has constructed an unrealistic and stereotypical por-trayal of immigrants (of colour) as dangerous and pathologically criminogenic. In 2005, the Institute of Public Policy Research (IPPR) revealed a growing habit of newspapers to taint people seeking refuge by linking them with 'Islamic fundamentalist terrorists' (Greenslade 2005; also see Moore et al. 2008). The report documented details of false and inaccurate commentary about refuge seekers and their alleged involvement in terrorist activities. Likewise, Migrant Observatory Report (2013) highlighted that coverage of immigration and asylum includes a vocabulary of numbers (words such as 'thousands' and even 'million') and discourses of security or illegality (words like Islamic terrorist, suspected, sham). The aligning of 'non-whiteness' to Islamic beliefs, "conspires to produce a visibly distinct and culturally different 'Other' that does not sit easily with the image of the 'true' Briton as it exists within the realm of common knowledge" (Lynn and Lea 2003: 429). When a visibly distinct and culturally different 'other' gets associated with crime and violence, it produces an overwhelming image of ethnic and racial differences as a social threat and the source of conflict and deviance (Poynting 2002). Tabloids exaggerate and strategically deploy these differences to instil fear, distortions and mystifications (Box 1983). The complexity of 'terrorism' and absolute lack of compelling research that links increases in refugee/migrant flows with increases in 'terrorist' incidents have not stopped the tabloids from turning refugees fleeing violence and conflict into 'terrorists suspects'. They have produced ideologically loaded misinformed articles, mirroring the 'clash of civilisation' effect (e.g. see the excellent analysis of media by Berry et al. (2016)).

The history of Calais, along with escalating populism, racisms and anti-immigrant sentiments, and the Conservative Party's promotion of a 'hostile environment' agenda for 'illegal' migrants (see Jones et al. 2017; Mondon and Winter 2017; Burnett 2017; Bruce-Jones 2018), has also influenced the coverage of the 'jungle'. At the same time, politicians and policy makers have attuned themselves to tabloids and right-wing newspapers and have deployed similar language in their speeches (for instance, use of words like 'swarms', 'swamped' and 'illegal'), to please the population and demonstrate 'leadership', but also to reinforce and maintain the white racial frames (see below). The figure of refuge seekers in the 'jungle' has transformed. Their status, their suffering, their resistance, all disguised and rendered invisible under the category of 'illegal' migrant. The following section will analyse ways in which tabloids/right-wing press have deployed 'illegal' migrant, turning refugees into a population that is socially dead.

From Refugees to 'Illegal' Migrants: Using Racial Frames to (Re)Produce Social Death

The 'illegal' migrant, a white racial framing, pushes refuge seekers out from the humanitarian and rights-based realm and pulls them into a racialised and criminalised sphere. It switches their status from at-risk individuals deserving of safety and security to those who are risks, criminals and a source of insecurity—one that needs to be detected, controlled and stopped from entering or living in the country. For instance, *The Telegraph* article published on 2 May 2016 headlined *7000 illegal immigrants smuggled into Britain on ferries*. The article argues that the number of people entering clandestinely has doubled in the past three years. It not only deploys the use of 'official' statistics (to make the article valid, objective, authoritative and unquestionable) to strengthen the central plank of the argument, making the 'security' problem appear urgent and real. By introducing a quote from a right-wing think tank MigrationWatch, the article dramatises and reproduces the notion of the country being under siege and demands that more measures be introduced to strengthen border 'security'. However, the reporting does not stop here and further highlights true numbers as "likely to be significantly higher as many illegal immigrants disappear after entering" Great Britain, and they are "never discovered by the authorities". The statement creates what Ahmed calls a 'bogeyman': a terrifying racialised figure that cannot be controlled, who could be anywhere and everywhere, like a ghostly presence, and induces nightmares and terror about the future. The very words 'illegal', 'entering', 'disappearing' create powerful and daunting synergies. They suggest that unknown but large numbers of criminal bodies have invaded borders and they are roaming freely, unhindered, invisible and unstoppable and likely to cause mayhem and misery. Of course, Calais and 'jungle' are highlighted as a source of the problem, where the 'illegal' migrant or bogeyman comes from, where they are based—making it a hyper-criminogenic space. Nowhere has the article mentioned that most individuals in Calais are refuge seekers, most fleeing wars and persecution and other threats to life. The article then speculates that "3m migrants to arrive by 2030", a projection with no explanation, which seeks to amplify the fears—three million bogeyman roaming the British streets. The end directs reader's attention to the *Telegraph*'s *Border Security Campaign*, which calls for the political leaders to address the 'porousness' of borders and ramp up the 'security'.

Before going any further, it is necessary to analyse the term 'illegal' migrants, as that will help understand the power of the 'illegal migrant' framing. The term needs a racialised migrant body,[9] without which it is meaningless and unrecognisable. The 'illegal' migrant is a peculiar criminal construct that targets the individual's existence and not their actions. Turning those seeking refuge into 'illegal' migrants not only results in criminalisation of racialised bodies but also racialisation of a 'crime' (of undocumented migration). Like most other crimes, it is constructed as an immoral act, undeserving of sympathy and attracting outrage and contempt. However, unlike most other crimes, being an 'illegal' migrant is a 'crime' in itself—it is a 'crime' of status—of racialised bodies not having a status: lack of status that is by default considered a 'crime', a 'crime' portrayed and understood as having no 'lawful' status. Whether 'illegal' migrants commit 'crime' or not, their very (lack of) status, their very (lack of) 'existence', their very (lack of) 'presence' or 'being', all of which is constructed as a 'crime'. According to a Latina/Latino Studies scholar Lisa Marie Cacho (2012), the law does not produce the 'crime' of being an 'illegal' migrant, and 'illegal' migrant is not a legal term. While this is equally the case in the UK, 'illegal' is considered as an epitome of 'un-Britishness'. When pushed into the realm of 'illegal', individual reasons and circumstances for migration simply do not matter, turning 'illegal' migrants into bodies that *do not matter* (such as refuge seekers in Calais turned 'illegal'). To target bodies for border controls and exclusion, deportation and banishment, detention and confinement, the state and the tabloid and right-wing press racialise and dehumanise them and construct or dramatise their 'threats', 'risks' or 'dangers' and consequently criminalise them. These individuals are excluded and marginalised and rendered invisible by the law, lacking protection, rights or status (Agamben 1998)—as explained in following paragraphs.

The 'illegal' migrant, is someone 'assigned' a criminalised status by those in power (i.e. white elites and media). Those seeking asylum are stereotyped and racially profiled as criminals, but more importantly, they are at the same time criminalised. There is a difference between the two—being stereotyped indicates that society misrecognises someone as a criminal, but to be criminalised indicates that someone by default is prevented from being considered lawful or given a chance to abide by the law (Cacho 2012). The category of 'illegal' migrant is a criminalised status because it creates a forced racialised exclusion of those bracketed as 'illegal' from being law abiding and also removes them from the protection of the law—since they are legally non-existent and therefore have no legal rights granted to citizens—but at the same time it confronts them with the law's disciplinary and control mechanisms (Cacho 2012). So, while there is no appetite for protecting 'illegal' migrants and ('bogus') asylum seekers, there is nonetheless ferocious hunger to subject them to higher deterrence and punitive controls, an aspect captured by various scholars (for instance, see Weber and Pickering 2011; Grewcock 2010; Bhatia 2014, 2015; Khosravi 2010; Canning 2017; Griffiths 2014; Aas and Bosworth 2013). The same applies to those 'living' in the 'jungle'. Following from the previous section it is apparent that tabloids, right-wing press and certain politicians have constructed and used the 'illegal' category for refuge seekers, to demand and enforce restrictive border controls and policing measures in and around the 'jungle'. This is to prevent the 'crime' of 'illegal' migration and 'illegal' migrants from coming or staying in the country and to block 'illegal' migrants from turning 'legal'. In the process, any violence directed against them (symbolic, cultural or 'real') is portrayed as valid, rightful and legitimate functions of crime control and prevention.

The 'jungle' and Calais borderlands have somewhat become spaces of exceptions. The 'jungle' refugees are rendered apolitical, rightless and unprotected. The 'crime' committed by them is entirely victimless (i.e. having no documents and status). However, they have yet achieved a criminalised status, and their bodies have become an object of racist repression. The populist press has hidden and denied their suffering and violence of exclusions, by moving them out of the humanitarian and rights-based realm and into a criminalised domain, as explained earlier.

This has also resulted in suffering and deaths of refugees presented as mere *collateral damage* of border controls or the outcome of their 'illegal' behaviour or 'presence'. They are blamed for their own deaths, and their deaths are portrayed as a hindrance. For instance, an article published in the *Mirror* dated October 2015 headlined: "Migrant found dead near Channel Tunnel as 6000 people mass at Calais seeking entry to Britain". It further states:

> A migrant trying to enter Britain was found dead near the tracks of the Channel Tunnel today amid a surge in people massing at Calais. Officials announced that the number of migrants at the Calais camp has doubled to close to 6,000 people just days after another suspected migrant died after being struck on the M20 motorway in Kent ... Many illegal migrants make repeated nightly attempts to break into the Channel Tunnel or the ferry port to sneak aboard lorries or trains to Britain. Mass raids of the tunnel site and rail track invasions in recent months have also led to long delays to freight and passenger trains to the UK.

The article does not highlight the desperation of those seeking refuge or lack of 'legal' and safe travel routes. More importantly, it does not recognise the deceased person as a refuge seeker. Stan Cohen (2013) argues that denial is a state in which an undesirable situation is unrecognised, ignored or made to seem normal. Once criminalised and pushed into the 'illegal' migration framework, those seeking refuge are denied victim status. The story not only follows this approach, but it further suggests that one migrant is found dead—however, there is a *surge in people massing at Calais* and hints that nation needs to be protected from their invasions. The language of war constructs the group as the racialised 'enemy other' (see Fekete and Webber 2010), it depersonalises their death, makes it appear insignificant and not worthy of attention. Such a portrayal removes refugees from compassion mind-set of readers and transforms them into 'undeserving victims'—('illegal') *migrant trying to enter Britain* ('illegally') *was found dead*—death caused due to 'illegal' behaviour. Therefore, while the article makes readers aware of the death, at the same time it equips them with tools to distance and deny the significance of his death. It presents information in a manner that adds on to the existing fears of invasions of 'illegal' migrants, who happen to be alive and in abundance, and marching their way into Great Britain.

Similarly, in another article published by the *Mirror* dated October 2016, days before the Calais demolition, the headlines read: 'Illegal immigrant' suffocates to death in back of lorry after 'being crushed by baby clothes magazines'. The articles further mentions:

> A suspected illegal migrant is believed to have suffocated under the weight of baby clothes catalogues as an HGV truck travelled across the English Channel. The panicked lorry driver found the body after he had travelled across the Channel through Calais hours before making the discovery at a busy Kent lorry park ... driver is believed to have discovered several people in the back of his truck at Calais, but Border Force failed to flush out all of the suspected migrants. Again when the truck was checked at the border in Dover, officers failed to find the stowaway ... Police believe the man, who was pronounced dead at the scene, had travelled from France...

The story was covered in several other tabloids and right-wing outlets, using the same frame and they replicated the distancing and denial strategies of the previous articles. What sets the story apart is the sensational portrayal of death. The article turns death into an example, to dramatise the deficiencies in border control operations and porousness of borders. On the surface, the article tends to highlight the failures of the border officials. However, on looking closer, the underlying message becomes clear—to stop the 'illegals' from dying, Britain needs tighter controls and tougher policing measures (as opposed to stating that escalating borders are forcing desperate refugees to take more risks and Britain needs a sensible humanitarian approach to save lives). The references to *stowaway* and Channel crossing turn the focus back to the 'jungle' as the source of 'crime'. Further, the publication date of article is close to the scheduled (or potential) demolition of the 'jungle', making it part of a wider tabloid frenzy over the 'jungle'.

The refugees turned 'illegals' are deprived from the status of 'living', and the 'jungle' has been transformed into space of the living dead and population 'dead to others' (Cacho 2012: 7)—a group that simply do not matter and are denied 'existence'. They are made what Tyler (2006) terms as "hyper-visible", and at the same time rendered hyper-invisible. The very criminalisation takes away their rights to have rights. Even in the death, their recognition is limited to the 'illegal' status. What we are witnessing is a brutal *social death* of Calais refugees—who are racialised, de-socialised, made non-existent and then re-introduced to society as 'criminals' and sub-human entities—a product of hostile and alien culture—an enemy wanting to bring harm. This racialised social death is a desired effect produced by the tabloid rehearsal of illegality and official practices and processes, through which individuals and groups become something other than humans and have been denied rights. The social death is a direct consequence of loss of dignity and personhood—achieved by subjecting them to violence(s), domination and exclusion, to the point that they are physically alive, but their lives considered and portrayed as meaningless and worthless.

The biological death of those who undergo *social death* is portrayed in a manner that it does not deserve sympathy and attention. As columnist Katie Hopkins commented in *The Sun* (dated 17 April 2015): "No I don't care. Show me pictures of coffins, show me bodies floating in water, play violins … I still don't care." This is obviously a grotesque portrayal of refugee deaths, which gained high level of criticism and public outrage[10] (Canning 2017). Not all right-wing and tabloid articles have portrayed asylum seekers' deaths and suffering in this manner. Nevertheless, they have adopted an equally grotesque approach by deploying the 'illegal' migrant racial frame and permanently excluded refugees from personhood, identity and belonging. The articles have demanded and legitimised draconian state actions and degraded refugees. In addition, when looked from a different angle, the columnist's words and ideas are also reflective of the sentiments of the British state (and Western governments in general) and its border control policies and refugee 'protection' regime (Canning 2017).

The socially dead live in a state of liminality and limbo, subjected to violence and rendered disposable. The tabloid portrayal of refuge seekers' deaths repeats and reaffirms this aspect. For instance, an article published by *the Express* (11 October 2016), days before the official dismantling of the 'jungle', headlined "Calais migrant dies in car crash after gang ambushes British driver in bid to reach UK". It further mentions:

> The Eritrean migrant was part of a gang who had spent Sunday evening installing makeshift barriers … to block traffic and force UK-bound cars

and lorries to hit the brakes. The British car driver said he was ambushed by a mob of Jungle migrants—including an Eritrean couple ... at which point he was "attacked" by the group of Calais migrants, who tried to jump inside his vehicle. He is said to have knocked down the Eritrean man and his partner after having panicked and attempted to flee the scene. The driver chose not to stop, the officials said. Instead, he raced to the Channel Tunnel and "immediately" reported the accident to members of the border police force.

The article's use of the term 'gang' indicates (violent) criminality and individuals involved in the incident being part of a larger criminal group. Just as 'illegal' migrants, the term 'gang' is a peculiar criminal construct. It racialises crime and criminalises racialised bodies. Regardless of whether these bodies are part of a 'gang' or not, they are by default associated with criminality (also see Williams and Clark's chapter in this book). Further, in the case of Calais any and every act (including acts of resistance) committed by these bodies could potentially be labelled as 'gang' related (violence). An overwhelming number of 2016 tabloid articles on the 'jungle' published visual images[11] of black and brown 'illegal' migrants in groups, who were termed as 'gangs', 'mob' or 'thugs'. The portrayal was that of extreme chaos, thereby strengthening the criminal construct, making the problem of 'crime' appear severe and inducing a sense of 'danger' and fear. The 'gang' in this case is also a gendered term, and it has leeched on to the behaviour depiction of male refugees of the 'jungle'. The unprotected individuals unable to challenge or reverse their criminal status as 'gang' members (not at least through legal means, since they are legally non-existent). The legal system has not assigned them a status of 'gang'; it is rather a tabloid construction. In this particular article, refuge seeker is associated with 'gang', which has automatically shifted the focus onto the criminal behaviour and devalued the death by racialising the deceased. Further, the recognition of death is strictly limited to the 'criminal' (and 'illegal') status, and there is no mention of the Eritrean man being a victim of a horrific accident.[12] Several tabloids/right-wing outlets published the story but failed to highlight the desperation of these individuals trying to reach safety and protection, taking life-threatening risks. Further, what is even more concerning is the fact that none of the articles included refugee voices or quotes or their lived experiences (at least not accurately) and have strictly enforced journalists' ideological viewpoints—resulting in deliberate and calculated denial and silencing of refugee suffering, resilience and resistance, and reinforcing white racial frames.

Criminalisation and fear work together in the production of social death and block the attempts of reviving those who are socially dead. The above articles do exactly this by constantly reproducing 'danger', or what Sara Ahmed (2000) calls "stranger danger". According to her analysis, strangers are familiar figures and someone that is already recognised as a stranger, as opposed to someone unknown and unfamiliar. The articles use techniques to make it easier for readers to recognise strangers: loitering bodies of colour, invaders, who are out of place and without a legitimate purpose or existence, posing danger to property, person and public life. The stranger is an object onto whom danger is projected. He is recognised as someone who lurks in the dark. It is easy to judge racialised bodies as dangerous as these constructions are inextricably connected with the racist history of Great Britain and historical framing of non-whites. In a rather lengthy article published by *the Daily Mail* dated 26 August 2016 (two months prior to the demolition), there is a repertoire of stranger danger. The columnist Hopkins has narrated her personal experience of driving through the Calais passage in a truck—she mentions:

> Leaving the truck park at 3am an hour outside Calais with my driver Vlad, we have strict instructions. Full tank of fuel. Do not stop. Do not slow down. Just drive. Vlad is grim. Barely speaking as he heads out into the night. Everyone making this journey is tense, peering out into the gloom, looking for the trouble they know is out there, waiting … in the early hours masked men wielding sticks felled a tree across the road outside the port. It's a driver's worst nightmare to be stationary. Left sitting vulnerable to the migrant hordes, vulnerable to being loaded with a new cargo for trade: humans … It's a story you will hear over and over. These gangs are unrelenting … [Calais is] A territory lost to invaders … Trucks simply cannot stop here now, cannot afford to be caught stationary on the road … Illegal migrants are everywhere in the darkness … After 28 hours on the road I have a new-found respect for these truckers … One tells me he can't tell his wife what he faces or she'd never let him in his cab again.

Calais is a fortress, but outside the safety of the gates the traffickers run free. This is bandit country. Every man for himself.

The strangers become an object of fear and their bodies a phobic object. The stranger is the black, the Muslim, the Arab, the 'illegal' migrant, all too familiar and known to be strangers. The article uses knowledge of these known strangers and projects danger on to it. The columnist states that 'illegal' 'migrant hoardes' and 'unrelenting' 'gangs' are roaming freely, and nothing is done to contain them, and nothing can contain them, making Calais a 'bandit country'. The threat of these freely roaming dangerous bodies of colour is overwhelming. By projecting danger on 'unrelenting' 'migrant hoardes', the article calls for even more restrictions and policing measures around Calais.

The tabloids have widely used several quotes from law enforcement to construct and strengthen the 'dangerous' criminal image of the Calais inhabitants—erasing their status of at-risk, vulnerable and victims. For example, the *Mirror* (12 August 2016) used a quote to highlight the fears of police and the 'growing numbers' of 'jihadi terrorists' that could be 'hiding' and 'lurking' amongst the 'thousands' of 'British-bound refugees' in Calais. Similarly, *The Sun* article on 13 August 2016 headlined "Jihadis in the Jungle" and further mentions about the 'anxious' cops, who 'fear' extremists in the 'unpoliceable black hole' of Calais.

The tabloids have also legitimised police/state violence against refugees. For instance, *The Daily Mail* published an article on 21 September 2016 (a month prior to the demolition) headlined "The Battle of Calais", which highlighted the criminal behaviour of the 'jungle' inhabitants. The online version[13] of the article contains a staggering 23 images and three videos depicting chaos, smoke firing up, people running around haphazardly, black men in groups and (white) police officers in full riot gear, carrying batons and tear gas. Furthermore, it describes the vulnerability of officers, whom migrants attacked with 'missiles' and 'objects', causing a shoulder injury to one officer. However, whilst this article (and many others) highlights the struggles of brave (white) police heroes in the 'battlefield', it fails to mention the sheer scale and severity of violence that refuge seekers have endured at the hands of law enforcement. On the contrary, the press has indicated that any violent treatment is a justified response to refugees' crime/criminal behaviour[14] and existence. This press strategy is what Thompson (1990) describes as "expurgation of the other"—which taints the victims of state violence and makes such violence appear as rational.

A recent report drafted by the Refugee Rights Data Project (2017) drawing upon responses of 213 Calais refugees reported that 89.2% of them said they had experienced police violence during their time in Calais. This was further broken into 84% experiencing tear gas, 52.7% other forms of physical violence and 27.7% verbal abuse. The police violence was higher for refugees from Eritrea (93%), Ethiopia (83%) and Sudan (92%), followed by Afghanistan (78%) and Pakistan (75%). Similarly, when questioned about the police treatment, 41.4% reported it to be 'bad' and 40% said it was 'very bad'—with one respondent commenting: "Is there an option that is worse than very bad? I choose that option" (p. 10).

The report further documents and explains in detail the cases of extreme physical violence inflicted by the police. One refugee reported shoulder dislocation, while another explained that his fingers had been dislocated in a similar fashion on a separate occasion. A 22-year-old Palestinian male spoke about beatings by police and being sprayed by tear gas directly onto his face, causing injury in one eye. Women also experienced police violence. A 27-year-old Eritrean woman spoke about physical abuse by police. Similarly, a 22-year-old Ethiopian woman said, "they pushed me to the floor and beat me." The quotes from refugee children also demonstrate the pain, suffering and state-sanctioned abuse:

I was sleeping with some others in the woods when the police came and told us to get up and move. I did what they asked but they still hit me with their baton on my legs which left me in pain for a while.

—Refugee from Eriteria, 16 years old

They gave me an electric shock. It happened in Calais port because they were searching the area.

—Refugee from Eriteria, 16 years old

I was on the road in the evening. They were many police and they verbally abused us, hit us with batons and sprayed tear gas.
—Refugee from Sudan, 16 years old

[The police] recognise me by my hair and they always come after me. They beat me up almost everyday. I have had tear gas sprayed on me several times.
—Refugee from Eriteria, 17 years old

According to Thompson (1990), 'expurgation of the other' is a symbolic construction of scapegoat that must be resisted or purged. The tabloid press and official narratives distort the image of refuge seekers and turn them from victims of violence to perpetrators and cause of violence, deserving brutal treatment. The press articles portray victims of state-sanctioned abuse as dangerous/threatening and thereby exhort their expurgation (also see Hirschfield and Simon 2010). At the same time, it vilifies and demonises refugees and depicts them as predatory and racialised villains, not deserving of compassion. This also legitimises police and border control tactics and physical force, making it appear legal and justified. Here the violence(s) is not portrayed as human rights violations, but rather a logical consequence of victim's unruly and animalistic behaviour and 'illegal' presence. The media have legitimised the use of force against and abuse of refuge seekers. This fits within Grewcock's (2010) definition of 'border crimes'—unjustified, systematic and racist violence(s) directed towards those in desperate need of protection. On looking closer, the real, substantive perpetrators are not refuge seekers, but rather the British and French state and the populist press.

Conclusion

Race is a social construct—constructed by those in power, to benefit by creating a social distance from those who are racialised, in order to rationalise their historical and ongoing oppression, expropriation and exploitation. From slavery to colonialism and beyond, whites have used racial framing and racial hierarchy for their power and gain. This is what Feagin (2013: 28) calls "racial capital"—reserved for the whites—benefiting from hierarchical system of racial operation. This hierarchy has persisted at the heart of systemic racism, from past to present, and used for maintaining racial power by degrading the racialised 'outsider' and subjecting them to violence(s). The powerful populist press in the West are part of this equation. They are driven by strong profit imperatives and have enriched themselves and thrived by circulating/selling racist ideologies and 'otherisation' discourses—producing fear (xenophobia, Islamophobia, etc.). They have greased the wheels of the 'immigration-industrial complex' (see Golash-Boza 2009). These discourses demand tighter immigration laws, even tougher border security and policing measures and greater government investments in technologies of control. The media, private security companies and (powerful, white) elites have become richer, and people of colour have suffered forced exclusion, marginalisation and social (and biological) death. This chapter has attempted to reverse the dominant racial gaze over the 'jungle' refuge seekers, by dissecting press narratives and turning the focus back to the crimes of powerful whites.

Notes

1. See the video here: http://www.telegraph.co.uk/news/2016/10/25/calais-jungle-demolition-france-to-begin-dismantling-migrant-cam/
2. Even when the word 'illegal' is not used in the articles, the illegal frame is still operative and illegality of migrants is implied.
3. http://www.eurotunnelgroup.com/uk/the-channel-tunnel/
4. On 24 June 2016, Britain voted to leave the European Union (termed as Brexit). This could potentially result in renegotiating the current freedom of movement agreement set in place.
5. https://ec.europa.eu/home-affairs/what-we-do/policies/borders-and-visas/schengen_en
6. This happened regardless of the fact that Le Touquet was not a European Treaty, but rather a bilateral agreement between two countries and had no direct relevance to Britain's exit from the European Union.
7. https://calaismigrantsolidarity.wordpress.com/

8. As per the deal, Britain agreed to grant work permits to 1000 Iraqi Kurds from the Sangatte centre and take a proportion of Afghan families.

9. Note: it is important to also recognise that post EU enlargement in 2004, the Eastern European migrants have come to represent 'degenerate' whiteness (just as Jews and Irish before them), and media coverage has often referred to 'cultural differences' in law breaking and associated them with illegal activities (Anderson 2013). Up until this stage, they have escaped the term 'illegal' migrants, due to being part of the EU. Nevertheless, this could change post-BREXIT, depending on the manner in which media and politicians racialise and represent their status and existence in the country.

10. A few months later, Donald Trump publicly declared her as a 'respected columnist' and praised her 'powerful writing'.

11. The online version contains videos as well as images.

12. In another article, a 14-year-old unaccompanied child from Afghanistan died in similar circumstances. The driver swerved left and right to knock him off the vehicle. Ironically, in this case, the tabloids acknowledged the desperation of children and dangers they face. However, such acknowledgement largely occurred after their deaths (another example would be that of a four-year-old child refugee Aylan Kurdi). Nevertheless, during the dismantling of the camp, Britain took handful of unaccompanied minors, and tabloids ended up waging a negative campaign, calling them fraudulent and adults posing to be children. As Berry et al. (2016) have highlighted, when compared to other European countries the portrayal of refugees in British press has been the most negative.

13. http://www.dailymail.co.uk/news/article-3800712/The-Battle-Calais-Police-use-tear-gas-repel-300-migrants-try-storm-road-leading-French-port.html

14. Important note: Even if the crime has occurred (as defined by the criminal law)—it needs to be contextualised against the dire circumstances in the 'jungle' wastelands, life in limbo, poverty and desperation (also see Bhatia 2015).

References

Aas, K. F., & Bosworth, M. (Eds.). (2013). *The Borders of Punishment: Migration, Citizenship, and Social Exclusion.* Oxford University Press.

Agamben, G. (1998). *Homo Sacer: Sovereign Power and Bare Life.* Stanford University Press.

Ahmed, S. (2000). *Strange Encounters: Embodied Others in Post-Coloniality.* Routledge.

Ahmed, S. (2004). Affective Economies. *Social Text, 22*(2), 117–139.

Allen, W., & Blinder, S. (2013). *Migration in the News: Portrayals of Immigrants, Migrants, Asylum Seekers and Refugees in National British Newspapers, 2010 to 2012.* Migration Observatory Report, COMPAS, University of Oxford.

Anderson, B. (2013). *Us and Them?: The Dangerous Politics of Immigration Control.* Oxford: Oxford University Press.

Bagot, M. (2015). *Migrant Found Dead Near Channel Tunnel as 6,000 People Mass at Calais.* Retrieved January 3, 2017, from http://www.mirror.co.uk/news/world-news/migrant-found-dead-near-channel-6648651

Barlow, M. H. (1998). Race and the Problem of Crime in "Time" and "Newsweek" Cover Stories, 1946 to 1995. *Social Justice, 25*(2 (72)), 149–183.

Bennett, A. (2016). *'Illegal Immigrant Crushed to Death by Baby Clothes Magazines' in Lorry.* Retrieved January 3, 2017, from http://www.mirror.co.uk/news/uk-news/illegal-immigrant-suffocates-death-back-9073463

Berry, M., Garcia-Blanco, I., & Moore, K. (2016). *Press Coverage of the Refugee and Migrant Crisis in the EU: A Content Analysis of Five European Countries.* Retrieved May 3, 2017, from http://orca.cf.ac.uk/87078/1/UNHCR-%20 FINAL%20REPORT.pdf

Bhatia, M. (2014). Creating and Managing 'Mad', 'Bad' and 'Dangerous': The Role of the Immigration System. In V. Canning (Ed.), *Sites of Confinement.* The European Group Press.

Bhatia, M. (2015). Turning Asylum Seekers into 'Dangerous Criminals': Experiences of the Criminal Justice System of Those Seeking Sanctuary. *International Journal for Crime, Justice and Social Democracy, 4*(3), 97–111.

Bhatia, M. (2016). Will Brexit Impact on Borders and the Control of Immigration? *British Society of Criminology Newsletter 78,* 97–111. Retrieved April 8, 2017, from http://www.britsoccrim.org/wp-content/uploads/2016/04/Bhatia_bscn78.pdf

Bosworth, M. (2008). Border Control and the Limits of the Sovereign State. *Social & Legal Studies, 17*(2), 199–215.

Box, S. (1983). *Power, Crime and Mystification.* London: Tavistock.

Bruce-Jones, E. (2018). Refugee Law in Crisis. In Bosworth et al. (Eds.), *Race, Criminal Justice, and Migration Control: Enforcing the Boundaries of Belonging* (pp. 176–196).

Brussels, P. (2007). *French Go Ahead with 'Sangatte 2'*. Retrieved January 3, 2017, from http://www.telegraph.co.uk/news/worldnews/1548603/French-go-ahead-with-Sangatte-2.html

Burnett, J. (2017). Racial Violence and the Brexit State. *Race & Class, 58*(4), 85–97.

Cacho, L. M. (2012). *Social Death: Racialized Rightlessness and the Criminalization of the Unprotected*. NYU Press.

Canning, V. (2017). *Gendered Harm and Structural Violence in the British Asylum System*. Routledge.

Chazan. (2016). 'Mission Accomplished': Calais Jungle Burns to Ashes and Dust in Its Final Hours. Retrieved January 3, 2017, from http://www.telegraph.co.uk/news/2016/10/26/migrants-start-fires-and-hurl-stones-at-firemen-as-demolition-cr/

Cohen, S. (2013). *States of Denial: Knowing About Atrocities and Suffering*. Polity Press.

Crawley, H., & Clochard, O. (2016). After the Calais Jungle: Is There a Long-Term Solution? Views from France and Britain. In *The Conversation*. Retrieved April 11, 2017, from https://theconversation.com/after-the-calais-jungle-is-there-a-long-term-solution-views-from-france-and-britain-67352

Department of Transport. (2015). Provisional Sea Passenger Statistics Report. Retrieved March 3, 2017, from https://www.gov.uk/government/statistics/provisional-sea-passenger-statistics-2015

Express. (2016). French to LET Migrants Head for Britain: Fury at Threat to Scrap Border Checks at Calais. Retrieved January 3, 2017, from http://www.express.co.uk/news/world/647094/Calais-EU-Brexit-border

Feagin, J. R. (2013). *The White Racial Frame: Centuries of Racial Framing and Counter-Framing*. Routledge.

Fekete, L., & Webber, F. (2010). Foreign Nationals, Enemy Penology and the Criminal Justice System. *Race & Class, 51*(4), 1–25.

Fricker, M. (2016). *Calais Jungle Migrant Camp Demolition Crews Move in as Riot Police form Guard*. Retrieved January 3, 2017, from http://www.mirror.co.uk/news/world-news/calais-jungle-migrant-camp-demolition-9122808

Gilroy, P. (2013). *There Ain't No Black in the Union Jack*. Routledge.

Godin, M., Møller Hansen, K., Lounasmaa, A., Squire, C., & Zaman, T. (Eds.). (2017). *Voices from the 'Jungle': Stories from the Calais Refugee Camp*. Pluto Press.

Golash-Boza, T. (2009). The Immigration Industrial Complex: Why We Enforce Immigration Policies Destined to Fail. *Sociology Compass, 3*(2), 295–309.

Greenslade, R. (2004). *Press Gang: How Newspapers Make Profits from Propaganda*. Pan Macmillan.

Greenslade, R. (2005). *Seeking Scapegoats: The Coverage of Asylum in the UK Press*. London: Institute for Public Policy Research.

Greer, C., & Jewkes, Y. (2005). Extremes of Otherness: Media Images of Social Exclusion. *Social Justice, 32*(1 (99)), 20–31.

Grewcock, M. (2010). *Border Crimes: Australia's War on Illicit Migrants*. Annandale: Federation Press.

Griffiths, M. B. (2014). Out of Time: The Temporal Uncertainties of Refused Asylum Seekers and Immigration Detainees. *Journal of Ethnic and Migration Studies, 40*(12), 1991–2009.

Hainmueller, J., & Hopkins, D. J. (2014). Public Attitudes Toward Immigration. *Annual Review of Political Science, 17*, 225–249.

Hall, S. (1992). The West and the Rest: Discourse and Power. The Indigenous Experience. *Global Perspectives*, 165–173.

Hall, S. (1997). The Work of Representation. In S. Hall (Ed.), *Cultural Representations and Signifying Practices*. Sage.

Hartmann, P., & Husband, C. (1974). *Racism and the Mass Media*. London: Davis-Poynter.

Hirschfield, P. J., & Simon, D. (2010). Legitimating Police Violence: Newspaper Narratives of Deadly Force. *Theoretical Criminology, 14*(2), 155–182.

Hopkins, K. (2016). *Katie Hopkins Runs the Migrant Calais Gauntlet with Truckers*. Retrieved January 3, 2017, from http://www.dailymail.co.uk/mostread/article-3760011/It-s-Jungle-Calais-right-desperate-migrants-menacing-truckers-aren-t-real-problem-s-one-s-never-need-worry-KATIE-HOPKINS-runs-gauntlet-lorry-drivers-Britain-s-border.html

Howarth, A., & Ibrahim, Y. (2012). Threat and Suffering: The Liminal Space of 'the Jungle'. In H. Andrews & L. Roberts (Eds.), *Liminal Landscapes: Travel, Experience and Spaces In-between*. Routledge.

Hughes, C. (2016). *Jihadi Terrorists Could Be Hiding in Calais Refugee Camp Ready to Attack Britain*. Retrieved January 3, 2017, from http://www.mirror.co.uk/news/uk-news/jihadi-terrorists-could-hiding-calais-8620074

Huysmans, J. (2006). *The Politics of Insecurity: Fear, Migration and Asylum in the EU*. Routledge.

Ibrahim, Y., & Howarth, A. (2015). Space Construction in Media Reporting. A Study of the Migrant Space in the 'Jungles' of Calais. *Fast Capitalism, 12*(1). Retrieved April 6, 2017, from http://www.fastcapitalism.com/

Ibrahim, Y., & Howarth, A. (2016). Imaging the Jungles of Calais: Media Visuality and the Refugee Camp. Networking Knowledge. *Journal of the MeCCSA Postgraduate Network, 9*(4), 1–22.

Iyengar, S., & Kinder, D. R. (1987). *News that Matters: Television and American Opinion*. Chicago, IL: University of Chicago Press.

Jones, H., Gunaratnam, Y., Bhattacharyya, G., Davies, W., Dhaliwal, S., Forkert, K., Jackson, E., & Saltus, R. (2017). *Go Home?: The Politics of Immigration Controversies*. Manchester University Press.

Khosravi, S. (2010). *'Illegal' Traveller: An Auto-Ethnography of Borders*. Routledge.

Kostakopoulou, T. (2000). The 'Protective Union'; Change and Continuity in Migration Law and Policy in Post-Amsterdam Europe. *JCMS: Journal of Common Market Studies, 38*(3), 497–518.

Kundnani, A. (2001). In a Foreign Land: The New Popular Racism. *Race & Class, 43*(2), 41–60.

Leapman, B. (2006). *Most Sangatte Migrants Are Out of Work*. Retrieved January 3, 2017, from http://www.telegraph.co.uk/news/uknews/1536473/Most-Sangatte-migrants-are-out-of-work.html

Lynn, N., & Lea, S. (2003). A Phantom Menace and the New Apartheid: The Social Construction of Asylum-Seekers in the United Kingdom. *Discourse & Society, 14*(4), 425–452.

Mail Online. (2014a). Complacent' Home Office Loses 175,000 Illegal Immigrants: Fresh Humiliation as Officials Admit How Many Went Missing After They Were Refused Permission to Stay. Retrieved January 3, 2017, from http://www.dailymail.co.uk/news/article-2742786/Complacent-Home-Office-loses-175-000-illegal-immigrants-Fresh-humiliation-officials-admit-went-missing-refused-permission-stay.html

Mail Online. (2014b). From Eritrea and Sudan, the New Migrant Queue at Calais: Latest Illegal Encampment to Spring Up Has Hundreds Who Are Currently Waiting for the First Chance to Escape. Retrieved January 3, 2017, from http://www.dailymail.co.uk/news/article-2713761/From-Eritrea-Sudan-new-migrant-queue-Calais-Latest-illegal-encampment-spring-hundreds-currently-waiting-chance-escape.html

Mail Online. (2016a). Calais Burning: Migrants Clash with Police in the Jungle Camp. Retrieved January 3, 2017, from http://www.dailymail.co.uk/news/article-3864084/Left-wing-British-anarchists-planning-trouble-against-Calais-police-French-authorities-prepare-raze-Jungle-ground.html

Mail Online. (2016b). Cleared ... at Last! Infamous Calais Jungle Camp Razed to the Ground. Retrieved January 3, 2017, from http://www.dailymail.co.uk/news/article-3890940/Cleared-Infamous-Calais-Jungle-camp-finally-destroyed-shelters-demolished.html

Mail Online. (2016c). Migrants to Spread Across France as They Filter Out of Calais Jungle. Retrieved January 3, 2017, from http://www.dailymail.co.uk/

news/article-3862226/With-belongings-bin-bags-shopping-trolleys-thousands-migrants-set-spread-Northern-France-forced-leave-Calais-Jungle-bulldozed.html

Mail Online. (2016d). The Battle of Calais: Police Use Tear Gas to Repel 300 Migrants. Retrieved January 3, 2017, from http://www.dailymail.co.uk/news/article-3800712/The-Battle-Calais-Police-use-tear-gas-repel-300-migrants-try-storm-road-leading-French-port.html

Malloch, M., & Stanley, E. (2005). The Detention of Asylum Seekers in the UK: Representing Risk, Managing the Dangerous. *Punishment & Society, 7*(1), 53–71.

McGuinness, R. (2016). *Calais Migrant Dies in Car Crash After Gang Ambushes British Driver in Bid to Reach UK*. Retrieved January 3, 2017, from http://www.express.co.uk/news/world/719493/Calais-Jungle-migrant-dies-car-crash-British-driver

McQuail, D. (2000). *Mass Communication Theory*. London: Thousand Oaks.

Mills, S. (1997). *Discourse*. London and New York: Routledge.

Mondon, A., & Winter, A. (2017). Articulations of Islamophobia: From the Extreme to the Mainstream? *Ethnic and Racial Studies*, 1–29.

Moore, K., Mason, P., & Lewis, J. M. W. (2008). *Images of Islam in the UK: The Representation of British Muslims in the National Print News Media 2000–2008*. Retrieved April 18, 2017, from http://orca.cf.ac.uk/53005/1/08channel4-dispatches.pdf

Peers, S. (2015). *The UK and the Schengen System*. Retrieved January 4, 2017, from http://ukandeu.ac.uk/the-uk-and-the-schengen-system/

Philo, G., & Beattie, L. (1999). Race, Migration and Media. In G. Philo (Ed.), *Message Received*. Edinburgh: Addison Wesley Longman.

Poynting, S. (2002). Bin Laden in the Suburbs: Attacks on Arab and Muslim Australians Before and After 11 September. *Current Issues in Criminal Justice, 14*(1). Retrieved June 7, 2017, from http://www.austlii.edu.au/au/journals/CICrimJust/2002/14.html

Refugee Rights Data Project. (2017). *Six Months on: Filing Information Gaps Relating to Children and Young Adults in Northern France Following the Demolition of the Calais Camp*. Retrieved June 12, 2017, from http://refu-geerights.org.uk/wp-content/uploads/2017/04/RRDP_SixMonthsOn.pdf

Said, E. (1978). *Orientalism: Western Representations of the Orient*. New York: Pantheon.

Schuster, L., & Solomos, J. (1999). The Politics of Refugee and Asylum Policies in Britain: Historical Patterns and Contemporary Realities. In *Refugees, Citizenship and Social Policy in Europe* (pp. 51–75). Palgrave.

Schuster, L. (2003). Asylum Seekers: Sangatte and the Tunnel. *Parliamentary Affairs, 56*(3), 506–522.

Schwenken, H. (2014). From Sangatte to 'The Jungle': Europe's Contested Borderlands. In H. Schwenken & S. Ruß-Sattar (Eds.), *New Border and Citizenship Politics*. Basingstoke, UK: Palgrave Macmillan.

Smith, A. M. (1994). *New Right Discourse on Race and Sexuality: Britain, 1968–1990* (No. 1). Cambridge University Press.

Smith, E., & Marmo, M. (2014). *Race, Gender and the Body in British Immigration Control*. Palgrave.

Solomos, J. (2003). *Race and Racism in Britain*. Palgrave.

Sparks, I. (2014). *Protest in Calais After Migrant Numbers QUADRUPLE*. Retrieved January 3, 2017, from http://www.express.co.uk/news/world/522264/Calais-police-protest-over-migrants

Swinford, S. (2016). *7,000 Illegal Immigrants Smuggled into Britain on Ferries*. Retrieved January 3, 2017, from http://www.telegraph.co.uk/news/2016/05/02/7000-illegal-immigrants-smuggled-into-britain-on-fer-ries/

The Sun. (2016a). Calais Jungle Migrant Camp Demolition Begins as Furious Refugees Torch Tents and Clash with Police in Last-Ditch Protests. [Online]. Retrieved January 3, 2017, from https://www.thesun.co.uk/news/2046884/calais-jungle-migrant-camp-demolition-begins-as-furious-refugees-torch-tents-and-clash-with-police-in-last-ditch-protests/

The Sun. (2016b). Chaos in Calais as Branches Are Hurled at Truckers by Migrant Gangs Determined to Halt Traffic and Board Lorries Bound for Britain. Retrieved January 3, 2017, from https://www.thesun.co.uk/news/1682984/shocking-moment-dozens-of-migrants-hurl-tree-branches-at-passing-truckers-outside-french-port-city-in-bid-to-board-lor-ries-and-sneak-into-britain/

The Sun. (2016c). Dozens of New Jungle-Style Camps Expected to Spring Up All Over France and Belgium as THOUSANDS of Migrants Scatter Following Destruction of Calais Shelters. Retrieved January 3, 2017, from https://www.thesun.co.uk/news/2047245/dozens-of-new-jungle-style-camps-expected-to-spring-up-all-over-france-and-belgium-as-thousands-of-migrants-scatter-following-destruction-of-calais-shelters/

The Sun. (2016d). Police Fear ISIS Terrorists Are Hiding Among 7,000 Migrants in Jungle Camp in Calais Poised to Attack Britain. Retrieved January 3, 2017, from https://www.thesun.co.uk/news/1604280/police-fear-isis-terrorists-are-hiding-among-7000-migrants-poised-to-attack-britain/

Thompson, J. B. (1990). *Ideology and Modern Culture: Critical Theory in the Era of Mass Communication*. Stanford, CA: Stanford University Press.

Tyler, I. (2006). Welcome to Britain' the Cultural Politics of Asylum. *European Journal of Cultural Studies, 9*(2), 185–202.

van Dijk, T. A. (1983). Discourse Analysis: Its Development and Application to the Structure of News. *Journal of Communication, 33*(2), 20–43.

van Dijk, T. A. (2015). *Racism and the Press* (Vol. 5). Routledge.

Webber, F. (1996). *Crimes of Arrival: Immigrants and Asylum-Seekers in the New Europe*. Statewatch Organisation.

Weber, L., & Pickering, S. (2011). *Globalization and Borders: Death at the Global Frontier*. Springer.

Welch, M., & Schuster, L. (2005). Detention of Asylum Seekers in the UK and USA: Deciphering Noisy and Quiet Constructions. *Punishment & Society, 7*(4), 397–417.

Check for
updates

11

Racism as a Crime in Britain's Right-Wing Press

Kerry Moore and Katy Greenland

Critical research of news media coverage has long highlighted the regular reproduction of hostile attitudes towards minority ethnic identities, immigrant groups and cultural and religious difference. Such studies often present compelling evidence demonstrating how the press construct and reproduce xenophobic or racist discourse through labelling and other language choices, the regular collocation of minorities with threats including terrorism, crime or anti-social behaviour and/or other negative narratives concerned with national vulnerability or social deterioration (e.g., Fox et al. 2012; Lynn and Lea 2003; Moore 2012; Moore et al. 2011; Poole 2011). Previous work also demonstrates how multifaceted and fluid discourses of racism in the press can be, with rhetorical defences to the accusation of racism readily at hand or embedded in the language through which racism is articulated (van Dijk 1992, 1993). The denial of racism as 'a slur', backlashes against 'political correctness', the endangerment of 'common sense' social criticism or 'free speech' and

K. Moore (✉) • K. Greenland
Cardiff University, Cardiff, UK

© The Author(s) 2018
M. Bhatia et al. (eds.), *Media, Crime and Racism*, Palgrave Studies in Crime,
Media and Culture, https://doi.org/10.1007/978-3-319-71776-0_11

counter-accusations of 'reverse racism' are classic examples of such strategies employed in the defence of or legitimisation of, especially elite, racist discourse (Augoustinos and Every 2007, 2010; Kobayashi 2009; Seidel 1988). This chapter examines a fundamental issue at the nexus of this conflict—the meaning of racism. What is racism understood *to be*, and how are these definitions of what *is* and *isn't* 'racism' constructed in crime and law and order news? Drawing upon findings from an extensive study examining the representation of racism in UK national newspapers, the *Daily Mail* and *The Mail on Sunday*, *The Daily Telegraph* and *Sunday Telegraph* and *The Sun*, it looks at the kinds of stories that feature racism, how racism is discussed, positioned and made sense of. What kinds of racist practice are represented as newsworthy? How are actors in narratives about racism characterised? What do the discursive boundaries of racism and their policing tell us about how racism is likely to be understood and addressed?

News Values, Racism and Law and Order

In some senses, the potential newsworthiness of racism is no different to that of any other topic. The expectations and interests of the perceived audience are synthesised with organisational and professional ideologies and routine production practices of journalism to inform the selection and priority afforded to stories and the 'public voice' through which they are expressed. For a story to be published, certain thresholds of 'newsworthiness' need to be met. According to classic studies of news values, these may be concerned with, for example, the timing or intensity of the story, the perceived proximity of issues to the audience and the involvement of celebrity or other public figures (Galtung and Ruge 1965; Galtung and Ruge 1981). Violence is assumed to further enhance news value, adding negativity and conflict, sensationalism and dramatic spectacle of the piece, whilst 'follow-up' stories supply reliably newsworthy developments on already familiar narratives (Harcup and O'Neill 2017). However, how and why racism weighs in decisions about newsworthiness is also subject to shifting cultural interpretations, norms and values about its relative importance. Whether racism is positioned as a pressing or escalating social issue in news agendas and how it is linked with or mediated through other newsworthy themes or values also matters. Moreover, the kinds of news in relation to which racism is likely to be seen will be conditioned by 'common sense' understandings of the meaning of racism itself (what it is commonly understood *to be* and the circumstances in which a response may be demanded)—discourses of racism that are historically and culturally contingent; that not only reflect but produce knowledge, shaping how ideas are 'put into practice' and 'used to regulate the conduct of others' (Hall 1997: 44). How discourses of racism are articulated within crime and law and order news is especially important due to crime news' often symbolic role in representing social authority, dominant values and reinforcing 'moral consensus' (Cohen 2004 [1972]; Critcher 2003; Hall et al. 1978; Jenkins 1992). As Jewkes notes, crime news often entails highly simplified, 'polarised frameworks of understanding' where binary oppositions of 'good versus evil' characterise news narratives and the portrayal of mutually exclusive narrative roles portray vulnerable, innocent victims threatened by 'deviant' shameful villains (Jewkes 2015: 53). Complex social or structural explanations for crime events, their causation or consequences are often eschewed in favour of highly personalised, psychological explanations focusing upon individual pathology, morality or motive. How victims and perpetrators are understood to behave can seem far removed from 'real-world' political, economic or cultural contexts—the law and its institutions providing the primary definitional framework through which reckless choices and injudicious risks of individuals are defined.

In relation to racism, such individualised and reductive frameworks for understanding conflict are clearly highly inadequate. Racism is cultural (Goldberg 1999 [1988]; Goldberg 2009): a complex ideology or discourse embedded in social structures and serving the reproduction of racialised group power (white privilege) and dominance. Its expression is plural, historically specific, yet draws upon shared historic cultural codes that subject minority ethnic, cultural and religious populations to experiences of 'economic social exclusion, racialised disadvantage, informal and institutional racism and cultural differentialism' (Hall 2000: 5). In mainstream British public culture, it is undoubtedly socially undesirable to be labelled 'a racist' and very few would be prepared to openly declare themselves as such. When accusations of racism emerge about public figures, it is considered highly damaging to those individuals' reputations. Not only are some expressions of racism against the law; to be 'against racism' is positioned as a 'social good'. However, this does not necessarily mean that an understanding of racism as 'cultural' is accepted. As Hill notes, when celebrities and other public figures face accusations of racism, it is experienced as 'profoundly unsettling' by many (Hill 2009). Social responses to such accusations are often panic, she argues, because dis-credit is shared by the many who have invested their attention, adulation and even money in those figures. Formerly self-affirming relations of identification are now profoundly shaken (Hill 2009: 92). In such a predicament, some leap to defend the accused with whom to preserve the 'credit and virtue' of their own selves. Others distance themselves as far as possible from their former associations, vociferously condemning the transgression in outrage. In both cases, an individualised discourse, 'personalism' prevails. Personalism directs attention to the intentionality behind the racism facilitating strategies of racism denial (it was 'light talk', a 'gaffe' or a misunderstanding of what the speaker *really* meant or believed) and detracting from the social or cultural context through which the power of such an utterance has developed and become meaningful (Dixon and Levine 2012). In racism 'scandals', rows or controversies, personalism further, tends to play a 'metacultural' role, where 'hyper-repetition' of racist language, slurs or stereotypes, condemned or otherwise, reinforce the circulation of 'everyday' racism ideas (Hill 2009). As a result, whilst racism is 'everywhere', it is always, apparently, somewhere else; almost always denied (van Dijk 1992) a racism without racists (Bonilla-Silva 2006) within a social milieu that protects, what DiAngelo (2011) calls, 'while fragility' from hurt when confronted with uncomfortable encounters with 'racism'. In interrogating these encounters within the right-wing press, as explained in the following section, this chapter builds upon the critical discourse, critical race and cultural theory literature, presenting systematically gathered, detailed empirical evidence about a key discursive site in UK culture.

Methodology

Between 3 April and 6 June 2013, an in-depth content analysis was conducted examining 585 news articles drawn from the *Daily Mail* and *Mail on Sunday*, *The Sun* and *The Telegraph/Sunday Telegraph*. This period was chosen to encompass the 20-year anniversary of the brutal racist murder of black teenager Stephen Lawrence. The UK press, and particularly the *Daily Mail* played a fundamental role in documenting and at times joining the Lawrence family's long and ongoing campaign for justice. The finding of systemic and institutionalised racism in the Metropolitan police force by the Macpherson report catalysed wider concerns about racism in British society—and, according to Cottle, a 'mediatised public crisis' about racism in national life with potentially transformative effects (Cottle 2005, 2006). The widest circulating tabloid, mid-market and broadsheet newspapers were chosen—each, generally speaking, right wing in their ideological tendencies. The analysis was designed to include a range of variables to investigate the kinds of news agendas within which racism now featured and to compare the news discourses through which meaning was attached to racism during this period.

As might be expected, the Lawrence case, arguably so cortical to public understandings of and attitudes towards racism, did arise as a main theme in the coverage in 4.6% (n = 27) of cases. However, no stories about Stephen Lawrence featured on the front page. As Table 11.1 below indicates, the news agenda during this period was dominated by sport and politics. This included, most notably, stories reporting and commenting upon unfolding racism rows involving premier league football players, clubs and referees as well as candidates standing for office from political parties—including, most conspicuously, UKIP.

Beyond the coverage of the Stephen Lawrence case, crime/law and order was identified as the third most significant theme—in 10.8% of articles (n = 63). The analysis that follows focuses specifically on this section of the coverage, providing a detailed critical analysis of right-wing press discourses on crime, law and order and racism during this period. It examines three key areas: (1) the 'news hooks' (or main issues carrying the news value of stories), (2) practices of racism (the acts, expressions or behaviours identified with or represented *as* racism) and (3) key narrative roles (how the attribution 'victim' and 'villain' are attached) within stories.

Table 11.1 Racism news main themes

	Mail	Sun	Telegraph	Total
Sport	68	112	72	43.1% (*n* = 252)
Politics	45	36	45	21.5% (*n* = 126)
Crime/law and order	**16**	**24**	**23**	**10.8% (*n* = 63)**
Media	10	14	17	7% (*n* = 41)
Stephen Lawrence	8	11	8	4.6% (*n* = 27)
Other	10	10	6	4.4% (*n* = 26)
International	1	8	16	4.3% (*n* = 25)
Migration/asylum	4	2	4	1.7% (*n* = 10)
Education	2	3	3	1.4% (*n* = 8)
Public opinion	1	2	2	0.9% (*n* = 5)
Religion	0	1	0	0.2% (*n* = 1)
Debates about multiculturalism	0	1	0	0.2% (*n* = 1)
Total	**165**	**224**	**196**	**585**

News Hooks[1]

The most featured 'news hook' and single most frequently covered crime/law and order story during monitoring (22.2% of articles) concerned revelations that the newly appointed Youth Crime Commissioner for Kent, 17-year-old Paris Brown, had published racist and homophobic comments on Twitter. A flagship initiative in Kent, the Youth PCC was intended to help 'bring more public accountability to police and crime policy' and to symbolise the decentralisation of power to young people as those most likely to be victims of crime. The story carried news value because of the potential damage to the reputation of a young woman and to the standing of the office of 'Youth PCC' in which such political investment had been made. Like other high profile 'rows', 'controversies' or 'scandals' featuring the alleged use of racist language by public figures (e.g., those involving Premiership footballers, John Terry and Luis Suárez in 2011–2012), this story promoted a clear interpretation of racism as a grave transgression of social norms and values. Yet the symbolic currency of mediated scandals are also dependent upon the degree to which social disapproval is expressed (Thompson 2000), a feature that in racism scandals, where personalism may play a role, may be lessened or amplified by the supposed intentionality, intelligence or moral competence of the perpetrator (e.g., a thoughtless teenager) and the circumstances in which they made the offensive utterance (e.g., poor humour, a 'gaffe' or ill-advised comment 'in the heat of the moment' or under pressure). In the case of Paris Brown, her racism denial, tearful apology and prostration in personal shame seems largely to have been accepted as factors mitigating her transgression:

> I deeply apologise for any offence caused by my use of inappropriate language and for any inference of inappropriate views. I am not homophobic, racist or violent and am against the taking of drugs. If I'm guilty of anything it's showing off and wildly exaggerating on Twitter and I am very ashamed of myself, but I can't imagine that I'm the only teenager to have done this. (*Daily Telegraph*, 8 April 2013)

Her personal testimony offers a strategic moral concession to rescue her essential sense of self from the disgrace of prejudice—confessing to be a 'normal', flawed teenager, simply making mistakes. Whilst on the one hand, then, racism is positioned as a signifier of moral depravity, on the other it is one simply expressed through insult—offensive individual behaviour, that can be avoided by learning life skills in 'appropriate' social conduct. In this calculation, when prejudicial attitudes are divorced from their outward expression, they potentially remain socially untroubling. Moreover, any notion of racism as anything other than 'prejudice'—irrationality or error in individual beliefs about culturally or ethnically 'other' categories of people—is absent from the discourse. The headlines demonstrate how what is represented as morally and socially reintegrating is the public shaming of individuals:

FORCE INSISTS: WE WERE RIGHT TO QUESTION PARIS [...]
shamed youth crime commissioner (*Mail on Sunday*, 21 April 2013)

CRYING SHAME OF CRIME TSAR AGE 17; Apology over violent rants; £15K teen: my tweets were stupid (*The Sun*, 8 April 2013)

The shift in focus of the scandal narrative onto the wisdom of the teenager's appointment also transfers the moral opprobrium away from the question of racism to the more general exercise of responsibility and political competence of the Kent PCC.

YOUTH CRIME CZAR POSTS RACIST TWEETS [...] One of Britain's new crime commissioners is under pressure to explain why she hired a teenager who posted violent and racist messages on the internet (*Sunday Telegraph*, 7 April, 2013)

TWEET 'N SOUR [...]...the violent, racist and homophobic tweets posted by Paris Brown would be unpleasant from any teenager, let alone one on the public payroll as a youth crime tsar. (*The Sun*, 8 April, 2013)

There is no space here for any notion of racism as a culture, a system of structural inequality embedded in social norms, values or institutions or as the everyday practices maintaining white privilege. Indeed, this is a tendency evidenced much more explicitly by the next most important news hook in the sample—the issue of 'sensitivity towards racism as a problem or danger to society'. Significantly, this news hook appeared in 20.6% of stories—significantly more than press discussions of racism itself as a danger or problem for society. Institutional racism was identified as a news hook in only two of the articles within this sample of crime/law and order news (Table 11.2).

Although arguably, the notion of racism as a threat or problem was implicitly signified within other stories (e.g., news of racially aggravated criminal acts), the prominence of a concern about (over)sensitivity nonetheless remains striking. Coverage included stories where sensitivity to racism was represented as a social threat in certain contexts, including the notion that it could be used to conceal criminal or anti-social activity. This idea was mainly conveyed through the Oxford abuse scandal—a widely reported, shocking story about the prolonged 'grooming' and sexual abuse of young girls by an organised gang of British Pakistani men. The news value of this investigation was compounded by the familiarity of the story with a similar scandal in Rotherham, which went to trial in 2010, and the serious failures to investigate on the part of police, social services and other authorities that rendered it a scandal. The story was

Table 11.2 News hooks in crime/law and order coverage

	Mail	Sun	Telegraph	Total
Youth PCC scandal	1.6%	11.1%	9.5%	22.2% (n = 14)
Sensitivity to racism as a danger/ problem for society	8.0%	4.8%	9.5%	20.6% (n = 13)
Other	7.9%	6.3%	4.8%	19.0% (n = 12)
Racially aggravated crime conviction(s)	0.0%	4.8%	4.8%	9.5% (n = 6)
Racism as a danger/problem for society	0.0%	4.8%	3.2%	8% (n = 5)
Racism is a crime	0.0%	3.2%	3.2%	6.3% (n = 4)
Racist murder	3.2%	1.6%	0.0%	4.8% (n = 3)
Institutional racism remains a problem/issue	0.0%	1.6%	1.6%	3.2% (n = 2)
Racism threatens/undermines reputation/position	3.2%	0.0%	0.0%	3.2% (n = 2)
UKIP	0.0%	0.0%	1.6%	1.6% (n = 1)
Racism in football	1.6%	0.0%	0.0%	1.6% (n = 1)
Total	25.4%	38.1%	36.5%	100.0% (n = 63)

not just one of incompetence, but of moral failing and confused priorities. Fashioned as an exposé of those failures, the news hook emphasised the damaging forces unleashed by supposed 'political correctness' and of privileging racism avoidance. Cultural sensitivities, reports suggested, had been 'exploited' by the abusers and used by those who sought to deny a more widespread problem in the British Pakistani Muslim community. A 'fear of racism', the *Daily Telegraph* claimed, had powerfully undermined the authorities responsible for protecting young women:

> There is growing concern that a wider issue is being brushed under the carpet because the authorities are fearful of being accused of racism (*Daily Telegraph*, May 18, 2013)

The primary concern of *Mail on Sunday* columnist Peter Hitchens too was to give voice to the fear of racism allegations—a demand for white middle-class vulnerability to be recognised set in a power play for justice against that for victims of sexual exploitation:

Like everyone who has any kind of public position, I know that an accusation of racism—even an entirely false one—could ruin my life… If Thames Valley Police or Oxfordshire County Council and its social workers deny that their wretched responses to these crimes were influenced by the same fear, then I simply do not believe them. It would be good if some of the newspapers of the Left would acknowledge this. In return, I'll agree with them that the law is a feeble protection for young girls exploited by older men. (*Mail on Sunday*, May 19, 2013)

Indeed, within this discourse, it is not self-protecting, reputation management per se that is positioned as the main problem (indeed, this is to varying degrees accepted as a rational, even if 'craven' priority) but a concern about racism accusations as the reputational threat in 'fearful, politically correct modern Britain' (*Daily Mail*, May 16, 2013). Furthermore, such concerns also provided a vehicle to reassert socially conservative prejudices about sexual politics and to reassert sweeping essentialist assumptions about anachronistic cultural values, ethnicity and violence:

We all know what happens next, don't we? Leaders of the Pakistani Muslim community—essentially a Victorian society that has landed like Doctor Who's Tardis on a liberal, permissive planet it despises—are at pains to deny that the grooming gang's behaviour has anything to do with ethnic origin or contemptible attitudes towards women. (*Daily Telegraph*, May 16, 2013)

However, an alternative strategy that featured within this news discourse was more directly to deny 'hate crime' as a legitimate social concern. On the potential prosecution of Paris Brown for hate crime, Rod Liddle asserted: 'Nobody other than a handful of far-Left loons in north London gives a monkey's about the sort of thing you call a "hate crime" […] so leave Paris alone—your police authority has already wasted enough money on the poor cow.' (*The Sun*, 11 April 2013).

Racist Practices

In each article, all practices represented as 'racism'—the acts, expressions or behaviours held to be 'racist'—were counted, with 79 in total identified across the sample. In three articles, no acts, expressions or behaviours were identified because racism was discussed in very general or abstract terms. The act or expression most often identified in 43% (*n* = 34) of the coverage was 'language' (43%, *n* = 34). This was in part attributable to the Paris Brown, Youth PCC story (Table 11.3).

However, a range of other stories, including the explicit reporting of investigations into alleged hate crimes, as well as other reports about racist 'slurs', 'taunts' and 'rants', were represented. These included the reporting of verbal attacks as serious and morally reprehensible, as, for example, in *The Sun* and the *Telegraph*'s 23 April articles about a white woman attacking an Asian passenger on the London underground (an incident video recorded and widely shared on YouTube) as a 'shameful rant'. However, they also included more glib coverage of alleged English anti-Welsh and Welsh anti-English 'racially aggravated disorderly behaviour', expressed through the distancing metadiscourse of reporting clauses and quotations in headlines, for example, 'SHEEP ABUSE WAS NOT

Table 11.3 Practices of racism in crime/law and order news

	Newspaper			
	Mail	Sun	Telegraph	Total
Language	7	16	11	43% (*n* = 34)
Killing(s)/murder(s)	2	3	4	11.4% (*n* = 9)
Other	4	0	3	8.9% (*n* = 7)
Attitudes/views	0	4	2	7.6% (*n* = 6)
Institutional racism	0	1	4	6.3% (*n* = 5)
Physical assault/violence/de-veiling	1	3	0	5.1% (*n* = 4)
Images/symbols	0	2	1	3.8% (*n* = 3)
Fascist org. membership/support	2	0	1	3.8% (*n* = 3)
Songs	0	0	2	2.5% (*n* = 2)
Assault on/damage to property	1	0	1	2.5% (*n* = 2)
UKIP membership/support	0	0	2	2.5% (*n* = 2)
Physical gestures	0	1	0	1.3% (*n* = 1)
Other org. membership/support	0	0	1	1.3% (*n* = 1)
Total	17	30	32	100% (*n* = 79)

AIMED ONLY AT WELSH, COURT TOLD' (*Daily Telegraph*, 29 April) and 'SEX JIBE "IS RACIST"' (*The Sun*, 28 April). Very few articles, by contrast, considered racism as an expression of institutional or social power, with those that did largely reporting the 20th anniversary of the killing of Stephen Lawrence. Yet, even in this coverage, the very idea of 'institutional racism' was rather distanced from the journalistic voice. In 'COPS ARE STILL RACIST SAY ETHNIC MINORITIES' (*The Sun*, 22 April), for example, the headline does not make it at all clear that it is the view of racism as a *systemic problem* that is being reported. It is through the results of a 'damning poll' that finds 'two in three black and Asian people deem police "institutionally racist"' that the term is introduced. Again, quotation marks play a metadiscursive, distancing role, as if the objectivity of journalistic discourse sensibly requires the label to be open to conjecture rather than settled or socially accepted as a result of the historic and transformative 1999 Macpherson inquiry: 'An inquiry called the Met "institutionally racist"'.

This was also reflected in the narrative focal points within stories, where only 10% focused on the social impact (*n* = 3) or institutional trend (*n* = 3) of racism. Overwhelmingly, the narrative focus of stories centred on individuals alleged to be racist (54%, *n* = 34), with the alleged targets or victims largely absent from the coverage (4.8%, *n* = 3) (Fig. 11.1).

Victim and Villain Roles

The nuanced narratives of right-wing press coverage about racism are brought into greater focus when we examine how oppositional roles in relation to which sympathy and identification on the one hand, and responsibility and blame on the other, are invited and attached to actors involved in or subjected to racism in crime/law and order stories. Given what we know about the usually polarised patterns of crime news, where the innocence of victims is represented in binary opposition to the villainy of perpetrators, the results are perhaps surprisingly equivocal. In

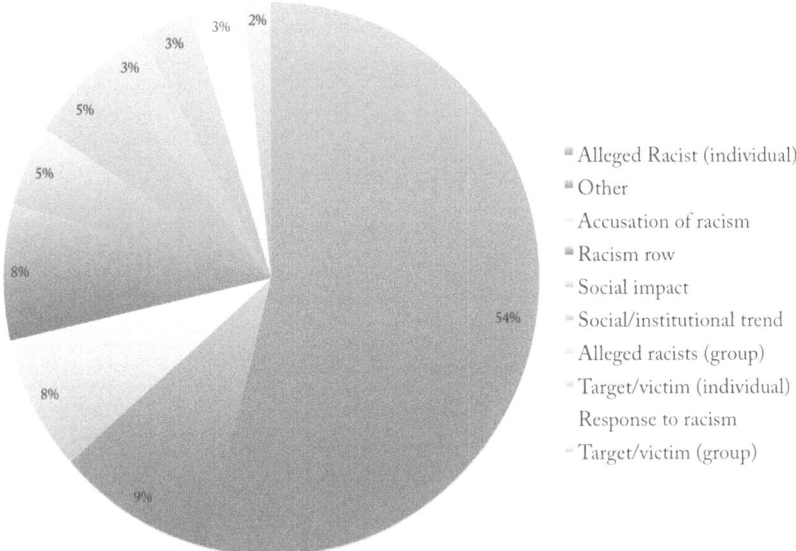

Fig. 11.1 Narrative focus

racism news, whilst we see that those identified as 'villains' are largely aligned with those accused of racism in relation to a range of different practices, we also see some instances when this is not the case (Fig. 11.2). Perhaps most surprisingly, in several articles, alleged targets of racism are represented as the 'villains' of the story—once in a story about a local campaign to close a gypsy camp and twice in relation to the Oxford abuse scandal. In each of these stories, the alleged victims of racism are positioned in a very negative context by other features of the story, and the journalistic voice is distanced from social ideas presupposed to be 'out there' representing particular groups as victims of racism.

More interestingly, perhaps, are those stories where those making accusations of racism are positioned as 'the villains'. One *Daily Telegraph* opinion piece sardonically reported Greater Manchester Police's suggestion for 'extending its definition of recordable hate crime to include alternative subcultures'. Contending that 'it's morality we need to invoke: not the law', the columnist seeks to demonstrate the partiality of such proposals:

Fig. 11.2   Villains of racist practices in crime news

Who is picked on automatically as uncaring, snobby and greedy? Who is jeered at and never given the benefit of the doubt (unless they're Boris)? Who never gets a fair hearing from the Left? Choose any of the following sample: posh people, Etonians, Tories or practitioners of field sports. Who are automatically identified as bigots? Orangemen and Tea Partiers. And as a sceptic who gets vilified as a "climate change denier" I want protection too. (*Daily Telegraph*, April 5 2013)

The notion that accusations of racism are essentially meaningful as an exercise of power, an insult to gain an advantage over one's opponent or an ill-conceived platform upon which to assume a moral high ground was also reinforced in articles where the 'villain' of the story was unclear. A *Daily Mail* article about clashes between football fans in the wake of a divisive managerial appointment, for example, notes how, 'local fans had taunted their Sunderland rivals with open-palm salutes, a reference to last month's controversial appointment of Paolo di Canio—who has described himself as a fascist, but not a racist' (*Daily Mail*, 15 April, 2013). In other articles, suspicions about the racist motivations of opposing immigration were at stake. One letter writer chastised Labour government policies as promoting an 'open door' on immigration, claiming indignantly: 'Anyone who doubted it was classed as a racist' (*The Sun*, 10 April 2013). Elsewhere, in the *Daily Telegraph*, an apology was demanded from Rotherham borough council for their alleged 'ridiculous mistake' of removing two children with minority ethnic backgrounds from the care of foster parents because their membership of UKIP meant 'they supported "racist" immigration policies' (22 May 2013). There were some instances where questioning the rationality of hate crime law was represented as a result of anachronistic ideas about acceptable behaviour (e.g., a 'great-grandfather' from Warwickshire who erected a sign stating 'No Eastern Europeans' as he suspected them of stealing his carp: 'I was staggered. I've never been racist in my entire life but I have to remove the signs because I don't want a criminal record') (*Daily Mail*, 11 April, 2013). However, it was largely with respect to 'hate crime', and more general concerns about accusations of racism or institutional change that figures other than 'alleged racists' were positioned as the 'villain of a story'.

Turning to how victims of racism were portrayed, we also see a some-what surprising picture. In 42.4% (n = 28) of articles, although racism featured, no clear identification of a victim or victims of racism was pos-sible—victims being either entirely absent from the narrative or too pas-sively invoked in its background to be accurately identified. Whilst this resulted, in part, from a small number of articles featuring abstract or general philosophical discussions about racism, mostly this does not account for the absence of victims from the narrative, including in hate crime, harassment stories and legal cases.

When we look in finer detail at the kinds of practices represented as racism when a victim role is and isn't clearly identified, we can see that the acts most likely to be disconnected from victims are verbal expressions, attitudes/views and symbolic acts/gestures, as well as membership of fas-cist organisations. A greater number of articles in which 'language' was identified as a racist practice had no clearly identified victim than the number of articles that did have a clearly identified victim, whereas phys-ical or violent attacks almost always involved the identification of the victim as the alleged target of the racist attack. As with the identification of 'villains', there were some surprising results, with the alleged racists sometimes identified as the victim within the narrative. Since most of these featured the news hook, 'sensitivity to racism as a danger or threat to society', they have been discussed above—including reflections about damage to personal reputations possibly due to accusations of racism, such as the Peter Hitchens' column (*Daily Mail*, 19 May, 2013) and those concerning supposed overzealous policing of opponents to immigration, such as the UKIP supporting Rotherham couple whose foster children were removed (*Daily Telegraph*, 22 May 2013) (Fig. 11.3).

In some examples, experiences of racism were reported to have pro-voked a violent response, for example, the *Sun* reported how 'A thug has been jailed for nine years for launching a hammer attack on a fellow party guest who made a "racist" joke' (13 April 2013). In another story, a cam-paign group seeking to prevent the development of a travellers' site in their area were represented as victims of alleged retaliation by those believing themselves to be racially persecuted:

> There have occasionally been ugly scenes. RAID's chairman, David McGrath, has received multiple death threats. Lawson Reading, an activist

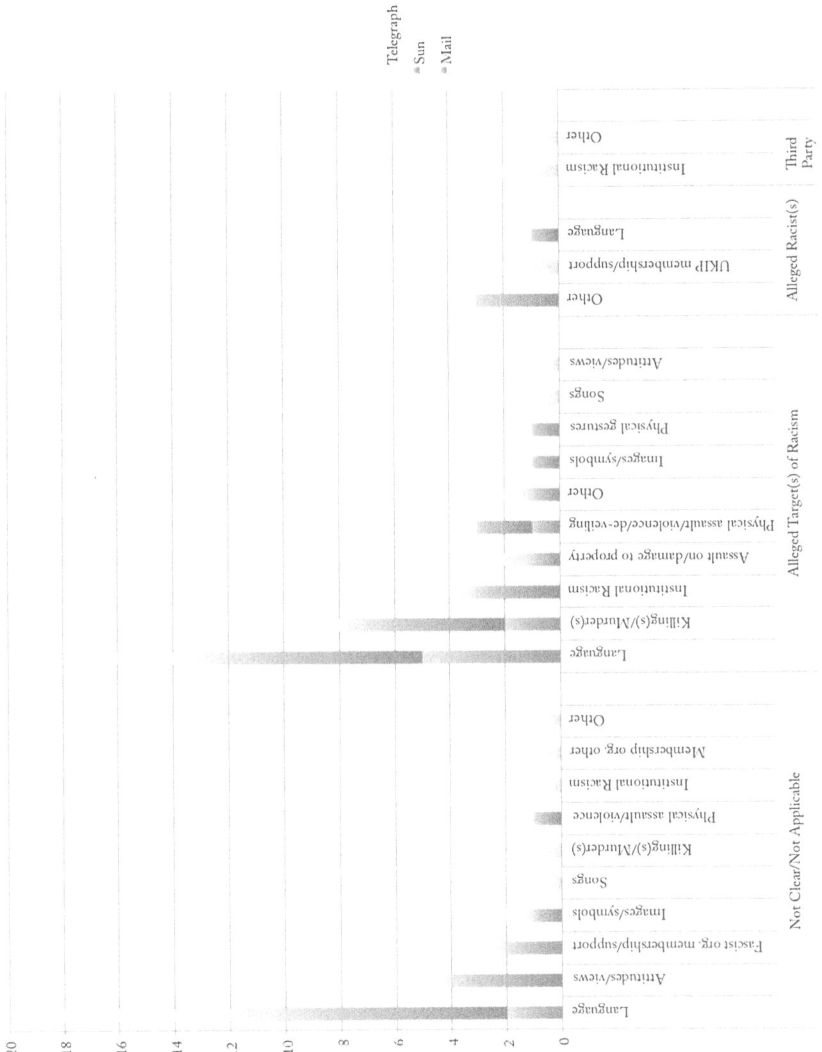

Fig. 11.3 Victims of racist practices in crime news

who lives near to the site, has seen his home vandalised. 'It's low-level stuff, he tells me, but stupid'. In his occasional public pronouncements, gipsy leader Mr Burton, who calls himself 'the Bin Laden of Meriden', has claimed his opponents are motivated by racism. 'They say they are flying the flag for the green belt, but it's just a cover up for their prejudice' he has said. The truth is that nobody wants a gipsy in their back garden. (*Daily Mail*, 30 March, 2013)

Through the use of quotation marks (i.e., 'racist') or by questioning the credibility and reliability of their testimony in both of these examples, the journalistic voice was distanced from the definition of racism suggested by those claiming to have experienced it, and the victimhood of the alleged racist therefore maintained as a legitimate narrative trope.

Conclusion

It is evidently *not* the case that right-wing press coverage of crime and law and order is simply dismissive of racism. Indeed, some extraordinarily vociferous condemnations of racism are to be found where racism is denounced, unambiguously, as socially offensive, represented as the moral responsibility of every decent individual. Indeed, through what Hill calls a 'personalist' discourse, the right-wing press demonstrate how the destructive potential of 'racism' is taken hugely seriously, although towards whom that violence is unleashed, with what degree of intentionality and to what end is not always so clear. Racism generally is 'bad', right-wing press discourse tells us, but how its result is suffered and by whom is infrequently explored. In crime news, racism further aggravates thuggish violence. More often, however, it is racist language (the enunciation of racist slurs, insults or words interpreted as such) in the news agenda. With respect to racist language, the moral discourse is less absolute and the lines between villainy and victimhood are sometimes less clear-cut. Accusations of racism can themselves be villainous, potentially doing violence to an individual's reputation. Alleged racists, the right-wing press remind us, can be victims too! On the other hand, reputation management is figured as a personal responsibility, about which being 'sensible' is a moral virtue par excellence. In failure, performing shame, contrition and learning quickly to mend your ways is essential. Having only oneself to blame is figured as a 'vulnerability' of 'us all'. Whilst 'institutional racism' may, occasionally, be sombrely acknowledged as a disgraceful cultural residue within some institutions, other news makes plain that to become too anxious about 'institutional racism' or to become *too sensitive* towards racism as a problem may be to invite exploitation, to impair 'common sense' thinking, or to induce serious failures in the face of greater evils (as, e.g., in Oxford or Rochdale).

'Racism' according to the image drawn in the right-wing press is morally abhorrent, but overwhelmingly, it is drawn very narrowly as the expression of individual prejudice in inappropriate or insulting language. There is little or no recognition of racism as a culture or as embedded in systems reproducing inequity and domination. This is a discourse that reinforces white privilege, not by denying racism entirely but in choosing to challenge it within very limited bounds, policed by defensive strategies that shore up white racial codes (van Dijk 1992). In this, the UK right-wing press protects the 'white fragility' of its readers, contributing to what DiAngelo identifies as 'the continual retreat from the discomfort of authentic racial engagement', promoting a culture with 'limited ability to form authentic connections across racial lines' and 'a cycle that works to hold racism in place.' (DiAngelo 2011: 66).

Notes

1. Included in the category 'other' is a range of news hooks relating to more general stories where racism was not the main reason for the story being newsworthy. These included, for example, coverage of the first speech of the new Chief Inspector of Constabulary, discussion of the unruly behaviour of football fans and a feature about the law breaking/anti-social behaviour of multiple members of a large family.

References

Augoustinos, M., & Every, D. (2007). The Language of 'Race' and Prejudice: A Discourse of Denial, Reason, and Liberal-Practical Politics. *Journal of Language and Social Psychology, 26*(2), 123–141.

Augoustinos, M., & Every, D. (2010). Accusations and Denials of Racism: Managing Moral Accountability in Public Discourse. *Discourse & Society, 21*(3), 251–256.

Bonilla-Silva, E. (2006). *Racism Without Racists: Color Blind Racism and the Persistence of Racial Inequality in the United States* (2nd ed.). New York: Rowman & Littlefield.

Cohen, S. (2004 [1972]). *Folk Devils and Moral Panics* (3rd ed.). London: Routledge.

Cottle, S. (2005). Mediatized Public Crisis and Civil Society Renewal: The Racist Murder of Stephen Lawrence. *Crime, Media, Culture, 1*(1), 49–71.

Cottle, S. (2006). *Mediatized Conflict.* Maidenhead and Berkshire: Open University Press.

Critcher, C. (2003). *Moral Panics and the Media.* Buckingham: Open University Press.

DiAngelo, R. (2011). White Fragility. *International Journal of Critical Pedagogy, 3*(3), 54–70.

Dixon, J., & Levine, M. (2012). *Beyond Prejudice: Extending the Social Psychology of Conflict, Inequality and Social Change.* Cambridge: Cambridge University Press.

Fox, J. E., Moroşanu, L., & Szilassy, E. (2012). The Racialization of the New European Migration to the UK. *Sociology, 46*(4), 680–695.

Galtung, J., & Ruge, M. (1965). The Structure of Foreign News: The Presentation of the Congo, Cuba and Cyprus Crises in Four Norwegian Newspapers. *Journal of International Peace Research, 2*(1), 64–91.

Galtung, J., & Ruge, M. (1981). Structuring and Selecting News. In S. Cohen & J. Young (Eds.), *The Manufacture of News.* London: Constable.

Goldberg, D. T. (1999 [1988]). The Social Formation of Racist Discourse. In D. T. Goldberg (Ed.), *Anatomy of Racism.* London and Minnesota: University of Minnesota Press.

Goldberg, D. T. (2009). *Racist Culture: Philosophy and the Politics of Meaning.* Hoboken, NJ: Wiley.

Hall, S. (1997). *Representation: Cultural Representations and Signifying Practices.* London: Sage.

Hall, S. (2000). *The Multicultural Question.* Paper Presented at the Political Economy Research Centre Annual Lecture, Firth Hall Sheffield. Retrieved July 7, 2017, from http://red.pucp.edu.pe/wp-content/uploads/biblioteca/Stuart_Hall_The_multicultural_question.pdf

Hall, S., Critcher, C., Jefferson, T., Clarke, J., & Roberts, B. (1978). *Policing the Crisis: Mugging, the State, and Law and Order.* Basingstoke and Hampshire: Palgrave Macmillan.

Harcup, T., & O'Neill, D. (2017). What Is News? *Journalism Studies, 18*(12), 1–19.

Hill, J. H. (2009). *The Everyday Language of White Racism.* Oxford: Wiley-Blackwell.

Jenkins, P. (1992). *Intimate Enemies: Moral Panics in Contemporary Great Britain.* New York: Aldine de Gruyter.

Jewkes, Y. (2015). *Media and Crime* (3rd ed.). London: Sage.

Kobayashi, A. (2009). 'Here We Go Again': Christchurch's Antiracism Rally as a Discursive Crisis. *New Zealand Geographer, 65*(1), 59–72.

Lynn, N., & Lea, S. (2003). 'A Phantom Menace and the New Apartheid': The Social Construction of Asylum-Seekers in the United Kingdom. *Discourse and Society, 14*(4), 425–452.

Moore, K. (2012). "Asylum Crisis", National Security and the Re-articulation of Human Rights. In K. Moore, B. Gross, & T. Threadgold (Eds.), *Migrations and the Media.* New York: Peter Lang.

Moore, K., Jewell, J., & Cushion, S. (2011). *Reach Media Monitoring Report.* Cardiff: Cardiff School of Journalism, Media and Cultural Studies.

Poole, E. (2011). Change and Continuity in the Representation of British Muslims Before and After 9/11: The UK Context. *Global Media Journal: Canadian Edition, 4*(2), 49–62.

Seidel, G. (1988). The British New Right's "Enemy Within": The Antiracists. In G. Smitherman-Donaldson & T. A. van Dijk (Eds.), *Discourse and Discrimination.* Detroit: Wayne State University Press.

Thompson, J. B. (2000). *Political Scandal: Power and Visibility in the Media Age.* Cambridge: Polity Press.

van Dijk, T. A. (1992). Discourse and the Denial of Racism. *Discourse and Society, 3*, 87–118.

van Dijk, T. A. (1993). Denying Racism: Elite Discourse and Racism. In J. Solomos & J. Wrench (Eds.), *Racism and Migration in Western Europe* (pp. 179–193). Oxford: Berg.

12

Closeness and Distance in Media Reports on the Trollhättan Attack

Marta Kolankiewicz

The first live footage from the town of Trollhättan in Sweden appeared in the private nationwide station TV4 just a couple of hours after the alarm about the attack at the Kronan school.[1] Shaky and blurred shots show a reporter—his brows knitted, his gaze feverish—describing the events in the elementary school in real time and space. A headline at the bottom of the screen announces: "Acts of violence in a school in Trollhättan". The immediate presence of the camera that follows the irregular movements and the improvised account of the reporter in the middle of the crowd gathering by the school directly evokes a sensation of closeness to the scene. Through the technological, narrative and aesthetic properties of live footage—"the genre of witness, par excellence"—spectators are placed in the middle of the drama as it unfolds (Chouliaraki 2006: 159). Moreover, by interrupting the scheduled broadcasts, breaking news confronts us with the extraordinary and produces a sense of emergency. In this way, the Trollhättan attack becomes of national concern and the spectator engages with the suffering other instantaneously and intensively.[2]

M. Kolankiewicz (✉)
Lund University, Lund, Sweden

© The Author(s) 2018
M. Bhatia et al. (eds.), *Media, Crime and Racism*, Palgrave Studies in Crime,
Media and Culture, https://doi.org/10.1007/978-3-319-71776-0_12

In this chapter, I will analyse the ways in which closeness and distance towards those affected by the attack in Trollhättan were produced in the media in the hours and days after the event. My point of departure is an insight that news not only represents or reports on the suffering but also shapes possible responses to this suffering. I am here inspired by Lilie Chouliaraki who treats media discourse as acts of identity that by "engaging the spectators and sufferers in various relationships of proximity and agency to one another,… ultimately construe some sufferings as being worthy of our pity and others as unworthy of it" (2006: 11). The workings of the media in such an approach consist in using an aesthetic and narrative spectacle to evoke affective responses in the audience. Following some feminist scholars, "affects" here, rather than being understood as natural emotions in the face of a scene of suffering, are defined as socially constructed dispositions to certain feelings, highly regulated by regimes of power (Butler 2009: 39). They constitute a peculiar force in the social relations not only between the audience and the media but also between the suffering and the spectators (Skeggs and Wood 2012: 6; Ahmed 2014). Thus, closeness and distance will be defined here as ways spectators are asked to relate to the suffering other, which are shaped by the aesthetic and narrative workings of the news spectacle by evoking particular affects and in this way conditioning public responses to the suffering.

One of the striking things about the first live footage from Trollhättan is how the disrupting and trembling form of the visual and audio contrasts with the stillness of the disclosed scene. The dramatic accounts of police searching the school for more perpetrators; ambulances rushing in and out, one of them hitting the wall of the building; a crowd trying to force its way into the school—all come to us through the narrative of the reporter. The background images captured by the camera reveal instead a gathering of people suspended in a tense state of waiting. What we would learn afterwards is that at that point the actual attack was already over, but the children and others present in the school at the time of the attack would be kept inside several hours until the police had secured the place. What the audience was invited to witness was thus the wait: the wait to find out what had actually happened, why and how, and what kind of consequences the event would have.

The condition of waiting informed however the first media reports in a more overwhelming and profound way. It was not only about showing the wait of those directly concerned, gathered in front of the school, in the local hospital and places specially prepared for the families. It was also the wait of the media audience before an official interpretation of the event had been established, which happened in the morning of the day after the attack, when the police declared that the attack had been a racist hate crime. I am interested in the media reporting during this time of waiting. I treat this time as a prolonged moment of interruption of the everyday, in which the spectators become intensively engaged in an extraordinary drama. It is also a time of tension before the unknown, of undecidability operating as "dialectics of openness and closure" (Chouliaraki 2006). A time in which what Chouliaraki calls "ecstatic news" operates, "that which seeks to resolve the radical undecidability of the event it reports during the act of reporting itself" (2006: 158). I claim that in this time—from the moment that the news about the attack breaks until the moment that a hegemonic knowledge about the attack is established—the media will play a special role in installing frames, through which the audience will look at the event. I use the term "frames", following Judith Butler, to denote interpretative schemes that seek to "contain, convey, and determine what is seen" (Butler 2009). Frames depend upon reproducibility, which means that they are culturally and politically anchored in existing knowledge and power regimes. In this sense, the media mobilise interpretations that are already accessible to and intelligible for audience, but they do it in discreet and suggestive ways rather than through persuasion and argumentation. What is important here is that frames enable affective responses to the suffering of the other, defining in this way some lives as grievable. I will argue that frames do this by producing closeness and distance between spectators and the suffering other, but also that closeness and distance draw on and re-establish certain hierarchies of belonging.

Thus, in this chapter, I will identify and analyse frames installed by the media in the first hours after the attack and explore narrative, aesthetic and affective ways in which distance and closeness are created by each of these frames.[3]

"This Can Happen in Sweden": The Compassionate Spectatorship

> What strikes me most is that … that this has happened. Everyone seems to be shocked in one way or another that this can happen in Sweden, in tiny, tiny Trollhättan, which is not a town that … if you hear about this type of event it is often abroad … in other towns. The fact that it happens here … there is a feeling of unreality that has settled over Kronogården.

The first frame emerges in conjunction with the closeness provoked by the extraordinary place that the news occupied in the media on the day of the event, interrupting the regular boundaries between what Chouliaraki calls the zone of safety and the zone of suffering (2006). It is from this location of closeness that an instantaneous identification emerged. The news reporters' ordinary distant objectivism was replaced by a testimonial style and an emotional tone. One way in which the effect of closeness was created was thus related to the fact that the scene of suffering took place within the national borders. The ordinary comfort of the distant spectatorship was thereby interrupted. The "shock" referred to in the above account was one of the most used words to describe the atmosphere in the town in the headlines all over the media, like the one from the Swedish News Agency: "Grief and shock after the school attack".

The personal tone in which the reporter of the public nationwide TV station SVT1, quoted above, referred to her own reactions and feelings returned in several reports during the first hours and days after the attack. Through the description of their own reaction, emotions and feelings, journalists created an intimate relation with the event as something that affected them personally. In this way, the emotions of those close to the attack, survivors and their families, were presented to the distant spectators through potential identification:

> We have spoken to pupils who saw this man stabbing people and who then barricaded themselves in classrooms … Of course such information does not leave anybody unaffected. We have all gone to school in our lives.

The identification was here possible through the establishment of a universal dimension of the experience. In a similar way, the experiences of relatives of the persons inside the school—horror and tension resulting from not knowing whether one's relative was safe—were often appropriated by newspapers in the form of personal accounts.

> The phone vibrates in my pocket. First once, twice, three times, four, five times. … It is news-flashes from all Swedish newspapers. At the top, one from Sydsvenskan [the largest newspaper in the southern region of Sweden]: "Many injured in a school". My brain immediately connects injured, a school and Sydsvenskan, and I am caught in a split-second horror—my daughter goes to an elementary school in Lund. What happened? It turns out to be an act of violence in a school in Trollhättan. My daughter is out of danger. I can breathe freely. The parents of the children in Trollhättan cannot.

The initial reports were imbued with the atmosphere at the scene and in the town and the reporters' testimonial accounts disclosed their own shock, fear and horror. Feelings were also the focus of many interviews with those who had seen the attack or the families of the victims, which, falling into commodified sentimentalism, risked reducing the spectators' witnessing of suffering to voyeurism, by "'appropriating' the sufferer as someone who shares our own humanity" (Silverstone in: Chouliaraki 2013: 141). The inclusive frame of such reporting consists thus in a universalisation of the suffering. And the attack becomes an attack against each and every one of us. All the spectators become vulnerable by the mere force of identification.

These accounts were quickly followed by the advice of professionals—psychologists and other experts working with crisis situations. Including online newspapers offering interactive spaces for sharing emotions: "Write here about your feelings about Trollhättan", or giving psychological advice: "How to talk to your children", the spectators were treated as those who suffered the trauma. In this way, the suffering becomes not only appropriated but also pushed towards the private sphere of each and every spectator, and the resolution is to take place on individual level and in psychological terms. Such an invocation of emotional reactions and psychological ways of dealing with them draws on popular therapeutic discourses. These have been saturating television in the last decades using a therapeutic and confessional strategy that "dislocates social and political conflicts onto individuals and families, privatises both the experience of oppression and possible modes of resistance to it, and translates political questions into psychological issues to be resolved through personal, psychological change" (Cloud in: Garde-Hansen and Gorton 2013: 50).

Parallel, however, the event is treated as a national tragedy, which almost immediately triggers public mourning. In the evening news bulletins, there are features about the attack displaying the Swedish flag at half mast with a voice-over informing of the school attack. Clips showing the Swedish prime minister paying tribute to the victims by leaving flowers on the scene and pronouncing that "This is a black day for Sweden" raise the status of the suffering into that of a national tragedy and define the zone of suffering as belonging to the nation.

How the identification works in this frame has much to do with the particular character of the space in which the attack took place. Schools are not only places that most of spectators are assumed to have some experience of. By being the daily space of children, schools, in particular elementary schools, are related to the idea of childhood as exceptionally innocent and vulnerable. From the very beginning of the media reporting on Trollhättan, the attack is presented in the media as a school attack and thereby mobilises the imaginary of school shootings, mainly connoted with the United States, but also influenced by recent school attacks in Germany and Finland. In the special coverage in the public nationwide TV station SVT1, the newsreader in the studio guests an expert from the National Operations Department. While the journalist is eager to discuss the possible nature and causes of the attack, the police expert shows himself reluctant to speculate further. His replies to the questions are laconic and vague: "no details", "too early to know", "it's impossible to say", "we don't know yet". Finally, he cuts the newsreader short: "I don't want to say what kind of event it is". He also questions whether one can in general talk about school attacks as a homogenous type of event. Still, the interpretation that we are dealing with a typical school attack seems to be quickly adopted by the media. Newspaper articles often include a fact box in which the Trollhättan school attack is placed in a chronology of cases of violence in schools in Sweden. Both the ways in which the fact boxes distinguish themselves from the rest of the articles that constitute more of a journalistically established knowledge and the historicised character of their narrative offer an authoritative interpretation of the attack as belonging to a specific history and category of violence.

Finally, framing the Trollhättan attack as a school attack has its implications for the ways in which the causes of and the responsibility for the attack are defined. The issue of responsibility is not limited to the urge to identify the perpetrator and disclose his motives, but also includes the broader question of responsibility for security. Framing the attack as a school attack in combination with the tone of national emergency embraced by the media leads to numerous discussions about school safety and the open nature of schools in Sweden. In this way, the Trollhättan school attack becomes a political issue concerning the ways of organising schools as a particularly important space for the nation.

"A Problem-Ridden School": Kronogården as a Threat

When the reporter on location in the live coverage in TV4, referred to in the opening of the chapter, has given the first overview of the scene of the attack, he passes to the studio in Stockholm. Behind the news desk, a newsreader together with a journalist responsible for collecting information about the attack, behind them flashing TV screens, bring us back to the stability and distanced tone of a regular news bulletin. The guest journalist is asked to provide some background to contextualise the event. He begins with some general information about the school that is enumerated in the convention of an objective comment, which— although using cautious epistemic modalities—deliver facts in a concise and dry form. The reliability of the presented information is supported by the source: a politician and a local freelance photographer.

> This is supposed to be a school from preschool to 9th grade, from what I understand … It is located in [the neighbourhood of] Kronogården and,

according to politicians in Trollhättan, it is a rather problem-ridden school. We heard here earlier a freelance photographer … who told us that it has been a rather vulnerable neighbourhood, with quite a lot of mess, a shooting two hundred meters away from the school earlier this autumn, but otherwise a very nice school, well-behaved and everything.

When the newsreader in the studio asks the reporter on location to confirm this information, he rephrases this description:

Maybe you could add something about this neighbourhood? About the neighbourhood? Because it is a segregated neighbourhood where there has been quite a lot of unrest, hasn't there?

The reporter on location answers these questions drawing on his personal experience of having worked in the neighbourhood:

Yes, that's right. I have periodically worked here in Trollhättan … When you went to Kronogården, the stories were about flourishing local association life, a successful integration project, but also quite a lot of what one could describe as suburban problems. There is a large share of people with immigrant background in this neighbourhood.

In this exchange between the three journalists, there is a shift from information about school as problematic to a definition of the neighbourhood as problematic. The problem is alternately described as vulnerability, messiness and unrest, evoking an imaginary of violence. It is also here that we are told that the neighbourhood is segregated and many of those living there are described as people with immigrant background. Back in the studio, the image of the area in which the school is located is again confirmed, but now a reservation is made that this does not necessarily explain the ongoing drama in Trollhättan.

Yes, we heard also [the freelance journalist] telling us that there had been car fires, there was a shooting as late as this autumn. So there has been unrest. But … this does not mean that we need to link this with the events today.

And we see the reporter on location nodding:

> Yes, indeed … yes, indeed … It's a mixture of people who are worried about their children and relatives. We don't know anything about the causes of this.

Already at this early stage of the live reporting about the Trollhättan attack, the school is being placed in a very particular space—the suburb. By bringing the imagery of burning cars and shootings and by describing the neighbourhood in terms of unrest and problems, an imaginary is set in motion. The use of the phrase: "what one could describe as suburban problems" by the reporter on location, suggests that he refers to a common knowledge that is already there—intelligible and recognisable to the spectators. A long tradition of media depictions of Swedish suburbs is brought about. Since the 1960s, when the public housing program known as *miljonprogrammet* was initiated, media reports have tended to represent suburbs in very special terms. The media focus was initially on the suburban landscape, with dirt and disorder as main attributes. With time, the very same attributes were projected onto those inhabiting this landscape and defined as characteristic of the social and moral terrain of the place, with class as an important marker (Ericsson in: Ericsson, Molina et al. 2002: 70). What Ericsson calls a "distant closeness" is created towards the suburbs, with media "connect[ing] people to a specific geographic space and portray[ing] both the individual and the suburb as separate and distinct from the rest of society" (Ericsson in: Ericsson et al. 2002: 91). When later the category of immigrant is added to this imaginary, the suburban space becomes racialised. In this way, the discursive topography of the suburb is constructed (Ericsson in: Ericsson et al. 2002). It has become widespread and well established in recent years, with media coverage of what was called unrest or riots in several suburbs in Sweden, often conflated with events in suburbs in other European countries. It is not accidental that the issue of the sufferers' racial or ethnic background is articulated for the first time on this occasion, and the way in which it is done is significant. The ethnicity or race is partly detached from those targeted in the attack to be projected on the school and the entire neighbourhood and associated with "what one could describe as suburban problems". The imaginary of the suburb mobilises particular politics of fear, as a consequence of which young people in the suburb emerge as bearers of threat and social disorder (for an analysis of similar dynamics in other places in Europe, see Back 2011). In this context, the early information provided by the media—that the victims are not children, but youngsters—may be telling. The innocence of children is here substituted by suspicion of young, racialised, suburban men.

Even though the suburb imaginary is here invoked in a suggestive and ambiguous way and even though it is almost directly questioned as potentially having no relevance to the story, the frame has already been set and a certain distance from the suffering other has been created. And thus, when the reporter at the end stresses that these are just people who are worried about their relatives, the spectator is pushed to know that these are not just any people. The boundary between the zone of suffering and the zone of safety is re-established and thereby the initial closeness and the possibility of a compassionate response disrupted. The neighbourhood of Kronogården becomes just another place located in the zone of suffering in which violence is a mundane and ordinary part of everyday life. But the frame does more than that: by describing the school as problem-ridden and the neighbourhood as a space of unrest, not only is the suffering other presented in a particular way but also the idea of who the spectators are changes. The audience is split into those located in the comfort zone "where people have the dubious privilege of being spectators, or of declining to be spectators, of other people's pain" (Sontag 2004: 85) and those who have some relation to the zone of suffering, often through association with the suburb. Moreover, these zones receive different statuses in the construction of the imagined national space. Particular hierarchies of belonging are established.

Furthermore, once the neighbourhood of Kronogården is portrayed as a source of problems and a daily scene of violence and disorder, the issue of the cause of the attack is approached in a different way. Here, the analytical use of the concept "frame" follows the meaning of the word in English. To frame, as Butler notices, also means to incriminate an innocent person through the use of false evidence. "If one is 'framed,' then a 'frame' is constructed around one's deed such that one's guilty status becomes the viewer's inevitable conclusion. Some way of organising and presenting a deed leads to an interpretative conclusion about the deed itself" (Butler 2009: 10).

It is in this sort of accusatory style that the evening bulletin in TV4, on the day of the attack, dedicates a longer story to an evaluation made by the Swedish School Inspectorate earlier that year. Apart from the summary of the evaluation presented in a voice-over, the program displays a document from the Inspectorate. Presented like a piece of evidence, the document is there to support the claim that the school is problem-ridden. The official character of the document shown in the header provides it with due credibility: "Order of a fine for the elementary school Kronan in the Trollhättan municipality". The camera zooms in on the relevant text that is highlighted in yellow, suggesting a finding of investigative journalism. The visual is accompanied by a voice that reads the highlighted text:

> In some classes, the study environment is so poor that teachers have difficulties in providing proper teaching. Moreover, the school's work against harassment is insufficient and there has been harassment among pupils. The school is therefore not a safe place for all the pupils.

While the media's attention on the problems with the school's environment in the past and on the neighbourhood as a space of unrest at least partly shifted after the attack was officially defined as a hate crime, it seems to have deeply informed subsequent reporting from Trollhättan, including the ways in which pupils and other inhabitants of the neighbourhood were portrayed. In this sense, the frame provides what Butler calls a field of representability, that is, a field delimited through "non-figurable and, to some extent, non-intentional operation of power" (Butler 2009: 73–74). The accounts of certain lives are only possible to narrate within this field. Such effects of the workings of the frame were visible in multiple features in the media on the victims of the Trollhättan attack. In particular, the teacher assistant Lavin Eskandar, who had tried to protected the children from the attacker and, was presented as an ordinary young man with dreams and hopes, creating music and films in his spare time. Such a portrayal functioned as an alternative account of one of those who work in the school and live in Kronogården: "a human being with dreams like everybody else", as Eskandar's cousin described him. This account remained in a dialogical relation with the accusatory frame, working as a counter-narrative to the usual narratives about young immigrant men from the suburbs.

The issue of responsibility is significantly transformed within this frame. It seems to be split along the lines that split the audiences. By projecting the guilt on the school and the neighbourhood, it becomes possible to disengage some segments of the audience. Thereby some of those spectators, who had just been invited to deeply identify with the suffering other, may now embark on detached witnessing in which suffering is located beyond them: neither affecting them, nor related to them.

Racism and Breaking from the Frame

When in the morning of the day after the attack the police hold a press conference at the local police station, the atmosphere is serious and heavy. Two police officers, a local police chief in uniform and the chief detective in civil clothes, sit behind a table on which several microphones are mounted. In a subdued voice, they report to the media on the state of the investigation. The main information for which the conference is called is that the deed has now been classified as a hate crime. This information is introduced through "we are completely convinced", which establishes the interpretation in categorical terms, leaving no space for discussion. Official knowledge of the attack is established in an authoritative mode, reflecting the police's authority to perform such interpretative speech acts. The press conference intends to explain the reasons for this interpretation, that is, to provide factual evidence gathered in the investigation and assessed as reliable according to the logics of legal knowledge regime, suggesting that a systematic and objective method has been used to establish the truth about the crime. The chief investigator begins with the first evidence: a document, "a kind of suicide letter", that has been found during the search of the perpetrator's house. The letter clearly indicates that this act was premeditated and that it was a hate crime. The other reason for classifying the crime as a hate crime is that the perpetrator "selected his victims so that those who had dark skin were subject to attack". The chief investigator continues, slowly, with his eyes fixed in the distance, carefully choosing his words: "he also met people with light skin and these were not attacked". During the later questions, another circumstance is mentioned: the perpetrator's clothes and the way in which he was marching in the school corridors during the attack "point in the Nazi direction". But this, the chief investigator adds, is only speculation.

The press conference represents a particular way of conveying an interpretation of the event. The media's role here seems to be limited to serving as an almost invisible channel for the authorities to establish official knowledge. The stable visuals make the spectator forget about the presence of the camera and thereby the medium, which enhances the impression of objectivity and impartiality. The frame in which the attack is captured as a racist crime is thus installed with much certitude, directly giving it the status of an authoritative account.

The information about the racist nature of the attack is repeated all over the media, almost always referring to the official police investigation as the source, and soon becomes an important part of the description of the causes of the attack and of the profile of the perpetrator. Interestingly, this frame will often figure side by side with the two other frames, in the same news bulletins, the same newspapers or even in the same articles. For instance, after the description of the event as a school attack targeting the whole of Sweden and revealing the necessity of a discussion about the openness of schools, the Kronan school could be described as problem-ridden and one of the worst rated in the country. This could be followed by a description of the perpetrator as having right-wing and Nazi sympathies and expressing negative opinions about refugees. Different frames are here combined in an eclectic way. This eclecticism seems to be related to a decomposition of the crime into discrete units: the event, the victims and the perpetrator. More importantly, the racist character of the crime is, in this type of accounts, limited to the racist subject, embodied by the villain, and to his explicit and overtly racist motives. Such an approach to racism builds on the idea of racist violence as identifiable through the presence of a racist subject as self-conscious and willing to give an open account of himself and his deeds (Kolankiewicz 2015: 146). Thereby racism becomes an issue of identity (Rattansi 2007: 119) attached to the figure of the racist and detached from the context of violent acts, the meaning they convey and their consequences for some communities.

In some cases, however, the frame imposed by the official definition of the crime, made by the law enforcement system, triggers a more profound reinterpretation of the attack. The chronology of school attacks is substituted by a chronology of racist violence in Sweden, including events that at the time had a profound impact on the entire country and in particular on racialised groups. The Trollhättan attack is now included in a series of events such as the serial shootings at immigrants by *Lasermannen* in the 1990s, the arson of the Trollhättan mosque in the 1990s, to which a group of young people related to the extreme right confessed, and the serial shootings at people with immigrant background by Peter Mangs in the 2000s. Thus the attack is redefined as belonging to the history of racist violence in Sweden. Also the choice of guests in different news bulletins and quotes in newspapers is affected, with experts on hate crime or right-wing extremism interpreting the event. Already in the evening of the day of the attack, the debate show *Debatt* (Debate), takes up two topics, the school attack in Trollhättan and the contemporary wave of the attacks on and arsons of refugee shelters all over Sweden, suggesting, albeit still implicitly, a connection between the two. In this way, the attack in Trollhättan is presented in the context of an anti-immigrant and anti-refugee climate in the midst of the "European refugee crisis".

The racist nature of the attack was also the focus of a few editorials and articles published on the cultural page. Kept in a debate tone, the pieces belong to the opinion section of the newspapers with less authority and a more complex relation to factuality and reliability. Many of these were written on a meta-level, providing a comment to previous media reports on the crime in the light of this new frame. With titles like: "The Fear in Our Country Is Unevenly Distributed", "The Fear in Our Dark Bodies" or "White Hypocrisy", these articles suggested that previous frames had misrepresented the event. They attempted to unmask the media's ambivalent position manifesting itself in either not noticing some groups' vulnerability and universalising the fear or contributing to a stigmatisation of dark people, who are treated as the source of problem.

In the media reporting that embraces the hate crime frame, the distance between those suffering and those not is put in place, but in a new way. Differences within audience are stressed: not every spectator belongs to the suffering zone, some are more vulnerable than others. So the audience is split up again, but this time making visible the fact that we do not fear in the same way. Vulnerability is redefined in terms of skin colour. Segregated neighbourhoods emerge as unsafe because they are a target of racism.

While the first two frames appear almost simultaneously in the first hours of the online reports from Trollhättan, the third seems to be triggered by the information from the police investigation and thereby receives a different status—that of a hegemonic interpretation of the event. Its effect goes deeper than that, however. The assertion of the racist nature of the attack is a moment of exposure of the previous frames, what Butler calls "breaking from the frame" (Butler 2009: 11–12). That which has been taken for granted is called into question.

In the first case, it is the universal vulnerability to violence. This frame, although inclusive and creating closeness to the suffering, apparently conceals the differences in vulnerability, which makes it impossible to attend to the very particular nature of the injury created by racist violence: an injury that goes beyond its immediate victims and spreads fear in some bodies, some communities and some spaces. As a result, the closeness produced by the affective workings of this frame turns out to be illusionary. In her essay on how pictures of war are used to raise sympathy in the Western public, Susan Sontag claims that the sympathy might work to obscure the real relations of power by proclaiming "our innocence as well as our impotence" and she urges instead for "a reflection on how our privileges are located on the same map as their suffering, and may—in ways we might prefer not to imagine—be linked to their suffering" (2004: 80). This discussion, despite the different context, sheds some light on the affective workings of the universal frame in media reporting on the Trollhättan attack. It seems that the frame inhibits spectators from situating themselves on the same map as those suffering, not as equally affected by fear, but as implicated in the suffering of the other through their own privilege. What is important, this happens almost unintentionally, or even despite good intentions, redefining in an important way the possibility of, and a road towards, anti-racist solidarity.

In the second case, the breaking from the frame consists in exposing how the media's way of describing the space in which the attack took place builds on an established narrative about the suburbs and those inhabiting them. As mentioned, this frame creates a distance towards those suffering through demonisation and othering but also through racialisation. The breaking from the frame therefore discloses the frame as a mechanism of power complicit in making some lives less grievable. It also reveals how responsibility for violence is projected onto those affected and, at the same time, detached from those located outside of the zone of suffering.

Epilogue: Media Self-Reflection and the Issue of Responsibility

When racism becomes the focus of media reports, the question of responsibility is redefined. Even though the responsibility for the attack is mostly treated according to the logics of legal criminal law as located exclusively in a particular racist subject, critical voices still open up for a redefinition of the question of responsibility beyond the individual perpetrator. In this context, maybe the most relevant issue is how ethics have been discussed in relation to the media's reporting on the Trollhättan attack.

Already three days after the attack, a larger feature was presented in the radio show *Medierna* (The Media) in the public station SR P1 that was highly critical of the media's "pursuit of own news angles". The feature discussed, among other things, an interview carried out on the day of the attack and broadcast in the main news bulletin on the same evening by the public nationwide TV station SVT1. Later, a complaint was filed against the interview with the Swedish Broadcasting Commission, a monitoring body for radio and TV. The controversial interview was a short exchange between a journalist and the spokesman of the Trollhättan municipality:

JOURNALIST: Yes, this school has had a lot of problems with safety and study environment and the School Inspectorate was here last spring and put fines on the local authorities because it is so unsafe. What do you have to say about this?

SPOKESMAN OF THE TROLLHÄTTAN MUNICIPALITY:	Yes … I think it should not be confused, since these are two completely separate things. What happened here today is an isolated event that cannot be linked to the other thing.
JOURNALIST:	How do you know?
SPOKESMAN:	It's much too early to discuss that right now. Right now we … we are a town in grief and a town in shock and this is a possible discussion we cannot have today.
JOURNALIST:	But this is exactly the question that many people ask today when they hear that the school has been unsafe. Also it is a very open school where there is both a library and a café where anyone can get in.
SPOKESMAN:	Anyone can get in to any public school in Sweden. I have a son that goes to another public school in another municipality and anyone can get in there and do a similar thing. So we can have this discussion later.
JOURNALIST:	It is an extremely segregated school with very few Swedish children. What do you have to say about this?
SPOKESMAN:	I can certify that it is a public school where many inhabitants of Trollhättan go and, it has worked very well before. It is no … Usually, there are no more incidents or more episodes or more indications than in other schools. It has been a very well-managed establishment.

According to the complaint, the interview, and in particular the formulation "an extremely segregated school with very few Swedish children", were "irrelevant, prejudiced and racist". In its response to the accusation, the representatives of the Swedish public television insisted that the interview was in agreement with legal regulations. In defence of the reporter, it was claimed that:

Under the time pressure, the reporter expressed herself in an unfortunate way. It is evident that she was looking for a better wording and paused to try to find a better expression. The expression was an attempt to describe the background to the issues of safety and study environment that the school had been fined for to the municipality's spokesman. The School Inspectorate's criticism concerned poor study results, lack of safety and bad study environment. The meaning of the question to the spokesman was whether the children could be more unsafe because they could be exposed to people with xenophobic motives. Regrettably, this was not clear due to the unfortunate wording of the reporter's question in the live broadcast.

(The Swedish Broadcasting Commission, Decision 2016-02-08 Nr: 15/02902 and 3015)

Despite these arguments, the Commission decided that the TV station had breached the ethical rules. What is striking, however, is that the defence strategy adopted by the TV station reduces the ethical problem with the interview to the issue of wording, unable to recognise the question of responsibility in relation to the racist attack in broader, social terms.

The complaint, the defence and the decision show that it has been possible in Sweden to attempt to hold the media responsible for how they report on events such as the Trollhättan attack. However, as the defence strategy suggests, such attempts are often contested. In this way, the competing frames discussed in this chapter not only determine how the reported events are interpreted and understood, they establish the relationship between the suffering other and the audience and decide whose lives are made grievable in the media. They also shape the very ways in which the media deal with the issues of responsibility and ethics in reporting on racist violence.

Notes

1. The attack started in the morning of 22 October 2015, when 21-year old Anton Lundin Pettersson approached the Kronan school located in a neighbourhood of Kronogården in Trollhättan—a town in mid-western Sweden. He was dressed in a black helmet and a mask and armed with a knife and a sword. Most of the pupils were inside the classrooms at that point. At 10:08 am the police received the first alarm, and few minutes later two police officers arrived at the scene. By then, Lundin Pettersson had stabbed two pupils Wahed Kosa and Ahmed Hassan; a teacher, Nazir Amso and a teacher assistant, Lavin Eskandar. Lundin Pettersson was shot by a police officer and died later that day in the hospital. Only the first victim survived the attack, the others died on the spot or in the hospital.

2. I would like to thank my colleagues from the Department of Gender Studies at the Lund University for their comments on a draft of this chapter and Scott Poynting for his insightful remarks and the editing work.

3. The analysis in this chapter has been inspired mainly by Lilie Chouliaraki's work on news and the spectatorship of suffering and Judith Butler's work on frames of war. In addition, Ruth Sheldon's analysis of the role of different recordings in mediating knowledge about certain events has been an important source of inspiration (Sheldon 2016: 108–109).

References

Ahmed, S. (2014). *The Cultural Politics of Emotion*. Edinburgh: Edinburgh University Press.

Back, L. (2011). *Reflecting on the Riots*. LSE British Politicast Episode 1. Retrieved July 6, 2017, from http://blogs.lse.ac.uk/politicsandpolicy/politicast-1/

Butler, J. (2009). *Frames of War: When Is Life Grievable?* London and New York: Verso.

Chouliaraki, L. (2006). *The Spectatorship of Suffering*. London and Thousand Oaks, CA: SAGE Publications.

Chouliaraki, L. (2013). *The Ironic Spectator: Solidarity in the Age of Post-Humanitarianism*. Cambridge and Malden, MA: Polity Press.

Ericsson, U., et al. (2002). *Miljonprogram Och Media: Föreställningar om Människor Och Förorter*. Stockholm: Riksantikvarieämbetet; Norrköping: Integrationsverket.

Garde-Hansen, J., & Gorton, K. (2013). *Emotion Online: Theorizing Affect on the Internet*. Houndmills, Basingstoke, Hampshire, and New York: Palgrave Macmillan.

Kolankiewicz, M. (2015). *Anti-Muslim Violence and the Possibility of Justice*. Lund: Lund University.

Rattansi, A. (2007). *Racism: A Very Short Introduction*. Oxford and New York: Oxford University Press.

Sheldon, R. (2016). *Tragic Encounters and Ordinary Ethics. Palestine-Israel in British Universities*. Manchester: Manchester University Press.

Skeggs, B., & Wood, H. (2012). *Reacting to Reality Television: Performance, Audience and Value*. Milton Park, Abingdon, Oxon, and New York: Routledge.

Sontag, S. (2004). *Regarding the Pain of Others*. New York: Picador.

13

Racism, the Press and Black Deaths in Police Custody in the United Kingdom

Ryan Erfani-Ghettani

In *Dying for Justice*, the Institute of Race Relations, looking at black and minority ethnic deaths in custody between 1991 and 2014, revealed that out of 509 cases, just ten had been considered unlawful killings at an inquest, only five prosecutions had been brought, and nobody had ever been convicted of an offence (Athwal and Bourne 2015). The media shares no small part in denying justice for the bereaved. Invariably, where one would expect the media to investigate police wrongdoing in a suspicious death in custody, the dead themselves are smeared as too strong, too volatile or too alien for their own good, and so having brought their death upon themselves. The police are able to frame the death in terms of a media narrative that portrays race, and not racism, as the problem. As family and community campaigns for justice emerge, police and the media collude to define their demands as extremist and therefore illegitimate. A potential crisis of legitimacy for the police is deflected by the press.

Though fatal police violence against back people has, since the 1980s, sparked riot after riot, police and media responses either parry criticism

R. Erfani-Ghettani (✉)
Institute of Race Relations, London, UK

© The Author(s) 2018
M. Bhatia et al. (eds.), *Media, Crime and Racism*, Palgrave Studies in Crime, Media and Culture, https://doi.org/10.1007/978-3-319-71776-0_13

of state violence back onto dissident communities or, through well-fired media campaigns, present technocratic tinkering as radical reform. Time and again, the police emerge from a legitimacy crisis having leapt 'towards a new ... stage of increased police power and prestige' (Gilmore and Gilmore 2016). To recognise the stories about violence and race woven in the aftermath of fatal police action by the police and their patrons in the press is to recognise one of the means by which the police regain legitimacy after deadly violence.

The police and media response to the killing of Jermaine Baker exemplified this process. In December 2015, Metropolitan police officers shot and killed Baker in the north London borough of Haringey. Alleged to have been involved in a conspiracy to free two prisoners from a van on its way to Wood Green crown court, Baker was sitting in a car with two associates when armed police sprang on the vehicle, taking lethal action. In the aftermath, Baker was described as a 'gangster-tattooed' affiliate of Mark Duggan, killed by the Met in 2011. The association with Duggan was pertinent; both fatally shot by armed officers, the notion that the two men were hardened outlaws was used as post-hoc justification for the extra-judicial killing of unarmed young black men.

During the next few days, the link between Baker and Duggan's gang activity was hotly contested. Some newspapers ascribed Baker first to the 'notorious Bloodline gang' (*Daily Mail* 2015), then suggested that this gang was associated with Duggan's 'Tottenham Man Dem'. Police vociferously denied that they had been responsible for this media briefing, before going on to state that Baker hadn't even featured on the Met's Matrix gangs database; any supposed links to Duggan were pure imagination, attempts to smear him by association (Scott 2015). Some papers went further. As rumours spread that Baker had been asleep at the time of the killing, *The Sun*'s Kelvin MacKenzie said that even if true, he cared 'not a jot' that Baker had been shot. 'In some ways', he continued, 'I'm quite pleased he's dead' (MacKenzie 2015).

The Sun's hostility—MacKenzie's assertion that whether guilty or not it was better that Baker was dead—drew censure from many of those who had previously subscribed to its narrative, even from those in whose defence the smear campaign was waged. Tottenham MP David Lammy, who had previously refused to attend a vigil for justice for Mark Duggan on the grounds that the event would be hijacked by 'anarchists' and 'criminals' (*Daily Mail* 2014), now accused the press of 'smearing' Baker. The Metropolitan police, eager to avoid the accusations of closing ranks, held a community meeting at Tottenham Town Hall to address the grief of the community, at which borough commander Victor Olisa denounced the reporting, stating that 'it does not help me, my officers, to continue to build the respect and trust that we seek, if there is emotional reporting that demonises a victim.'

The episode highlighted the different approaches taken by press and police. Compared to the ferocity of the right-wing press's attack on a victim of police violence, the Metropolitan police *appeared* to do the right thing. The media's defence of the police rested on smearing Tottenham's black community. The Met, however, presented itself as accountable, liaising with the community and arresting the officer who had taken lethal action against Baker, aware that its legitimacy rested on *being seen* to serve in partnership, not police by force. This approach drew cautious praise from stalwart black justice activists, whose interpretation was that lessons may have been learned from the disastrous approaches of the past. Yet five days later, Prime Minister David Cameron announced a review into whether armed officers who shoot terrorist or criminal suspects should get more protection from the law. This came after Met Commissioner Bernard Hogan-Howe, in discussions with Cameron, decried the treatment of armed officers that had used lethal force at the hands of the criminal justice system. On the basis that officers should 'protect the safety of the public … with the full support of the law and the state', the argument attempted to shield armed officers from legal procedures of investigation and accountability. In the space of a week, the question had been turned from whether the black community was safe while police were not held accountable, to whether 'the public' could feel safe while armed officers, 'heroes' in Hogan-Howe's words (BBC News 2016), were constrained by the demand that they justify their actions (Fekete 2016). A crisis of police legitimacy was used as an opportunity to demand further police impunity.

Compared with the Met's obdurate lack of communication with Mark Duggan's family in the wake of his death in 2011, this engagement with Tottenham's black community after Baker's death was certainly an improvement, in terms of the attitude towards the grieving friends and relatives of the deceased. But it would be a mistake to consider the response to Baker's death an attempt to improve procedures of accountability. Rather, the community meeting at Tottenham Town Hall was a performance. As a piece of public relations, the meeting—and its contrast with the media's performance—can be considered a strategy of 'winning by appearing to lose'. While the right-wing media attacks black Tottenham in defence of the police force and in the name of 'muscular liberalism', the police present themselves as the victims of a misdirected grief and judicial scrutiny, suffered in the line of the duty of arbitrating between warring factions.

Policing by consent has allowed the police to appear above the fray. But over the course of the last decade and a half, British police have positioned themselves as acting in defence of a way of life, which necessitates more powers and a relaxation of accountability procedures. This shift in terrain promises to make policing ever more unaccountable, ironically in defence of 'liberal values'. The call for further police impunity is a plea to white Britain: 'protect us so that we can protect *you* from *them*'.

Consent and the Representation of Black Dissent

Two years after the 1985 Brixton rebellion, sparked by the police shooting of unarmed mother Cherry Groce in her own home, A. Sivanandan took the measure of society's freedom: 'where [the] shift to authoritarianism first manifests itself is in the distinction the police makes between its publics, as to whom it shall serve by consent and whom control by force—and, in forcing, remove them from the public domain, "decitizenise" them' (Sivanandan 1987). Key to police evasion of accountability has been the notion of 'policing by consent'. This notion was at the heart of the police's attempt to cultivate a more co-operative relationship with the media over the course of the twentieth century (Reiner 1985). Managing the media was crucial for regaining legitimacy after the newspapers investigated the police following a series of corruption scandals during the 1960s. Commissioner Robert Mark, mandated to 'clean up' the Met's image, deployed a broad range of strategies to this end. A mixture of censorship on the one hand, and supply of information on the other, allowed the Met to manipulate the information war in a liberal democratic society by 'appearing to lose' (Reiner 1985). By adopting an air of openness, encouraging police officers to communicate freely with members of the press and develop relationships with journalists independent of the Met's internal bureaucracy, Mark was able to engage with the media to ensure its coverage was in sympathy with policing priorities.

This strategy, pursued in the name of democratising access to the police and freeing the flow of information, masked a simultaneous process by which access to information was selective. Under Mark's tenure, access to proceedings at the Old Bailey, to reporting on demonstrations, and to the visits of foreign dignitaries—areas in which police activity was susceptible to scrutiny—was restricted, with many left-wing journalists turned away (Bunyan 1977). Police Press Cards allowed journalists access to these events, but newspaper editors were forced to nominate journalists who would then be vetted according to police prerogatives. Those granted access were to be provided with special briefings by the police. In reviewing the new landscape of police-press relations, Mark concluded in 1974 that 'many more responsibly written articles and well-researched features about the Metropolitan police are now being seen by the public' (Bunyan 1977).

Mark recognised that decentralising the communications strategy would allow the police to avoid media charges of excessive control, of having something to hide. Indeed, Mark made a virtue of admitting to police wrongdoing. These moments of candour, however, were not strictly in the spirit of accountability. Rather they were an opportunity to present the police as a beleaguered and under-resourced force. Mark's strategy was to 'attract attention to the conditions which govern an urban policeman's life', conditions in which the police force, charged with delivering the lawful expression of dissent—in Mark's words 'the very essence of democracy'—are faced daily with the frustrations of the 'dissenter' (Mark 1978). Mark's success was in painting the police as democracy's midwife, the impartial adjudicator between warring factions, managing dissent according to the 'pendulum principle of aversion to extremism in any form', while allowing its free expression in the name of a 'free country'. Within such a context, the grievance of those experiencing police violence was transformed into the vented anger of a community, 'fed with a continuous diet of dissent for … political purposes', cast unfairly upon a force striving to be the 'embodiment' of 'truth and impartiality'.

Mark's approach strengthened the notion of policing by consent by appearing to foster reporting that challenged police legitimacy; *being seen* to be accountable bore the fruit of being able to both acknowledge wrongdoing and offer an alternative portrayal of the terrain upon which officers operated, which, if it did not justify police malpractice, offered an explanation that sustained the image of the police as victimised for their role as impartial adjudicator. In doing so, police relied upon 'a popular morality that ha[d] come to define black people out of society': 'the police no longer just reflect or reinforce that morality: they re-create it' (Sivanandan 1979). The media and the police, working in tandem, reinforced a narrative that presented black communities as sites of criminality. And when the political and criminal lines were blurred, as in the case of the Spaghetti House Siege, Mark's media allies removed politics from the equation outright. In September 1975, three armed black activists raided a Spaghetti House restaurant to fund their political activities. In the face of political support for the robbers, later dubbed in Mark's autobiography an 'ethnic press which was frequently prejudicial and unfair', the commissioner insisted that it was an 'ordinary armed robbery with no racial or political connotations' (Bourne 2011). Rather than considering the role of racism in the heavy policing of black communities, such practices were justified by narratives that claimed that these were communities in which social order had broken down (by fecklessness, absentee parenting or cultures of poverty). Black dissent against racist policing is therefore suspect, an evasion of responsibility by a community that has failed to integrate, politically motivated even. Any attempt to scrutinise police power in black communities creates a hostile environment in which the police are considered the perpetrators of violence, and the perpetrators of crime are their victims, further justifying Mark's narrative of police victimhood.

Black political organisation against police abuse of power was met by state-led attempts by the media to restore the legitimacy of the police by challenging not only the form that black dissent takes (violent, criminal, etc.) but also the articulation of that anger. Black struggle has been historically marred by accusations, from the police, press and the political classes, that it is the outcome of political agitators with ideological agendas, rather than the legitimate anger of those at the front line of state racism. Take the self-defence campaigns in East London from 1968 to 1970, necessitated by the state's failure to protect Pakistani communities from a spate of racial violence. These campaigns led to a split between those who favoured an integrationist approach (forging a 'collaborative relationship' with the state and political establishment, 'thereby assimilat[ing] the recently settled Pakistani migrant community into the so-called "British values" of law and order and the authority of the police), and those who favoured an autonomous approach, with a wider anti-racist analysis, 'bypassing the state, mainstream party politics and the apparatuses of the race relations industry'. The integrationists attempted to create consent for the police by condemning the autonomous defence campaigns as '"extremist outsiders"' and by recasting, if not criminalising, the politics of self-defence as mindless violence' (Ashe et al. 2016).

At another pivotal moment in the forging of black anti-racist politics, violent confrontations at the 1977 Battle of Lewisham between young black people and a National Front march protected by heavy police ranks were credited by the press to the Socialist Workers Party (SWP). Yet historical accounts of the day's events suggest that Lewisham's black youth, 'harassed by the police near daily' and 'seeing the force arrive in numbers reminiscent of an occupation to enable a neo-Nazi parade' needed 'little encouragement to go on the offensive'. The subsequent launch of the Anti-Nazi League, which was to give anti-fascism 'a tremendous public boost', 'emerged when it did on the back of what was essentially a black protest against the state and the police' (Higgs 2016). Not only did the media reverse the flow of violence at the demonstration, making out that anti-fascist violence was aggressive rather than defensive, they then delegitimised that violence by making it appear ideological and co-ordinated, a brushstroke which negated the contribution of black-led protest to the political culture that followed it. The black experience, and black peoples' articulation of that experience during the 1970s and 1980s, was crucial to informing, challenging and redefining white analysis and activism not just around racism but around the role of state power more generally. The muting of black protest in the mainstream popular press has obscured the vanguardist role of black politics in a wider political culture.

A Problem of Perception

When, during the 1980s and 1990s, police violence against black people, sometimes with fatal consequences, propelled communities into spontaneous street demonstrations, the police's approach was to follow Mark's strategy, spinning a loss of legitimacy into a problem of black perception rather than state malpractice. Smearing black protest as politically suspect bolstered a narrative that the police, rather than the community, were under siege. This mandated further attacks on the grassroots support network that came to the community's aid, whose analysis—that the state was the root of the black community's problems—was thought to have gained too much influence. In the aftermath of the 1981 Brixton rebellion, Metropolitan Commissioner David McNee, briefing the press, appealed to the 'decent and law-abiding people of Brixton' (as opposed to the 'looters' and 'arsonists'), to 'support the police … [and] get back to normality as quickly as possible', before claiming that the 'events were not spontaneous but orchestrated … locals were helped by persons from outside the area' (McNee 1981). The insinuation—that this was not about police treatment of black people at all but had been manipulated by political agents—was eagerly picked up by the press. The *Sunday Express* reported of the 'Terror Plan' and '"Anarchy" clue' behind the unrest, while the *News of the World* claimed police were hunting for left-wing 'extremists' who had organised the 'riot' (26 April 1981). Italian anarchist Patricia Giambi was arrested outside her Railton Road home during the unrest, and in the days that followed, her case was used to justify claims of an 'international link' to organised anarchist terrorist groups that had orchestrated the events. Giambi was issued with a deportation order. During her appeal against it, the court was told of the 'leftist posters' decorating her flat, and her love letters from a 'known Italian agitator'. A police source briefed the *Daily Mail* that she was a 'professional troublemaker', 'very anti-police' (17 October 1981).

Again, in 1985, after Tottenham's Broadwater Farm uprising following the death of Cynthia Jarrett during a police raid on her home, police sources fed the media with narratives that exonerated the force and fitted into long established racist narratives that had become a common sense in the press. Jarrett had suffered a fatal heart attack after police officers illegally entered her home and violently pushed her to the ground. Yet officers on the scene briefed the media that it had been her daughter's 'aggressive', 'anti-police' attitude that had triggered the angina (Rose 1992). The right-wing media effectively wrote out police culpability for the 'riot': the community's critique, that they had been pushed too far, that Jarrett's death was the logical conclusion to the 'colonial-style' policing they had endured—a community on edge after the shooting of Cherry Groce in Brixton eight days earlier—was explained instead as the 'savagery' of the 'jungle' (*Daily Mail*, 8 October 1985). Again, the notion that the depth of anger was manipulated by outside agitators reared its head when a cartoon book, *How Racism Came to Britain*, was found in a home on the farm. Those who had erupted, according to the *Daily Mail*, had been 'Brainwashed to hate the police' because of the 'relentless anti-police propaganda pumped into many inner-city school children' (Bourne 2015). This led to an attempt to dismantle the burgeoning anti-racist police monitoring infrastructure, which was said to be to blame for the *perception* of racist police practices that didn't exist. The Greater London Council came under fire for its police committee support unit; its head, Tony Bunyan, was attacked for his links to the radical journal *Race & Class*; the Institute of Race Relations, which had published the cartoon book, had its funders named and shamed in the press.

The then Met Commissioner Kenneth Newman, echoing McNee's comments four years earlier, said the Broadwater Farm unrest was orchestrated by 'groups of Trotskyists and anarchists', while the *Police Review* explained it as a by-product of a policy of appeasement towards the 'ethnic criminal' (24 October 1985). Popular black MP for Tottenham, Bernie Grant, defending the community, claimed in parliament that 'what the police got was a bloody good hiding.' The *Sun* responded with a front page splash: 'Don't call me Barmy Bernie', describing him as 'peeling a banana and juggling with an orange'. An unnamed Labour councillor was quoted as describing him as 'like the leader of a Black tribe—always looking for battles and shaking his spear. He sees all whites as his enemy' (Lord Gifford 1986). Eight years later, in 1993, Grant was again attacked for his role in the aftermath of the death of Joy Gardner, again in Tottenham, after police officers trussed her up in shackles and wrapped 13 feet of tape around her nose and mouth. Grant responded to the call by then Commissioner Paul Condon to counsel calm amongst the black community to prevent another 'riot'. There was no violent unrest, but there was committed protest to call the Metropolitan police to account. Despite the non-violent nature of the demonstrations, the press still deemed it illegitimate; it was, commentators said, manipulated by outsiders, ideologically anti-police agents, who sought to manoeuvre community organising onto violent terrain. A meeting, hosted in Tottenham by the Socialist Workers Party in conjunction with Gardner's mother Myrna Simpson, was branded a 'gospel of violence', an attempt to 'fan the flames of inter-communal hatred' (Rose and Gerard 1993). Grant was presented as manipulating black grievance from above, part of a politically motivated extreme that made capital from orchestrating violence: Richard Littlejohn, for example, repeatedly asked Grant 'Did you want a riot?' on LBC radio (Littlejohn 1993a). Anti-racists were to blame for stoking emotion around a perceived racism that did not exist (Erfani-Ghettani 2015a), and their role in aiding community organising made such activity prone to public disorder of the kind seen in 1985. The demands of anti-racist activism that the state hold itself to account were spun as necessitating coercive policing measures to curtail the threat posed to public safety.

Though the legitimacy of black grievance was still questioned, whether it was legitimate or not was beside the point. Black protest was now seen as a public order issue. The dissent of black communities had to be fought in order to prevent the kinds of rebellions that had been seen in St Pauls, Brixton, Toxteth, Moss Side, Chapeltown, Handsworth and Tottenham. All had been sparked by heavy policing, yet all had been written off by the police and the right-wing press as criminal and ideological in nature. The warnings issued by the press in the wake of Gardner's death that those protesting 'wanted a riot' and should be dealt a 'healthy dose of police brutality' prescribed state violence as the solution to the problem (Littlejohn 1993b). At such moments of candour, the right-wing press betrayed the narrative it had constructed to explain black unrest, one which had divorced state violence from the political violence that followed. The press heard the black community's complaint that it had been dealt 'heavy manners', but they deserved it.

The response to these instances of urban unrest and black activism— sparked by police impunity and closed ranks after often fatal violence— involved the development of a common sense narrative that saw race, not racism, as the problem. The police did not suffer from a crisis of legitimacy of their own making but from a breakdown of trust within the black community, stoked by politically motivated agitators—from the anti-racist lobby to ideologically anti-state anarchists—manipulating black anger from behind the scenes. Those within the community who voiced their anger were part of a 'minority of dissidents', against whom the majority must be co-opted onto 'the side of law and order' and coerced into 'believing they have a moral duty to … control and discipline the "criminal minority"' (John 1986). Such a narrative made illegitimate the black community's cry: 'we do not consent'. The implication that black people could not be trusted to articulate their own grief legitimised police demands for further protection from legal duress, which seemed a necessary bulwark against the anger that had been channelled their way.

The Construction of Police Impunity

Throughout the 1990s, community protest in response to black deaths in custody was deemed illegitimate by the police and the media. The received wisdom of the 1980s held that black protest against police violence was a pretext for riot, a public order threat that necessitated pre-emptive criminal justice procedures. As the Campaign Against Racism and Fascism (CARF) warned in 1996, 'incitement laws brought in to protect minorities are now being used against black people and anti-racists … there appears to be a systematic attempt to close down criticism of the policing of black people' (*CARF* Collective 1996). In December 1995, following

the death of Wayne Douglas at the hands of the police, black people protested on the streets of Brixton. Both police and media reinforced each
other's plans to bring incitement charges against Rudy Narayan, a bar-
rister who had spoken at the protest. Initial media reports focussed on the
damage caused by 'rioters', but after Commissioner Condon said that he
was 'considering incitement charges because of the inflammatory nature
of the speeches', the media began to focus on a broad conspiracy insti-
gated by the 'firebrand' Narayan. This was, according to CARF, a 'Trial
by "white" media' (*CARF* Collective 1996). Black newspapers, such as
the *Voice*, were found by the *Sunday Express* to be the 'extremists behind
the chaos' by virtue of reporting on police brutality in the run-up to the
demonstration. Commissioner Condon went on to attack the *Voice* for
being 'irresponsible', 'inflammatory' and 'fuelling discontent'.

It was clear that what infrastructure had been built by anti-racist struggle—legislation, the black press, a grassroots support network: hard-won
tools with which to hold the state to account—was being dismantled or
turned against the struggle itself. Not even the landmark 1999 Macpherson
report into the racist murder of Stephen Lawrence in 1993, which found
the police to be an 'institutionally racist' force, could halt the backlash
against anti-racist struggle. That finding was a huge boon to anti-racist
campaigning and vindicated the years-long battle fought by the Lawrences
and their allies. Yet the finding of institutional racism was resisted at the
time by Commissioner Condon on the grounds that such 'labels can
cause more problems than they solve' (Macpherson 1999), in other
words, highlighting racism would further fuel the *perception* that the
police were racist. The police lost the battle, but the force's grudging mea
culpa became a kind of year zero, after which their racism could be presented as a thing of the pre-Macpherson past. The Macpherson moment
has now 'become part of the UK's self-congratulatory narrative'. In 2012,
when two of Lawrence's murderers were finally convicted, 'their incarceration was celebrated almost universally by the press, the government,
the police, the establishment, as a shared national victory, as evidence
that a scar of injustice had at last begun to heal' (Burnett 2014). But the
promotion of the 'colorblind or postracial' state has been 'used to justify
dismantling the state's capacity to challenge discrimination' (Taylor
2016). The media's narrative appropriated the historical struggle of black

campaigners, obscuring their role as drivers of change. Instead, where activism couldn't be integrated into state-friendly narratives, the narrative replaced activists with a benevolent political class that bestowed justice on black victims of racism. The liberal myth that Britain is now a colour-blind society has been used to cast a pall over the role of political struggle and to silence any analysis of institutional racism as an ongoing injustice (Bergin and Rupprecht 2016). The British media's acknowledgement of *historic* injustice is complicit in the silencing of activism *today* (Bolton 2016).

Such was the case in the aftermath of Duggan's killing in 2011, which led to days of rioting across the country. David Lammy, now MP for Tottenham, compared the riots to those of 1985, the earlier unrest 'a race riot, given its energy by an explosive relationship between the black community and the police', the latter the 'lawlessness' of 'criminals' in a context in which 'the relationship between the local force and the local community had improved immeasurably' (Lammy 2011). Since then, the Justice for Mark Duggan Campaign's years of protest have been consistently denigrated as the hijacked anger of a grieving community, manipulated by 'extremists', 'anarchists' and the 'race lobby'. In 2014 an inquest into Duggan's death found that he had been lawfully killed despite being unarmed at the time he was shot. As supporters of the Duggan family congregated in protest outside the Royal Courts of Justice, television crews broadcast the fraught scenes on the evening's news. Carole Duggan, Mark's aunt, told cameras that her family would continue to campaign for justice, not just for Mark but for the families of others killed in police custody. Her declaration, 'No justice, no peace', was intended as an indictment of Britain's criminal justice system; instead, it was presented as a threat of further violent protest. After attacking her for her 'council-estate facelift' and 'Manc meets Jafaican' accent, the *Daily Mail*'s Richard Littlejohn condemned those who had been 'stoking the flames of dissent' before petitioning that 'Justice has been done. Now let's pray for peace' (Littlejohn 2014).

As had happened so often over the years, the media presented protest over the inquest verdict as a riot waiting to happen. The potential for violent unrest overshadowed the black community's demands for justice. At a vigil commemorating Duggan's memory two days after the inquest verdict, the media appeared to have been prepped by the police and local elected officials that there were 'those who will try to seek advantage of the vigil to try to cause trouble.' The vigil proceeded without trouble, yet as attendees milled about at the closing of the day's events, Channel 4 News' Darshna Soni announced in a live TV broadcast that 'the real test now for the police is whether they can persuade them to go home quietly and quickly' (11 January 2014). A BBC documentary on the Met's handling of the aftermath of the inquest verdict also focussed on the threat the community's protest posed to public order. Yet the BBC's understanding of the role of the police—a neutral force 'stretched too thin' and 'facing daily criticism'—allowed it to see only the threat of a riot. This analysis blinded the BBC to the role of police and judicial culpability in potentially causing one. It had then to look elsewhere for the causes of a riot, allowing the Met itself to supply the analysis, institutional racism is a thing of the past, and the corollary, black rage is abetted by a narrative that blames racism where it doesn't exist (Erfani-Ghettani 2015b). Black critiques of racist policing are dismissed out of hand. The media is forced then to pathologise the black community's anger so that it becomes a *belief in* rather than *reaction to* actual institutional racism. By defining institutional culpability out of institutional racism, black protest is narrated according to the principles of 'public disorder' and thus justifies further heavy-handed policing in black communities.

Police Power and the War over Liberalism

Such perspectives have justified the further shoring up of powers of public order policing. The approach after 2011's riots was that justice must be delivered and offenders held accountable no matter the social cost: 24-hour courts handing out severe sentences. It was emblematic of the 'circular racial logic' that has 'conflated the racialized poor with spacialized disorder'; the 'wanton criminality' of the rioters was divorced from the stop-and-search practices targeted at black communities that many rioters cited as cause for unrest. While racist policing practices had sparked disorder, any analysis of institutional culpability—let alone racism—was substituted for an attack instead on criminogenic sites of disorder (Camp and Heatherton 2016; Burnett 2012). The zero-tolerance and pre-emptive policing that has since been emblematic of Hogan-Howe's 'Total Policing' strategy in black communities allows for the surveillance and, ultimately, displacement of poor communities from now-desirable urban space (Operation Shield's planned eviction of suspected gang members' families from social housing, for instance, was resisted by the London Campaign Against Police and State Violence on the grounds that it constituted collective punishment).

Alongside this, anti-racist campaigning has been increasingly derided as the 'multicultural tolerance' of extremism and become 'in itself a national security risk' (Kundnani 2014). In the same way as the policing of the inner cities became a means of controlling pre-crime behaviours deemed anti-social, the narrative around terrorism has extended to argue for the proscription of modes of thinking deemed antithetical to liberal values which have not yet led to political violence but lead inevitably to this end. A 2015 BBC Panorama special, taking its cue from government rhetoric, declared that Muslim anti-racist activism was 'non-violent extremism', the activity of 'activists disdainful of western values … a grievance narrative which seems to seduce some Muslim students' (Ware 2015). The war on terror is said to have 'come home', necessitating the greater scrutiny of British Muslims by the security services. After the murder of the soldier Lee Rigby in south London in 2013 by black British citizens Michael Adebolajo and Michael Adebowale, Adebolajo's threat that 'You people will never be safe' was emblazoned on the front pages of multiple national newspapers. What followed was a spike in far-right vigilante activity, racist abuse and assault. The police too seemed emboldened by the national mood. In the days after Rigby's death, two black brothers driving through the district in which he was killed, Asanti and Husani Williams, were pulled over by police officers in a 'hard stop' of the kind used to apprehend both Azelle Rodney and Mark Duggan. The Williams brothers were tasered, accused of being terrorists and repeatedly racially abused, before being charged with possession of drugs. Charges were later dropped, but activists warned that 'It looks very much like a racist assault by the Police, which could have resulted in the death of an innocent man' (LCAPSV 2014). BBC Political Editor Nick Robinson's description of Rigby's killers as being 'of Muslim appearance', though derided by anti-racists at the time, reflected the realities of policing in the city: being black, in a pair, and on the wrong street in south London marked the Williams brothers as suspect.

The consolidation of police impunity behind the notion of 'muscular liberalism' has been clear since the acquittal of officer Anthony Long for the murder of Azelle Rodney. Long was cast in the media as victim to malicious prosecution, thus reinforcing the case for further immunity from legal duress. Twenty-four-year-old Azelle Rodney was killed in a car during a policing operation in north London in April 2005. Unarmed at the time, Rodney was shot six times after police stopped his vehicle, sustaining four shots to the head. Within hours of his death, news agencies misreported that Rodney was holding a gun when he was shot. The few newspapers that noted the incident subsequently described Rodney as a crack-dealing 'drugs baron' (Barkham 2006). It took state prosecutors nine years to decide to charge Long, dubbed by senior Metropolitan police chiefs as their 'very own serial killer' for his history of shooting suspects dead. This was only the third such murder charge brought against an on-duty officer. While a judge-led public inquiry had found that he had no lawful reason to shoot, in 2015, after a lengthy legal battle, Long was cleared of murder.

Long was granted numerous interviews in the national press where he was able to claim his actions had been self-defence and therefore necessary. Flawed intelligence had led him to believe that the car had been used to pick up three MAC-10 sub-machine guns and Long told the press that he had feared for his life and those of fellow officers when he decided to take lethal action. Reporting of the case emphasised the sincerity of Long's fears that he would be shot and therefore made repeated reference to the 'strength' of the intelligence that he had been briefed with. Yet no media outlet took it upon itself to investigate why this intelligence had proved untrue, and to then connect this to the repercussions this had on policing operations. Long's version of events, that Rodney had ducked down in the car and re-emerged, as though grabbing a gun, justified his presumption that his life was in imminent danger. Despite an inquiry's forensic study of police footage, which found that Long had fired before Rodney had been able to move, Long's narrative was sustained on the basis that such painstaking analysis ten years after the event failed to take into account the lived experience of armed officers. The press gave us a 'ride-along' story, inviting us to put ourselves in the place of the brave officer as he puts his life on the line. In a feature commending him for his bravery, Long expressed no remorse: 'These young men went out to take the short cut to wealth. Well, it backfired ... If it comes down to a choice between the public, one of my colleagues and people like Rodney, then Rodney is going to come a poor third' (Luck 2015). We were told that Rodney lived by the gun and died by the gun; the reality was that the police force had planted a weapon in the minds of its officers, pre-emptively justifying his death.

In the months after Long was cleared, the terms of debate shifted. The previous judge-led inquiry that had found his actions unlawful was cast as a kangaroo court. Met Commissioner Hogan-Howe suggested review-ing the law around the prosecution of firearms officers who make the decision to shoot to kill, stating that he was worried that 'we're putting officers in a position that is the same as the criminal who decided to go out with a firearm' (Hogan-Howe 2015). Hogan-Howe went so far as to portray Long as the real victim of the criminal justice system, criticising the court's 'forensic analysis' of his actions, stating that, when 'the officer takes the right action', 'it still seems as though they're having to explain it 10 years later' (Long later went on to release an autobiography, *Lethal Force*, and was the subject of a Channel 4 documentary, *Secrets of a Police Marksman*). This was the public debate about deaths in police custody in the months and weeks leading up to the shooting of Jermaine Baker in December 2015 in Haringey, which shaped the police response to his death. While the officer who shot Baker was immediately suspended pending a criminal investigation by the Independent Police Complaints Commission, the Police Federation warned the press that the measure would have a 'chilling effect' on armed enforcement recruitment. Emboldened by this climate, two days later rank-and-file armed officers took to the *Daily Mail* with a threat to 'lay down' their weapons if the officer in question was charged.

The Police Federation's implications of mutiny rested on the claim that officers would now be fearful of volunteering for the position 'just at the time when the MPS is looking at expanding its capabilities ... because of the terror threat' (*Telegraph* 2015). That the Federation was able to muddy the demand for institutional accountability with a potential terrorist threat reflected its confidence in the media's renewed support for armed officers and lethal force. This was a media which, in a bid to extend police powers, had already raised the spectre of terrorism to justify police killings of black people. After the November 2015 Paris terror attacks on the Bataclan music hall, London's Met Police lobbied for further powers to aid the emergency response to a possible attack in the UK. A measure of how far the media had rehabilitated armed counter-terrorism response units can be found in the attack on Labour leader Jeremy Corbyn for his opposition to a shoot-to-kill policy, for which he was denigrated not only by Prime Minister Cameron, but by sections of the Parliamentary Labour Party, who found sympathetic hearing in much of the media. So, too, the relative absence in public debate of Jean Charles de Menezes, the Brazilian plumber mistaken for a terrorist and shot dead by trigger-happy shoot-to-kill cops in the aftermath of London's 2005 bombings, testified to the media's collective amnesia. After David Cameron announced in late November that the police must be free to 'take out a terrorist to save lives', the *Mail*'s Richard Littlejohn drove the case against Anthony Long into the debate, claiming he was 'thrown to the wolves' after 'a concerted campaign by Rodney's family, "community leaders" and an inquiry which ruled he had been unlawfully killed … Police chiefs and prosecutors decided that this decorated officer, who went to work daily prepared to put his life on the line to protect the rest of us, should be charged with murder' (Littlejohn 2015) The question now posed by the state and echoed by the press is whether the public has enough confidence that the police can protect society if they cannot kill without fear of reprisal.

Conclusion

In order to make the case that the state should be able to kill with impunity, those who campaign for justice against state violence—anti-racists, human rights lawyers and their civil society advocates—have been cast as treasonous. It is rare that the Crown Prosecution Service considers bringing charges against police officers for their role in an unlawful killing. When officers are charged, it is usually as a result of tireless community campaigning and innumerable legal battles, led by the relatives of the dead. This campaigning is represented in the media as politically motivated; rather than the claim of the bereaved for justice, the press denigrates the process as the usurpation of the judiciary by an anti-racist lobby seeking to victimise state agents in pursuit of a wider anti-police agenda. So powerful is this lobby, the argument goes, that the police are fearful to tackle the black offender lest they are targeted by an anti-racist backlash, thus creating a two-tier justice system. Attacks in the media on the bereaved, the campaigners who support them and on the wider enabling culture of political correctness are deployed in order to ward off the threat of prosecution or form the backdrop of puff-pieces aimed at rehabilitating the reputations of the few officers, inevitably acquitted, to be brought to trial (Barkas 2013; Erfani-Ghettani 2015b). This arsenal rests upon portraying the delivery of community-based justice as a deviation from a 'common sense' intuitive justice.

References

Ashe, S., Virdee, S., & Brown, L. (2016). Striking Back Against Racist Violence in the East End of London, 1968–1970. *Race & Class, 58*(1), 34–54.

Athwal, H., & Bourne, J. (2015). *Dying for Justice*. London: Institute of Race Relations.

Barkas, B. (2013). Powell Family's Police Complaint Upheld. *IRR News*, 7 November.

Barkham, P. (2006). He Was Shot Six Times. Why? *The Guardian*, 7 December.

Bergin, C., & Rupprecht, A. (2016). History, Agency and the Representation of "Race" – An Introduction. *Race & Class, 57*(3), 3–17.

Bolton, M. (2016). Media Bias and the "News" form: A Historical Critique. *Novara Media*, 20 May.

Bourne, J. (2011). Spaghetti House Siege: Making the Rhetoric Real. *Race & Class, 53*(2), 1–13.

Bourne, J. (2015). Anti-Racist Witchcraft. *Race & Class, 57*(1), 67–77.

Bunyan, T. (1977). *The Political Police in Britain*. London: Quartet.

Burnett, J. (2012). Total Disaster. *IRR News*, 18 January.

Burnett, J. (2014). The Violence of Denial. *Open Democracy*, 13 March.

Camp, J. T., & Heatherton, C. (2016). Introduction. In *Policing the Planet: Why the Policing Crisis Led to Black Lives Matter*. London: Verso.

CARF Collective. (1996). Incitement – The New State Weapon. *CARF*, 31.

Daily Mail, 15 December 2015.

Erfani-Ghettani, R. (2015a). The Defamation of Joy Gardner: Press, Police and Black Deaths in Custody. *Race & Class, 56*(3), 102–112.

Erfani-Ghettani, R. (2015b). Public Order Broadcasting: *The Met* and the Press. *IRR News*, 17 July.

Fekete, L. (2016). Policing with Accountability or Policing with Impunity? *IRR News*, 14 January.

Gilmore, R. W., & Gilmore, C. (2016). Beyond Bratton. In J. T. Camp & C. Heatherton (Eds.), *Policing the Planet: Why the Policing Crisis Led to Black Lives Matter*. London: Verso.

Greenwood, C. (2014). Tottenham MP Snubbed Vigil for Duggan Over Fears it Would end in Anarchy. *Daily Mail*, January 13.

Higgs, M. (2016). From the Street to the State: Making Anti-Fascism Anti-Racist in 1970s Britain. *Race & Class, 58*(1), 66–84.

Hogan-Howe, B. (2015). *Victoria Derbyshire Show*, BBC, 6 July.

Hogan-Howe, B. (2016). *BBC News*, 14 January.

John, G. (1986). Oh Dear! That "Criminal Minority" Again. *Race Today*, January.

Kundnani, A. (2014). *The Muslims Are Coming! Islamophobia, Extremism, and the Domestic War on Terror*. London: Verso.

Lammy, D. (2011). *Out of the Ashes: Britain After the Riots*. London: Guardian Books.

Littlejohn, R. (1993a). *The Sun*, 6 August.

Littlejohn, R. (1993b). Barmy Bernie and a Dose of the Trots. *The Sun*, 5 August.

Littlejohn, R. (2014). Duggan Was a Gangster not Nelson Mandela. *Daily Mail*, 10 January.

Littlejohn, R. (2015). Don't Shackle Our Shoot-to-Kill Cops. *Daily Mail*, 20 November.

London Campaign Against Police and State Violence (LCAPSV, 2014) Statement, 13 January.

Lord Gifford, Q. C. (1986). *The Broadwater Farm Inquiry*. London: Karia.

Luck, A. (2015). The Met's Own Serial Killer. *Daily Mail*, 25 July.

Macpherson, W. (1999). *The Stephen Lawrence Inquiry: Report of an Inquiry by Sir William Macpherson of Cluny*, s. 6.25.

Mark, R. (1978). *In the Office of Constable*. Glasgow: William Collins Sons & Co.

MacKenzie, K. (2015). *The Sun*, 18 December.

McNee, D. (1981). *Commissioner's Press Briefing*, 12 April.

Reiner, R. (1985). *The Politics of the Police*. Brighton: Wheatsheaf.

Rose, D. (1992). *Climate of Fear: The Murder of PC Blakelock and the Case of the Tottenham Three*. London: Bloomsbury.

Rose, D., & Gerard, L. (1993). *Observer*, 8 August.

Scott, S. (2015). What Do Police Know About Jermaine Baker's Killing That We Don't. *The Guardian*, 21 December.

Sivanandan, A. (1979). *Police Against Black People*. London: Institute of Race Relations.

Sivanandan, A. (1987). *Policing Against Black People*. London: Institute of Race Relations.

Taylor, K.-Y. (2016). *From #blacklivesmatter to Black Liberation*. Chicago, IL: Haymarket Books.

Ware, J. (2015). *The Battle for British Islam*, BBC Panorama, 12 January.

14

Indigenous People, Resistance and Racialised Criminality

Chris Cunneen

Racism and racial discrimination is a common experience for many Indigenous people. Recent Australian research found that, depending in which state they lived, between one in three and one in four Aboriginal and Torres Strait Islander people identified experiencing racial discrimination over the previous two years in a range of areas from abuse in public places to denial of access to goods and services, including employment and housing (Allison et al. 2012; Cunneen et al. 2014; Schwartz et al. 2013). Racism has material outcomes (in the denial of goods and services) and further entrenches social and economic marginalisation. It can directly contribute to Indigenous anger and criminal offending (Day et al. 2008: 98) and has specific effects on poorer physical and mental health, including increased psychological distress, depression and anxiety (Paradies et al. 2008: 3). Racism and discrimination is an ongoing manifestation of the historically excluded position of Indigenous people as colonised peoples. It is the active denial of the humanity of the affected person and their collective

C. Cunneen (✉)
University of Technology Sydney (UTS), Sydney, NSW, Australia

© The Author(s) 2018
M. Bhatia et al. (eds.), *Media, Crime and Racism*, Palgrave Studies in Crime,
Media and Culture, https://doi.org/10.1007/978-3-319-71776-0_14

277

cultural identity, with negative impacts on political, economic, social and emotional wellbeing (Paradies et al. 2008: 6).

This chapter focusses on one particular aspect of racism: the ways in which racialised criminality is both constructed and reproduced in the media. I focus specifically on racialised criminality and Indigenous peoples in Australia. The chapter takes a broad approach to media and includes mainstream media outlets (both print and television) and other media forms including social media and film. It looks at both non-Indigenous and Indigenous media, the latter being particularly important in understanding Indigenous resistance and challenges to mainstream representations. We have argued elsewhere that criminalisation and penality are part of the relations of power which produce and reproduce racialised social relations (Cunneen et al. 2013). The criminal justice system constitutes social groups as threats and reproduces a society built on racialised boundaries. Indeed, processes of criminalisation and penality constitute a significant racialising discourse—that is, we understand 'race' through discourses about crime and punishment (black men as violent; Indigenous culture as criminogenic) and we understand crime and punishment through images of race (e.g. the dominant cultural image of the violent offender/prisoner as being young, male and from a minority background). The media convey various representations of criminalisation and penality, and it is this role of the media (in its various contradictory ways) that is the centre of this chapter. The chapter focusses on a number of areas including reporting of Indigenous deaths in custody, reporting on riots and the growing use of social media as a means of constructing racialised criminality. Finally, the chapter considers the growth of Indigenous and alternative media in challenging mainstream representations of Indigenous people and crime.

Reporting Deaths in Custody

The Royal Commission into Aboriginal Deaths in Custody (RCIADIC) (Johnston 1991) was one of the most comprehensive inquiries held into the situation of Indigenous peoples in Australia. The Royal Commission investigated 99 Indigenous deaths in police, prison and juvenile justice custody during the period 1980 to 1989 and made widespread recommendations relating to the criminal justice system and social, economic and political affairs more generally. The establishment of the Royal Commission was the result of a long national campaign by Indigenous people (Wootten 1991). In the lead-up to the Royal Commission, investigative journalism played an important part in raising questions about the causes of Indigenous deaths in custody and the failure of authorities to respond to those deaths. As Bacon (2005: 23) notes, 'Mayman won a Golden Walkley, Australia's highest journalism award, for an investigation of John Pat's death published in *The Age* [and] ABC's *Four Corners* team took up the story and also won a Walkley award for their report'.

This critical role of the media in the establishment of the RCIADIC was acknowledged by the Commission:

> By its coverage of the issues, from the death of John Pat to that of Lloyd Boney, by placing them in their broader social and moral context, and by its presentation of the campaign of the Committee to Defend Black Rights, the media has acted as one of the protagonists in the process of achieving greater justice for Aboriginal people that is the goal of this Commission. (Johnston 1991: (2) 185)

However, the Royal Commission noted that this progressive role by sections of the media was overshadowed by more problematic approaches. The far more common media approach was to either ignore Indigenous issues completely or when they were reported upon to treat Indigenous people as a 'problem', that is, to represent 'Aboriginal people as a dissident, disruptive, or criminal element' (Johnston 1991: (2) 186). The Royal Commission noted the increase in the use of the word 'riot' in relation to confrontations involving Aboriginal people during the late 1980s. An analysis conducted for the Commission of the *Sydney Morning Herald* from January 1987 to April 1990 (the period the RCIADIC was investigating deaths and coincidentally also covering the 1988 Australian Bicentennial celebrations) showed that 40 per cent of all references to the word 'riot' within Australia were related to Aboriginal people (Johnston 1991: (2) 186).

Other research around this time confirmed the strong association between Indigenous people and crime and disorder. In an examination of newspaper reporting about youth in Western Australia between 1990 and 1992, Sercombe (1995) found that the major issue reported in relation to young people was crime. However, the 'face' of youth crime was also heavily racialised. Some 85 per cent of stories that referred to Aboriginal youth were principally about crime (Sercombe 1995: 78). A media study for the Australian Human Rights Commission's National Inquiry into Racist Violence revealed that 38 per cent of newspaper articles which mentioned Redfern during 1988 and 1989 were articles which were 'stereotypically negative stories' about Aboriginal people (Jakubowicz 1990: 18). Within these stories, the largest subject category identified Aboriginal people with crime and violence. A study of newspaper reporting in northwest NSW (Cunneen 1987) found that the major daily newspaper in the area (the *Daily Liberal*) engaged in discriminatory reporting: Aboriginal people were the only identifiable group who had their ethnicity or racial background mentioned in newspaper reports on crime: the only 'offenders' who were linguistically marked and separated by 'race' were Indigenous people. Thus analysis of various media confirmed the association of Indigenous people with crime, criminality, irrationality and riots (see also Goodall 1993). The National Inquiry into Racist Violence also raised a number of issues relating to the media portrayal of Aboriginal people.

> Discriminatory reporting in relation to crime stories was cited as being particularly likely to generate a climate conducive to racist violence. Terms such as 'black terror' or 'black crime wave' clearly convey a sense of racial hostility and threat… Aborigines in many rural areas complained that local media reinforced racist attitudes and generated fear and tension in their reporting of race issues. (HREOC 1991: 357)

By contrast, analysis of newspaper reporting of Indigenous deaths in custody in the period following the RCIADIC showed that many deaths were not reported upon at all, and when they were reported on the stories were brief, often less than 100 words (Bacon 2005: 32). This is despite the fact that Indigenous deaths in custody remain a significant problem.

The number of Indigenous deaths increased during the 1990s after the RCIADIC. Notwithstanding a decline during the early 2000s, the number of Indigenous deaths in custody has again increased (Lyneham and Chan 2013: xviii). One of the few in-depth media investigations of deaths in custody in recent years has not appeared in the mainstream media, but rather in the independent online news service *Crikey*. Inga Ting (2011), in an 11-part series of articles, investigated 132 coronial inquests into deaths in NSW prison custody between 2001 and 2009. Many of these involved the deaths of Indigenous prisoners. She discovered that prisoners were still dying in custody from the same failed practices that the RCIADIC had sought to eliminate. Ting found that coronial investigations documented more than 60 cases in which 'bureaucratic bungling, a failure or absence of policy, breaches of procedure or lack of communication between government agencies contributed to the death' (Ting 2011: 2). Many of the deaths occurred because custodial or health staff failed to adequately screen inmates, failed to consult inmate's medical and other files, failed to transfer files or failed to communicate important information about prisoner's health and safety. As a result, in many cases prisoners died because of incompetence or neglect. Their deaths 'could have been avoided had custodial and health authorities exercised proper duty of care and adhered to policies implemented as a result of Royal Commission recommendations' (Ting 2011: 2). The work of independent investigative journalists, like Ting, stands in contrast to the relative silence around deaths in custody found in the mainstream media.

The Media, Deaths in Custody and Indigenous Resistance

Of particular importance is not only the silence of the mainstream media around deaths in custody but also the factors that appear to pique media interest. The moment when the mainstream media becomes interested in deaths in custody is when there are Indigenous protests (usually referred to as riots by the media) after a death has occurred. While the events and circumstances surrounding deaths in custody appear of little interest to the media, this changes dramatically if there are public protests concerning those deaths. Indigenous resistance to policing, imprisonment and deaths in custody in Australia is recast through the mainstream media and the criminal justice system as instances of racialised criminality. Indigenous resistance is represented as lawless and the political dimension of resistance is denied. Representing Indigenous resistance to colonial power as 'criminal' has a long history in Australia and rests on particular racialised assumptions about Indigenous people as being without law and civilisation and the nature of the Australian state being founded in discovery and settlement, rather than through invasion.

The violence of the colonial state, both historically and contemporaneously through deaths in custody, is recast as the colonial state upholding law and order against rioting and lawless 'natives'. Goodall's (1993) analysis of the Brewarrina protests and 'riot' after the death in custody of Lloyd Boney in 1987 showed that television footage of the events was cut and repeatedly reused in such a way as to show Aboriginal people as irrational and criminal. The televised message had a powerful symbolic meaning well beyond any aim to simply report 'what happened'. Similar issues can be seen in coverage of the Redfern and Palm Island 'riots' discussed in more detail below.

Redfern Riot 2004

The riot in Redfern in February 2004 occurred after the death of TJ Hickey. Seventeen-year-old 'TJ' had died after impaling himself on a metal fence whilst riding his bicycle in the inner Sydney suburb of Redfern. On the night following his death, a serious riot erupted in Redfern between Aboriginal people and police which caused widespread injury. At the time of TJ's death, there was a police operation in the vicinity arising from an earlier assault and robbery which had allegedly involved an Aboriginal offender. A number of vehicle patrols were active in the area at the time, and one had followed TJ although he was not a 'person of interest' in relation to the robbery. There was a widespread belief at the time that TJ was being chased by police at the time of his death, and indeed the Coroner subsequently found that TJ's death was a death in custody, occurring as it did during police operations.

The subsequent riot after TJ's death received widespread publicity, with various 'causes' discussed by media and politicians. There were a group of common explanations and solutions to the riot which dominated the public domain. One set of explanations used motivational causes for rioting behaviour such as drugs, alcohol and hot weather. Another set of explanations blamed social disadvantage. And the third set of explanations blamed the lack of effective policing in the area. These explanatory narratives have been used previously to account for anti-police riots in Redfern (Cunneen 1990).

One explanation put forward by police, politicians and media commentators was that the riot was caused by drugs. According to a source from Redfern police, the heroin trade was the 'true cause' of the riot and poor relations with police because of a police crackdown on the heroin trade in Redfern (*Sydney Morning Herald* 2004a, 17 May 2004). Similarly, an editorial in *The Australian* stated simply, 'the riot was caused by heroin' (18 May 2004). Other reports blamed a 'softly, softly' approach to policing in Redfern (*Sydney Morning Herald* 2004b, 18 February 2004). Alternatively, the 'Block' (an area in Redfern where many Aboriginal people live) was portrayed as a no-go area, with the only solution being to increase the number of police and the number of street patrols (*Sydney Morning Herald* 2004c, 24 February 2004). Both these explanations saw the cause of the riot as a failure of an inadequate police presence.

The question of disadvantage and the lack of 'hope' for people in Redfern was also a theme: summarised in the newspaper heading 'Kids Need Hope, Assistance and Education' (*Sydney Morning Herald* 2004d, 22 February 2004). It was common in this narrative for police to 'blame' other government departments for their lack of support in Redfern. The assumption was that if young people had educational and employment opportunities then there would be no rioting behaviour. In the months following the riot there was a strong emphasis on increasing police capabilities in Redfern. The building of a new $6 million seven-storey police station was announced. Police numbers in Redfern were increased by one third from 170 to 226, and a new riot squad (the Operational Support Group) was formed. In relation to social policy, the Redfern Waterloo Partnership Project was further strengthened and funded.

Virtually no attention was paid in these official explanations to the long history of volatile conflict between Aboriginal people and the police in Redfern. Instances of police abuse of Aboriginal people, first documented by the New South Wales Council for Civil Liberties, date back to the 1960s. In the early 1970s, the first Aboriginal Legal Service in Australia was established in Redfern because of police harassment of Aboriginal people in the area. By the mid to late 1980s, riots between police and Aboriginal young people were relatively common (Cunneen 1990). An investigation by the Federal Race Discrimination Commission in 1990 over the use of tactical response police in raids around the 'Block' found that the police used excessive force and that the justifications for the raids exhibited institutional racism. Some local police were found to refer to Redfern as 'coon county' (Cunneen 1990: 11).

The death of TJ Hickey sparked a riot, but did so in the context of constant complaints of police harassment, particularly of Aboriginal youth. Part of this harassment derived from a renewed focus on 'zero tolerance' style police operations and the use of public order legislation that clearly targeted young people. The fact that TJ was classified as a 'High Risk Offender' by police meant that he was subject to constant scrutiny. His bail requirement not to visit a particular housing area where his mother resided almost certainly imposed a condition that he would constantly breach. The 2004 riot in Redfern was a clear case of moral indignation and collective protest against what was seen to be police involvement in the death of a young Indigenous boy. It demonstrated the depth of collective anger at the way the justice system operates. Yet the media representations of the riot provided no context or discussion of this sense of injustice. Indeed, the apparent lawlessness of Indigenous people lent itself well to the arguments for a greater police presence in the area. The fact that policing might be part of the problem was erased from public policy consideration.

Palm Island Riot 2004

Thirty-six-year-old Mulrunji Doomadgee died in police custody on Palm Island in November 2004. He had been arrested for drunk and disorderly behaviour. He was healthy man when arrested and was not known as a troublemaker on the island and had not been previously arrested on the island. The riot occurred a week after Mulrunji's death, when the results of the autopsy became known to the community. The post-mortem examination revealed that Mulrunji suffered four broken ribs, a ruptured spleen and that his liver was almost cleaved in two.

The riot which occurred on Palm Island was clearly a protest against what was seen at the time as police involvement in the death of Mulrunji. During the protest, the local police station was set on fire, and the courthouse extensively damaged. As a result of the riot, the Queensland government established a Palm Island Select Committee. The terms of reference for the committee did not include an examination of policing on the island, but rather local government arrangements, infrastructure development and options to improve the coordination of government services on the island. The government developed a five-point plan for Palm Island. The first point and 'absolute priority' was the restoration of law and order on the island. The other four points included re-establishing services, rebuilding infrastructure (the first of which was to build a new police station and courthouse), the development of an alcohol management plan (to restrict access to alcohol) and to establish new governance arrangements.

The dominant view presented by government was the social and economic 'problems' of Palm Island led to the riot. The rioters were seen as lawless with media depictions such as a 'war zone', 'rioting mobs' and 'rioters… in a rampage' (Porter 2015: 292). However, people on Palm Island were also seen passive victims of disadvantage. Newspaper reports of Palm Island such as 'Tropic of Despair: Decades of oppression have the people of beautiful Palm Island dispirited and desperate' (*Sydney Morning Herald* 2004e, 4 December 2004: 31) reinforced this view. There are serious social and economic issues on Palm Island including unemployment, over-crowded housing and poor health. Yet the basic cause of the riot was a death in police custody where there was a strong community belief that police were directly responsible for the death. Contrary to dominant view of 'despair', the riot on Palm Island can also be interpreted as the community standing up assertively and clearly expressing its outrage at the death of Mulrunji, and what it saw to be an attempted cover-up by the authorities.

Indeed, the community's anger was vindicated by the coronial report. The state coroner found that Mulrunji had punched Sergeant Hurley after being arrested and transported to the police station and that Hurley had punched Mulrunji in response. Both men fell to the ground and Hurley lost his temper and hit Mulrunji several times after falling to the floor. 'I conclude that these actions of Senior Sergeant Hurley caused the fatal injuries' (Clements 2006: 27). The coroner found that the decision to arrest Mulrunji for drunk and disorder could easily have been addressed by means other than arrest. According to the coroner, the arrest was an inappropriate use of police discretion. In other words, Mulrunji should never have been in police custody in the first place.

The coroner was critical of the failure to check on the health of Mulrunji after the fall and the assault.

> Mulrunji cried out for help from the cell after being fatally injured, and no help came. The images from the cell video tape of Mulrunji, writhing in pain as he lay dying on the cell floor, were shocking and terribly distressing to family and anyone who sat through that portion of the evidence. The sounds from the cell surveillance tape are unlikely to be forgotten by anyone who was in court and heard that tape played. There is clear evidence that this must have been able to be heard from the police station dayroom where the monitor was running. Indeed, the timing of Senior Sergeant Hurley's visit to the cell suggests that the sounds were heard. But the response was completely inadequate and offered no proper review of Mulrunji's condition or call for medical attention. The inspections were cursory and dangerous even had Mulrunji been merely intoxicated. The so called arousal technique of nudging Mulrunji with a foot is not appropriate. It cannot be sanctioned. (Clements 2006: 32)

After it was suspected that Mulrunji was dead, there was no attempt at resuscitation. The Coroner was highly critical of the investigation which failed to meet the standards of thoroughness, competency or impartiality. One investigating officer was a friend of Hurley—the police officer most likely to be under investigation.

In an important analysis of media representation of Indigenous people in Australia, Porter (2015) has contrasted the way mainstream media in Australia portrayed the riots on Palm Island after the death of Mulrunji Doomadgee with the portrayal of the riots in Ferguson, Missouri, after the police shooting of Michael Brown: a contrast in portrayal between riotous (Palm Island) and righteous (Ferguson) behaviour. As Porter (2015: 294) notes the disturbances in Ferguson are contextualised within a framework of civil disobedience, political demonstrations and the civil rights movement, while the event is placed more generally within the US history of Jim Crow and institutional racism. In contrast, the people of Palm Island are depicted as 'rioters' and therefore lack legitimacy to their claims. 'Indigeneity was portrayed as itself being synonymous with criminality… The police and media were constructed as victims, focusing on the fear and terror felt by these parties' (Porter 2015: 292). The media construction of the events created suitable scapegoats and 'justified the state's heavy-handed response that follows' (Porter 2015: 294).

The problems identified by the RCADIC in media representations of Indigenous people and criminality have not abated. Indeed, in the 25 years since the Royal Commission it is commonplace for Indigenous people to be constantly framed within a discourse of criminality—a point highlighted by the relative neglect of deaths in custody except when there is community outrage and protests over specific deaths. In these cases Indigenous protests are recast as examples of lawlessness and criminality.

Racism and Social Media

Social media has provided an important medium for Indigenous groups and supporters. For example, the Facebook groups like the *Indigenous Human Rights Network* and *Australians against Aboriginal Racism and Forced Land Acquisition* advocate and promote the awareness of Indigenous human rights in Australia. The social media platform *IndigenousX* began life as a Twitter account founded by Indigenous teacher Luke Pearson in 2012 with over 18,000 followers. *IndigenousX* has expanded to Facebook, Instagram and YouTube, and a partnership with *The Guardian Australia*. However, social media has also been used to flame racial tensions and denigrate Aboriginal people. ABC reporter Norman Hermant (2015) has noted that when the ABC posts stories about Indigenous justice on Facebook, 'the flood gates open'. In this instance, Hermant had written a number of stories on an Amnesty International report which was critical of the levels of juvenile detention of Indigenous young people in Australia. The stories were posted on the ABC News Facebook page. Hermant details some of the many comments that were posted from people across Australia, including the following:

> White man built this country up and made it what it is today. What has ANY aboriginal ever built?? The laws is meant for all Australians as equals, but then that's why you don't like it, and you don't like it, the bush is wide open and waiting for you. Hey, you can go walk-about and just keep walking.
> Well, if we start summery (sic) executions for these crimes they won't need to go to jail.
> They can practice their war dances in prison.

Hermant (2015) notes that the comments 'expose an uncomfortable reality many of us prefer to ignore. After reading these comments, and hearing from my colleagues at ABC Online, it's hard to conclude anything but this: the racially charged and hostile opinions expressed in these comments are not marginal'. They also reflect a long running trope of colonial ideology within Australia, namely, that Indigenous people are a racially inferior, crime-prone group who require either incarceration or removal—themes which are repeated below in the discussion of a local 'anti-crime' Facebook group.

The Townsville Crime Alerts and Discussion Facebook Group

The Townsville Crime Alerts and Discussions (TCAD) is an active online Facebook group using social media to promote and lobby for more punitive approaches to law and order particularly focusing on harsher penalties for [Indigenous] juveniles. The Facebook page was created in 2012 and at October 2016 had nearly 35,000 members. Townsville has an estimated population of 180,000. The TCAD have successfully organised petitions and protests and received considerable media attention (e.g. ABC News 2013; Gillham 2013; SBS 2014). Their primary message is that current legislation does not allow for 'young criminals' to be punished adequately for serious crimes and that laws need to be toughened.

The Facebook group's founder, Ms Parkinson, personally met with then Premier, Campbell Newman, and Mr Bleijie, the then Attorney General. She was specifically referred to during the second reading of new punitive juvenile justice legislation. It was noted that the TCAD was 'very much in favour of the government's actions on youth offending' (Queensland Parliament 2014: 596). Parkinson claimed that the reforms would not have occurred without the pressure of the TCAD (Anderson 2014). The state government's draconian youth justice reforms at the time included, among other changes, removing the principle of juvenile detention as a sanction of last resort, introducing 'naming and shaming' of young offenders, mandatory boot camps for repeat offenders and the abolition of both the Indigenous Murri Youth Court and the court-ordered Youth Justice Conferencing programme. In 2014, a splinter Facebook group, the Townsville Crime Alerts and Discussions Without Hitler Admin, was established. It is generally more extreme and overtly racist than the TCAD. It currently has over 3000 members.

Some posts on these Facebook pages explicitly refer to 'ATSI' (a generally unacceptable abbreviation of Aboriginal and Torres Strait Islander people), and many refer specifically to Indigenous young people; others, while not explicitly referencing Indigenous people, post photos which makes it clear who is being discussed in the posts. Overwhelmingly the posts are highly derogatory, referring to young people allegedly involved in offences as 'pieces of crap', 'ATSI ferals', 'scum bags' and 'pieces of shit'. A perhaps well-rehearsed litany of complaints includes lenient judges and magistrates, 'holiday camp' detention centres and the lack of tough legislation. However, it is the racialised heart of the Facebook posts which is most pronounced and provides a deeper symbolic colonialist resonance to various claims such as 'the only thing that is going to deter these mongrels is a bullet', or calls to train dogs to attack Indigenous young people, or the need to bring the army onto the streets and allow them 'to use any force should they come across trouble' as one post stated. Images on the site, such as the one reproduced below, condone and legitimise violence. In this atmosphere, vigilante responses are hardly surprising. When an Indigenous man was reported in the local media to have been attacked by a group of masked men, racially taunted and then impaled on a fence (McMahon 2016), many of the Facebook posts either doubted the veracity of the claim or thought the injured man had committed an offence and was therefore deserving of the response.

Facebook groups condoning vigilante violence against Indigenous people are not restricted to the TCAD. Similar Facebook groups can be found in the Northern Territory (NT) and Western Australia (WA). Facebook groups in Kalgoorlie, WA, became the focus of attention recently after the death of a 14-year-old Aboriginal boy in August 2016. Elijah Doughty was killed when struck by a vehicle driven by the owner of a motorcycle the boy had allegedly stolen. The driver was charged with manslaughter. Following a protest outside the courthouse which turned violent, Aboriginal community members blamed Facebook groups and social media for inflaming racial tensions in the town (Bembridge 2016). Kalgoorlie has a population of about 30,000 with the two main Facebook groups having about 18,000 members. Prior to Elijah Doughty's death, the two Facebook groups were full of similar posts to those found on the TCAD—a focus on crime and Aboriginal people and various appeals to vigilante action. Some of the posts included: 'There is going to be revenge of some sort very soon!'; 'How many human bodies would it take to fill the mineshafts around Kalgoorlie? A: We're one theft closer to finding out!'; 'Feel free to run the oxygen thieves off the road if you see them'; 'We need a vigilante, like The Punisher'; 'Things will never change unless there is annual cull' and 'Everyone talks about hunting down these sub human mutts, but no one ever does' (cited in Purtill 2016).

After Elijah's death, posts included 'Condolences to the driver trying to get his bike back. Went a bit to far' and another by same person 'I have more sympathy for the ute driver than I do for a thieving little scrote who was on the wrong place at the wrong time' (cited in Graham 2016) and 'Good job you thieving bastard. Don't think you'll be touching another bike anytime soon ahaha. About time someone took it into their own hands hope it happens again' (cited in Purtill 2016). Both Facebook groups have now been closed.

Andrew Bolt and Hate Speech

At the other end of the spectrum to the Facebook groups discussed above are the more institutionalised attacks on Indigenous people. The well-known media commentator Andrew Bolt crosses over the use of mainstream and social media with a newspaper column, television program and blog site. The blog site in particular facilitates not only Bolt's attacks on Indigenous people but opens up a site where unrestrained racist response from contributors proliferate (e.g. see Bolt 2009).

In 2011 Andrew Bolt was brought before the Federal Court of Australia for breaching s18C of the *Racial Discrimination Act*. The section of the Act makes it unlawful to 'offend, insult, humiliate or intimidate' a person because of their 'race, colour or national or ethnic origin'. Bolt has used his position in the media for a considerable time to attack what he sees as 'light-skinned' Indigenous people who have no right to claim their Aboriginality and only do so because of a financial or other benefit

(Langton n.d.). Nine Aboriginal people took Bolt to court in relation to two articles he had written for the *Herald Sun* attacking 'light-skinned' Indigenous people.

The media commentator was found guilty. The Federal Court found that the articles were not written in good faith and contained factual errors. Bromberg J was 'satisfied that fair-skinned Aboriginal people… were reasonably likely… to have been offended, insulted, humiliated or intimidated by the imputations conveyed by the newspaper articles' (*Eatock v Bolt* [2011] FCA 1103 at 17). Bromberg J was especially concerned with the 'intimidatory effect… in particular [on] young Aboriginal persons or others with vulnerability in relation to their identity' (*Eatock v Bolt* at 24). Andrew Bolt, along with some conservative and ultra-right politicians, has campaigned for the repeal of s18C of the *Racial Discrimination Act* (see e.g. Patel 2016).

The growth of social media has allowed the representations of Indigenous racialised criminality to flourish, especially at a more localised level and largely without any form of moderation and regulation. Both the discussion by Hermant and the Bolt case also show that social media connected to mainstream media outlets allows the expression of a relatively unrestrained racism against Indigenous people. While the successful prosecution of Andrew Bolt related to pieces published in the *Herald Sun*, it is perhaps the public's response to his blogs which are more concerning. In commenting on the racism evident in public responses to the ABC Facebook stories on Indigenous people, Hermant notes that 'many of them list their names, where they live, even where they work on their Facebook accounts. They're not hiding'.

Indigenous Media and Resistance

A significant contribution to challenging representations of the racialised criminality of Indigenous people has been through the development of Indigenous media. This media takes various forms including newspapers, television, radio and film. Indigenous-run community radio dates back to the early 1970s and has developed now to over 130 community radio stations. In 1996 the National Indigenous Radio Service (NIRS) was established, providing a 24-hour-a-day service and an independent voice for Indigenous commentators nationwide on a range of issues including matters such as policing, over-representation in the criminal justice system and deaths in custody. Indigenous television dates back to 1988 with the establishment of Imparja in Alice Springs. National Indigenous Television (NITV) was established in 2007. Like the NIRS, NITV provides an important voice for Indigenous people. Its news service and current affairs programmes regularly broadcast on Indigenous criminal justice matters. For example, Stan Grant's programme, *The Point*, has investigations and analysis of topics such as Indigenous juveniles in detention, unsolved Indigenous murders, criminalisation and deaths in custody. A range of Indigenous-operated newspapers (online and print) have also developed since the *Koori Mail* was established in 1991 and the *National Indigenous Times* in 2002. As Porter (2015: 299) noted in relation to the riots on Palm Island after the death of Mulrunji, 'Indigenous media was particularly critical of the labelling of all participants as 'rioters', and stressed the moral righteousness of Palm Islanders… In these ways, Indigenous media provided a powerful source in questioning misinformation within the mainstream media portrayal'.

Indigenous media has been important in providing alternative information on deaths in custody. In the case of the death of Julieka Dhu in Western Australia in 2014, NITV has provided extensive coverage and established a dedicated Facebook page. Twenty-two-year-old Ms. Dhu died in a police watch house after being arrested for unpaid fines. Ms Dhu complained to police about severe pain, vomiting and partial paralysis and was twice taken to hospital but on both occasions was sent back to prison. On the third occasion she was taken to hospital, she was dying from septicaemia and pneumonia. Police believed her transfer to hospital was not urgent and reportedly told nursing staff she was 'faking' her illness (Gartry and Trigger 2015). At the time of writing, the coronial inquiry is yet to be completed.

Another medium through which Indigenous deaths in custody, imprisonment and criminal justice responses more generally have been explored by Indigenous people is through films such as *Who Killed Malcolm Smith?* (1992), *Innocence Betrayed* (2014) and *Prison Songs* (2015). *Prison Songs* focusses on inmates of Berrimah prison in the Northern Territory.

Aboriginal people make up over 80 per cent of the prison's population. The inmates share their stories through song. Kelrick Martin, the writer and director of the film, notes that, 'A lot of people in prison tend to be quite reflective, because they have a lot of time to think about where they've come from and how they've gotten where they are. The participants were therefore open to confronting their pasts and actions, and talking about it in an honest way' (Molloy 2015). *Innocence Betrayed* (2014) follows the story of three families' search for justice after a botched police investigation and failed prosecution following the murders of three Aboriginal children in Bowraville, NSW, in the early 1990s.

Who Killed Malcolm Smith? deals explicitly with Aboriginal deaths in custody. It was written and narrated by Richard Franklin. The film traces the story of Malcolm Smith from his early life, his removal from family and institutionalisation and his subsequent imprisonment and death while in prison. Franklin helped investigate Smith's death for the Royal Commission into Aboriginal Deaths in Custody. In the film he narrates the story of Smith's life and death. Smith died from self-inflicted injuries after the handle of a paint brush had been driven into his left eye. While the facts concerning how Malcolm Smith died are relatively straightforward, the film explores the far more difficult question is *why* he died. Smith had been removed and isolated from his family at the age of 11. He spent time 'in despotic institutions of various kinds [which] left him illiterate and innumerate, unskilled, and without experience of normal society' (Wootten 1989).

After being made a state ward, Smith was first sent to Kinchela Boys' Home. After four years the Home's achievements were summarised in a manager's report which stated, 'taking into account Malcolm's lack of academic qualifications, being a persistent liar and his habits of perversion, it is difficult to be able to recommend anything for the future for him'. The film contrasts this view with what we know of Malcolm's early life before state intervention. There was no indication of ill treatment or unhappiness. The worst 'crimes' of 11-year-old Malcolm were that he truanted from school and had gone joyriding on another child's bicycle.

The film traces the periods of Malcolm's imprisonment in Mt. Penang Training Centre and then Tamworth Boys' Home, both described as paramilitary institutions designed to turn boys into 'automatons'. During the nine years and eight months of his adult life, Smith spent nine years in adult gaols, often as a result of prison sentences which were extremely harsh. It was during the period of his adult imprisonment that Malcolm's psychotic symptoms developed. Yet, no thorough psychiatric assessment was conducted, despite numerous serious attempts at self-injury. The film, following the Royal Commission report, argues that his particular death is part of a continuing legacy of the 'brutal cruelty of what was done in the name of protection and welfare by a smug, self-righteous and racist community'.

Conclusion

The 'media' is not a monolithic entity. There are times when investigative journalism by publicly owned media organisations, the ABC and SBS, has played an important role in uncovering injustices against Aboriginal people. This has been exemplified most recently by the ABC's 2016 *Four Corners* program exposing the abuse of children in detention in the Northern Territory. Indigenous media and alternative online media has also been important in providing a different discourse and voice for Indigenous people, particularly around deaths in custody and when there has been open conflict between Indigenous people and state authorities.

However, the dominant discourse in mainstream media presents a racialised view of criminality. The problems identified by the RCADIC in media representations of Indigenous people and criminality have not abated. Indeed, representations of racialised criminality have been popularised in new forms through the growth of social media. The widespread reach in local communities of Facebook shows the power of these mediums. Representations of Indigenous racialised criminality have flourished, largely without any form of moderation and regulation. Indeed, some posts on these Facebook sites call for or support vigilante violence against Indigenous people. Such depictions of Indigenous people as criminal, and the call for stronger state responses and the potential resort to violence, resonate with longer historical colonialist views of Aboriginal people as racially inferior and as a threat to property and social order.

References

ABC News. (2013). Anti-Crime Group Keen for Youth Curfew Commitment. *ABC News*, 8 October. Retrieved from http://www.abc.net.au/news/2013-10-08/anti-crime-group-keen-for-youth-curfew-commitment/5008908

Allison, F., Cunneen, C., Schwartz, M., & Behrendt, L. (2012). *Indigenous Legal Needs Project: Northern Territory Report*. Cairns: James Cook University.

Anderson, C. (2014). Online Warriors Fighting Crime with the Click of a Mouse. *Townsville Bulletin*, 29 March. Retrieved from http://www.townsvillebulletin.com.au/news/online-warriors-fighting-crime-with-the-click-of-a-mouse/story-fnjfzs4b-1226868519996

Bacon, W. (2005). A Case Study in Ethical Failure: Twenty Years of Media Coverage of Aboriginal Deaths in Custody. *Pacific Journalism Review, 11*(2), 17–40.

Bembridge, C. (2016). Kalgoorlie Protest: Community Mourns as Elders Call for Action Against Online Racism. *ABC News*, 31 August. Retrieved from http://www.abc.net.au/news/2016-08-30/community-mourns-as-elders-call-for-justice-after-riot/7799942

Bolt, A. (2009). The New Tribe of White Blacks. *Andrew Bolt Blog Posts*, 21 August. Retrieved from http://www.heraldsun.com.au/blogs/andrew-bolt/column--the-new-tribe-of-white-blacks/news-story/2084e333d698f20fafd8b0a3f88c77b4

Clements, C. (2006). *Inquest into the Death of Mulrunji*. Brisbane: Office of the State Coroner. Retrieved from http://www.justice.qld.gov.au/courts/coroner/findings/mulrunji270906.doc

Cunneen, C. (1987). Newspaper Reporting of Crime, Law and Order in North West NSW. *Journal for Social Justice Studies, 2*, 14–32.

Cunneen, C. (1990). *Aboriginal/Police Relations in Redfern with Special Reference to the Police Raid of 8 February 1990*. Report Commissioned by the National Inquiry into Racist Violence. Sydney: Human Rights and Equal Opportunity Commission.

Cunneen, C., Baldry, E., Brown, D., Brown, M., Schwartz, M., & Steel, A. (2013). *Penal Culture and Hyperincarceration*. London: Ashgate.

Cunneen, C., Allison, F., & Schwartz, M. (2014). *Indigenous Legal Needs Project: Queensland Report*. Cairns: James Cook University.

Day, A., Davey, L., Wanganeen, R., Howells, K., De Santolo, J., & Nakata, M. (2008). The Significance of Context: Stories from South Australia. In A. Day, M. Nakata, & K. Howells (Eds.), *Anger and Indigenous Men* (pp. 88–102). Leichhardt: Federation Press.

Gartry, L., & Trigger, R. (2015). Police Thought Dying Woman Ms Dhu Was Faking It, Coronial Inquest Told. *ABC News*, 23 November. Retrieved from http://www.abc.net.au/news/2015-11-23/inquest-into-death-of-dhu-in-police-custody/6963244

Gillham, A. (2013). Townsville Youth Crime Protesters Get a Hearing. *ABC North Queensland*, 26 February. Retrieved from http://www.abc.net.au/local/photos/2013/02/26/3698793.htm

Goodall, H. (1993). Constructing a Riot: Television News and Aborigines. *Media Information Australia, 68*, 70–77.

Graham, C. (2016). White Man's Manslaughter. Black Man's Murder. White Man's Riot. *Black Man's Uprising, New Matilda*, 31 August. Retrieved from https://newmatilda.com/2016/08/31/the-kalgoorlie-uprising-a-rational-response-to-another-black-death/

Hermant, N. (2015). It Doesn't Take Much to Find Australia's Racial Divide on Facebook. *The Drum, ABC News*, 5 June. Retrieved from http://www.abc.net.au/news/2015-06-05/hermant-exposing-australias-racial-divide-on-facebook/6524358

Human Rights and Equal Opportunity Commission (HREOC). (1991). *Racist Violence*. Report of the National Inquiry into Racist Violence, Canberra: AGPS.

Innocence Betrayed. (2014). Director: Larissa Behrendt, Frontyard Films.

Jakubowicz, A. (1990). *Racist Violence, Racism and the Media*. Unpublished Paper Commissioned by the National Inquiry into Racist Violence, Sydney: Human Rights and Equal Opportunity Commission.

Johnston, E. (1991). *Final Report*. Royal Commission into Aboriginal Deaths in Custody, Canberra: AGPS.

Langton, M. (n.d.). *The Nature of My Apology*. Retrieved from http://www.abc.net.au/tv/qanda/pdf/Marcia_Langton_on_Bolt.pdf

Lyneham, M., & Chan, A. (2013). *Deaths in Custody in Australia to 30 June 2011*. Canberra: Australian Institute of Criminology.

McMahon, C. (2016). Man Claims Serious Injuries Behind Racial Attack from Masked Men. *Townsville Bulletin*, 2 June. Retrieved from http://www.townsvillebulletin.com.au/news/man-claims-serious-injuries-behind-racial-attack-from-masked-men/news-story/afeda78c89ce975430fe332c6ec617a1

Molloy, S. (2015). *Prison Songs Is the Groundbreaking Musical Documentary Filmed Inside a Darwin Jail*. Retrieved from http://www.news.com.au/entertainment/tv/reality-tv/prison-songs-is-the-groundbreaking-musical-documentary-filmed-inside-a-darwin-jail/news-story/c350469c9d9ee82bf79a78e2be7a03ca

Paradies, Y., Harris, R., & Anderson, I. (2008). *The Impact of Racism on Indigenous Health in Australia and Aotearoa: Towards a Research Agenda.* Discussion Paper No. 4, Darwin: Cooperative Research Centre for Aboriginal Health.

Patel, U. (2016). David Leyonhjelm, Malcolm Roberts Push for Section 18C of Racial Discrimination Act to Be Removed. *ABC News*, 7 August. Retrieved from http://www.abc.net.au/news/2016-08-07/leyonhjelm-roberts-tell-insiders-18c-racial-discrimination-act/7698252

Porter, A. (2015). Riotous or Righteous Behaviour? Representations of Subaltern Resistance in the Australian Mainstream Media. *Current Issues in Criminal Justice, 26*(3), 289–304.

Prison Songs. (2015). Director: Kelrick Martin, Spear Point Productions/Screen Australia.

Purtill, J. (2016). Racist. Violent. Deleted: The Facebook Posts Dividing Kalgoorlie. *Triple J Hack, ABC Online*, 1 September. Retrieved from http://www.abc.net.au/triplej/programs/hack/the-facebook-posts-dividing-kalgoorlie/7805346

Queensland Parliament. (2014). *Record of Proceedings (Hansard)*, 18 March. Retrieved from http://www.parliament.qld.gov.au/documents/hansard/2014/2014_03_18_WEEKLY.pdf

SBS. (2014). New QLD Laws Aims to Stop Young Offenders. *SBS*, 11 February. Retrieved from http://www.sbs.com.au/news/article/2014/02/11/new-qld-laws-aim-stop-young-offenders

Schwartz, M., Cunneen, C., & Allison, F. (2013). *Indigenous Legal Needs Project: Victorian Report.* Cairns: James Cook University.

Sercombe, H. (1995). The Face of the Criminal is Aboriginal. In J. Bessant, K. Carrington, & S. Cook (Eds.), *Cultures of Crime and Violence: The Australian Experience.* Melbourne: La Trobe University Press.

Sydney Morning Herald. (2004a). Redfern Riot Blamed on Heroin Trade. *Sydney Morning Herald*, 17 May. Retrieved from http://www.smh.com.au/articles/2004/05/16/1084646071049.html

Sydney Morning Herald. (2004b). Redfern Violence Blamed on 'Softly–Softly' Approach. *Sydney Morning Herald*, 18 February 2004, Retrieved from http://www.smh.com.au/articles/2004/02/17/1076779978733.html

Sydney Morning Herald. (2004c). Time to Start Again, Say Redfern Police. *Sydney Morning Herald*, 24 February. Retrieved from http://www.smh.com.au/articles/2004/02/23/1077497517473.html

Sydney Morning Herald. (2004d). Kids Need Hope, Assistance and Education. *Sydney Morning Herald*, 22 February. Retrieved from http://www.smh.com.au/articles/2004/02/21/1077072890380.html

Sydney Morning Herald. (2004e). Tropic of Despair. *Sydney Morning Herald*, 4 December. Retrieved from http://www.smh.com.au/news/National/Tropic-of-despair/2004/12/03/1101923341699.html

The Australian. (2004). The Real Racists Are Dealing Drugs. *The Australian*, 18 May 2004.

Ting, I. (2011). *Deaths in Custody*, An Eleven Part *Crikey* Investigation. Retrieved from http://www.crikey.com.au/deaths-in-custody/

Who Killed Malcolm Smith? (1992). Directors: Adler, N and C. Sherwood, Film Australia/Titus Films.

Wootten, H. (1989). *Report of Inquiry into the Death of Malcolm Charles Smith*, Royal Commission into Aboriginal Deaths in Custody. Canberra: AGPS.

Wootten, H. (1991). 99 Reasons: The Royal Commission into Aboriginal Deaths in Custody. *Polemic*, *3*(3), 124–127.

Cases

Eatock v Bolt [2011] FCA 1103 (28 September 2011).

15

An Analysis of Anti-Black Crime Reporting in Toronto: Evidence from News Frames and Critical Race Theory

Wesley Crichlow and Sharon Lauricella

Introduction

Modern media representations of Blacks as violent and criminal (Crichlow 2009, 2014) have contributed to the construction of Blacks, and particularly Black males, as ensconced in a life of crime, poverty, and violence. The issue of media depiction of Black males is particularly important in the present age—coined "post-racial"—after Barack Obama's presidential victory in 2008. Politics constitutes a variant of the post-racial era in Canada, where political parties have sought out racial minority candidates in predominantly Black, ethnic, and racialised communities. This was most evident in the appointment of Canada's first Black Governor, General Michaelle Jean, in 2005. In general, however, media reports about Toronto's Black communities address violence, gangs, and crime, and are anecdotally recognised as reporting Blacks as academic underachievers, recipients of child welfare, overrepresented in youth correctional facilities, and living in abject poverty (Crichlow 2014). Entman

W. Crichlow (✉) • S. Lauricella
University of Ontario Institute of Technology, Oshawa, ON, Canada

© The Author(s) 2018   **301**
M. Bhatia et al. (eds.), *Media, Crime and Racism*, Palgrave Studies in Crime,
Media and Culture, https://doi.org/10.1007/978-3-319-71776-0_15

and Rojecki (2000) suggest that print media and television visually construct poverty as nearly synonymous with Blacks and that surveys show that whites typically accept this view. In this sense, news—whether print or visual—encourages the acceptance of the prototypical Black as poor and the prototypical poor person as Black (Entman and Rojecki 2000, p. 102). These anti-black working class racist stereotypes besmirch the image of Black men who are either not poor or are from middle and upper class groups (Collins 2004; Poindexter et al. 2003).

It is arguable that Blacks have been pathologised, demonised, and vilified (Drummond 1990; Crichlow 2014) in the media. Stereotypical depictions of Black masculinity as wanton and stigmatised are held responsible for the social problems that beset them, rather than the everyday state lynching and racist violence that diminishes their sense of self-worth. These negative portrayals and perceptions are important, because public mass-mediated perceptions have the potential to exaggerate people's perceptions. Therefore, stereotypes often become the distorted dominant viewpoint whether they are accurate or not, and so all forms of new and old media complements what one reads in textbooks at schools, colleges, and universities (Ribeau et al. 1997, p. 149). Further, the media's stereotypical portrayal of Blacks as criminals is also political, which operates to produce anxiety, moral panic, and antiblackracism in Canada (Tator and Henry 2006). Racist stereotypical perceptions of Black males construct the lens through which the media, as a dominant institution, dehumanises Blacks.

Antiblackracism is a conceptual framework for understanding a dialectic which involves "a particular form of systemic and structural racism in Canadian society, which historically and contemporarily has been perpetrated against Blacks" (Benjamin 2003, ii). Antiblackracism highlights the "resistance against dominant and hegemonic systems of Whiteness and the building of agency and social transformation against racism and other forms of oppression" (Benjamin 2003, ii). When Blacks are continually portrayed in the context of crime, it becomes impossible to maintain the critical analysis to recognise and confront the ideological (read: media) repressive apparatus of the private sector and government. These hegemonic parameters make it difficult for the black male—particularly the financially poor—to escape the race/poverty/crime nexus.

Media narratives situate social problems such that they arise solely from the actions of Blacks (and in particular, Black youth); typically, the media does not represent social problems as emanating from the structural, systemic, and social conditions in which poor working class Blacks live.

Critical race theory (CRT) is integral to the approach taken in this research to demonstrate how state violence on the Blackbody constitutes crime news worthiness. CRT is a conceptual tool designed to challenge the color-blind notion of law, the neutrality of law, subtle forms of racism, racial discrimination in law, and how law can be used as a tool to challenge racism. Legal scholars (Delgado and Stefancic 1995; Crenshaw et al. 1995; Matsuda 1996; Valdes et al. 2002; Bell 1992) contest the absence of attention to race in the courts and the law; however, its use and influence has extended to other disciplines (Iverson 2007, p. 588). Bell (1992) and Delgado and Stefancic (1995) among other legal scholars began writing about liberalism defects and the way the western system of civil rights statutes and case law reinforces white-over-black domination (Delgado et al. 1995). In this paper, CRT informs how we come to the data—we consider how the news represents Blacks—and how racism can be challenged by considering the relationship between media portrayal and socially constructed hegemonic values.

This study addresses qualitative coding of mainstream news articles collected for the period of ten years and helps to consider the accuracy of W.E. Du Bois's (1903) suggestion that the problem of the twentieth century [and beyond] is "the problem of the colour line." We seek to more deeply understand the media's representation of Blacks, which in previous studies has been shown to be negative and demoralising. This analysis is important because media reporting contributes to creating white anxiety and a less just and equitable concept of Blacks. Employing frame theory analysis of crime reporting, together with antiblackracism and CRT frameworks, this article examines coverage of crime and portrayal of Blacks in Toronto print media. We examine here whether reporting of Blacks and criminal justice is racially informed and whether racist policing and news reporting of Black folks remains an everyday disarticulating reality for Blacks in Toronto; in other words, we consider whether racism is not an issue of the past but rather of the present and future, particularly in Canada. This consideration is anathema to the reality that crime is not a "normal" part of Black male youth identities—even in an urban Canadian area.

In order to consider the interplay between media reporting and the race/crime nexus, we attempt to answer the following research question (RQ1):

RQ1:   How has Canada's largest newspaper framed news as it relates to blacks, police, and race?

Specifically, we focus on (a) the tone of media coverage (positive, negative, or neutral) and (b) reporting of "gangs," "guns," "poverty," "drugs," "unemployment," "violence," and "crime reduction" as frames constructed by news media reports about race and crime in Toronto. An investigation of how mainstream Toronto media cover issues relative to Blacks, police, and race remains meaningful because of media frames' notable effects on the audience, including opinion leaders and those engaged in policy (Entman 2004). The current research seeks to bring attention to broad issues surrounding contemporary Canadian media's framing of race and policing, including does media coverage inform Canadians about the economic and social issues surrounding race and policing? What kinds of contextual information does this coverage provide to Canadian readers? How do these reports enhance audiences' understanding of race, police, and the relationship between the two? How would news stories add to non-Blacks' understanding of the issues facing blacks in contemporary culture, thereby leading to a more nuanced understanding of race issues in Canada? These meaningful questions inform this investigation and its goal to provide a more well-rounded understanding of contemporary race issues in Canada, and the greater Toronto area in particular.

This investigation considers print news coverage of issues pertaining to race (specifically Blacks) and police in a Canadian newspaper. *The Globe and Mail* is a Toronto-based Canadian newspaper with a nationwide distribution, and has been in print for 172 years. With a readership of over 3.5 million, it is Canada's most-read newspaper, and is the only Canadian paper to demonstrate an increase in readership over the past five years (globelink.ca 2016). In 2015, *The Globe and Mail* was awarded five

National Newspaper Awards—making it the most awarded newspaper in Canada. Editor-in-Chief David Walmsley states that the newspaper takes on "brave, independent work that challenges conventional narrative" (Globe Tops National Newspaper Awards 2015). *The Globe and Mail* is therefore positioned as forward-thinking and rigorous in its approach to news reporting, with an educated readership, thus making it an ideal venue for research on race- and police-related reporting.

Method

Data Collection

To answer RQ1, we analysed data collected from *The Globe and Mail*. The unit of analysis in this investigation is the individual news article. Data collection processes aimed to collect the largest set of news articles relative to the RQ. The LexisNexis database was employed to retrieve articles from *The Globe and Mail* over the ten-year period from 2005 to 2015 containing all keywords "black" *and* "police" *and* "race" either in headlines or in the body of the article. These specific search terms were employed in order that the data reflected articles specifically relating to Blacks and their interaction with police, either literally or via legal policy. The search term "race" was included in order that articles with a direct reference to race relations or race issues were captured.

A total of 448 articles containing all such search terms were retrieved for the ten-year period. Data was cleansed in order that opinion and editorial articles were removed, as they are congruent with personal opinion rather than objective reporting as is associated with large newspapers in Canada. News articles such as film or book reviews which were captured by the database search but irrelevant to the present study were also removed. The careful elimination of articles that were opinion rather than reflective of the ideology of the newspaper ensured that the data was limited to robust articles produced exclusively for *The Globe and Mail*. Similarly, articles relevant to the "black market" (e.g. in art) or Conrad Black were removed; such articles were captured in the database search though were irrelevant to this study. The resultant articles were *n* = 155.

Data Analysis

Frame theory has characterised research which seeks to examine and explain the ways in which news media favor particular "frames," or vantage points, in their coverage (e.g. Goffman 1974; Entman 1991). In keeping with previous research employing frame analysis methodology (e.g. Dimitrova and Connolly-Ahern 2007; Douai and Lauricella 2014), we first examined the tone toward Blacks and the tone toward police in each article. We considered whether the article is written in such a way that it frames Blacks as "positive," "negative," "both positive and negative," or "neutral." For example, if an article asserted that blacks were "violent," "looking for trouble," or "dangerous," then the tone toward Blacks was coded as "negative" toward blacks. Similarly, if the overall tone of an article indicated that Blacks were "cooperative" or "hard working," then the tone toward Blacks was coded as "positive" toward blacks. If an article contained both tones, it was coded as "both positive and negative," or if no discernible tone was evident, it was coded as "neutral." The same practice was applied to the tone toward police. If an article made reference to the police as "careful" or "responsible," it was coded as positive toward the police. If the overall tone of the article indicated that the police were "brutal" or "petty," then the article was coded as "negative" toward police. If an article contained both tones, it was coded as "both positive and negative," and if no overarching tone was evident, the article's tone was coded as "neutral."

The second stage in the data analysis addressed the overarching frames employed to categorise the various news stories addressing Blacks, police, and race in Toronto. Articles underwent an initial coding process (Glaser and Strauss 1967; Charmaz 2006) whereby all potential frames were identified. The authors and three independent coders discussed the codes in detail and identified the five overarching themes present in the data. Data were then coded as to whether they utilised the following frames: gangs, guns, poverty, drugs, unemployment, (general) violence, or crime reduction. Each of the categories addressed specific key issues relative to each news story. For example, articles that addressed blacks, police, and race were coded with the "gang" frame when the main tenets of the reporting were gang issues (or more specifically, problems). Similarly, articles coded with the "guns" category addressed weapons and violence specifically relative to a gun or guns. Articles that gave particular attention to issues of poverty in the Black community were coded with the "poverty" frame. When drugs were an issue to either the police or Black individuals, the "drugs" frame was applied to the article. Unemployment is a particular area of concern in detecting bias in media reporting; when articles referred to unemployed Blacks or youth, the article was allocated to the "unemployment" frame. General violence was another overarching frame in the data, so articles indicating non-specific violence such as "street violence" were coded as fitting with the "violence" frame. Finally, crime reduction is a particular effort on the part of police, and so articles framed with the overall objective to curb violence were coded as "crime reduction."

Given that three independent coders assessed the data, inter-rater reliability was essential in assessing the integrity of the research process. After creating a mutually agreed upon coding guide, the coders met to discuss cases in which disagreement in frame codes occurred. Pursuant to discussion and adjustments to codes allocated to each article, inter-rater reliability was high among the coders at 98%.

Results

This study examines how Toronto's Globe and Mail covers issues relative to Blacks and police in Toronto. The study considered a total of $n = 155$ articles that addressed police, Blacks, and race. In keeping with prior studies of news media frames (e.g. Entman 1991; Pan and Kosicki 1996; Douai and Lauricella 2014), we attempt to maintain rigorous research standards by considering both the tone and the dominant news frames present in the corpus of news reporting. In this project, "tone" refers to the overall positive, neutral, or negative tone in the article regarding both Blacks and police. The complimentary element in this research focused on how *The Globe and Mail* articles framed significant issues present in the intersection of Blacks, race, and police issues.

Tone of Coverage

Blacks

The clear majority of news reports in the Globe and Mail were neither overwhelmingly positive nor negative toward Blacks; a combined 50% of articles were either both positive and negative (27%) or neutral (23%) in tone. While 29% of news coverage about Blacks as they related to the police was positive, about 1/5 (21%) of news coverage was negative. If an overall figure of positive coverage of Blacks in the context of the police is considered (i.e. unambiguously positive articles plus articles that were both positive and negative), the figure becomes 56% of all news coverage in this data from *The Globe and Mail*. Similarly, an overall figure of negative coverage (unambiguously negative articles plus articles that were both positive and negative) amounts to 48% of all news stories in the data.

Police

Just over 1/3 (35%) of all news articles in the data indicated a clear neutral tone toward the police. If the neutral figure is combined with articles containing both positive and negative tones in the same piece, the figure becomes 62%. However, only 18% of the articles indicated an unambiguously positive tone to the police, while 20% of the articles in the data indicated a clearly negative tone. Articles with any positive tone (i.e. unambiguously positive articles plus articles containing both positive and negative tones) comprised 45% of the data, while 47% of articles in the data contained either an overall negative tone or contained a negative tone alongside a positive (Table 15.1).

Framing Blacks and Police in Toronto News Reports

A framing analysis of the Globe and Mail's coverage relating to Blacks, police, and race revealed clear issues associated with violence. A

Table 15.1 Articles' tone toward Blacks and police in *The Globe and Mail* coverage

	Positive		Negative		Both positive and negative		Neutral		Total	
	N	%	N	%	N	%	N	%	N	%
Blacks	(45)	29	(32)	21	(42)	27	(36)	23	155	100
Police	(28)	18	(31)	20	(42)	27	(54)	35	155	100

preliminary reading of the data suggested that we focus on issues associated with violence; these issues were made more specific by considering problems traditionally associated with violence, such as gangs, guns, and drugs. Data analysis shows that the general "violence" frame most frequently dominated coverage of Blacks, the police, and race in this data at 52% of the news stories over the ten-year period examined.

In more specific terms, 44% of the articles were framed by means of gun violence. The "gangs" frame represented almost 1/3 (30%) of the articles in the data. The poverty frame comprised 19% of the articles, the "drugs" frame 15%, and 5% of the articles were framed by means of "unemployment" issues. Despite the significant number of articles framed in general terms of violence and specific frames relative to violence, the "crime reduction" frame represented just over 1/3 (33%) of the articles in this data. In both mainstream and alternative or community media framing of Black lives and crime, none of these efforts have been directed to Black LGBTQ persons and criminal justice. We see this as one shortcoming of this analysis, because ignoring this population will only maintain the exclusion and alienation this group faces within criminal justice (Table 15.2).

Discussion

The general tone of news stories examined in this study was largely neutral. This neutral tone indicates that neither Blacks nor the police are depicted in positive or negative ways in *The Globe and Mail*. However, this neutral tone demands that we pay more attention to the frames incorporated in the news stories in order to gain a fuller understanding of

Table 15.2 News frames in *The Globe and Mail* coverage of Blacks and police and race

News frame	N	%
Violence	(81)	52
Guns	(68)	44
Crime reduction	(52)	34
Gangs	(7)	30
Poverty	(29)	19
Drugs	(24)	15
Unemployment	(8)	5

how news is communicated and meaning of relevant issues is constructed. The media's frames of reference—in this investigation seen via Canada's the *The Globe* and *Mail*—are widely present to construct newsworthy stories (Turnage 2009; Dickerson 2001). While the tone of news reporting in this investigation is overall a neutral one, it is evident that *The Globe* and *Mail's* frames in news relative to Blacks are constructed to reflect the skin color of urban Blacks in Toronto as indicative of trouble. Both the news frames and the narrative of Blacks as socialised troublemakers comes from the media's ability to frame and reify a debate without the audience or its readers realising that the media has this power (Poindexter et al. 2003, p. 527). Indeed, the frames evident in relation to Blacks and the police are overwhelmingly violent; the only potentially positive frame is that of "crime reduction," though it is indicative of inherent violence in the Black community.

The framing of Blacks, even and perhaps especially in the context of news, allows for media consumers, including politicians and policy makers, to use both media and narrative against Black and racialised communities of race/racism/violence. News reporting then serves to create an ideological divide between political parties and ethnic groups. Hall (2003) argues that framing news stories is accomplished through "representations of the social world, images, descriptions, explanations and frames for understanding how the world is and why it works as it [does]" (p. 91). Data in this study indicate that *The Globe* and *Mail's* mass media language, narrative, and grammar about Black youth violence in Toronto are grounded in a language that equates Blacks with violence. The news articles communicate to readers nothing, or at best very little, about the social conditions and structural context of the violence and crime within communities. In particular, the Black community suffers from lack of state investment in meaningful rehabilitation programs, affordable housing, abject poverty, state neglect, and racist policing in these communities. None of this is addressed in the frames inherent in the media stories examined here.

Many Toronto youth explore a number of social possibilities, identities, and experiments while coming of age in order to make it in life; these include associations with gangs, use or dealing of drugs, or theft. Such behaviors are seen as risky by law enforcement and the police—not to mention that some are illegal—which leads to both criminalising and hopelessness of Black youth. (It should be noted that some alternative experiments include attendance and participation in school, which is scarcely reported in the media.) *The Globe* and *Mail*'s nature of framing, combined with issues of stereotypes and crime, is evident in the framing of news articles in this study. Previous research has demonstrated how African-American males are overly represented in media crime reports. The reinforcing of these negative stereotypes toward Blacks in Canadian and American contexts only serves to give white audience members an "identity advantage" over Black audience members (Mastro et al. 2011). Ryan, Carragee, and Meinhofer (2001) argue that "frames organize discourse, including news stories, by their patterns of selection, emphasis and exclusion" (p. 175). Thus, by "select[ing] some aspects of a perceived reality and mak[es] them more salient in a communicating text" (Entman 1993, p. 52).

The media's framing of race in crime reporting to construct and deconstruct realities of Blacks in Toronto has the potential to contribute to reinforcing a discriminatory culture. Minority neighborhoods endure the challenge of a disproportionate amount of television news coverage devoted to crime within their communities (Entman 1992); an examination of frames in this study indicates that the same is true of print news media. Recently a Toronto chapter of #BlackLivesMatter was formed in order to respond to the social injustices of Blacks in Toronto. #BlackLivesMatter can be seen as a counter-hegemonic movement in order to address the need to turn framing negative messages associated with Blacks into positive ones. The #BlackLivesMatter movement used the media to advance their own definitions of political issues through mainstream news media.

#BlackLivesMatter: Reframing the Message

The media is a powerful influencer in hegemonic values and structure, and the issues addressed in this data suggest the perpetual nature of negative stereotypes by the media about Black people's lives. Following the death of Trayvon Martin in 2013, Patrisee Cullors reposted the hashtag #BlackLivesMatter from her friend Alicia Garza's Facebook page, which served as the beginning of a rehumanising project (Robinson 2015). When #BlackLivesMatter was reposted, Cullors and Garza did not know the magnitude of its potential to make a positive impact via social media outlets. The #Blacklivesmatter hashtag and resultant movement is a cross-generational struggle for rethinking and redefining Black people's lives void of state violence with a positive message about themselves.

#BlackLivesMatter explains on their website: "When we say Black Lives Matter, we are broadening the conversation around state violence to include all of the ways in which Black people are intentionally left powerless at the hands of the state… #BlackLivesMatter is working for a world where Black lives are no longer systematically and intentionally targeted for demise #BlackLivesMatter" (http://blacklivesmatter.com/about/). Judith Butler, in an interview with George Yancy, reframes the meaning of #BlackLivesMatter: "according to Butler: one reason the chant "#BlackLivesMatter" is so important is that it states the obvious but the obvious has not yet been historically realized. So it is a statement of outrage and a demand for equality, for the right to live free of constraint, neutralization and degradation of black lives, but also a police system that more and more easily and often can take away a black life in the flash all because some officer perceives a threat" (Yancy and Butler 2015, p. 2).

Traditional media, portraying Blacks as stereotypically violent and incompetent, lost traction in its political power and social control to the #BlackLivesMatter movement. The hashtag and resultant movement had (and still has) the ability to build an online following and consensus among its followers with a positive political and ideological message. The

American Dialect society even voted the #BlacklivesMatter as the Word of the Year in 2014, making for a Twitter hashtag a "word" for the first time (Evans 2015). This significant movement has had effects on traditional print news. The framing of crime stories and violence associated with the Black community in this study indicates a fertile ground for the #BlackLivesMatter movement in Canada.

We argue that news framing—in this case, via news stories involving Blacks and the police—tells only half the story. Accounts of gun violence, gangs, and illegal activity without explicit acknowledgment of their connection to underlying social and economic issues undermine and disguise the impact of racism on Blacks. The failure to link stories of violence to other broader issues serves to make such events appear as isolated incidents among "bad" people who have failed to be civically engaged. The emergent frames in this investigation demonstrate the negative issues associated with Blacks and police in Toronto. The lack of social networks that provide encouragement and opportunities alternative to violence is lacking in the greater Toronto area. In order to reduce violence in Black lives, communities must work on providing what has been missing, not perpetuate media frames which criminalise Blacks (and particularly Black men and youth) and frame them as violent. The failure to recognise and depict the complexity of structural, systemic, and social issues facing Black men is currently being addressed by #Blacklivesmatter. This movement in both Canada and the USA is an example of the rallying call for those who see the possibility of transformation through transforming the living conditions in Black communities, and as a way to talk about the prevalence of Black crime.

Conclusion

Mainstream media's ability to frame news stories can be used to shape public opinion and serve as a foundation for public discourse. This paper sought to answer how Canada's largest newspaper framed news as it relates to Blacks, police, and race. Overall, the tone in news stories toward both Blacks and the police was neutral. However, the news frames demonstrated an overall violent culture, with stories of guns and gangs pervasive in the data. These stories and their inherent notion of violence serves to keep Blacks "where they are" in the current political discourse. Without explanation of the inherent issues facing Blacks, including economic, educational, and community challenges, the media is only communicating a fraction of the story. This fraction then continues the cycle of racism whereby the public narrative is such that Blacks are overwhelmingly violent, uneducated, troublesome, and problematic. While this paper did not examine the role that new media plays in the reproduction of racist crime stereotypes of Black males, we are cognizant of the implications for future new media studies and critical race theory. This is most evident with the emergence of the #Blacklivesmatter movement, which started as a new social media activist platform. With the increase in citizen-led media and mobilisation via social media (in this case, via a powerful hashtag), we suggest that it can become possible to communicate the larger picture of race and racism. We hope that mainstream media, including major print news outlets, will then accept the responsibility of communicating the meaning of race issues and racism in Canada.

References

Bell, D. A. (1992). *Faces at the Bottom of the Well: The Permanence of Racism*. New York: Basic Books.

Benjamin, A. (2003). *The Black/Jamaican Criminal: The Making of Ideology*. Unpublished Doctoral Dissertation. Toronto: University of Toronto.

Charmaz, K. (2006). *Constructing Grounded Theory: A Practical Guide Through Qualitative Analysis*. London: Sage.

Collins, P. (2004). *Black Sexual Politics: African Americans, Gender and the New Racism*. New York: Routledge.

Crenshaw, K., Gotanda, N., Peller, G., & Thomas, K. (Eds.). (1995). *Critical Race Theory: The Key Writings*. New York, NY: The New Press.

Crichlow, W. (2009). How Far Have Our Courts Come and How Far Will They Go? Racializing Courts and Racializing Judgments. In R. Barmaki (Ed.), *Racism Culture & Law: Critical Readings – A Collection of Essays* (pp. 43–67). Toronto, ON: APF Press.

Crichlow, W. (2014). Weaponization & Prisonization of Toronto Black Youth. *International Journal for Crime, Justice and Social Democracy, 3*(3), 113–113. Retrieved from https://www.crimejusticejournal.com/issue/view/14

Delgado, R., & Stefancic, J. (1995). *Critical Race Theory*. New York, NY: New York University Press.

Delgado, D. J., Lin, W. Y., & Coffey, M. (1995). The Role of Hispanic Race/Ethnicity and Poverty in Breast Cancer Survival. *Puerto Rico Health Sciences Journal, 14*(2), 103–116.

Dickerson, D. L. (2001). Framing "Political Correctness": The New York Times' Tale of Two Professors. In S. D. Reese, O. H. Gandy Jr., & A. E. Grant (Eds.), *Framing Public Life: Perspectives on Media and Our Understanding of the Social World* (pp. 163–174). New York: Digital Printing 2010 by Routledge.

Dimitrova, D. V., & Connolly-Ahern, C. (2007). A Tale of Two Wars: Framing Analysis of Online News Sites in Coalition Countries and the Arab World During the Iraq War. *The Howard Journal of Communication, 18*(2), 153–168.

Douai, A., & Lauricella, S. (2014). The "Terrorism" Frame in "Neo-Orientalism": Western News and the Sunni-Shia Muslim Sectarian Relations After 9/11. *International Journal of Media & Cultural Politics, 10*(1), 7–24.

Drummond, W. (1990). About Face: From Alliance to Alienation Blacks in the News Media. *The American Enterprise, 1*(4), 24–29.

Du Bois, W. E. B. (1903). *The Souls of Black Folk*. New York: Dover Publications, Inc.

Entman, R. M. (1991). Framing U.S. Coverage of International News: Contrasts in Narratives of the KAL and Iran Air Incidents. *Journal of Communication, 41*(4), 6–26.

Entman, R. M. (1992). Blacks in the News: Television, Modern Racism and Cultural Change. *Journalism Quarterly, 69*(2), 341–361.

Entman, R. (1993). Framing: Toward Clarification of a Fractured Paradigm. *Journal of Communication, 43*, 41–58.

Entman, R. M. (2004). *Projections of Power: Framing News, Public Opinion, and US Foreign Policy*. University of Chicago Press.

Entman, R. M., & Rojecki, A. (2000). *The Black Image in the White Mind: Media and Race in America*. Chicago: University of Chicago.

Evans, C. K. (2015). Past President, American Name Society. cevans@bellevue.edu, (402), 557–7524.

Glaser, B. G., & Strauss, A. L. (1967). *The Discovery of Grounded Theory: Strategies for Qualitative Research*. Chicago: Aldine Publishing.

Globe Tops National Newspaper Awards with Five Winners. (2015, May 22). *The Globe and Mail*. Retrieved from http://www.theglobeandmail.com/awards/national-newspaper-awards/article24579253/

Globelink.ca. (2016). *The Globe and Mail*. Retrieved from http://globelink.ca/platforms/newspaper/?source=gamnewspaper

Goffman, E. (1974). *Frame Analysis: An Essay on the Organization of Experience.* New York: Harper & Row.

Hall, S. (2003). The Whites of Their Eyes: Racist Ideologies and the Media. In G. Dines & J. M. Humez (Eds.), *Gender, Race, and Class in Media: A Text Reader* (pp. 89–93). Thousand Oaks, CA: Sage.

Iverson, S. V. (2007). Camouflaging Power and Privilege: A Critical Race Analysis of University Diversity Policies. *Educational Administration Quarterly, 43*(5), 586–611.

Mastro, D. E., Blecha, E., & Atwell Seate, A. (2011). Characterizations of Criminal Athletes: A Systematic Examination of Sports News Depictions of Race and Crime. *Journal of Broadcasting & Electronic Media, 55*(4), 526–542.

Matsuda, M. (1996). *Where is Your Body: And Other Essays on Race, Gender, and the Law.* Boston: Beacon Press.

Pan, Z., & Kosicki, G. M. (1996). Assessing News Media Influences on the Formation of Whites' Racial Policy Preferences. *Communication Research, 23*(2), 147–178.

Poindexter, P., Smith, L., & Heider, D. (2003). Race and Ethnicity in Local Television News: Framing, Story Assignments, and Source Selections. *Journal of Broadcast & Electronic Media, 47*, 524–540.

Ribeau, S., Baldwin, J., & Hecht, M. (1997). An African-American Communication Perspective. In L. Samovar & R. Porter (Eds.), *Intercultural Communication: A Reader* (8th ed., pp. 147–153). Belmont CA: Wadsworth.

Robinson, A. (2015, March 16). BlackLivesMatter: The Evolution of a Movement. *Occupy.* Retrieved from http://www.occupy.com/article/black-lives-matter-evolution-movement

Ryan, C., Carragee, K. M., & Meinhofer, W. (2001). Theory into Practice: Framing, the News Media, and Collective Action. *Journal of Broadcasting and Electronic Media, 45*, 175–182.

Tator, C., & Henry, F. (2006). *Racial Profiling in Canada: Challenging the Myth of a Few Bad Apples.* Toronto: University of Toronto Press.

Turnage, A. K. (2009). Scene, Act, and the Tragic Frame in the Duke Rape Case. *Southern Communication Journal, 74*(2), 141–156.

2014 Word of the Year Is "#BlackLivesMatter." (2015, January 9). *American Dialect Society.* Retrieved from http://www.americandialect.org/2014-word-of-the-year-is-blacklivesmatter

Valdes, F., Culp, J. M., & Harris, A. (Eds.). (2002). Crossroads, Directions and a New Critical Race Theory. Temple University Press.

Yancy, G., & Butler, J. (2015, January 12). What's Wrong with 'All Lives Matter?' *New York Times.* Retrieved from http://opinionator.blogs.nytimes.com/2015/01/12/whats-wrong-with-all-lives-matter/?r=0

16

Contesting the Single Story: Collective Punishment, Myth-Making and Racialised Criminalisation

Patrick Williams and Becky Clarke

Introduction

On the 31 January 2016, British Prime Minister David Cameron announced a review, to be led by the Labour MP David Lammy, to investigate "evidence of possible bias against black defendants and other ethnic minorities". He continued,

> If you're black, you're more likely to be in a prison cell than studying at a top university. And if you're black, it seems you're more likely to be sentenced to custody for a crime than if you're white. We should investigate why this is and how we can end this possible discrimination. (Ross 2016)

The concept of the black male as crime prone remains one of the enduring mediated realities of contemporary British society. Traces of such imagery are historically located within the British conscience, presenting as a powerful discourse episodically evoked, repackaged, looped and (re)presented as an infallible myth, transcendental folklore, the single

P. Williams (✉) • B. Clarke
Manchester Metropolitan University, Manchester, UK

© The Author(s) 2018
M. Bhatia et al. (eds.), *Media, Crime and Racism*, Palgrave Studies in Crime,
Media and Culture, https://doi.org/10.1007/978-3-319-71776-0_16

story to explain the crime problem within British society (Ngozi-Adichie 2009; Hall et al. 1978; Gilroy 2002). Whilst the character names have shifted from 'coloured' to 'black' to 'BAME', and the 'reported' (offending) behaviours of concern traverse from 'pimps' to 'muggers', 'drug dealers' to violent 'gangs', the inevitable consequence of the story remains the same. The story succeeds in the presentation of a simplistic and consumable explanation, which accentuates and reaffirms 'them' from 'us' (Keith 1993), demanding penal solutions to protect the public from the dangerous criminal black other.

Within this chapter, we set about to disrupt this story. From the outset, we position the media as omnipresent in latently mediating cues and signs of the presence of a threatening other within British society. Contemporaneously, this mediating function is pivotal to the process of criminalisation where print and television media communicate, and prime members of the public as to the individuals, groups and communities are responsible for the 'crime problem'. In addition, we draw attention to the concerning trend where (social) media profiles are utilised by the State to perpetuate the myth of black people as culturally predisposed and involved with gang-enabled violence and serious offending behaviour. Within this chapter then, we argue that the maintenance of the singular story serves to legitimise the imposition of powerful penal strategies. To this end, we utilise the police construct of the gang and in particular the use of Joint Enterprise (JE) as a resource through which to elicit the precise processes that drive the overrepresentation of black men and women in prisons, many for offences that they did not commit. By way of structure, the chapter will revisit the question of racialised 'bias' within the Criminal Justice System (CJS) of England and Wales. However, of importance we highlight what we define as a series of 'strategic silences' which conceal the CJ practices that facilitate differential treatment of minority ethnic groups. It is from this point that we focus attention on the emergent use of JE as a penal device in response to the 'gang' and the problem of serious youth violence in England and Wales. Through this endeavour, we attempt to present the racialised nature of contemporary CJ responses to the gang. In addition, we will show how such constructions are developed, mediated and maintained through the articulation of dangerous associations through the media, CJ practitioners and more recently third sector organisations.

Race and Criminality: A Hardwired Bias[1]

The publication of "Statistics on Race in the Criminal Justice System" (Sec 95) marks a statutory obligation enacted through Section 95 of the Criminal Justice Act (1991) that:

> The Secretary of State shall in each year publish such information as he considers expedient for the purpose ... of facilitating the performance of those engaged in the administration of justice to *avoid discriminating* against any persons on the ground of race or sex or any other improper ground... (MOJ 2015: 10 emphasis added)

Now in its 25th year, the report has consistently demonstrated the disparity of CJS experience between black, Asian and minority ethnic (BAME) people and their white counterparts in England and Wales.[2] In this regard, the 2015 publication shows that BAME people are up to four times more likely to be subject to stop and search by the police when compared to their white counterparts. In addition, BAME people were three times more likely to be arrested and sentenced for indictable offences. A discussion of imprisonment rates points to significant over-representation of BAME people when compared to both their white counterparts and their proportions within the general population. Where 15 people per 10,000 of the population are serving a custodial sentence, this figure increases to 44 per 10,000 for the 'mixed' group and 55 per 10,000 for the 'black' group (MOJ 2015).

Importantly, the now almost predictable outputs of Sec 95 are often (mis)read as indicative of black criminality. They are not. They are at best, a representation of an individual's encounters with the agencies of the CJS, serving a bureaucratic function of monitoring the system's throughput. Such statistics cannot explain the *processes* that result in differential outcomes for BAME people, a point acknowledged within the report, where "no causative links can be drawn from these summary statistics"

(MOJ 2015: 7). Of concern then, the report ambiguously alludes to racial disparities, yet neglects to offer any meaningful explanation for this apparent 'discrimination'. For example, the vexed issue of police stop and search and in particular the use of s60 of the Police and Criminal Evidence (PACE) Act, 1984 empowers the police to undertake 'suspicionless' (Bowling 2014) stop and searches of individuals where,

> the police believe, with good reason, that there is a possibility of serious violence; that a person is carrying a dangerous object or offensive weapon; or that an incident involving serious violence has taken place and a dangerous instrument or offensive weapon used in the incident is being carried in the locality. (MOJ 2012: 44)

Recent data shows an overwhelmingly disproportionate use of s60 against black people. In 2007/2008, just over a quarter (28%) of s60 stops were recorded as being carried out on BAME people, with 65% conducted on white people. Markedly, there has been a gradual reversal in this trend where by 2010/2011, 64% of s60 stops involved BAME people against 31% for white people. Whilst we note the bi-annual 'empirical haggling' (Gilroy 1982) which accompanies the publication of sec 95, the report serves to silence activists claims of police racism and discrimination, yet serves to mediate to the reader an association between BAME people with criminal behaviour. However, nowhere is such a strategic silencing more prevalent than in the contemporary use of JE and the statutory response to gangs and serious youth violence, a point to which we will now turn.

Joint Enterprise and Gangs

JE is a doctrine of common law developed by the courts where more than one person is to be prosecuted for the same offence. Controversially, it applies even where the 'suspects' have played different roles and (in many cases) where a suspect was not in the proximity of the offence committed. Intrinsic to the application of the doctrine is the principle of 'common purpose' where it is the alleged individuals have planned to commit a crime together. Where such a 'common purpose' is demonstrable, associated individuals may then be held liable for crimes committed by a member of the group, even though they may not have participated in or intended that the crime should have been committed (Williams and Clarke 2015). Recent evidence of the increasing use of JE prosecutions has found that at "least 1800 and up to 4590" people were prosecuted for JE homicide over the period 2005/2006 and 2012/2013 [Bureau of Investigative Journalists 2013]. Indeed, since 2005 there has been a marked increase in the use of JE reaching a peak in 2008, when approximately 20% of all homicides involving four or more defendants were prosecuted as JE cases. Arguably, the emergence of such powers can be located within the political ruminations of the New Labour government (1997–2010) rhetoric and commitment to be 'tough on crime'

> The message that the law is sending out is that we are very willing to see people convicted if they are a part of gang violence—and that violence ends in somebody's death. Is it unfair? Well, what you've got to decide is not, 'Does the system lead to people being wrongly convicted?' I think the real question is: 'Do you want a law as draconian as our law is, which says juries can convict even if you are quite a peripheral member of the gang which killed?' And I think broadly the view of reasonable people is that you probably do need a quite draconian law in that respect.
>
> (BIJ 2014: 46)

Whilst we concede that those individuals who perpetrate serious violent offences should face sanctions, we find Lord Faulkner's unashamed acknowledgement of the probability of wrongful convictions both staggering and alarming, particularly where individuals have not perpetrated violence. Detected herein is a deliberate shift towards a 'crime control' function of the CJS (Garland 2001) which forsakes the legal principles of justice enshrined in 'due process' by empowering control agents to deliver (in)justice by whatever means. The disjuncture between political posturing and CJ policy and practice, alongside the conflation of gangs and serious violence above is of significance here. Such deterrent-based policies, underpinned as they are by the threat of 'draconian powers' are legitimised through a professed need to deter those 'unreasonable people' deemed to perpetrate serious gang-enabled violence and hence are deserving of punitive punishments. JE powers then, whilst concealed away from members of the public (no data is published on its use), communicates a message that the state is 'effectively' responding to the problem of serious violence. More recently, such political rhetoric has become manifest through the practical reality of Operation Shield where the Metropolitan police will,

> [T]arget gangs as a whole (rather than individual members). This will see every known member of the gang penalised through a range of civil and criminal penalties when one gang member commits a violent crime, such as a stabbing.

The implementation then of such draconian policy is illuminated through the following extract of a letter (provided to the authors) sent to the home of a young man by the Metropolitan police.

> Information indicates that you have or are associated to a gang that is linked to crime. If you are involved with crime and do not stop, you may be targeted by police and partner agencies. Under a piece of legislation called "Joint Enterprise" you may be convicted of a crime and sent to prison; for just being present when a serious crime is committed, or being with those persons who commit a crime and you don't try to stop it. Methods (known as tactics) we may use to target individuals involved with crime, guns or knives or linked to others involved with these are listed at the end of this letter.

However, the emergence of such powers is not without criticism. Crewe et al. (2015: 252–269) point to the ways "the state of the law is unnecessarily confused" in relation to the application of JE. Through a series of hypothetical 'gang' scenarios, Crewe et al. demonstrate the significant tension between proving individual culpability and establishing collective responsibility. Moreover, the paper tentatively points towards the racialised use of JE where, "many of the interviewees felt that joint enterprise was being used as an indiscriminate ethnic vacuum cleaner". For Pitts (2014: 50), "the central question in the case of joint enterprise concerns how the police and prosecution establish who is, and who is not, a 'gang member". Pitts expresses concern for those individuals 'who are uninvolved in gang illegalities" yet are drawn into the prosecution of 'gang-related' offences. Similar to our findings to follow, Pitts quotes a case where young people contest the gang associations placed on them, revealing how being on 'nodding terms', playing Sunday league football, or even being entirely unknown to someone can result in individuals becoming co-defendants on a JE charge. Whilst Pitts acknowledges the phenomena of gang 'myth-making' by young people themselves, the centrality of the paper rests upon developing a "taxonomy of descriptors of gang involvement" to assist police, prosecution teams and sentencers to understand the level of gang involvement of charged individuals. Whilst valuable, there is little attempt in the work of Pitts to appreciate the significance of everyday encounters and interactions between young black men and the police, which we believe drives the prosecution narrative of the racialised black gang. Moreover, there is little acknowledgement of the 'myth-making' tendencies of State actors and in particular, policing processes of 'intelligence' making, which are critical in securing JE convictions (Fraser and Atkinson 2014). Academically then, the thorny issue of ethnic overrepresentation in localised gang narratives and its nexus to JE violence is again silenced and concealed.

A Racialised Gang Narrative: The Engine for Joint Enterprise Prosecutions

In 2015, the authors published the findings of a research study, which explored the relationship between JE prosecutions and gangs (Williams and Clarke 2015). By way of method, the study undertook analysis of official criminal justice data sources alongside a survey of 241 prisoners who were serving JE prison sentences. Participants were identified through the monitoring database of the campaign organisation Joint Enterprise Not guilty by Association (JENGbA) who had gathered the details of over 600 prisoners convicted of JE offences. From its inception, the study was concerned with developing an understanding of those processes of criminalisation that contribute to the discriminatory use of JE.

Over half of the prisoners self-disclosed as belonging to a BAME group (53%). Three quarters of the group were serving average prison sentences of 15 years. However, it is evident that BAME prisoners were serving on average longer sentences (22.3 years) when compared to their white counterparts (19.6 years). The BAME group were also more likely to be younger with 62% under the age of 25 years (against 41% for the white cohort). For those prisoners aged 17 years of age and under (*n* = 21), the average prison sentence was 14 years, with one child serving a prison sentence of 26 years. The length of sentence in part reflects convictions for the committal of violent offences, with over 90% of respondents imprisoned for JE murder. Yet strikingly, almost half (45%) of our respondents reported that they were 'not at the scene' when the offence was committed. Furthermore, of those who reported not being at the scene, 70% disclosed that "they had no contact with the co-defendants ahead of or during the event". The findings summarised above raise serious questions of justice and the legitimacy of harsh punishments endured by those men, women and children who responded to our research. However, our central research question was to elucidate the relationship between JE convictions and the construct of the gang. To this end, JE prisoners were asked to consider the extent to which the language of the 'gang' was evoked during their court case. In response, over half of the prisoners (59%) recognised the presence of a gang narrative during their court case. Significantly, over three quarters (78.9%) of BAME prisoners disclosed the use of 'gang-speak', whilst the figure is reduced to 39% for the white group. The implications of this finding cannot be overstated. Our research found that collective punishments were disproportionately disposed against young black people because of (police) intelligence that suggested gang membership or gang association. Whilst a small minority of prisoners acknowledge gang involvement (*n* = 5), the vast majority of prisoners contested prosecution attempts to attribute the gang label to them.

'I don't agree with the prosecution constantly using the word gang because we were not a gang. One was a friend and the other my customer.'
    'I disagree with this description. This is because only [two] people out of the group of nine I was in were gang members. I have never classed myself as a gang member.'

'We are a group of young lads who smoke weed and fuck around, and we get labelled a gang!'

'I was brought up with the same group of people through school to holidays with family, we were very close and always together so the prosecution found it easy to call us gang members.'

'One of my [co-defendants] was an active 'gang member' but I was not. I was a friend of a gang member, so I was also judged to be a gang member.'

'There was no gang, it was just two people from the same area.'

'My 3 [co-defendants] I grew up with and that is what the prosecution described as a gang. We were friends.'

'To me a gang is a group of mates but the prosecutor made it sound as if we are a gang walking around with weapons protecting the area.'

'We knew each other from school and two of my [co-defendants] I'd never met.'

The multiple accounts captured above represent only a small sample of the individual counter-claims of JE prisoners. Yet the similarity in the language used to describe their court experience reflects a striking commonality and consistency. Analysis of official CJ data offers a further insight into the inconsistencies between prosecution team narratives of black prisoners as gang-involved and the challenges from survey respondents. Data gathered from police gun and gang units further highlights an array of contradictions in the ethnic profile of those individuals who were convicted of serious violent offences. Drawing upon police gang databases from Manchester, the Metropolitan Police's Trident Unit (Matrix) and Nottingham police reveal that it is black people who populate police gang databases (Williams and Clarke 2015; Williams 2015). In Manchester, 81% of those people registered to the police gang database were black. In London, 72% of those registered to the Matrix were defined as black. Similarly, in Nottingham, 65% of registered gang members were of a BAME background.[3] However, when we examined the ethnic profiles of people who were convicted of serious violent (SV) offences,[4] within the same geographical areas, using data produced during a similar time-period, a different picture develops. Within Manchester, 94% of SV offenders were 'non-black',[5] and in London 73% of SV offences were committed by 'non-black' people. Finally, a recent publication by the London Assembly (21 September 2016) shows that of the serious violence offences perpetrated across London, less than 5% is gang-enabled (Mayor's Office for Police and Crime 2016). The imposition of the gang label has a profound impact upon the life chances and opportunities afforded to those young people so labelled (Smithson et al. 2013).

How can we account for the over representation of JE collective punishments for black people who were not present at the scene of the offence? Why are seemingly unrelated individuals who are not criminally associated or active, made subject to such harsh collective punishments? It is in response to such questions that we consider the interplay between the police, academic and politicians' narratives, which coalesce to produce an infallible narrative of the criminal black other.

Processes of Black Otherisation

It seems implausible to us that criminology as a discipline can contribute a coherent understanding of the complex relationships between JE, gangs and young black people outside of the historical context within which contemporary penal practice is both constructed and delivered (Garland 2001; Spalek 2008). The earlier calls of politicians to understand 'discrimination' and 'bias' require a more critical appreciation of the continuities and contradictions inherent within the recent history of the policing of black communities in England and Wales. Criminological endeavours to comprehend the race and crime nexus without due cognisance of racism(s) and racialisation are futile and can only serve to consolidate pathological constructs of black people as crime prone. It is our view that the ideas of more critical scholars such as Alexander (2008), Gilroy (1982), Hall et al. (1978), and Gutzmore (1983) provide a valuable framework through which to understand the contemporary realities of racialised encounters between the crime control industry and black communities.

Racialisation recognises the interplay of power relations through which negative and detrimental constructions of particular groups are created and sustained (Phillips 2011; Quraishi and Philburn 2015: 13). Its cumulative effects result in the presentation of black people as 'suspect' consequently demanding increased surveillance and regulation due to the 'ascription of criminal characteristics'. The racialisation of crime then emerges as a feature of the interactions, encounters and social constructions, aroused through dominant CJ discourses and narratives, which coalesce to preserve a consciousness, which propagates the black criminal other (Phillips 2012; Alexander 2008). Haining and Law (2007: 13) notes that "police perceptions may be influenced by particular past experiences and attitudes as well as what is or is not remembered". Of importance here, the study found that police respondents believed that 'high intensity' areas for serious violence were those that were characterised by 'high ethnic heterogeneity', despite contradictory evidence presented by police recorded crime data. In other words, the police perception of 'unsafe areas' was premised upon the 'degree of concentration of minority ethnic people'. From here, criminal behaviours 'racialised as black' become an imagined quotidian feature of 'what is remembered' and of what is concealed within the collective memories of local police areas.

To develop upon this theme, the English riots of 6–11 August 2011 followed the fatal shooting of Mark Duggan by the Metropolitan police. Yet, whilst media and academic attention was confined to 'reading the riots' through which to explore 'the most serious bout of civil unrest for a generation' (Lewis et al. 2011), less scrutiny was paid to the misleading police/media construction of Mark Duggan as a 'well known gangster' who was 'heavily involved with criminality' (Barkas 2014). Through an excellent commentary in 'Framing the death of Mark Duggan', Barkas reconstructs the significance of a concerted strategy of (mis)information or 'gang-making' (Williams 2015) from 'unnamed police sources' to media outlets which presented Mark Duggan as "part of a gang linked to Jamaica's 'Yardies'" and associated with 'Manchester gangsters'. Within this process, the attribution of the gang label necessitates a motive, which emerges through police 'intelligence' that Duggan 'intended to kill someone with a gun' with this story furthered by the *Telegraph* newspaper which announced that this was to be a retaliatory 'tit-for-tat murder'. The 'spectre' of Mark Duggan as a 'violent gangster' became amplified and cemented through media 'gang-speak' with the funeral of Mark Duggan reported as "Gansta salute for a 'fallen soldier'". It is noteworthy that

Mark Duggan had never served a custodial sentence, having only two minor convictions, one for handing stolen goods and another for cannabis possession (Barkas 2014).

Memorised recollection of riots and urban popular uprisings are often precipitated by instances of extreme police violence and over-policing perpetrated against black and brown people living within communities characterised by 'high ethnic heterogeneity'. The vexed history of police-community relations, the infamous myths of local 'gangs' endure within police 'canteens' and the multi-agency gang units and in recent times are amplified by an ever increasing range of mass media. Racialised criminalisation is not only confined to the collective memory of police but can also be detected within the contemporary work of sociologists and criminologists. Within this context, criminologies have maintained as its normative agenda, the identification and ontologisation of the other (Spalek 2008; Bowling and Phillips 2002). That is, those characterised as outsiders who infringe the normative boundaries of contemporary British society. Conceptually, the 'other' corresponds as a feature of a dominant 'community of values' which serves to articulate the 'non-citizen', the 'failed citizen' and the 'them' from the 'us'. The identification and attribution of (an)other as 'failed' or as non (citizen) are communicated and augment the evocation of State regulatory penal strategies through which to manage the outsider to preserve 'us' (Anderson 2013; Jewkes 2011).

The above arguments demand we reconnect with the work of those aforementioned critical scholars who observed the internal obstructions of a sociology that reproduces negative constructions of black people. Such obstructions (re)emerge through the concealment and 'arguing away' of racism(s) as an explanatory framework through which to understand the prevalence of criminalising constructs pertaining to black people and black communities (Gilroy 2002). At present there is a criminological reluctance to name racism and racialisation as an intrinsic feature of the CJS in England and Wales which therefore renders contemporary criminology 'pathological' and "dangerous and in our opinion of little normative value" (Keith 1993; Bourne and Sivanandan 1980). Such criminologies pathologise the outsider by locating the (social, economic and personal) problems experienced and endured within a 'structurally neutral' cultural framework that accentuates a plethora of assumed cultural-criminogenic peculiarities and idiosyncrasies (Amos et al. 1982). In addition, Gutzmore (1983: 26) notes the convergence of a powerful and "crucial ideological and repressive state apparatus" of academics, the police, Home Office, the media and others—collectively providing a critical function in both the identification and ontologising of the black 'folk devil'. Significantly, for Gutzmore, there is a discursive blurring where, "academics share both language and concepts with police ideologues" (ibid). So in the disclosures of Sir Kenneth Newman where "in the Jamaicans you have people who are constitutionally disorderly, disposed to be anti-authority" (ibid), sits seamlessly alongside self-styled 'radical' sociologists of that time who profess that,

> [T]here is a penchant for violence in the West Indian culture, possibly stemming from the days of slavery…Whatever the source of the proclivity there can be no denying its existence: black youth do have a certain fascination with violence.
>
> (Cashmore and Troyna 1982: 32)

Such hegemonic convergence can also be found within the new 'criminologies of the other' (Garland 2001) which profess an explanatory framework within which serious violence becomes an undeniable feature of black 'West Indian' culture. It is perhaps unsurprising then that senior politicians adopt the 'single story'. Akin to the deviancy amplification thesis developed by Wilkins in 1968, and appropriated by Cohen (1972) and Hall in 1978, where politicians emerge as moral entrepreneurs exploiting popularised media narratives, predicated upon moral panics to further political ends. The story is appropriated presented as a simple, digestible construct of black communities as violent and crime prone, repeatedly, replayed and evoked as the other approximates towards the imagined ideals and boundaries of British society. So for Tony Blair commentating in *The Guardian* 2007 "…the spate of knife crimes in London was not being caused by poverty, but a distinctive black culture" (Webbe 2007). This theme is echoed by David Starkey in 2011 where the 'English riots' were communicated as a product of a 'particular sort of violent, nihilistic gangster culture'. The outputs of such hegemonic collectives facilitates the (re)constructions of imagined black criminality which are mediated through a range of media.

The Media: Rehearsal and Amplification of the Racialised 'Gang' Narrative

Now, if a jury sees five young black friends in the dock, they don't see five individuals, but one black gang. The jury might be influenced by racist media stereotypes, and because of this they may find it difficult to separate, apportion responsibility, determine culpability. Seven black kids in the dock immediately becomes a dangerous black gang, because that is exactly the way members of the jury are taught to see black boys by the media. (Fekete 2012)

As highlighted above, Gloria Morrison of the JENGbA campaign group has long recognised the racialised nature of JE prosecutions. Our findings confirm the utility of the gang in the prosecution of JE cases. The durability of this nexus is imbued with a racism, concealed within elaborate processes of 'evidence-building' against black defendants, the like of which white prisoners did not report. The race and gang nexus is therefore established by the police, prosecution teams and the media— through a manipulation of social media images, cultural references to 'hip hop' music and online 'rap videos'.

'St Anns where we are from has this reputation.'
    'The term 'St Anns' was used to group us together.'
    They said we was Gooch, but I ain't no Gooch member and I wasn't even there.'
    'Burger Bar Boys'
    'Kray Twins'
    'Just because we are from the same area and are of a certain colour does not make us a gang'

The (un)intentional reference to place names synonymous with black communities and serious violence are the very same areas synonymous with the 'riot' and uprisings of the 1980s. The stories are mediated, rehearsed and retold alluding to an association to be made within the court arena and in the consciousness of the public. On 20 July 2016, The *Daily Mail* ran the header "A genteel setting blighted by sex, mayhem and the shooting of a Brixton 'gangster': How several blind eyes—and political correctness—helped Yardies invade a Surrey village idyll". The article focuses attention on the murder of a 34-year-old at a party in Headley, Surrey. Sadly, the article is (again) less concerned with the fatal shooting of a partygoer, than the "impact" of guests who were "mainly from the Caribbean community in Brixton" upon the "unsuspecting folk of Headley many of them retired". The newspaper article deftly presents the image of a quintessentially English village subjected to an organised party where the "earth began to shake with the sound of Reggae music". Of particular relevance is that "Witnesses said several guests were suspected of being Yardies, a term for Jamaican-born gangsters originally from the backyards of Kingston, the capital of the Caribbean island". Significantly, "Detectives from Scotland Yard's Trident unit, which specialises in gang-related crime, are now helping the Surrey force with the investigation". Such newspaper articles metaphorically mediate contemporary concerns of an 'invasion' of white Englishness by the 'Jamaican' black other. What accompanies the Jamaican 'Yardies' incursion to the 'wealthy hamlet' is serious, gun-enabled violence. For the *Daily Mail* and its readers, the black gang is the signifying explanation for the violence, which was brought to this English village from the 'ganglands' of Brixton. The newspaper and media more widely, presents us with a masterclass in 'melodramatic techniques', with stories of 'over the top' conflict, hyperbole and melancholia', furnishing members of the public with an authoritative grasp of the causes and risks posed by black people. The imagined black gang in such circumstances is a construct that requires little explanation to members of the public or a court jury. Quite simply, such ideas have always been communicated on a daily basis, yet are consumed as new(s).

As Gutzmore (1983) noted in relation to the black mugger of the late 1970's, local news media are key to building the localised codes which today are played out in JE cases. In Manchester, on the 16th August 2007, the *Manchester Evening News* graphically presented the images of predominantly black faces of people killed by guns under the banner 'How Many More?' Significantly, throughout the article there is no reference to 'race', but the story is situated within a 'gang' discourse providing the reader with an analytical short cut, away from the contextual realities of each fatality. The news editor, Sarah Lester, reports that "in showing the faces, it made people see them [the victims] not just as "gang members", but people". The racialised dimensions of the story are relayed, again through intermittent references to the ethnically heterogeneous locations of Moss Side, Hulme, Longsight and Old Trafford in Manchester. The news effect is to associate the victims of gun violence in Manchester as gang members, residing in those communities predominated by black people (Williams 2015).

On the 15th February 2016, The *London Evening Standard* ran the headline "London is facing 'a new surge' of gang killings, warns Chuka Umunna". Within the piece, the Labour MP Umunna offers a 'chilling warning' of a surge in gang-related violence. Umunna's intervention follows the *London Evening Standard's* serialisation of 'Gangs in London' which presented an ill-defined but graphic commentary of gang feuds and 'gang wars' in London, replete with the images of young black men concentrated within the marginalised and economically deprived areas of the nation's capital. Elsewhere, in the *Birmingham Mail* under the headline "Inside the gangs who bring fear and misery to parts of Birmingham" (22 May 2013), Detective Chief Inspector Wallis takes the reader through the names and areas of newly emerging gangs including "The Hutton Boys, Unstoppable Terrorist Soldiers, Slash, Bang-Bang, B515s, Raiders, and the Wolf Pack". Unhelpfully, Wallis offers a professional insight where "If you go to the east area where there is undoubtedly a higher percentage of Asian people, then it's no great surprise that some of the gangs there are Asian-based". In a city already infamous for "The Johnson Crew and The Burger Bar Boys", such media representations reaffirm the 'dog-whistle' to conjure the imagined black gang within the consciousness of the public and significantly to jury members within the court arena.

Conclusion

Within England and Wales, strategies to arrest serious violence through the prism of the 'gang' remain woefully ineffective (MOJ 2015; MOPAC 2016; Medina and Shute 2013). Yet, such approaches continue resulting in a number of profound consequences. Firstly, they have legitimised the introduction of unjust collective punishments resulting in the wrongful imprisonment of many young men, women and children. Second, such approaches have racialised serious violence, legitimising the increased yet concealed criminalisation of black people and black communities. Third, such penal strategies reaffirmed the mediated constructions of (an)other, who, whilst historically derived, are (re)presented as responsible for society's contemporary ills. Serious violence persists irrespective of 'race', gender, class, sexuality and (dis)ability. Therefore, we resist the simplistic and culturally derived (criminological) explanations of violence as occurring as a result of advanced marginalisation. Rather, through a series of 'dangerous associations', we find a racialised dragnet underpinned by the penal resource of the 'black gang' through which JE prosecutions and collective punishments are both demanded and sanctioned. Moreover, the 'success' of JE enabled collective punishments is contingent upon the converging discourses of CJ practitioners, academics and third sector organisations. Critically, such discourses are unceremoniously mediated through print and social media, a series of 'dog-whistles', arousing entrenched racist constructions of those deemed as outsiders. For Jewkes (2011: 270), the media is not a window on the world but a "prism subtly bending and distorting our picture of reality". Significantly then, crime is mediated and consumed to permit the reader to side-step reality, rather than confront it. For Jewkes, the media-recipient relationship is one of the collusion, not passivity, utilised to perennially "define the parameters of social (in)tolerance".

There is a single story hegemonically exploited to justify the State's damaging incursions into the lives of people racialised as black. The story serves to conceal the true nature and extent of interpersonal and State violence within England and Wales. The findings of 'dangerous associations' demonstrates that it is only through naming racism(s) that we can understand the *why* of joint enterprise and expose the trope of the gang as the *how* that historical continuities become exposed, demanding critical explanation and radical alteration.

Notes

1. We acknowledge Mark Blake from BTEG for his astute conceptualisation of racialised discrimination as hardwired within the systems and structures of British society.
2. Whilst we acknowledge the criminal justice 'system' in England and Wales encompasses a large and varied number of organisations, for our purpose, we isolate the police service, Her Majesty's Court Services (HMCS) inclusive of Crown and Magistrates Courts, the Crown Prosecution Service (CPS), the National Offender Management Service (NOMS) and Her Majesty's Prison Service (HMPS).
3. It was not possible to break down the Nottingham data beyond the omnibus BAME category.
4. Serious violence is defined by the Home Office as the offence types of murder, attempted murder, manslaughter, wounding and actual bodily and grievous bodily harm.
5. The 'non-black' group includes all those who were NOT identified as black African, black Caribbean, black other or of mixed heritage with one of the black groupings.

References

Anderson, B. (2013). *Us & Them: The Dangerous Politics of Immigration Control*. Oxford: Oxford University Press.

Alexander, C. (2008). *Re-Thinking "Gangs"*. London: Runnymede Trust. http://www.runnymedetrust.org/uploads/publications/pdfs/RethinkingGangs-2008.pdf

Amos, V., Gilroy, P., & Lawrence, E. (1982). White Sociology, Black Struggle. In D. Robbins (Ed.), *Rethinking Social Inequality*. Aldershot: Gower Publishing Company Ltd.

Barkas, B. (2014). *Framing the Death of Mark Duggan*. [Online] London: Institute for Race Relations. Retrieved from http://www.irr.org.uk/news/framing-the-death-of-mark-duggan/

Bourne, J., & Sivanandan, A. (1980). Cheerleaders and Ombudsmen: The Sociology of Race Relations in Britain. *Race and Class, 21*, 331.

Bowling, B., & Phillips, C. (2002). *Racism, Crime and Justice*. London: Pearson.

Bowling, B. (2014). *There Is Much Still to Do on Stop and Search*. London: Centre for Crime and Justice Studies. Retrieved from https://www.crimeandjustice. org.uk/resources/there-much-still-do-stop-and-search

Bureau of Investigative Journalism. (2014). *Joint Enterprise: An Investigation into the Legal Doctrine of Joint Enterprise in Criminal Convictions*. London. Retrieved from https://www.documentcloud.org/documents/1100186-joint-enterprise-investigation.html

Cashmore, E., & Troyna, B. (1982). *Black Youth in Crisis*. London: Routledge.

Cohen, S. (1972). *Folk Devils and Moral Panics*. London: Routledge.

Crewe, B., Liebling, A., Padfield, N., & Virgo, G. (2015). Joint Enterprise: The Implications of an Unfair and Unclear Law. *Criminal Law Review Issue, 4*, 252–269.

Fekete, L. (2012). *Joint Enterprise, Racism and BME Communities* [Interview]. Institute for Race Relations. Retrieved from http://www.irr.org.uk/news/joint-enterprise-racism-and-bme-communities/

Fraser, A., & Atkinson, C. (2014). Making Up Gangs: Looping, Labelling and the New Politics of Intelligence Led Policing. *Youth Justice, 14*(2), 2.

Garland, D. (2001). *The Culture of Control*. Oxford: OUP.

Gilroy, P. (1982). The Myth of Black Criminality. *Socialist Register*. London: Merlin.

Gilroy, P. (2002). *There Ain't No Black in the Union Jack*. Oxfordshire: Routledge.

Gutzmore, C. (1983). Capital, 'Black Youth' and Crime. *Race and Class, 25*(2), 13–30.

Haining, R., & Law, J. (2007). Combining Police Perception with Police Records of Serious Crime Records of Serious Crime Areas: A Modelling Approach. *Journal of the Royal Statistical Society, 170*(4), 1019–1034.

Hall, S., Critcher, C., Jefferson, T., Clarke, J., & Roberts, B. (1978). *Policing the Crisis: Mugging, the State and Law and Order*. London: Macmillan.

Keith, M. (1993). *Race, Riots and Policing*. London: UCL Press.

Jewkes, Y. (2011). *Crime and Media: Overview*. SAGE Publications Limited.

Mayor's Office for Police and Crime. (2016, February 2). *MOPAC Challenge: Gangs*. Greater London Authority. Retrieved from https://www.london.gov.uk/sites/default/files/mopac_challenge_gangs_2_february_2016_-_presentation.pdf

Medina, J., & Shute, J. (2013). *"Utterly Appalling": Why Official Review of UK Gang Policy is Barely Credible*. Manchester Policy Blogs: University of Manchester. Retrieved from http://blog.policy.manchester.ac.uk/featured/2013/12/utterly-appalling-why-official-review-of-uk-gang-policy-isbarely-credible

Ministry of Justice. (2015). *Statistics on Race and the Criminal Justice System 2014: A Ministry of Justice Publication Under Section 95 of the Criminal Justice Act 1991*. London: MOJ. Retrieved from https://www.gov.uk/government/uploads/system/uploads/attachment_data/file/480250/bulletin.pdf

Ngozi-Adichie, C. (2009). *The Danger of a Single Story*. Tedtalks: New York. Retrieved from https://www.ted.com/talks/chimamanda_adichie_the_danger_of_a_single_story/transcript?language=en

Lewis, P., Newburn, T., Taylor, M., Mcgillivray, C., Greenhill, A., Frayman, H., & Proctor, R. (2011). *Reading the Riots: Investigating England's Summer of Disorder Reading the Riots*. London: The London School of Economics and Political Science and The Guardian.

Phillips, C. (2011). Institutional Racism and Ethnic Inequalities: An Expanded Multilevel Framework. *Journal of Social Policy, 40*(1), 173–192.

Phillips, C. (2012). *The Multicultural Prison: Ethnicity, Masculinity, and Social Relations Among Prisoners*. Oxford University Press.

Pitts, J. (2014). Who Dunnit? Gangs, Joint Enterprise, Bad Character and Duress. *Youth and Policy, 113*, 48–59.

Quraishi, M., & Philburn, R. (2015). *Researching Racism: A Guidebook for Academics and Professional Investigators*. SAGE.

Ross, T. (2016). David Cameron: 'Black People More Likely to Be in Prison than at a Top University. *The Telegraph*, 31 January. [Online]. Retrieved from http://www.telegraph.co.uk/news/politics/david-cameron/12131928/Labours-David-Lammy-to-lead-government-race-review.html

Smithson, H., Ralphs, R., & Williams, P. (2013). Used and Abused: The Problematic Usage of Gang Terminology in the United Kingdom and Its Implications for Ethnic Minority Youth. *British Journal of Criminology, 53*(1), 113–128.

Spalek, B. (2008). *Communities, Identities and Crime*. Bristol: The Policy Press.

Webbe, C. (2007). Blair Blames Spate of Murders on Black Culture. *The Guardian*, 12 April. [Online]. Retrieved from https://www.theguardian.com/politics/2007/apr/12/ukcrime.race

Williams, P. (2015). Criminalising the Other: Challenging the Race and Crime Nexus. *Race and Class, 56*(3), 18–35.

Williams, P., & Clarke, B. (2015). *Dangerous Associations: Joint Enterprise, Gangs and Racism*. London: Centre for Crime and Justice Studies. Retrieved from https://www.crimeandjustice.org.uk/

17

The Figure of the 'Foreign Criminal': Race, Gender and the FNP

Luke de Noronha

Introduction

The UK's 'Foreign National Prisoner crisis' erupted on 25 April 2006, when it emerged that 1023 foreign offenders, who had been recommended for deportation by the courts or the prison service, had been released upon completion of their sentences. The following day's newspapers declared a 'crisis', with coverage exposing the government's incompetence and the danger that grew from it. In the weeks that followed, the Home Secretary, Charles Clarke, was forced to resign and his replacement proclaimed the Home Office was 'not fit for purpose' (BBC 2006).

The Foreign National Prisoner (FNP from here on) 'crisis' inspired a 'moral panic' (Cohen 1972), in which a range of emergency measures and new policies were hastily instituted (Kaufman 2013). After the 'crisis', 'foreign criminals' became increasingly salient in migration debates in the UK. This chapter is based on my analysis of articles from the most widely read dailies in each newspaper group identified by The Migration

L. de Noronha (✉)
University of Oxford, Oxford, UK

© The Author(s) 2018
M. Bhatia et al. (eds.), *Media, Crime and Racism*, Palgrave Studies in Crime, Media and Culture, https://doi.org/10.1007/978-3-319-71776-0_17

Observatory (2013). The most popular tabloid, mid-market and broadsheet newspapers are The Sun, The Daily Mail and The Daily Telegraph, respectively. I searched for the terms 'Foreign Criminal', 'Foreign Prisoner' and 'Foreign National Prisoner' through Nexis, and selected my time frame (26 April to 30 June 2006) based on the most intense period of reportage—yielding over 400 articles in the three papers. The aim of this chapter is to explore the mechanics of race and gender in the construction of the 'foreign criminal'.

The Emergence of the FNP and Its Consequences

Foreign offenders had been labelled the 'forgotten prisoners' (Cheney 1993; Prison Reform Trust 2004), but they came to occupy centre stage in national consciousness following the 'crisis' (Bhui 2007). Newspaper articles on 'foreign criminals' and 'foreign prisoners' skyrocketed in 2006, ushering in a new 'folk devil' (see Fig. 17.1). The 'foreign criminal', a

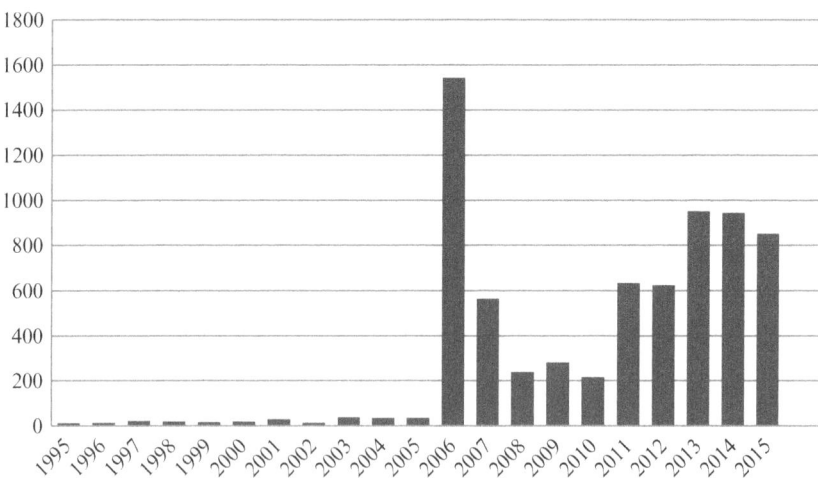

Fig. 17.1 Articles featuring the terms 'foreign prisoner' or 'foreign criminal' in UK national newspapers

figure produced during the FNP 'crisis', is now central to British media commentary on the 'problem of immigration'.

This media attention was met with a range of policy responses. In the months and years following the 'crisis', the Home Office prioritised the management and deportation of foreign offenders; its Criminal Casework Directorate expanded to 35 times its original size (Kaufman 2013). Moreover, the number of foreign ex-offenders deported increased five-fold, from 1000 in 2005 to around 5400 in 2008 (Fekete and Webber 2009: 6). Numbers remained relatively stable in subsequent years, averaging over 5000 in the four years following the scandal (Vine 2011). Clearly then, the mushrooming of media stories on 'foreign criminals' was mirrored in deportation practices.

This drive to deport FNPs, often with complete disregard for length of residence, personal circumstances and ties to the country (Gibney 2013), was facilitated by provisions introduced in the UK Borders Act 2007. The Act signalled the most important change in policies surrounding the deportation of foreign offenders since the Immigration Act 1971 (Dubinsky 2012: 69). Any non-EEA citizen sentenced to 12 months or more was now subject to 'automatic' deportation. Before the scandal, a wide range of factors would be weighed in the balance when determining whether to deport (Fekete and Webber 2009). The Borders Act, however, made deportation 'automatic', save for when expulsion would contravene the UK's human rights obligations under EU law or the refugee convention.

After the FNP 'crisis', the Home Office feared the political consequences of releasing non-citizens post-sentence (Vine 2011: 22). Consequently, many ex-offenders were kept in immigration detention indefinitely, while the Home Office pursued their deportation (London Detainee Support Group 2009). The FNP 'crisis' also catalysed a significant shift in the British penal estate (Kaufman 2012a). In early 2009, the Prison Service announced new plans to distribute foreign prisoners according to a policy called 'hubs and spokes' (Ministry of Justice and United Kingdom Border Agency 2009). The 'hub' prisons were to house a majority of foreign nationals and 'spoke' prisons were to direct foreign nationals to 'hub' prisons where possible (Bosworth 2011). 'Hub' prisons, and the 'foreign-national only' prisons which emerged at the same time, were to be furnished with immigration personnel who could facilitate the deportation process (Ministry of Justice and United Kingdom Border Agency 2009). This policy "constructed 'the foreigner' as a distinct category of existence in the prison" (Kaufman 2012b: 189). The prison is now a key bordering site which manages and disciplines foreignness (Bosworth 2012; Kaufman 2012a, b).

The Immigration Act 2014 saw sweeping cuts to the rights of appeal in immigration cases, and Theresa May promised to 'deport foreign criminals first, and hear their appeals later' (BBC 2013). This group was targeted specifically and denied an in-country right of appeal. The effects of this policy have been swift and effective—most people simply do not bring appeals to the tribunal from abroad, for a number of practical and financial reasons (Joint Council for the Welfare of Immigrants 2015).

As a direct result of these policy responses to the FNP crisis, an increasing number people have been (and are being) exiled from their homes in the UK, often to unfamiliar and forgotten countries of origin. As a result of policies designed to expedite the removal of 'foreign offenders', people who moved to the UK as children, and have British children of their own, are being deported from all that they know, often on the basis of relatively minor convictions. As I have argued elsewhere, deportation is often experienced as banishment (de Noronha 2016). To understand the UK's extraordinarily draconian approach to the deportation of foreign offenders we have to analyse the genesis of the 'foreign criminal', during the FNP 'crisis' of 2006/2007 (explained in the following subsections).

The FNP Scandal and the Consensus

Charles Clarke walked into the House of Commons on 26 April 2006 to a chorus of shouts to 'resign' (House of Commons Debate, (26 April) 2006, column 573). The morning's papers were awash with the news of 1023 'dangerous' foreign criminals, released and "free to roam our streets" (*Daily Mail* 2006a). This wilful neglect of the public's safety was indicative of a "government in meltdown" (Daily Mail 2006b); in what Richard

Littlejohn (2006) of the Mail would call "one of the worst ever political scandals in history".

In the weeks that followed, parliament was consumed by the scandal and the media coverage was unrelenting. The FNP 'crisis' came at a bad time for Labour, who went on to suffer severe losses in local elections on the 4 May, precipitating a cabinet reshuffle. Shadow Home Secretary David Davies would later claim: "this has been the year from hell in the Home Office, possibly the worst in its 224-year history" (House of Common Debate (23 November) 2006, column.700).

As MPs argued, and journalists offered their commentary on the causes and implications of the crisis, the underlying consensus was that this was, indeed, a monumental calamity. The issue was seen by most to be rather simple. The government had released over 1000 dangerous criminals to commit more crime in a country they had no right to reside in.

The language employed, both in parliament and the media, depicted 'foreign criminals' through animal metaphors (see Olson 2013); they were 'let loose', 'roaming', 'alien predators' who should be 'rounded up'. Richard Littlejohn (2006) expressed his "rage and a degree of guilt about being a citizen of a country which allows such animals to roam free— indeed, rolls out the red carpet for them". The danger posed was unequivocal and both journalists and politicians expressed disgust at the foreigners who endangered 'our' streets, 'our' public and 'our' nation; 'we' had a right to answers, and, more importantly, 'we' had a right to action.

In the next section, I will unpick some of the different narratives at play during the so-called FNP crisis. While the coverage was almost completely uniform in its condemnation of the government and of 'foreign criminals', different articles and authors summoned and engaged different tropes. 'Foreign criminals' were portrayed as bad migrants, undeserving asylum seekers, evil criminals, rapists, murderers and paedophiles. I argue we cannot interpret these different narratives without accounting for the implicit work that racialised and gendered stereotypes perform. During the 'crisis', foreign offenders were constructed as specific kinds of migrants and specific kinds of criminals, and these images are fundamentally about race and gender.

'Bad Migrants'

Migrants, in general, are non-members on probation (Kanstroom 2007) and must prove their deservingness. They should "work hard, play by the rules, speak English and get on through merit" (Home Office 2007: 2). Migrants must elude association with 'internal others': the 'criminals' and 'welfare-scroungers' (Anderson 2013). The 'good migrant' should "walk on eggshells" when in Britain (Hastings 2006 Mail), and any misbehaviour proves that which was always feared about their foreignness, that it renders them a threat to the nation's values and value (Anderson 2013; Gibney 2013). Importantly here however, the type of migrant abusing 'our' hospitality really was important.

FNPs were most commonly described as, and conflated with, asylum seekers:

> It's no coincidence that a quarter of these foreign criminals were failed asylum seekers. (*Daily Mail* 2006a)

> It was its failure to get to grips with the abuse of the asylum system for many years that was the principal driver behind the influx of criminal elements, who exploited the shambles to get into the country and set up their networks. (Johnston 2006, *Telegraph*)

It was suggested that "serious criminals were seeking asylum and then vanishing" (Reid et al. 2006, Mail), and that the asylum system became "a ruse favoured by foreign convicts to avoid deportation" (Reid 2006a, Mail). This deep mistrust of the asylum system pervades media coverage on migration in the UK (Philo et al. 2013; Migration Observatory 2013). Asylum seekers are portrayed as scroungers, taking advantage of Britain's soft-touch hospitality, bringing only insecurity and offering nothing in return (Kushner 2003; Pirouet 2001).

Framing the FNP 'crisis' through the lens of asylum opens a wider debate about human rights:

> He'd [Tony Blair] rather play Russian roulette with our safety than return murderous foreign scum to their homeland if they claim they face torture. (Shanahan 2006, Sun)

Will he [Tony Blair] also make a commitment to scrap the Human Rights Act 1998, which in the public's mind has done so much to entrench a culture in which people believe that the system favours giving rights to criminals, prisoners and illegal immigrants at the expense of the ordinary, decent, law- abiding citizens of this country? (Philip Davies, MP for Shipley, House of Commons Debate (20 July) 2006 column 485)

The Human Rights Act (HRA) was introduced by New Labour in 1998. It simply codified the European Convention of Human Rights into primary British legislation, thus reducing the need for claimants to take their cases to Strasbourg. In much of the coverage, the HRA was described as an enemy of ordinary, law-abiding citizens and as a get-out-of-gaol-free-card for criminals and immigrants. The HRA had always been controversial (*The Sun* 2001), but the FNP crisis acted as a conduit for this animosity.

The HRA was described as a 'curse' making it impossible to deport anyone. It was argued that the "human rights industry" (Hastings 2006, Daily Mail) had "quite simply altered the entire legal and moral culture of this country and taken an axe to common sense" (Phillips 2006, Mail); the HRA was described as a form of "tyranny" with profoundly perverse consequences, "a principle [sic] weapon against the culture and identity of the nation" (Phillips 2006, Daily Mail). The FNP 'crisis' provided ammunition for the anti-HRA onslaught, which is now manifest in the Conservative government's promising to scrap the HRA, leave the European Convention on Human Rights and introduce a new British Bill of Rights (Travis 2013). The UK's decision to leave the EU can be traced and explained in different ways. But I would argue that the idea that liberal EU law prevented the deportation of dangerous 'foreign offenders' was more consequential than most recognise.

The reason FNPs served so well in this assault on the HRA is because they were so often constructed as asylum seekers. The FNP as the asylum seeker provides conclusive evidence of the exploitation faced by ordinary, hard-working British citizens by those who abuse the 'human rights industry'. The 'criminal asylum seeker' confirms that migrants claiming to be 'victims' are often, in fact, 'villains'.

In general, migrants are conceptualised as either victims or villains (Anderson 2008; Pupavac 2008; Judge 2010). Most migrants are portrayed as deceitful and dangerous. They are claiming something which is not theirs—jobs, resources, land—and they will break the rules to get access. The migrant as villain is always ready to break the rules and take what is not theirs, and they make things difficult for the 'genuine refugees'—however impossibly small this group is imagined to be in number. The migrant as victim, much like the ordinary British taxpayer, is violated by bad migrants (Anderson 2013): by those bogus and deceitful migrants, who abuse the system, break the rules and cut the queue.[1] The asylum seeker as offender plays his part in this discourse, confirming the fears of the sceptics, who knew that many crying 'victim' were in fact villains all along.

Importantly, this victim-villain binary is profoundly gendered: the released FNP villains, who never really made convincing victims, were men. Asylum seekers, like 'victims of trafficking', are most frequently 'good migrants', the referent of the receiving state's hospitality, when they are vulnerable, suffering and unthreatening (Fassin 2001). Men, especially young men, are always potentially dangerous, morally deviant and sexually violent (Hubbard 2005; Pupavac 2008). Put simply, the asylum-seeking 'foreign criminal' is a man. This is hardly surprising, given that both 'criminals' and 'bad migrants' are overwhelmingly imagined as male. The point is that through gendering the FNP as an asylum-seeking man, as a victim turned villain, a wolf in sheep's clothing, the 'foreign criminal' was produced as dangerous, deceitful and undeserving.

It is important to note that women do not appear only as victims; indeed women appear as specific kinds of villains—as benefit-scroungers and irresponsible mothers (see e.g. Reid 2006b). However, in general, in media representations of immigrants, men appear as villains, women as victims (Judge 2010; Pupavac 2008; de Noronha 2015). The FNP scandal did not only incense commentators because FNPs were migrants but because they were specific kinds of migrants—almost always men, usually asylum seekers—who could be situated within the gendered victim-villain binary. Given that gender and race work through one another, these 'bad migrant men' were also implicitly racialised:

Coming from societies in which men live by what they are strong enough to take, they seek to live by the same principle in Britain. (Hastings 2006, Mail)

This appeal to the dangerous, culturally depraved, 'bad migrant' chimes with a set of intersecting fears regarding racialised men (Alexander 2004). The British people need to be vigilant in ensuring that the few victims worthy of their support really are victims. FNPs, quite crudely, prove that the system for ascertaining who goes where is rotten to its core. Framing the FNP 'crisis' in terms of asylum, and in terms of victims-turned-villains, allowed journalists and politicians to position the scandal in familiar territory.

'Evil Criminals'

It is clear that journalists and parliamentarians alike were quick to relate the FNP scandal to broader crises in crime control:

It is not only foreign offenders who have enjoyed lenient treatment at the hands of your government. Labour's crazy early release scheme, whereby criminals are let off part of their sentences, has needlessly increased the crime rate. (Davies 2006, Telegraph)

Here we see a more general complaint about the prison system: there are not enough prison beds, sentences are far too lenient and criminals are getting off scot-free. Much concern was raised regarding recidivism: the result of this scandal was seen to be more crime, more danger and more victims. Fear of crime has become a 'political motif' in late modern societies; crime is seen to affect us all and is a prominent issue in politics (Garland 2001: 12). Simon (2007) notes that "people are seen as acting legitimately when they act to prevent crimes" and that "we can expect people to deploy the category of crime to legitimate interventions that have other motivations" (2007: 4). We see this clearly in the FNP scandal: deportation becomes necessary, even righteous, not only or even primarily as a measure to control migration, but primarily as a means of reducing crime (Warner 2005). Crime is bad, its reduction is good, and hence the deportation of 'foreign criminals' is necessary:

> The law should state that non-citizens who break the law should be instantly deported, without conditions, to the place from which they came. Crime is voluntary, and they will have volunteered for whatever they then face. (Hitchens 2006, Mail, emphasis added)

> Let's be clear, if someone comes to our country and abuses our hospitality by committing serious crimes, I don't give a toss what happens to them when they are thrown out. I'm willing to pay their airfare and for the bullet when they get home. We've got enough of our own villains without importing or releasing back into the community the rapists, muggers and murderers of the world … I am sick to death of paying to support these leeches, criminals and terrorists. (Shanahan 2006, Sun)

'Foreign criminals' elicit intense hostility largely because of the broader discursive construction of 'criminals'. Profoundly illiberal approaches to 'crime' provide one of the main explanations for the FNP 'crisis', and we should situate the FNP scandal within these broader narratives on crime and 'criminals'. However, we should stay alert to the work that foreignness is doing in conversations about FNPs. What is the relationship between foreignness and criminality and how are 'foreign criminals' different to 'home-grown' ones? To examine the foreignness in the 'foreign criminal', we should question what types of 'criminals' and crimes exercised the media.

What Work Does the 'Foreignness' of the 'Foreign Criminal Do?

The clause 'including murderers, rapists and paedophiles' (or some variation thereof) was repeated time and time again in the coverage; journalists and parliamentarians consistently invoked the rapist and murderer. While a number of articles detailed the number of offenders in each category (three for murder and nine for rape by most accounts, out of a total of 1023), the ceaseless discussion of rape and murder had the effect of inflating the significance of these offenders within the population. Some articles carelessly exaggerated the numbers: suggesting the British government was "letting hundreds of foreign rapists and murderers out of prison" (Letts 2006, Mail).

In my main data set—in articles from The Sun, Daily Mail and Daily Telegraph—134 of the 438 articles included the word 'rape' or 'rapist' (roughly 31%). Across all national newspapers in the selected time frame, the proportion was similar—that is, just under one third of articles referenced rape and/or rapists in reporting on the FNP scandal. This suggests that foreign criminals are especially likely to be guilty of rape; however rates of sexual and violent offences among non-citizens are either comparable to or lower than for citizens (Banks 2011).

Arguably however, this emphasis is common to media reporting on crime in general. The types of crime that are least common tend to be reported the most, in what has been termed the 'law of opposites' (Surette 1998: 47). Sexual attacks receive an inordinate amount of coverage (Carrabine 2008: 2), especially when the assailant is a stranger, imperilling weak, 'ideal victims' (Christie 1986). However, we need to consider how 'the criminal' takes on contorted forms when foreign. While crime is generally reported in a sensationalist tone, and the media exhibit a fascination with sexual violence (Carrabine 2008), the recurrent individual stories of the 'foreign criminal' as rapist cannot be read as simply sensationalist crime stories; they echo deeply entrenched fears about the dangerous sexuality of racialised men (Hubbard 2005: 61).

Social events "must be brought within the horizon of the 'meaningful'" (Hall et al. 1978: 54), and we should think critically about race and the 'horizon of the meaningful' in contemporary Britain. I agree with Stuart Hall when he argues that British "culture does partly live off a reservoir of unconscious feelings about race, and in particular those feelings remain unconscious because they are about race. It's difficult for them to get expressed somehow" (Hall and Back 2009). Journalists and politicians rarely invoked the 'race' of 'foreign villains' in crude terms, but "in Britain the concepts of race and foreignness cannot be separated" (Kaufman 2013: 181).

My argument, simply put, is that the foreigner is racialised and that foreigners are racialised through gender. In thinking about the way foreignness and race are inextricably linked, we should think about what is meant by 'the migrant' in public debate. After all, 'the migrant' in discourse encompasses much more and much less than the non-citizen in law (Anderson and Blinder 2014)—'the migrant' in discourse is a foreigner. "In public debate [the] 'migrant' is not simply about either legal status or where a person is born but is about being one of the global poor" (Anderson 2014: 3). I would add that race is central to the discursive construction of 'the migrant', and suggest that race and class are hard to disentangle in this conversation. Race, nationality and poverty are not independent variables (Anderson 2013: 3), and even if the debate is couched in terms of nationality, legal status, social class or 'integration', race matters. As De Genova notes, "race need not always speak its name" (2010: 55).

We should also note that there are lots of migrants who rarely feature in debates about migration, who don't really count as foreigners. Australian backpackers and visiting academics are not considered migrants or foreigners in discourse (or perhaps rather they are invisible in conversations about migration), and yet some British citizens cannot shed their foreignness—they are the second and third generation migrants with the wrong kind of values (read foreign). Not all non-citizens are foreign, and some citizens are (Honig 2002). In other words, foreignness and legal citizenship do not map onto one another neatly; citizens and non-citizens alike are made foreign through racialisation.

Importantly here, gender is central to processes of racialisation. Groups subject to racist discourse are routinely described as displaying problematic, backwards and debased gender norms. If we think of the figure of the 'black brute' invoked to justify lynching in the antebellum South (Gunning 1997), or the mugger in 1970s Britain (Hall et al. 1978), or the 'Muslim grooming gangs' that have served as the platform for new modes of far-right activism in the UK (see e.g. Pidd 2014; Tufail and Poynting 2016), we realise that the dangerous sexuality of foreign men is a narrative with many historical precedents; it is a motif undergirding the whole FNP 'crisis' and the visceral response to it. The impulse to frame the FNP as a rapist cannot be interpreted without a critical reading of British national identity and the spectre of race.

Victims and Villains

So far, I have argued that FNPs were constructed as specific kinds of 'bad migrants', regularly depicted as male asylum seekers who had fraudulently claimed victim status. FNPs were constructed as specific kinds of criminals, as rapists, murderers and paedophiles—despite the widely available statistics. Images of the FNP as rapist reflect deeply entrenched fears about the dangerous sexuality of racialised men (see e.g. Collins 1990). Hopefully, in examining some of the individual cases commented upon by journalists and parliamentarians, I will be able to explore the interplay of migration, criminality, race and gender in the discursive construction of the 'foreign criminal'.

The victim has become the voice of the law-abiding citizen, the representative of the nation (Garland 2001; Walklate 2007), and this was manifest in the platform given to victims in the coverage:

> Perhaps if Mr Clarke saw a picture of my daughter it would be more real for him. Maybe then he might understand how I feel. (Pyatt 2006, Sun)

> If the Home Office and the prison authorities had done their jobs, then my son would still be alive. (Dolan 2006, Mail)

Victims, friends and families and victim support groups were given significant voice, to air their anger, to tell their stories, to condemn and to represent the readership (Reiner 2007). Victims must be protected, heard and their fears addressed (Reiner et al. 2003); they are the representatives of ordinary citizens:

> Publicized images of actual victims serve as the personalized, real-life, it-could- be-you metonym for a problem of security that has become a defining feature of contemporary culture. (Garland 2001: 11)

Yet all victims are not equal; some people are easier to feel sorry for than others (Butler 2010) and are thus more likely to receive media coverage. Nils Christie (1986) suggests that the ideal victim is weak, respectable and innocent and the ideal offender is big, bad and unknown to the victim. As Christie notes, the more ideal the villain, the more ideal the victim (and vice versa). Moreover, ideal victims and villains bear little relation to the majority of real offenders and victims. Importantly for this paper, Christie notes that the ideal victim is almost always female, and the ideal villain almost always male:

> The ideal offender differs from the victim. He is, morally speaking, black against the white victim. He is a dangerous man coming from far away. He is a human being close to not being one. (1986: 26)

Ideal villains were depicted in media reports, as journalists drew on specific cases to ground the catastrophe in the real lives of ordinary, innocent British citizens.

The Cases that Said It All

The foreign villains who served as case studies in the coverage were invariably hypermasculinised; their crimes were violent and often sexually violent. Articles were devoted to criminal histories, details of offences, descriptions of brutality and the anguish of victims and their families. Rapists were by far the most (un)popular criminals in the coverage. The nationality of villains was almost always referred to, with a notable number of stories on Jamaicans and Somalis. In the Daily Express (2006) article 'Gallery of Shame', a number of criminals were depicted as representative of the FNP 'crisis', all of them guilty of rape and sexual violence, all of them with 'Muslim-sounding' names.

Rashid Musa, a "fake asylum-seeker … released to rape" (Nugent 2006, Times), was found guilty of "raping a 46-year-old mother and a 16-year-old schoolboy in separate attacks" (Gardham 2006, Telegraph). The brutality of his offences, coupled with his status as asylum seeker, provided ammunition for the broader attack on the asylum system and the 'human rights industry'. Musa was sentenced back in 1999, yet his case surfaced in the coverage of the FNP scandal. The media were quite clearly scouring recent history for abhorrent crimes committed by non-citizens, yet the effect was to represent the FNP 'crisis' in terms of rape, murder and violence—often perpetrated by those who had claimed asylum.

Courtney Burry was described as the 'Jamaican paedophile' whose case said it all (Daily Mail 2006c). He was sentenced to four years imprisonment for gross indecency and recommended for deportation; however, he went on to marry (while facing deportation, the coverage notes) and claimed it would be unsafe for him to return to Jamaica. Burry was framed as a monster, whose family life was a sham and whose presence near a primary school was an outrage (Grant 2006, Mail). The fact that Burry claimed it would be unsafe for him to return to Jamaica, because he would be persecuted for his criminal history, was offered to illustrate the absurdity of the human rights laws which protect those who deserve no sympathy.

The villain who garnered the most media attention was undoubtedly Mustaf Jama—another Somali asylum seeker—who was prime suspect in the murder of the female police officer Sharon Beshenivsky. "The whole nation was horrified by what happened to WPC Beshenivsky (Pascoe-Watson 2006, Sun); "she had swapped her shift on the day of the murder last November so that she could get home in time for her daughter Lydia's fourth birthday party" (Stokes 2006, Telegraph). Sharon was described as a good mother in a 'decent family' (Daily Mail 2006d), while Jama was described as a career criminal who had abused the asylum system. It was later reported that Jama escaped the country under the cover of a veil, perhaps sealing his fate as the ultimate ideal villain.

We should think about what work these stories do in discursively constituting the 'crisis'. The victims in these anecdotes were overwhelmingly British women and children. Victims were commonly described as law-abiding 'mothers', with strong family values. Women are seen as bearers of the ethnic community, transmitters of culture and mothers of the nation (Yuval-Davis and Anthias 1990), and this might explain why these violent sexual attacks by foreign men had such purchase among journalists and politicians. The threats were existential.

The villains were often depicted as deceitful asylum seekers who abused 'our' misplaced regard for human rights. Their stories framed the 'crisis' in terms of rape, murder and paedophilia. Race was rarely mentioned explicitly, but Somalis, Jamaicans and Arabs are hardly race-less categorisations—nationality stands in for race here (Gilroy 1987). These stories highlight that the FNP 'crisis' cannot be interpreted as just the latest in a series of immigration scandals, nor a simple marriage of concerns about migration and crime—the specific kinds of migrants and criminals made to represent the 'crisis' animated 'the nation' at a much deeper level.

In the 'foreign criminal' a number of fears crystallise: fears around asylum seekers, Muslims, dark men, terrorists and paedophiles. These terms and labels are used in emphatic ways, sometimes interchangeably, creating a set of associations which produce an intense climate of fear and 'moral panic'. It is in this sense that racist media reportage, even if implicit, is able to animate the British public at a kind of gut level. It is now almost impossible to have a measured discussion about foreign offenders and deportation. Any non-citizen with a criminal record (even criminal association), is now the 'foreign criminal', a figure which is deeply racialised and saturated with negative connotations.

Conclusion

It is hardly surprising that 'foreign criminals' animate the British media. Concerns surrounding crime and immigration have long been central to British politics. But suggesting that 'foreign criminals' are simply the product of 'the migrant' plus 'the criminal' does not get us far enough.

During the 'crisis', FNPs were depicted as specific kinds of undeserving migrants, usually male asylum seekers, who had deceitfully and callously abused 'our' hospitality. These 'bad migrant men' dirtied the entire system for assigning victimhood status, proving just how dangerous 'human rights' can be. FNPs were also constructed as 'evil criminals' and profoundly illiberal approaches to crime legitimate deportation as a decisive form of crime control.

Further however, FNPs incensed public commentators because they were described as specific kinds of violent criminals. These rapists, paedophiles and murderers were seen to endanger innocent, law-abiding citizens. In the individual cases of 'foreign criminals' discussed by journalists and politicians, these narratives were combined in the construction of 'ideal villains'. We can only interpret the work these stories do through exposing the 'common sense' ideas about race and gender on which they play.

Commentators consistently appealed to 'common sense' when discussing, or more accurately creating, the 'crisis'. 'Common sense' ideas about who belongs, who deserves, who is good and who is bad offer insights into dominant conceptions of Britishness. The 'community of value' is peopled by good citizens who work hard, respect one another, abide by the law and cherish family values (Anderson 2013). 'Common sense' also defines those who do not and cannot belong (Lawrence 1982). Importantly, 'common sense' harbours racist attitudes which justify and even celebrate the incarceration, indefinite detention and forced expulsion of certain bodies.

The FNP 'crisis' incensed the media and politicians who framed the issue in terms of dangerous foreign men whose hypermasculinist violence presented a severe and existential threat to the British people. These constructions of 'bad migrants' relied upon race for their intelligibility and these racialised stereotypes were articulated through gender. Put simply, 'foreign criminals' are dangerous racialised men and the violent state practices implemented to protect the British public from these 'monsters'—that is, prison, indefinite detention and deportation—can only be understood in reference to the racialised and gendered stereotypes that construct them as such.

Notes

1. The migrant victim may well be the 'genuine refugee' but is perhaps more likely to be the 'victim of trafficking' (de Noronha 2015). Dominant discourse on trafficking and smuggling work to imply that migrant victims did not want to move in the first place, they were coerced, and so the solution is to send them home (O'Connell Davidson).

References

Alexander, C. (2004). Imagining the Asian Gang: Ethnicity, Masculinity and Youth After "the Riots". *Critical Social Policy, 24*(4), 526–549.

Anderson, B. (2008). *'Illegal Immigrant': Victim or Villain?* Working Paper Series No. 64, COMPAS, University of Oxford.

Anderson, B. (2013). *Us and Them? The Dangerous Politics of Immigration Control.* Oxford: OUP.

Anderson, B. (2014). *Exclusion, Failure, and the Politics of Citizenship.* RCIS Working Paper No.1. Retrieved December 23, 2014, from http://www.ryerson.ca/content/dam/rcis/documents/RCIS_WP_Anderson_No_2014_1.pdf

Anderson, B., & Blinder, S. (2014). 'Who Counts as a Migrant? Definitions and Their Consequences' the Migration Observatory Briefing, The University of Oxford.

Banks, J. (2011). Foreign National Prisoners in the UK: Explanations and Implications. *The Howard Journal of Criminal Justice, 50*(2), 184–198.

BBC. (2006). *Immigration System Unfit* (Online). Retrieved June 12, 2014, from http://news.bbc.co.uk/1/hi/uk_politics/5007148.stm

BBC. (2013). *Theresa May: Deport Foreign Criminals Before Appeal* (Online). Retrieved January 5, 2017, from http://www.bbc.co.uk/news/uk-politics-24335368

Bhui, H. (2007). Alien Experience: Foreign National Prisoners After the Deportation Crisis. *Probation Journal, 54*(4), 368–382.

Bosworth, M. (2011). Deportation, Detention and Foreign-National Prisoners in England and Wales. *Citizenship Studies, 15*(5), 583–596.

Bosworth, M. (2012). Subjectivity and Identity in Detention: Punishment and Society in a Global Age. *Theoretical Criminology, 16*(2), 123–140.

Butler, J. (2010). *Frames of War: When Is Life Grievable?* London: Verso.

Carrabine, E. (2008). *Crime, Culture and the Media.* Cambridge: Polity.

Cheney, D. (1993). *Into the Dark Tunnel: Foreign Prisoners in the British Prison System.* London: Prison Reform Trust.

Christie, N. (1986). The Ideal Victim. In E. Fattah (Ed.), *From Crime Policy to Victim Policy: Reorienting the Justice System* (pp. 17–30). Basingstoke: Macmillan.

Cohen, S. (1972). *Folk Devils and Moral Panics.* London: Routledge.

Collins, P. H. (1990). *Black Feminist Thought.* New York: Routledge.

Daily Express. (2006). Gallery of Shame, April 3.

Daily Mail. (2006a). A Home Secretary Failing in This Duty, April 26.

Daily Mail. (2006b). A Government in Meltdown, April 27.

Daily Mail. (2006c). Case that Say It All, June 15.

Daily Mail. (2006d). A Sorry Legacy of Rank Incompetence, May 3.

Davies, D. (2006). Do Away with Weakness, Bluster and the Gimmicks' David Davis, the Shadow Home Secretary, Offers John Reid Some Advice for His New Cabinet Role. *Sunday Telegraph*, May 7.

De Genova, N. (2010). The Deportation Regime: Sovereignty, Space, and the Freedom of Movement. In N. De Genova & N. Peutz (Eds.), *The Deportation Regime: Sovereignty, Space and the Freedom of Movement* (pp. 33–68). Durham: Duke University Press.

de Noronha, L. (2015). 'Victims of Trafficking' and 'Foreign Criminals' – Constructing the State as Our (Masculine) Saviour. *COMPAS blog*. Retrieved January 18, 2017, from http://www.compas.ox.ac.uk/2015/victims-of-trafficking-and-foreign-criminals-constructing-the-state-as-our-masculine-saviour/

de Noronha, L. (2016). Deportation and Multi-Status Britain. *Discover Society* (Online). Retrieved January 5, 2017, from http://discoversociety.org/2016/10/04/deportation-and-multi-status-britain/

Dolan, A. (2006). My Son's Blood is on Your Hands, Mr Clarke, Says Murder Victim's Mother. *Daily Mail*, May 2.

Dubinsky, L. (2012). *Foreign National Prisoners: Law and Practice*. London: Legal Action Group.

Fassin, D. (2001). The Biopolitics of Otherness: Undocumented Foreigners and Racial Discrimination in French Public Debate. *Anthropology Today, 17*(1), 3–7.

Fekete, L., & Webber, F. (2009). Foreign Nationals, Enemy Penology and the Criminal Justice System. *IRR European Race Bulletin, 69*(Autumn), 2–17.

Gardham, D. (2006). Freed to Rape and Kill: Two Men Who Should Have Been Deported. *Daily Telegraph*, April 2.

Garland, D. (2001). *The Culture of Control: Crime and Social Order in Contemporary Society*. Oxford: Clarendon Press.

Gibney, M. (2013). Deportation, Crime, and the Changing Character of Membership in the United Kingdom. In K. Aas & M. Bosworth (Eds.), *The Borders of Punishment: Migration, Citizenship and Social Exclusion* (pp. 218–236). Oxford: OUP.

Gilroy, P. (1987). *There Ain't No Black in the Union Jack: The Cultural Politics of Race and Nation*. London: Routledge.

Grant, G. (2006). Why Won't the Police Arrest Him? This Paedophile Should Have Been Deported from Scotland Six Years Ago. *Daily Mail*, June 14.

Gunning, S. (1997). *Race, Rape, and Lynching: The Red Record of American Literature, 1890–1912*. New York: OUP.

Hall, H., & Back, L. (2009). At Home and Not at Home: Stuart Hall in Conversation with Les Back. *Cultural Studies, 23*(4), 658–687.

Hall, S., Critcher, C., Jefferson, T., Clarke, J., & Roberts, B. (1978). *Policing the Crisis: Mugging, the State and Law and Order*. London: Palgrave Macmillan.

Hastings, M. (2006). We'll Continue to Pay in Blood and the Peace of Mind of Ordinary People Until We Come to Our Senses Over the Loss of Control of Our Borders. *Daily Mail*, May 4.

HC Deb (House of Commons Debates). (2006, April 26). HC Deb (House of Commons Debates). 2006, 20 July HC Deb (House of Commons Debates). 2006, 23 November HC Deb (House of Commons Debates). 2007, 8 October.

Hitchens, P. (2006). We Need a Reshuffle of Minds, Not Ministers. *Mail on Sunday*, May 7.

Home Office. (2007). *Enforcing the Rules: A Strategy to Ensure and Enforce Compliance with Our Immigration Laws*. London: COI.

Honig, B. (2002). A Legacy of Xenophobia. *Boston Review* (December 2002/January 2003).

Hubbard, P. (2005). Accommodating Otherness: Anti-Asylum Centre Protest and the Maintenance of White Privilege. *Transactions of the Institute of British Geographers, 30*(1), 52–65.

Johnston, P. (2006). The Home Office Failure Is Criminal. *Daily Telegraph*, April 2.

Joint Council for the Welfare of Immigrants. (2015). *House of Lords Second Reading Briefing Immigration Bill: Appeals* (Online). Retrieved January 4, 2017, from https://www.jcwi.org.uk/policy/parliamentary-briefings/immigration-bill-2015-house-lords-2nd-reading-briefing-appeals

Judge, R. (2010). *Refugee Advocacy and the Biopolitics of Asylum in Britain*. Working Paper Series No. 60, Refugee Studies Centre, University of Oxford.

Kanstroom, D. (2007). *Deportation Nation: Outsiders in American History*. Cambridge: Harvard University Press.

Kaufman, E. (2012a). Finding Foreigners: Race and the Politics of Memory in British Prisons. *Population, Space and Place, 18*(6), 701–714.

Kaufman, E. (2012b). *Foreign Bodies: The Prison's Place in a Global World*. DPhil Thesis, University of Oxford.

Kaufman, E. (2013). Hubs and Spokes: The Transformation of the British Prison. In K. Aas & M. Bosworth (Eds.), *The Borders of Punishment: Migration, Citizenship, and Social Exclusion* (pp. 166–182). Oxford: OUP.

Kushner, T. (2003). Meaning Nothing but Good: Ethics, History and Asylum-Seeker Phobia in Britain. *Patterns of Prejudice, 37*(3), 257–276.

Lawrence, E. (1982). Just Plain Common Sense: The 'Roots' of Racism. In Centre for Contemporary Cultural Studies (Ed.), *The Empire Strikes Back: Race and Racism in 70s Britain* (pp. 45–92). London: Routledge.

Letts, Q. (2006). Asked About His Friend Condoleezza, Mr Straw Blushed Like a Teenager. *Daily Mail*, April 26.

Littlejohn, R. (2006). How CAN Charles Clarke Face Himself in the Mirror? *Daily Mail*, May 2. IMI Working Papers Series 2015, No. 111 23.

London Detainee Support Group. (2009). *Detained Lives: The Real Cost of Immigration Detention*. London: LDSG.

Migration Observatory. (2013). *Migration in the News: Portrayals of Immigrants, Migrants, Asylum Seekers and Refugees in National British Newspapers, 2010–2012*. University of Oxford.

Ministry of Justice and United Kingdom Border Agency. (2009). Service Level Agreement to Support the Effective and Speedy Removal of Foreign National Prisoners, May 1.

Nugent, H. (2006). Fake Asylum-Seeker Was Released to Rape. *The Times*, April 26.

Olson, G. (2013). *Criminals as Animals from Shakespeare to Lombroso*. Berlin: Walter de Gruyter.

Pascoe-Watson, G. (2006). WPC Sharon 'Killer' Should Have Been Deported. *Sun*, May 3.

Phillips, M. (2006). If We Really Want to Escape the Grip of Human Rights Law We Must Quit the EU. *Daily Mail*, May 15.

Philo, G., Briant, E., & Donald, P. (2013). *Bad News for Refugees*. London: Pluto Press.

Pidd, H. (2014). Police Investigate Far-Right 'Invasions' of Bradford and Glasgow Mosques. *Guardian*, 13 May 2014. Retrieved December 22, 2014, from http://www.theguardian.com/world/2014/may/13/police-far-right-invasions-bradford-glasgow-mosques-britain-first

Pirouet, L. (2001). *Whatever Happened to Asylum in Britain? A Tale of Two Walls*. Oxford: Berghahn.

Prison Reform Trust. (2004). *Forgotten Prisoners: The Plight of Foreign National Prisoners in England and Wales (Briefing Paper)*. London: Prison Reform Trust.

Pupavac, V. (2008). Refugee Advocacy, Traumatic Representations and Political Disenchantment. *Government and Opposition, 43*(2), 270–292.

Pyatt, J. (2006). Clarke Must Share Blame for My Girl's Brutal Murder. *Sun*, April 27.

Reid, S. (2006a). What Kind of System Lets a Jailed Foreign Rapist Claim Asylum to Avoid Being Deported? *Daily Mail*, May 3.

Reid, S. (2006b). My Fake Passport into Britain. *Daily Mail*, June 3.

Reid, S., Camber, B., & Salkeld, L. (2006). Foreign Villains Roam Our Street. *Daily Mail*, June 24.

Reiner, R. (2007). 'Media-Made Criminality: The Representation of Crime' in the Mass Media. In M. Maguire, R. Morgan, & R. Reiner (Eds.), *The Oxford Handbook of Criminology* (4th ed., pp. 302–340). Oxford: OUP.

Reiner, R., Livingstone, S., & Allen, J. (2003). From Law and Order to Lynch Mobs: Crime News Since the Second World War. In P. Mason (Ed.), *Criminal Visions: Media Representations of Crime and Justice* (pp. 13–32). Cullompton: Willan.

Shanahan, F. (2006). Blair Talks the Talk but Won't Walk the Walk. *Sun*, May 2.

Simon, J. (2007). *Governing Through Crime: How the War on Crime Transformed American Democracy and Created a Culture of Fear*. Oxford: OUP.

Stokes, P. (2006). Outrage at the Murder of an Unarmed Policewoman. Crime that Shocked Nation Need Not have Happened. *Daily Telegraph*, May 3.

Surette, R. (1998). *Media, Crime, and Criminal Justice: Images and Realities*. Belmont: Wadsworth Press.

The Sun. (2001). *Scrap the Act*, August 21.

Travis, A. (2013). Conservatives Promise to Scrap Human Rights Act After Next Election. *Guardian*, 30 September. Retrieved June 6, 2014, from http://www.theguardian.com/law/2013/sep/30/conservitives-scrap-human-rights-act

Tufail, W., & Poynting, S. (2016). The Rochdale 'Grooming' Case and the Politics of Racialisation. In D. Pratt & R. Woodlock (Eds.), *Fear of Muslims: International Perspectives on Islamophobia* (pp. 79–92). Berlin: Springer.

Vine, J. (2011). *A Thematic Inspection of How the UK Border Agency Manages Foreign National Prisoners*. London: Independent Chief Inspector of the UK Border Agency.

Walklate, S. (2007). *Imagining the Victim of Crime*. Maidenhead: Open University Press.

Warner, J. (2005). The Social Construction of the Criminal Alien in Immigration Law, Enforcement and Practice and Statistical Enumeration: Consequences for Immigrant Stereotyping. *Journal of Social and Ecological Boundaries, 1*(2), 56–80.

Yuval-Davis, N., & Anthias, F. (Eds.). (1990). *Woman-Nation-State*. London: Palgrave Macmillan.

18

Beyond Media Discourse: Locating Race and Racism in Criminal Justice Systems

Vicki Sentas

Introduction

Identifying racism through the critique of elite discourses (including media, political and institutional discourses) has been a key concern in the study of race and racism since the 1960s. Teun Van Dijk, an influential scholar of discourse analysis and race, situates racism within discourse:

> Racism, defined as a system of racial and ethnic inequality, can survive, only when it is daily reproduced through multiple sources of exclusion, inferiorization, or marginalization. Such acts need to be sustained by an ideological system, and by a set of attitudes that legitimate difference and dominance. Discourse is the principle means for the construction and reproduction of this socio-cognitive framework. (2002, pp. 322–323)

Media representations of race and crime are routinely used as primary discursive sources across disciplines for understanding the relation

V. Sentas (✉)
University of New South Wales, Sydney, NSW, Australia

© The Author(s) 2018
M. Bhatia et al. (eds.), *Media, Crime and Racism*, Palgrave Studies in Crime, Media and Culture, https://doi.org/10.1007/978-3-319-71776-0_18

between race and crime. The political and cultural power of media makes this focus unsurprising. However, a number of questions can be asked of this methodological choice. Are there limits in what media can tell us about the social relations of race and about institutional racism, power and domination? Do media practices shape criminalisation and racialisation in different ways and with different effects, to criminal justice institutions and practices? Is the point of anti-racism to change social representation, or is it to change institutional practices? In short, is media discourse the right place to begin/focus when considering racism in the criminal justice system?

This chapter revisits key concepts and methods in race and racism in order to consider the limits of media discourse and of discourse analysis more broadly, for understanding race and racism in criminal justice systems. I argue that a reliance on media and other textual sources in isolation from study of the particular dynamics of criminal justice systems can contain understandings of racism to being a mode of social representation of belief systems. I argue that beginning and ending with media ill-equips us to understand the social formations of racism, including the diverse material practices that criminalise race and institutionalise racism through state agencies as well as racialised people's experiences of these dynamics. Unlike most primers on race in criminology, my approach is to assess how the received wisdom of ideology critique of race as a social construction might inadvertently blind-side us from asking the questions that connect, in Fairclough's classic formulation, 'text to context', let alone *invert this relationship*. In other words, the role of criminal justice institutions and practices in subjugating marginalised and racialised peoples may bare very little relation to the form of express media propositions or media denials.

The chapter first briefly characterises some of the diverse approaches to the relationship between media discourse and race. It then sets out how the work media does in representing race is not the same as the material reproductions enabled by diverse criminal justice institutions (and their discourses) in criminalising race and generating racial hierarchies. I explain why these distinctions matter, by considering debates around institutional racism, differential racism and anti-essentialism. The chapter concludes with a proposal to decentre media representations as an organising framework for understanding racialisation, in favour of recentring theoretically and empirically connected studies of diverse criminalisation practices in state and civil society domains. In addition—putting media to one side—by examining criminal justice institutions and practices together with their discursive manifestations, we can better use critical discourse analysis to understand race as a material set of social practices.

Media, Race and Criminal Justice

There are a number of ways that the relationship between media, racism and criminal justice has been understood in critical scholarship across sociology and criminology, in particular. In a somewhat oversimplified and select characterisation, I set out three aspects of media critiques on race and reflect on some approaches to the relationship between discourses and social practices.

First, race in media discourse is readily identifiable and critiqued through linguistic analysis of both direct and indirect forms of discriminatory assumptions when crime or criminal justice is reported upon. For example, the most obvious forms of racism by media are when demeaning or inferiorising language and stereotypes are used to describe either an individual or a group of people by virtue of their ethnic or racial background and links to an imputed criminality. In this register, (akin to interpersonal racism), texts can be understood as a discriminatory harm and may or may not breach a range of laws on anti-discrimination, vilification or hate crime. Regardless of the inadequacies of anti-discrimination law, in an age of social media saturation, racist language is both readily promulgated and 'called out' as an illiberal harm.

Second, there is a well-established critical scholarship drawing on media and other elite discourse as sources that racialise crime and criminalise race. These two concepts, racialisation and criminalisation, have been fruitful since their development in the early twentieth century to explain the social processes by which race and crime have come to be co-constituted. In short, criminalisation refers to the processes by which, through law or institutional practices (like policing, court process and corrections), certain types of behaviour are made into prohibited acts and penalised, so that 'anyone engaging in any of these types of behaviour may be defined as a criminal' (Hillyard 1993, p. 260). The starting point for criminalisation as method is that the concept of 'crime' is neither neutral nor objective and rather reflects conduct prioritised by the state for detection, prosecution and punishment (Cohen 1988, pp. 256–258). Cohen drew attention to how some forms of life are criminalised and other behaviours are not. Criminalisation requires understanding the laws and institutional processes by which crime is defined and by which marginalised populations are detected and regulated and/or charged, convicted and sentenced. Criminalisation is a key method for interrogating institutional processes and decisions over what and who is criminalised.

Criminalisation does not simply repress pre-existing behaviours or activities. By acting on collective identities, diverse institutional practices construct ethnic or racial difference as criminal, associating racial identity with crime (Keith 1993)—with media practices and other discourses being but one mode of criminalisation and racialisation that give insight into broader social structures (Collins et al. 2000; Poynting et al. 2004). The last section of this chapter will discuss how study of the combined effects of criminalisation and racialisation in criminal justice institutions and practices provide different anti-racism tools in contrast to a focus on social representations of race and crime, such as those in the media.

The concept of racialisation has been long used to analyse the varied processes where 'ideas about race are constructed, come to be regarded as meaningful and are acted upon' (Murji and Solomos 2005, p. 1). Race is predominantly considered in contemporary race and ethnicity scholarship as a historically contingent social construction produced through cultural, economic and political practices. Social relations of race in this view are 'socially constructed' as 'real' biological or cultural categories and naturalised as fixed and immutable, as elaborated shortly. Consequently, racialisation as method focuses on race as a process of becoming rather than one of being and identity (Murji and Solomos 2005, p. 8). Importantly, racialisation is not simply an external ascription of inferiorising characteristics for the purpose of subjugation. There is no necessary equation or relation between racialisation and racism. Processes of racialisation do not necessarily reveal racism: a point I return to shortly in discussing the importance of connecting practices of marginalisation in the criminal justice with inconsistencies, as well as consistencies, in discursive practices.

The methodological utility of racialisation in connecting the structural with social representation is helpfully captured by Collins and colleagues' definition:

> a complex social dynamic which takes place between the structural dimensions of social, economic and political marginalisation, and the cultural representation of social relations—the 'ways of seeing' which frame the experience of social relations but which are negotiated through a process of self identification. (2000, pp. 17–18)

What Collins et al. effectively highlight is that social contestations over racial power are also played out through collective self-identification and the subject formation of racialised peoples themselves. It also means that the resistance of racialised people against the criminal justice system is just as important (if not more so) as what criminal justice institutions do, say or how they might be represented through media.

Racialised discourses of crime may be less overtly inferiorising than the first category—but no less productive of social reality and knowledge. Media texts are identified as a source for understanding the 'ways of seeing' race and the ways that media racialise crime. Most critical approaches that take media discourse as empirical sites of race and racism are consistent with social constructivist theories of race as culturally and historically determined. There is no universal or general structure to racism, only historically specific 'racisms' (Hall 2002b, p. 56). For social constructionists, the particular and specific formation of racism in a particular context focused attention to the ideologies that sustained those specific forms of racism.

The idea of race in social constructionism is largely located within historic shifts in the ideology of racism from biology to culture (Barker 1981). The various descriptions of racism as 'new racism', 'neo-racism' or 'racism without race' characterise a discursive shift to a notion of racism as bounded and fixed in culture, largely replacing biological determinants as the basis for exclusion and the assignment of inferiority (Barker 1981, p. 22). The story that social constructionism tells is that, as a result of the defeat of fascism, the end of formal segregation in the US South, the global processes of decolonisation, the vast population movements from the Third World to the centres of the world economy and the rise of social movements, the biologically based theories of race entered a paradigmatic decline and were no longer dominant by the 1960s (Balibar 1991, pp. 17–27). This kind of racism, largely supported by overt formal exclusionary legislation and policy measures, gave way to 'race neutrality' or 'colour blindness' and formal equality in the law (Haney Lopez 1996).

Cultural racism as a variant of biological racism deploys polarisations about progressive or primitive peoples to cultural categories, focusing on the 'insurmountability of cultural differences' (Balibar 1991, p. 9). In Etienne Balibar's terms, we see 'the play of substitutions between race, people, culture and nations' as ways of representing modern subjects (1991, p. 26). The interchangeability between race, nation and ethnicity as signifiers highlights the permanence of phenotypic indicators of race alongside the cultural.

Media routinely portray race as an explainer for complex social problems, whether it be through explicit forms of biological racism or attributing so-called 'cultural' explanations for crimes. For example, media contribute to dominant understandings of Muslim and ethnic identifications as a national security problem that conflict with 'our way of life'. Essentialist characterisations of Islam in dominant public discourses as inherently violent, culturally regressive and anti-modern have been extensively documented (see e.g. Poynting et al. 2004). Consequently, Islam is inscribed with monolithic immutable and inferior characteristics that effectively 'religionises' race (Chon and Arzt 2005) or racialises religion, a phenomenon that crowds the pages of newspapers and magazines globally. In this way, Islam is criminalised through media and political discourses as an ideological source of political violence and in turn critiqued as the dominant ideological form of anti-Muslim racism—an analysis of racial discourse that we return to shortly.

There is a third dimension of approaches to media that go beyond merely identifying media discourse as sites of racialised ideology and open out readings of texts to institutional, social and political analysis and their purported effects. Broadly speaking, approaches to racialisation grounded in examining representation employ a critical discourse analysis framework. As exemplified in Collins et al.'s quote above, critical discourse analysis is concerned with how social relations (in this case, social relations of race), identity, knowledge and power are constructed through texts as a form of sociocultural practice, as well as remaking material structures. While complex and requiring more detailed consideration than is possible here, the conceptual underpinnings of this approach are worth briefly noting in order to flag some productive tensions.

Marxist approaches to doing ideology critique through discourse analysis foreground social, historic and economic structures in relation to the production of discourse, notably shaped by the work of Gramsci, Althusser and Hall. These connected threads of materialist social theory revised classical Marxist ideas of ideology away from a symbolic system of distorted beliefs and ideas epiphenomenal to and in distinction from socio-economic and historic structures of production. Rather, these currents of Marxist thought are concerned with how ideologies arise and depend on material social conditions; that is, the productive resources and social relations of the economy but also the social reproduction of life. Althusser's concern with ideology was not as systems of belief but as the implicit categories by which material conditions are represented and understood. Ideological belief is itself a product of material conditions, of the practices of subjects, in turn regulated by practices of the state (Althusser 1971). In sum, the influence of Marxist currents on critical discourse analysis has been an approach that sees ideology as the *interface* between the representations of social practices and processes within discourse on the one hand and social structures and material conditions on the other.

In contrast, (and indeed, developed in direct opposition to Marxist conceptions of ideology), Foucault's influential concept of discourse has had an abiding effect on academia and diverse approaches to discourse analysis. Putting a complex concept simply, discourse encompasses the knowledge and power relations expressed in language and social practices and reflects the material traces of history (Foucault 2002). One of Foucault's most enduring insights is that discourses have disciplining effects, governing what can be said and done, shaping identities and practices, in productive as well as coercive ways. For Foucault, discourses not only construct subjectivity, relations of power and knowledge, but social relations are not outside of, or prior to, their representations and reality in discourse. Whilst drawing, attention to the specific materiality of symbolic practices, for Foucault there was no truth or reality outside of the power of discourse (Foucault 1991). At best ideology is an effect of discourse, and ideological stances 'emerge as the result of a complex inter-action of discursive procedures' (Vighi and Feldner 2007, p. 148). As Vighi and Feldner point out, Foucault offers no externality or route to a non-discursive realm: discourse is 'self-enclosed' in the operation of its 'micro-powers' (2007, p. 153). One result of the influence of Foucauldian discourse analysis has been a method that tends to treat discourse as self-contained, giving the impressions that texts are sufficient sources for understanding material social relations.

Allan Luke describes the ideal analytics in critical discursive methods to be the movement between the micro linguistic analysis of text and the macro analysis of the social, institutional and political relations that texts signify. For Luke, texts can only be understood if the institutions and material and historical formations under study have been theorised. Hence discourse analysis can only be political if it explains how such discourses do ideological work (Luke 2002, pp. 101–102). Critical dis-course analysis is a concern however, largely with the material conse-quences and *effects of texts*, as the primary unit of analysis.

For critical discourse analysis, the relationship between media dis-courses and practices of criminalisation and racialisation needs to be studied in relation to structural and systemic operations of criminal jus-tice and institutional interests and contexts. These explorations take het-erogeneous lines of inquiry. In one register of critique, criminal justice institutions and media work strategically *in tandem* to present race as naturalised sites of criminality. In one helpful example, Poynting, Noble, Tabar and Collins's influential work, *Bin Laden in the Suburbs*, argues that the 'Arab other' functioned as the deposit of historical antipathy towards those of 'Middle Eastern appearance' (2004). The authors situ-ated the emergence of the Arab Other as a pre-eminent folk devil in contemporary Australia since the 1970s, making links between the gen-eration of 'moral panics' from 1998 over 'ethnic gangs', 'race rape' in

Sydney in 2000–2001, asylum seekers and the attacks of 9/11. They argued these events enabled the racist imaging of a singular criminalising category for those of Arab, Muslim or Middle Eastern background—a hegemonic status upon which to project a host of social anxieties.

The result is that while the media blames entire communities for criminal acts, certain actions based on perceived visible and threatening difference are made criminal by the police. The Other is thus subject to hostility and fear and also functions as ideological explanation for a range of social antagonisms and problems including terrorism. Conflicting media representations of police as at once victims and military aggressors figure as part of an intricate system of public blaming, situating the Other as both cause and effect. The authors argue that this process of criminalisation based on essentialised categories is facilitated by the ways in which police are situated within the media narrative of war with the Arab Other (Poynting et al. 2004, pp. 69–70, 79). For example, the authors connect the naturalisation of terrorism with Islam in discourse, with the targeting of Muslims by police and for racist attacks in the general body politic and, more broadly, the legitimation of draconian counter-terrorism laws (Poynting et al. 2004, p. 32).[1]

There are diverse ways in which the connection between media texts and criminal justice practices are set out. The concept of legitimation is often used in media discourse analysis to generally refer to the processes by which the ideology of race is normalised and made socially acceptable. Media *legitimate* the institutional racism of key criminal justice institutions such as the police, courts and corrections. First, media discourses are understood to represent what criminal justice institutions, or laws do, regenerate dominant ideologies and smooth over possibilities for the public to recognise truths. Second, the inverse relationship is also apparent in many studies—that there is an identifiable connection between what the media say and what diverse criminal justice institutions and government do in response.

In related yet distinct lines of inquiry, media discourse has been a focal point because it plays a significant role in the denial of the function of racism in society (Van Dijk 2002). The denial of racism by media is a foundational expression of liberal democratic ideals that 'we are not racists'. For Van Dijk 'When they want to say something negative about minorities, they will tend to use denials, disclaimers, or other forms that are intended to avoid a negative impression with their listeners or their readers' (2002, p. 308). Media denials explain away racism by confining the harm to ideological racism based on notions of superiority and inferiority, with cultural or new racism at best understood as intolerance. Through denials the media routinely express 'ingroup allegiances and white group solidarity' in ways that mark social boundaries and construct social identities. Media denials of racism have an important 'sociopolitical function' in critical discourse analysis, including managing ethnopolitical affairs and delegitimising resistance to racism (Van Dijk 2002, pp. 311–313).

In these conceptual registers, media discourses of race and crime provide important sources for understanding what the representations of social relations of race, class and gender signify for diverse modes of alienation and oppression. But media representations alone are a limited source for understanding broader discourses that circulate through diverse criminal justice institutions and practices and processes that have *non-discursive* dimensions. Media is a limited standpoint for analysing what race and racism mean and how race and racism are remade as relations of power through criminal justice institutions and practices that are constantly reshaped in response to those it criminalises. I set out in the next section how the criminalisation of race and racialisation of crime are most powerfully enacted through criminal justice institutions, including the police, the courts, corrections and prisons as well as law and the processes, practices and knowledges that sustain criminalisation in action. The work that media discourse does to remake ideas of race is neither equivalent to, nor a signifier for, the work that diverse criminal justice institutions, discourses and processes do, in remaking racial power.

The theory of critical discourse analysis notably sets out the need to articulate the precise relationships between these readily identifiable essentialised discourses of race and the resulting (or prior) criminal justice practices that are asserted to be in relation to the text. But the critical discourse approach is largely concerned with the material consequences and effects of *texts*. Texts are the starting point with which to make connections to the social. Instead, discourse analysts ought to reverse the relationship and begin with the criminal justice system. This is because prioritising media representations of race take very particular under-standings of race and racism as coherent categories of ideology under-stood through language as beliefs. There is a complexity to the concepts of race and racism that is in danger of being left out all together when we start or end our inquiry with media discourse.

Racism, Ideology and the Material

Within the sociology of race, it is well established that racism suffers from what Robert Miles has described as both 'conceptual inflation' and 'con-ceptual deflation': either being made to do too little or conversely to explain too much (58; in relation to criminology, see Holdaway 1997). One of the key debates in the twentieth century in social constructionist approaches to race was that rejecting race as biological 'fact' drew theo-rists to understanding race as an 'ideology'—as an illusion, a false con-sciousness, something that was not true. Consequently, one of the basic misunderstandings of the concept of racism is that racism is attributed to a moral failing or a pathology or other forms of irrationality (Rattansi 2005, p. 294). The first characterisation of the ways in which social media readily identifies and condemns racism in language is a prominent exam-ple of anti-racism from a moral standpoint. Ghassan Hage identifies that in traditional approaches to sociology, the concept of racism was largely deployed as a mode of thinking or classification, which detaches racism from the examination of everyday practices and relations of power (1989, pp. 30–36). Hage argues that neither do relations of power alone make racism a useful analytic tool. Racist practice is not in itself a *motivating* ideology and does not answer the question of precisely what racism empowers, that is racism's 'power to do what?' (Hage 1989, p. 35). Earlier work on racism also critiques the view of 'racism as a passive element used to realise political goals' (Banton 1970, p. 22).

Due to the influence of Hall (1996, 2002a, b), Omni and Winant (2005) and others, the material reality of social constructs—the institu-tional practices, lived experiences, structures and agency which make race real—refuted the idea of racial ideology as a false illusion. 'Real' here does not refer to biological categories but to a recognition of the social, economic and political realities that institute race as an embodied lived reality. In this methodology, race is not simply socially constructed, it is material. The defunct biological idea of race endures in social structures imbued with racial meaning. For Hall, 'race … is a discursive system, which has "real" social, economic and political conditions of existence, and "real" material and symbolic effects' (Hall 2002b, p. 453). These Marxist and materialist approaches to race do not simplistically privilege the study of the real over the study of representation but are rather interested in the material character of signification. In other words, race is not simply *about* representation, nor an ideological *effect*, nor an effect of *something else*, such as racism or class. If we take as our starting point, the social processes and practices which differentiate individuals, the social and structural features of race are assembled through and after these processes (Chang 1985). This point is important because the strategies of political institutions which may be intended to be non-discriminatory nevertheless contribute to social relationships saturated in differential, racialised or racist outcomes. Furthermore, the *absence* of 'bad words' or identifiable discriminatory representations in media or political discourse does not mean that there is not racism. This is important for how we understand the relationships—if any—between particular media discourses and diverse criminal justice practices that racialise. I return to this in detail.

What is distinctive about 'new racism' is its declaratory anti-racism and universality. Under liberalism, all 'cultural identities' are equal before the law and law is declared race-neutral. Critical race scholarship has elaborated how race is not only socially constructed but legally produced (Haney Lopez 1996). The dominance of race neutrality means that racialisation in the law, policy and criminal justice practices like policing and corrections are effaced and non-propositional. While many scholars understand law to translate racial meanings in a dynamic of coercion and ideology, (Haney Lopez 1996, p. 13) the simultaneous regulatory function of the law and criminal justice in practice is an even more important aspect of the 'new racism'. Relations of domination and power can circulate over racialised peoples, *without* being in tandem with, or consistent with, racialised texts.

Institutionalised Racism

The concept of institutional or institutionalised racism points not to the intentions of individuals or the expressed purpose of policies or institutions but the effects and outcomes of pervasive conventions that reinforce racial inequality, exclusion and inclusion in relation to resources, services and policies (Bowling and Phillips 2002, pp. 40–41; Rowe 2004, pp. 9–11). Racism inscribes onto state practices a political reality structuring the social, economic and political domination and marginalisation of minorities. Institutional racism is one specific process of racialisation (Rattansi 2005, p. 288) that tells us about the particular mode of racism in operation through the criminal justice system. While definitions vary, institutional racism generally refers to discrimination which disadvantages ethnic minorities.[2] The definition of Islamophobia below, for example, explicitly draws on this shared conceptual framework of institutional racism:

> Institutional Islamophobia may be defined as those established laws, customs and practices which systematically reflect and produce inequalities in society between Muslims and non-Muslims. If such inequalities accrue to institutional laws, customs or practices, an institution is Islamophobic whether or not the individuals maintaining those practices have Islamophobic intentions. (Commission on British Muslims and Islamophobia 2004, p. 14)

This in-built pervasiveness of differential treatment may be neither conscious nor intentional and may take subtle and concealed forms at the institutional and organisational level. Suggested manifestations of institutional Islamophobia include routine and widespread negative stereotyping of Muslims in the media and by politicians; negative stereotypes that imply Muslims are less committed to democracy and the rule of law; discrimination in recruitment and employment; lack of attention to the way that Muslims are disproportionately affected by poverty and social exclusion; non-recognition of Muslim and religious discrimination in the law and legal curtailing of civil liberties disproportionately affecting Muslims (Commission on British Muslims and Islamophobia 2004,

p. 8). As a result of this institutional Islamophobia, Muslims feel under siege, are constructed as outsiders and suffer disproportionate socio-economic exclusion. The understanding of Islamophobia as a particular form of institutional racism identifies such racism as both direct and indirect forms of religious *discrimination*.

The concept of institutional racism has been subject to critique within the sociology of race and ethnicity. Robert Miles and Malcolm Brown argue that by insisting on unintentional practices and the outcomes of exclusion, the notion of institutional racism simply *asserts* racism and simultaneously inflates and decontextualises its meaning (Miles and Brown 2003, pp. 68–71). But locating racism institutionally places an important conceptual emphasis on outcomes that make sense of the coded, implicit and non-propositional or non-discursive operations of power. In other words, analysis of institutionalised forms of racism is a better starting point for understanding the interaction between practices and texts.

For this reason institutional racism as a concept remains an important tool for examining the shifting social relation of race. I disagree with Miles's concerns with the emphasis institutional racism gives to effects and outcomes; however, he rightly points out that ideological transformations have not been a site of analysis within most studies of practices of institutional racism. The focus has rather mostly been on the continuation of structural subordination in the form of discrimination (Miles and Brown 2003, pp. 71–72). Can ideas of race, and racial power, circulate without being readily identifiable as *discrimination*? If we ask Ghassan Hage's question of the concept of racism—the power to do *what?*—then the answer is yes.

Differential Racism and Essentialism

The concept of institutional racism ought not to focus solely on self-evident discrimination, exclusion and essentialist ideas of race. To do so would miss the nuances of modern racial power where liberal states might keenly recognise cultural or racial 'difference' and use seemingly positive discourses to do so, without a hint of inferiorising language.

French sociologist, Pierre Taguieff's distinction between 'discriminatory' and 'differentialist' racism is helpful in unpacking what racism without 'bad words' looks like. Taguieff acknowledges that discriminatory racism locates the Other in a hierarchy of inequality, while differentialist racism appreciates, tolerates and values the cultural distinctiveness of difference (1990). Taguieff's study of right-wing factions in the French Government in the late 1980s demonstrated the predication of racist ideas *entirely* on valorising ethnic difference. In practice, Taguieff concluded, the deployment of difference was far from benign. Difference is categorised, evaluated and ranked and through the superficial respect for difference and other nuanced appeals to distinctive group identity, authoritarian projects promoted as liberal and anti-racist secured representation of the official French values of autonomy, freedom and equality (Taguieff 1990). While such discourses may be formulated as politically inclusive, the material *effects* of acting on 'difference' in practice are necessarily neither progressive nor anti-racist (St Louis 2005, p. 44; Pitcher 2008). In the domain of criminal justice, this requires examining the effects of particular laws, policies and practices and targeted people's experiences, as a primary method.

The harm of racism has been situated within theories of recognition, most commonly associated with debates on Charles Taylor's influential essay, *The Politics of Recognition* (1994). A key aspect of recognition relates to claims made to democratic states to recognise the cultural distinctiveness of identity as the basis of freedom from the harms of racism. For example, the Commission on British Muslims in their approach to institutional racism, discussed above, characterised Islamophobia as a form of misrecognition which shapes identity. The Commission drew on Taylor's suggestion that: 'Non recognition or misrecognition can inflict harm, can be a form of oppression, imprisoning someone in a false, distorted and reduced mode of being' (Taylor, quoted in Commission on British Muslims and Islamophobia 2004, p. 27).

However, this characterisation of racism, and specifically here anti-Muslim racism, as misrecognition forecloses the possibility that *recognition* of Islamic 'cultural' difference can make 'suspect communities'. Taylor noted that the demand to be judged as worthy, to be recognised, can simply keep the status quo intact. To be the object of recognition can homogenise and categorise those demanding worth (Taylor 1994, pp. 100–101). The recognition of difference provides no intervention into the regulatory structures of criminal justice. The recognition of difference may in fact, sustain the extension of criminal justice institutions, laws or policies into people's lives. Discourse analysis—of either media or political or institutional discourse—is unable to account for these modes of racialised state power.

The politics of difference and identity are arguably a dominant mode of racism in liberal, multicultural democracies, alongside identifiable modes of discrimination and biological inferiorisation. The normative framework of the regressive racial political project structured by discourses of inferiority is limited conceptually because it ignores the reality of the hegemony of 'new racism' and its moral stance of anti-race(ism). Ben Pitcher argues that

> an impeccably anti-essentialist vocabulary has effectively become installed as hegemonic in a variety of contemporary social contexts—and in particular mainstream political discourse. (2008, p. 2)

The anti-essentialist commitment of race theory has historically galvanised important critiques of the reductive tendencies of law and institutions. Hence the contributions of race theory towards understanding hybridity and shifting forms of self-identification readily identify and critique essentialist classifications of race and culture. However, Pitcher argues that while the political context has successfully mobilised anti-essentialist discourses, race theory on the whole continues to privilege 'an abstract, doctrinal anti-essentialism' as innately progressive (2008, p. 3).

The absence of media discourse that *essentialises* ethnic/racial identity does not mean that there are not essentialising practices at play. Nor does the presence of non-essentialising discourse (e.g. cultural diversity talk) indicate the absence of institutional racism. Non-essentialising discourse is a key feature of life in liberal, plural democracy where multiculturalism might be simultaneously vilified, as well as welcomed, commodified or showcased as a feature of national tolerance and inclusion. My argument is that the politics of difference does not solely or predominantly function as racial or religious discrimination based on essentialised or exclusionary identity constructs. A primary conceptual emphasis on discrimination or 'racist discourse' in media or other discourses will miss the exclusionary or coercive effects of nominally inclusive strategies. There is now a diverse body of work demonstrating how varied criminal justice institutions rely on strategies of integration and the incorporation of difference into liberal pluralism, as much as they rely on strategies of exclusion and coercion.

'Doctrinal anti-essentialism' has limited our understanding of the mechanisms by which race is reproduced in diverse criminal justice institutions. For example, I have argued elsewhere that it has become routine for socio-criminological scholarship on the war on terror to map elite discourses which essentialise or homogenise Islam as violent, anti-Western and pre-modern (Sentas 2014). For counter-terrorism to function hegemonically, it does not as a matter of course rely on essentialised approaches to Islam and even less so on discourses of inferiority/superiority. Homogenous and generalised constructs of Islam no doubt served and continue to serve varied political purposes for governments. However, the racialisation of Muslims takes the form of a number of contingent and often contradictory state strategies. In practice, the racialisation of Muslims is less monolithic, often drawing on well informed and nuanced conceptions of Islam particularly held by police, which could not be characterised as racist or discriminatory. These practices look very different to media representations. Nonetheless, these anti-essentialist strategies racialise Muslims as the over-policed subjects of intensive state regulation in ways that normalise, extend and deepen racial power across criminal justice institutions and discourses (Sentas 2014). Investigations into the diverse realities and strategies of identity and identification must account for the state's *recognition* of the diversity of difference as much as towards state misrecognition.

In another example, strategies that are designed to be inclusive and non-racist, such as community policing, largely rely on discourses that recognise and value minority ethnic communities. People's experiences of these institutional practices provide key sites for understanding inclusive and, apparently, non-racialising discourse. Empirical studies of community policing in several jurisdictions demonstrate the particular racialising and exclusionary effects that can be sustained when community policing functions as over-policing (Reside and Smith 2010). In relation to another domain of criminal justice, that of prisons, the recognition of cultural and gender diversity can function to entrench structural racism. Studies of gender-responsive discourses and strategies have found they function to reinforce 'pathologizing and risk focused practices' that 'yield more racializing, interventionist and expansionist responses' that reproduce structural racism through individual rehabilitation programmes premised on cultural diversity (Russell and Carlton 2013).

More broadly, hegemonic developments whereby state institutions have adopted strategic anti-essentialism raise conceptual challenges for criminologists studying state practices through the lens of discrimination and inferiorisation alone. Of methodological interest here is how the politics of valuing and recognising cultural difference can organise the discourses, strategies and practices of diverse components of criminal justice. As researchers into race and crime, we can ask the question of how any criminal justice institutions that value and recognise the cultural differences of diverse racialised groups deploy strategies that in effect deepen forms of regulation or oppression.

Conclusion

What are the dominant modes of racism operating in any specific aspect of a particular criminal justice system today? How can we answer this question when '… it is now possible to perpetuate racial domination without explicit reference to race'? (Omni and Winant 2005, p. 7). An emphasis with the study of action, practices and experiences of criminal justice, rather than with discourses alone, can lead researchers to formations of race and racism that may look very different to ideas of race represented through media. Conceptions of race as a social construction have emphasised analyses of discourses and practices that essentialise race in cultural, national, religious or biological terms. But in liberal democracies today, criminal justice institutions increasingly valorise diversity and produce non-essentialising discourses in line with 'new racism'. These discourses can support modes of state racism that although attentive to heterogeneous diversity and inclusion, subject racialised people to diverse forms of regulation, management, surveillance and control. The specific forms, processes and knowledges of institutional practices are vital starting points for understanding any potential relationship criminal justice systems have to media texts. One broad set of methods for interrogating the operation of race and racism in criminal justice is to begin with the interaction between power and meaning produced by institutional practices and the diverse social groups who interact with them.

Notes

1. With the advance of the war on terror, Poynting and Mason trace the transition in racialised representation in Australia from the Arab Other to the Muslim Other and similarly in the UK from the Asian to the Muslim Other (2006, p. 366). A large international literature has followed, identifying media's Islamophobic discourse in concert with counter-terrorism practices producing suspect communities (see e.g. Hickman et al. 2011).
2. In the United Kingdom, the 1999 MacPherson inquiry into the investigation of the murder of Stephen Lawrence in 1993 found out that institutional racism was embedded in the Metropolitan Police.

References

Althusser, L. (1971). *Lenin and Philosophy*. New York: Monthly Review Press.

Balibar, E. (1991). Is There a Neo-Racism? In E. Balibar & I. Wallerstein (Eds.), *Race, Nation, Class*. London: Verso.

Banton, M. (1970). The Concept of Racism. In S. Zubaida (Ed.), *Race and Racialism* (pp. 17–33). Sydney: Tavistock Publications.

Barker, M. (1981). *The New Racism: Conservatives and the Ideology of the Tribe*. London: Junction Books.

Bowling, B., & Phillips, C. (2002). *Racism, Crime and Justice*. Harlow: Pearson Education Limited.

Chang, H. (1985). In Liem, P. and Montague, E. (eds). Toward a Marxist Theory of Racism: Two Essays by Harry Chang. *Review of Radical Political Economics, 17*(3), 34–45.

Chon, M., & Arzt, D. E. (2005). Walking While Muslim. *Law and Contemporary Problems, 68,* 215–254.

Cohen, S. (1988). *Against Criminology.* New Brunswick: Transaction Books.

Collins, J., Noble, G., Poynting, S., & Tabar, P. (2000). *Kebabs, Kids, Cops and Crime: Youth, Ethnicity and Crime.* Sydney: Pluto Press.

Commission on British Muslims and Islamophobia. (2004). In R. Richardson (Ed.), *Islamophobia: Issues, Challenges and Action.* Sterling: Trentham Books.

Foucault, M. (1991). *Discipline and Punish.* London: Penguin.

Foucault, M. (2002). *The Archaeology of Knowledge.* London and New York: Routledge.

Hage, G. (1989). *White Nation: Fantasies of White Supremacy in a Multicultural Society.* Sydney: Pluto Press.

Hall, S. (1996). Gramsci's Relevance for the Study of Race and Ethnicity. In D. Morley & K. H. Chan (Eds.), *Stuart Hall: Critical Dialogues in Cultural Studies* (pp. 411–441). London: Routledge.

Hall, S. (2002a). Race, Articulation and Societies Structured in Dominance. In P. Essed & D. T. Goldberg (Eds.), *Race Critical Theories* (pp. 38–68). Massachusetts: Blackwell.

Hall, S. (2002b). Reflections on Race, Articulation and Societies Structured in Dominance. In P. Essed & D. T. Goldberg (Eds.), *Race Critical Theories* (pp. 449–454). Massachusetts: Blackwell.

Haney Lopez, F. (1996). *White by Law: The Legal Construction of Race.* New York: New York University Press.

Hickman, M., Thomas, L., Silvestri, S., & Nickels, H. (2011). *Suspect Communities? Counter-Terrorism Policy, the Press, and the Impact on Irish and Muslim Communities in Britain: A Report for Policy Makers and the Public.* Retrieved from http://www.city.ac.uk/__data/assets/pdf_file/0005/96287/suspect-communities-report-july2011.pdf

Hillyard, P. (1993). *Suspect Community: People's Experience of the Prevention of Terrorism Acts in Britain.* London: Pluto Press.

Holdaway, S. (1997). Some Recent Approaches to the Study of Race in Criminological Research. *British Journal of Criminology, 37*(3), 383–400.

Keith, M. (1993). *Race, Riots and Policing: Lore and Disorder in a Multi-Racist Society.* London: University College London Press.

Luke, A. (2002). Beyond Science and Ideology Critique: Developments in Critical Discourse Analysis. *Annual Review of Applied Linguistics, 22,* 96–110.

Miles, R., & Brown, M. (2003). *Racism* (2nd ed.). London: Routledge.

Murji, K., & Solomos, J. (2005). Introduction: Racialization in Theory and Practice. In K. Murji & J. Solomos (Eds.), *Racialization: Studies in Theory and Practice* (pp. 1–28). Oxford: Oxford University Press.

Omni, M., & Winant, H. (2005). The Theoretical Status of the Concept of Race. In W. Crichlow (Ed.), *Race Identity and Representation in Education.* New York: Routledge.

Pitcher, B. (2008). The Materiality of Race Theory. *Darkmatter, 2,* 1–7. Retrieved from http://www.darkmatter101.org/site/2008/02/23/the-materiality-of-race-theory/

Poynting, S., & Mason, V. (2006). Tolerance, Freedom, Justice and Peace? Britain, Australia and Anti-Muslim Racism Since 11 September 2001. *Journal of Intercultural Studies, 27*(4), 365–391.

Poynting, S., Noble, G., Tabar, P., & Collins, J. (2004). *Bin Laden in the Suburbs: Criminalising the Arab Other.* Sydney: Sydney Institute of Criminology.

Rattansi, A. (2005). The Uses of Racialization: The Time, Spaces and Subject Objects of the Raced Body. In K. Murji & J. Solomos (Eds.), *Racialization: Studies in Theory and Practice.* Oxford: Oxford University Press.

Reside, S., & Smith, B. (2010). *Boys You Want to Give Me Some Action? Interventions into Policing of Racialised Communities in Melbourne.* Fitzroy Legal Service, Western Suburbs Legal Service & Springvale Monash Legal Service, Victoria.

Rowe, M. (2004). *Policing, Race and Racism.* Devon: Willan Publishing.

Russell, E., & Carlton, B. (2013). Pathways, Race and Gender Responsive Reform: Through an Abolitionist Lens. *Theoretical Criminology, 17*(4), 474–492.

Sentas, V. (2014). *Traces of Terror: Counter-Terrorism Law, Policing and Race.* Oxford: Oxford University Press.

St Louis, B. (2005). Racialization in the "Zone of Ambiguity". In K. Murji & J. Solomos (Eds.), *Racialization: Studies in Theory and Practice* (pp. 29–50). Oxford: Oxford University Press.

Taguieff, P. (1990). The New Cultural Racism in France. *Telos, 83,* 109–122.

Taylor, C. (1994). The Politics of Recognition. In D. T. Goldberg (Ed.), *Multiculturalism: A Critical Reader* (pp. 75–106). Oxford: Blackwell.

Van Dijk, T. (2002). Denying Racism: Elite Discourse and Racism. In P. Essed & D. T. Goldberg (Eds.), *Race Critical Theories* (pp. 307–324). Massachusetts: Blackwell.

Vighi, F., & Feldner, H. M. (2007). Ideology Critique or Discourse Analysis? Žižek Against Foucault. *European Journal of Political Theory, 6*(2), 141–159.

Index[1]

---

[1]Note: Page number followed by 'n' refers to notes.

© The Author(s) 2018   **381**
M. Bhatia et al. (eds.), *Media, Crime and Racism*, Palgrave Studies in Crime, Media and Culture, https://doi.org/10.1007/978-3-319-71776-0

The manufacturer's authorised representative in the EU is Springer
Nature Customer Service Centre GmbH, Europaplatz 3, 69115 Heidelberg,
Germany. If you have any concerns regarding our products, please
contact ProductSafety@springernature.com

Printed and bound by CPI Group (UK) Ltd, Croydon, CR0 4YY
29/04/2026
02099514-0005